John Sinclair, John Adams

The History of the Public Revenue of the British Empire

John Sinclair, John Adams

The History of the Public Revenue of the British Empire

ISBN/EAN: 9783337272692

Printed in Europe, USA, Canada, Australia, Japan

Cover: Foto ©Suzi / pixelio.de

More available books at **www.hansebooks.com**

THE

HISTORY

OF THE

PUBLIC REVENUE

OF THE

BRITISH EMPIRE.

By JOHN SINCLAIR, Efq.

CAVENDUM EST, NE EXHAUSTO ÆRARIO, REPENTINA CALAMITATE RESPUBLICA
DESERATUR.
Bodin. *De Repub.* Lib. vi. Cap. 2.

———————————

LONDON:
PRINTED BY W. AND A. STRAHAN, FOR T. CADELL IN THE STRAND.
M DCC LXXXV.

ADVERTISEMENT.

THIS Work was begun in the month of Auguſt 1784, ſoon after the concluſion of the laſt Seſſion of Parliament. When it was originally undertaken, the Author had no conception of the immenſe difficulties attending it; and they have increaſed to ſuch a degree, that he has found it impoſſible to purſue it farther at preſent. He has judged it expedient, however, to lay before the Public the *Firſt* and *Second* Parts of the Work: and, if the preſent publication ſhould meet with a favourable reception, he propoſes attempting a *Third* Part, containing—A Hiſtory of the Progreſs of the National Revenue, together with ſome Obſervations on its preſent State—An Hiſtorical Account of the Progreſs of our National Expences—Obſervations on the Reſources of

A 2   the

the Nation—An Analyfis of our Public Debts; and an Enquiry into the real Nature and Amount of the Burden—A Plan for re-eftablifhing the Public Credit and Finances of the Country; together with fome Account of the Progrefs and Prefent State of the Revenue of Scotland and Ireland.

It is impoffible that a Work of this nature, which comprehends fuch a number of objects, and includes fuch an extent and variety of matter, fhould be perfected at once. To complete it in a manner fuited to the Author's ideas and wifhes; to compofe fuch a Hiftory of our Revenue as may clear up many doubtful points, correct the miftakes of former hiftorians upon the fubject, and minutely afcertain the real ftate of the national income in every æra of our hiftory, would require many years of severe labour and intenfe application. The prefent Work is indeed little more than the firft fketch or outlines of fuch a performance: and as the Author may, perhaps, be unable to execute fo laborious a tafk himfelf, it is his intention to add to the Third Part, a full Account of all the various Writings which have been publifhed upon the Finances of this Country, which may be of ufe to any other perfon who, with more leifure and happier talents, may alfo have courage and induftry equal to fo arduous an undertaking.

It

It is only farther to be remarked, that although we have had many naval, military, commercial, ecclefiaftical, and parliamentary hiftories, yet this may be faid to be the firft attempt at a financial hiftory on an enlarged fcale; and, it may be hoped, will, on that account, be received with the greater candour and indulgence by the Public.

TABLE of the SOVEREIGNS of ENGLAND, from the Conquest.

Norman Line.

King's Names.	When their Reigns began.	Years.	Reigned Months.	Days.
William the Conqueror -	- 1066 October 14.	20	10	26
William Rufus -	- 1087 September 9.	12	10	24
Henry I. - -	- 1100 August 2.	35	4	—
Stephen - -	- 1135 December 1.	18	10	24

The Saxon or Plantagenet Line.

Henry II. - -	- 1154 October 25.	34	8	11
Richard I. - -	- 1189 July 6.	9	9	—
John - -	- 1199 April 6.	7	—	12
Henry III. -	- 1216 October 19.	56	1	—
Edward I. - -	- 1272 November 16.	34	7	21
Edward II. -	- 1307 July 7.	19	6	20
Edward III. -	- 1327 January 27.	50	5	25
Richard II. -	- 1377 June 21.	12	3	8

The Line of Lancaster.

Henry IV. - -	- 1399 September 29.	13	5	21
Henry V. - -	- 1413 March 20.	9	5	11
Henry VI. - -	- 1422 August 31.	38	6	4

The Line of York.

Edward IV. - -	- 1460 March 4.	22	1	5
Edward V. - -	- 1483 April 9.	—	2	13
Richard III. -	- 1483 June 22.	2	2	—

The

The Houſe of Tudor.

Kings Names.	When their Reigns began.	Years.	Reigned Months.	Days.
Henry VII. -	- 1485 Auguſt 22.	23	8	—
Henry VIII. -	- 1509 April 22.	37	9	6
Edward VI. -	- 1547 January 28.	6	5	8
Queen Mary -	- 1553 July 6.	5	4	11
Queen Elizabeth -	- 1558 November 17.	44	4	7

The Houſe of Stuart.

James I. -	- 1602 March 24.	22	—	3
Charles I. - -	- 1625 March 27.	22	10	3
Charles II. - -	- 1648 January 30.	36	—	7
James II. - -	- 1684 February 6.	4	—	7

Since the Revolution.

William III. -	- 1688 February 13.	13	—	23
Queen Anne -	- 1701 March 8.	12	4	24
George I. -	- 1714 Auguſt 1.	12	10	10
George II. -	- 1727 June 11.	33	4	14
George III. -	- 1760 October 25.			

CON-

C O N T E N T S.

PART I.

a   CHAP.

THE

THE

H I S T O R Y

OF THE

PUBLIC REVENUE

OF THE

BRITISH EMPIRE.

PART I.

B

INTRODUCTION,

AND

PLAN of the WORK.

THE power of a State muft greatly depend on the income it poffeffes. If it enjoys a confiderable and unencumbered revenue, it can employ a greater proportion of its fubjects to carry on war, or may cultivate to greater advantage, the arts of peace, when unembarraffed with hoftilities: Whereas, with a fmall income, it can neither reward the fervices, nor encourage the exertions of its people; and it muft principally truft, both for its improvement and protection, to the natural activity of mankind, or to the voluntary and difinterefted zeal of public-fpirited individuals.

But however numerous the advantages of a great Revenue, they are dearly purchafed if they cannot be procured without oppreffion. A certain fhare of his annual income no individual can refufe to contribute for the general purpofes of the State. Sometimes alfo a flight additional burden may prove an incentive to labour, and a fpur to greater diligence and activity. But if the load becomes too heavy, either in confequence of the greatnefs of the amount, or the impolitic mode of laying it on, the induftry of a nation diminifhes, its wealth quickly difappears, the number of its people decreafes, and the greater the occafion it has for refources, the fewer it will actually enjoy.

Unfortunately, the fyftem of finance fo prevalent in Modern Europe, has an unavoidable tendency to public oppreffion: Wars are perpetually arifing, and the conteft generally is, who can firft drain the Exchequer, and deftroy the credit of the enemy. It is foon difcovered,

that

that war is not a favourable feafon for impofing heavy taxes on the property of the people, and that the beft means of commanding the neceffary fupplies is, to borrow from thofe who have confidence in the faith of the nation and the fecurity it can afford ; and confequently who are willing to leave their capitals unclaimed, provided they are regularly paid a certain annual intereft. , To pay that intereft, new taxes muft be devifed ; and as little care is taken by ignorant, by interefted, or by timid minifters, to leffen the incumbrances of war during the fhort intervals of peace, the burden perpetually increafes ; and the unhappy fubject finds himfelf obliged, not only to affift in defraying the charges neceffary for fupporting the government under which he lives, but is alfo compelled to contribute to the payment of expences incurred for expeditions which took place a century ago, and for wars, commenced, perhaps, contrary to the intereft of the nation ; conducted with profufion and weaknefs, and, of courfe, terminated with difgrace.

In no country has the fyftem I allude to been carried to fuch an excefs as in Great Britain. From the year 1684 to the prefent time, it has been under the neceffity of increafing its revenue from about Two, to at leaft *Fifteen Millions per Annum.* Fortunately the State can ftill bear that burden, heavy as it is ; but as any confiderable addition to it would probably be found unfupportable, and, at any rate, as fuch a fyftem muft fooner or later end in total bankruptcy, or the moft grievous oppreffion, it is full time for the nation at large to confider what plan is the moft likely to relieve us and our pofterity from the danger either of infamy or diftrefs.——To affift the public in fo important a difcuffion, the following Work has been compofed.

In attempting to give an hiftorical account of the finances of this country, the fubject naturally divides itfelf into two branches : The firft will relate to our public Revenue prior to the Revolution 1688 : The fecond, to our fyftem of finance fince that period. During the the firft æra, the expences of the State were principally defrayed by the ordinary revenue of the crown. It feldom happened that any extraordinary tax was laid upon the people ; and even then, it was only a temporary grant to the monarch upon the throne. The period fince the Revolution is diftinguifhed by principles of a very different nature.

The

The State has aſſumed the appearance of a great corporation : it extends its views beyond the immediate events, and preſſing exigencies of the moment—it forms ſyſtems of remote, as well as of immediate profit—it borrows money to cultivate, to defend, or to acquire diſtant poſſeſſions, in hopes that it will be amply repaid by the advantages they may be brought to yield.   At one time it protects a nation whoſe trade it conſiders as beneficial : at another, it engages in war, leſt the commerce of a neighbour and a rival ſhould be too great : in ſhort, it propoſes to itſelf a plan of perpetual accumulation and aggrandizement, which, according as it is well or ill conducted, muſt either end in the poſſeſſion of an extenſive and a powerful empire, or in total ruin.

How far ſuch a ſyſtem can boaſt of advantages adequate to the hazards with which it is accompanied, and the conſequences to which it leads, will more fully appear in the courſe of the following inveſtigation.

C. H A P.

CHAP. I.

Of the Modes made use of by the Ancient Britons for raising a public Revenue.

THE original inhabitants of the fouthern part of this ifland, it is probable, were defcended from the ancient Gauls or Celtæ, to whom they bore a ftrong refemblance in refpect to manners, language, government, and religion. They were divided into many tribes, or fmall communities, who being engaged in perpetual hoftilities with each other, could make but little progrefs in the arts of cultivation and improvement. Their commerce principally confifted in the exportation of hides, tin, and other articles of little value, and from which little profit was derived. Their hiftory remains involved in fable and obfcurity, until they became objects of importance fufficient to draw upon them the notice and the arms of Rome, when, after a gallant ftruggle, they found themfelves obliged to refign their independence, and fubmit to its yoke.

The government of the Ancient Britons, like that of every nation in a fimilar ftage of fociety, was of a mixed nature. Each little tribe had a prince or leader, who conducted the operations of war; and who, in proportion to his ability and fuccefs in that department, acquired influence and authority over the community in times of peace. But the weight of fuch princes was of little avail, unlefs it accorded with the general wifhes and prejudices of their fubjects; and their income was of too fcanty and limited a nature to furnifh them with the means of increafing the little power they were able to obtain.

The domain, or perfonal eftate of the monarch, was the principal fupport on which he placed his dependence. It enabled him to maintain the followers of his court, and occafionally to reward their fidelity and attachment with beneficial grants. If any addition was made to the territory of the State, the greater part of it in general fell to the fhare of the fovereign, by which that domain would be not a little increafed; and when his authority came to be more confirmed, im-

3   portant

portant acceſſions would arife from the frequent confiſcations which muſt have taken place in fuch turbulent communities.

The Britiſh kings drew fome advantage from the exercife of certain prerogatives with which they were inveſted. They commanded the forces of the community, and enjoyed a confiderable ſhare of the plunder that was taken; and the exclufive privilege they poſſeſſed of coining money, was probably attended with fome pecuniary benefit[1].

Prefents and fubfidies from foreign nations are alfo accounted by fuch monarchs an important branch of their revenue. " The German " princes (we are informed by a great hiſtorian) chiefly rejoice in the " gifts which come from neighbouring countries, not only fuch as are " fent by particular perfons, but in the name of the State[2]." To the monarch of a fmall tribe, a fuit of fplendid armour, rich harnefs, and chains of gold, are matters of great moment; and the tranfition is not difficult from the receiving of fuch prefents, to that of an annual fubfidy in money. The Romans were the firſt who taught the northern nations that mercenary fyſtem.

Before taxes exiſt to any great amount, a politic and popular fove-reign may draw a precarious revenue from the voluntary contributions of his fubjeſts. The northern nations, as defcribed by Tacitus, be-ſtowed on their princes, of their own accord, a certain number of cattle, or a certain portion of grain, with a view, under the appearance of honour and of reverence, to fupply their neceſſities[3]. There is every reafon to believe, that fuch contributions were cuſtomary among the Ancient Britons, and indeed they are the real fpring from which, in almoſt every country, taxes are derived.

Such, joined to perfonal fervices in war, were the ſlender fources on which alone the ancient inhabitants of this country depended, in order to protect themfelves and their poſſeſſions from the ambition, the mili-tary force, and the opulence of Rome. Yet poor as the Britons were, and feldom united with each other, they were not fubdued without making a gallant and obſtinate refiſtance. If the conqueſt was fo dif-ficult in their ſtate of poverty and difunion, it is fcarcely to be doubted

[1] Henry's Hiſt. of Great Britain, vol. i. p. 206.
[2] Tacit. de Morib. Germ. c. 15.   '   [3] Ibid.

that

that they would have been able to have repelled their invaders, had they been the fubjects of one monarch poffeffed of valour and ability in war, and enjoying an income fufficient to have enabled him to reward the zeal and exertions of his fubjects. But, in the words of Tacitus, " they rarely united their forces againft the common enemy; " and by this means, while each community fought feparately, they " were all fucceffively fubdued *."

CHAP. II.

Of the Revenues of Britain under the Roman Government.

IN examining the various political diftinctions between ancient and modern nations, none is more ftriking, or perhaps better intitled to attention, than the great difproportion between them, in regard to their public revenues. It is a fingular and aftonifhing circumftance, that the province of Gaul alone fhould have been able, about a century ago, to maintain a body of men equal to the whole military and naval eftablifhments of the Roman empire '; and it is more than probable, that the revenues of France, of Spain, and of Great Britain, joined together, are at this time equal in amount to the whole income of that empire, when it was moft flourifhing and moft extended '.

It is natural to afcribe this circumftance, in fome meafure, to the difcovery of America, and the great increafe of fpecie in confequence of that event; and it is not to be doubted, that fuch an increafe muft have enabled modern nations to pay, with greater facility, the demands

---

* Tacit. vita Agric. c. 12. Thofe who wifh farther information with regard to the revenue of the Ancient Britons, may confult Campbell's Political Survey, book iv. ch. 1. and Henry's Hift. of Great Britain, vol. i. p. 204.

' Gibbon's Hift. vol. i. p. 18.

' A great modern hiftorian calculates the amount of the Roman revenue at only fifteen or twenty millions of our money. Gibbon, vol. i. p. 164. But it muft have become more confiderable, particularly during the reign of Dioclefian, when a general fyftem of exaction was fpread over the whole empire.

of their refpective governments. But notwithftanding the great influx of money into Europe, fince the fuccefsful difcoveries of Columbus, unlefs ancient hiftorians deceive us, more fpecie muft have actually exifted in the various provinces of the Roman empire, during the reign of Auguftus, or of Trajan, than now circulates in the three monarchies above-mentioned; and confequently other caufes, perhaps the following in particular, muft have produced fo great a difproportion.

A warlike nation like the Romans confidered commerce, and the arts depending on it, as but fecondary objects of attention. With them valour in war, and a knowledge of the jurifprudence and political interefts of their country, were the only eftimable qualifications; whilft the fkill neceffary for carrying on traffic, was looked upon in a light the moft contemptible. The profeffion of a merchant being held in difrepute, it was purfued by none who had fpirit or abilities calculated for more popular and refpectable employments: hence little encouragement was given to commercial exertions. The principles of trade were but little known, and inftead of any addition and improvement to the progrefs made by other nations of antiquity, the difcoveries they had brought to light were neglected, and the fpirit of enterprife they had difplayed, remained unrivaled by their conquerors. But in modern times the cafe is different: trade is no longer confidered as difhonourable; it is undertaken by men of the greateft capacity, and of the moft refpectable characters; the principles of commerce are developed, and thoroughly underftood: a fpirit of induftry is excited; the efforts of the merchant and of the manufacturer meet with every poffible countenance and fupport: a new ftruggle has arifen among nations, and the conteft is, not only who fhall acquire the greateft extent of territory, but alfo who fhall poffefs the greateft number of active and induftrious fubjects. The confequence is, a confiderable addition to the general wealth of thofe countries where fuch objects have been attended to; and hence they have been enabled to furnifh a greater revenue for the purpofes of the State.

The extenfion of paper credit, and the eftablifhment of public debts, are alfo circumftances which have not a little contributed to increafe the oftenfible income of feveral modern nations. By the eafier circulation which paper-money and credit produced, individuals are better enabled

C

to pay the public burdens impofed upon them. If taxes were paid in kind, as is ftill the cafe in poor and uncultivated countries, paper-money would be of lefs advantage to individuals or to the Public. But as the exchequer muft have money from the people, and as it receives with equal facility paper-money and fpecie, the increafe of the one, in a financial view, is equally ufeful as a proportionable addition to the other.

In a country where taxes are laid upon articles of confumption, and where the intereft of the national incumbrances is paid chiefly to the natives, the public debt itfelf contributes to the increafe of the revenue. This feeming paradox, it is not difficult to account for. In Britain, for example, every individual who confumes his income, muft pay, in taxes to the State, about one-fifth part of what he expends. If, therefore, there is paid to the natives of this country eight millions *per annum*, as the intereft of their fhare of the national debt, a fifth part of that fum, or one million fix hundred thoufand pounds, will be repaid by thofe creditors in taxes to the very government from which it is received. This circumftance greatly contributes to render our national incumbrances much lefs burthenfome than otherwife they would be. A new debt thus produces a new fource of revenue, at leaft in proportion as the annual intereft of fuch a debt is paid to the natives of the kingdom.

Though Great Britain, France, and Spain cannot boaft, like the ancient Romans, of contiguous provinces fubject to their yoke, yet at the fame time they enjoy diftant colonies and poffeffions, which, in many refpects, are equally beneficial. The furplus of the products of thefe poffeffions, after maintaining their inhabitants, it is well known, centre in the capital. The commerce carried on between the mother-country and the colonies, furnifhes income and employment to many individuals in the former, who are thus better enabled to pay the burdens to which they are fubject. The wealthieft colonifts are in general fond of refiding at the feat of government, and contribute, by the taxes levied on their confumption, to increafe the income of the State ; and in fome cafes, fuch colonies pay no inconfiderable fum (after fupporting their own eftablifhments) into the coffers of their fovereign.

Not

Not only have means been invented to increafe the wealth, the induftry, and the refources of nations in modern times, but better modes
have alfo been devifed for raifing public revenues.

The ancient Romans fhewed no mercy to the nations they conquered. No fooner were the natives completely difarmed, and a little
inured to the yoke, than they found how fatal it was to be fubject to
diftant rulers, ignorant of their fituation, and carelefs of their complaints. Provided a revenue was raifed, they were little anxious about
the means by which it was effected : but tyranny defeats its own object; and thofe countries are uniformly.the moft productive of revenue, where there is the leaft oppreffion, and where the greateft attention is paid to the happinefs and profperity of the people.

It is not propofed to give any particular account of the Roman fyftem
of taxation, as it is a fubject which belongs more properly to the Roman, than to the Britifh hiftory, and would require a performance of
no contemptible fize to elucidate. It is fufficient for our prefent purpofe to remark, that the taxes paid by Britain, and the other provinces
of the empire, were partly levied in kind, and partly in money : that
thofe who paid taxes in kind, were obliged to furnifh about a tenth
part of the produce of their lands, and to carry the quantity they were
rated at, to any diftance however great, according to the fuppofed neceffities of the State, or to the caprice of thofe who were in power : that
fo heavy a duty was laid upon cattle (in which Britain particularly
abounded), that, joined to other grievances, it was the occafion of a
very dangerous revolt, which was not extinguifhed but with the greateft
difficulty : that heavy cuftoms were paid upon goods both imported
and exported : that the proprietors of mines were obliged to pay a
certain fhare of their profits, for the benefit of the State : that a duty
was laid upon commodities fold by auction, or in the public market,
above a certain value : that capitation taxes were rigoroufly executed;
to which might be added a variety of other impofts on legacies, flaves,
houfes, pillars, hearths, air, artifts, animals, and other articles too tedious
to mention [3]: "Nay, fuch, it was faid, is the exquifite tyranny, and

[3] See Henry's Hiftory of Great Britain, vol. i. p. 237.   Campbell's Political Survey, Book iv. chap. 2.   Whitaker's Hiftory of Manchefter, vol. i. p. 212.

" infatiable

" infatiable avarice of the Romans, that they extort taxes even from the " dead [4];" alluding to a duty upon the body of the deceafed, before it was fuffered to be buried.

At firft, the income of the province of Britain did not pay the whole expence of the eftablifhment [5]; but it came at length to be fo confiderable, as to furnifh the Imperial treafury with fome valuable remittances. It is fuppofed by a modern hiftorian, who founds his calculations upon the authority of Lipfius, that the whole revenue could not be lefs than two millions of pounds fterling [6]. Our information, however, as to the finances of the Roman empire in general, and in particular with regard to the fpecific fum drawn from each different province, is too fcanty and defective to furnifh us with the materials neceffary to form any exact computation.

CHAP. III.

Of the Revenue of England, during the government of the Saxons.

FROM the departure of the Romans, to the invafion of England by William of Normandy, comprizes a period of about fix hundred and twenty years ; an Æra diftinguifhed above all others in the Englifh, and perhaps in any other hiftory, for perpetual wars, ravages, and bloodfhed.

On the final retreat of the Romans, the northern parts of England were laid wafte by the defultory, but deftructive incurfions of the Scots and Picts. Upon their repulfion, a defperate and fatal difpute arofe, between the original natives of the country, and the Saxons, their auxiliaries. The latter had no fooner fecured the moft fertile provinces of

---

[4] Xiphil. ex Dione Nicolo, in Nerone.   [5] Appian. in Pref. p. 3.

[6] Henry's Hiftory, vol. i. p. 238. But Campbell fays, that it is impoffible at prefent, to form any probable guefs, of the Roman income from this ifland. Political Survey, vol. ii. p. 493, note 9.

the

the ifland, than the little kingdoms into which they were divided, began to contend with each other, for the fole poffeffion and intire government of the country. This important difpute was no fooner
brought to a conclufion, than the Saxons were attacked by a dangerous
enemy, who haraffed their coafts with the moft deftructive inroads,
and, after much flaughter, compelled them to fwear allegiance to the fovereigns of Denmark. At laft, William of Normandy, boldly determined to attempt another revolution, and actually fecured for himfelf and
his pofterity, the government of a country, thus ftained with the blood
of fo many conquerors, who were fucceffively vanquifhed in their
turn.

Little or no advantage could arife from a review of the reigns, or an
account of the revenues, of the innumerable multitude of monarchs,
who, in a greater or lefs degree, wielded the fceptre of England during
the Æra above mentioned. It will be fufficient to give a general fketch
of the refources from which their income arofe, without entering into
minute and unimportant details.

The demefnes of the Anglo-Saxon monarchs were very great: which
is a circumftance not difficult to be accounted for. The kingdoms of the
Heptarchy were founded by Chieftains, who commanded troops attached
to them by the ties of confanguinity, who were born with an hereditary
regard for the family they reprefented, or were led to join in the incurfion from the high idea they entertained of their courage, character,
and good conduct. In other words, they were the heads of clans
or little tribes, fuch as now exift among the Tartars, and fome veftiges
of which ftill remain in the mountains of Scotland. Such commanders, it is probable, would claim a confiderable fhare of the territory that
was conquered; and as, befides the plaufibility of their original pretenfions, it was difcovered in the courfe of the war, that many advantages refulted from fubordination on the one hand, and pre-eminence
on the other, it was natural to fuppofe that a confiderable portion of
the new acquifition would be given to the leader, not only to preferve
fo ufeful a pre-eminence, but alfo to fupport the dignity of his office,
and to reward his valour in the field. Thus each petty monarch of
the Heptarchy came to be poffeffed of a landed eftate of great value and
extent; and when all the domains of thefe different kingdoms, united

4. to

to enrich one fovereign, the whole muft have yielded a very confiderablé revenue.

The power of a monarch to determine queftions litigated among his fubjects, is one of the firft prerogatives with which he is entrufted. Employed in diftributing juftice among the people, in procefs of time ‑he is accounted the preferver and guardian of the public peace, and gradually becomes intitled to a fhare of the fines, impofed upon thofe, who difturb the quiet and good order of his government. Among the Saxons and other northern nations, criminals of every defcription, were only fubject to pecuniary punifhments, in proportion to the fuppofed atrocioufnefs of their offences: nay, 30,000 thrimfas were fuppofed to be a fufficient atonement for the unpremeditated murder of a monarch, of which 15,000 were paid to his kindred, and 15,000 went into the public ftock, or enriched his fucceffor [1]. Among a rude and licentious people, fuch as the Saxons, it is probable that crimes of every dye and denomination were not unfrequent; and, as a great proportion of the mulcts impofed on the offenders belonged to the king, it muft have added not a little to his income.

By the original conftitution of the Anglo-Saxon government, there were three important duties, commonly known by the name of the *Trinoda Neceffitas*, to which every proprietor of land was fubject. At firft, they were exacted in kind, and every individual was obliged to appear in perfon, when legally called upon, for the purpofe of repelling the enemy, of conftructing fortreffes for the public defence, or repairing the bridges neceffary for the internal commerce of the country. Such fervices, both for the advantage of the State, and the convenience of its more opulent and induftrious members, were gradually converted into money; and hence arofe the taxes known under the name of *Heregeld*, *Burg-bote* and *Brig-bote*, which it appears were occafionally levied by the Saxon monarchs [2].

---

[1] Bifhop Fleetwood (Chron. prec. p. 29.) fuppofes 30,000 thrimfas to be equal to 150 Saxon pounds of filver.   Hume (Append. vol. i. p. 219.) converts this fine into 1300l. of our money.   But another hiftorian calculates it only at £. 351 : 11 : 3. Henry's Hiftory of Great Britain, vol. ii. p. 511.   Rapin remarks, that *wilful murder* was punifhed, not by a fine, but with death.

[2] The word *Bote*, in the Saxon language, fignifies to repair; Rapin's Hiftory, vol. i. p. 119, note 3.

But

But the ordinary revenues of the crown, and the perfonal fervices of the people, were not adequate to the defence of the country, againft the incurfions of the Danes. They naturally began their depredations in the weakeft parts of the kingdom, where they flattered themfelves with the greateft booty, or where they were the leaft expected ; and as their progrefs was marked with every fpecies of devaftation and horror, it was found neceffary, when the kingdom was unable or unprepared to oppofe them, to purchafe their departure almoft on any terms. In order to raife the money wanted for that purpofe, each hide of land ³ (of which it is faid there were 243,600 during the Saxon government) was made fubject to a tax of one fhilling or more, according to the peculiar exigencies of the times. This impofition, which was called Danegeld, or Dane-money, was firft raifed by Ethelred, *anno* 991, and enabled him to purchafe an ignominious truce from the Danes, for the fum of £. 10,000, equal to about £. 300,000 of our modern money. *Anno* 994, a fimilar agreement was made at the price of £. 16,000 ⁴. But fuch bribes only ferved to expofe the miferable Saxons to frefh infults, and greater extortion. For gratifying the avarice increafed the hopes, and fwelled the demands of the invaders ⁵; and, on the whole, thefe events furnifh an ufeful leffon to other nations, not to truft for their fafety and protection, to the wealth they are poffeffed of, but rather to depend on the vigour of their councils, and their valour in the field.

³ A hide of land is by fome authors calculated to be as as much as one plough can manage in a year. Bede fixes it at the quantity neceffary to maintain a family. Some are fo particular as to fay that it contained one hundred acres ; others again affert, that the number of acres was uncertain. This tax was fometimes called Hidagium. See Mort. Hift. of England, vol. i. p. 93. Brady (Hift. of England, vol. i. p. 270, note) fays, that there were about 274,950 hides of land in England. See alfo Lytt. Hiftory of Henry II. vol. iii. p. 82.

⁴ See Brady's Hiftory, vol. i. p. 123.

⁵ The tribute paid to the Danes *anno* 1002, was £.24,000; *anno* 1007, £.36,000 ; *anno* 1012, £.48,000. The laft tribute of this kind raifed for the purpofe of bribing the Danes, was *anno* 1018, when Canute exacted the fum of £.72,000 from the kingdom in general, and about £.11,000 from the city of London befides, with a view of rewarding his Danifh followers, and of inducing them to leave England, which, without fome pecuniary recompence, would not eafily have been effected. Brady's Hift. of England, vol. i. p. 123.

A.t

At firft, this tax was laid on folely to bribe the Danes to defift from their depredations; but afterwards, under the pretence of making preparations to prevent their inroads, it became an annual branch of the revenue, and was levied by the fucceffors of Ethelred, until Edward the Confeffor, anno 1051, in order to render himfelf popular, not only abolifhed it, but reftored to the feveral proprietors from whom it had been collected, as much of the produce of the tax as remained in the exchequer [6]. It will be feen, in a future period of the hiftory of our revenue, that this odious and oppreffive burden was revived by William the Norman; a circumftance which greatly contributed to render him obnoxious to the Englifh.

' It is impoffible to form any accurate calculation of the income that would arife from thefe and other fources of revenue [7], which the king of England enjoyed from the landing of the Saxons, to the deftruction of the Heptarchy, and from thence to the Norman Conqueft. It is computed that the tax called Danegeld, at the rate of a fhilling for each hide of land; raifed 12,180 Saxon pounds, equal in point of real value to £.360,000 of our modern money; and confequently the tax laid on by Canute anno 1018, amounting to 83,000 Saxon pounds, was equal to a modern land tax of two millions and a half. It was found, however, too great a burden for the country to bear; and Danegeld, until the reign of William the Norman, never afterwards exceeded four fhillings per hide; but whatever was the income of the Saxon monarchs (when they poffeffed abilities adequate to their fituation), their revenue amply furnifhed them with the means of being refpected both at home and abroad, and enabled a prince poffeffed of Alfred's genius and capacity, to rival the fame, and to fhare in the immortality, of the greateft heroes and legiflators of antiquity [8].

C H A P.

[6] See Webb's account of Danegeld. Madox Excheq. chap. xvii. p. 1. Mort. Hift. of England, vol. i. p. 118.

[7] It is fuppofed that the Saxon monarchs exacted fome taxes of a feudal nature, particularly reliefs, then known under the name of heriots. It is alfo probable, that fome cuftoms were paid on merchandife, and fome profit drawn from vacant benefices.

[8] We are told that Alfred divided his revenue into two parts: he referved one part for himfelf, the other he gave to the poor. His own fhare was thrown into three divifions, which he expended, in maintaining his houfehold, in paying his architects, and

other

CHAP. IV.

General View of the ancient Revenue of the Crown of England.

UNDER every great political fyftem of government there are four principal fources of public revenue. The firft is, the income derived from property vefted in the public; the fecond, the emoluments of certain lucrative prerogatives annexed to the fovereignty; the third, voluntary contributions from the people; the fourth, taxes or impofts, not fpontaneoufly given, but legally exacted. From one or other of thefe great fources all public revenue muft arife. Without entering into any particular difcuffion of the principles on which they are refpectively founded, or enquiring where they are peculiarly productive, or which of them are the leaft burthenfome to a nation, the fole intent of the prefent chapter is to give a general view of the fources from which the ancient revenue of the Crown of England was derived; including alfo the firft dawning of our prefent fyftem of taxation.

I. Property vefted in the Sovereign.

In the preceding chapter it was obferved, that the royal domains of the Saxon monarchs were very confiderable. It is faid, that the crown was poffeffed of 1422 manors, befides other lands and quit rents, in the time of Edward the Confeffor; and great additions muft have arifen

1. Crown lands.

other curious workmen, and in penfions to ftrangers united to his court, for the inftruction of his fubjects. The portion of his revenue appropriated for charitable ufes, was divided into four parts. The firft was affigned for the relief of the poor in general; the fecond, for the maintenance of the monafteries he had founded; the third, for the fubfiftence of the profeffors and fcholars at Oxford; the fourth, for poor monks, whether Englifh or foreigners. Hearne's Life of Alfred, p. 204.

Such as wifh to be more fully informed with regard to the revenue of England under the Saxon government, may confult Henry's Hiftory of Great Britain, vol. ii. p. 258. Campbell's Political Survey, vol. ii. p. 499. and Stuart's Hiftorical Differtation on the Englifh Conftitution, p. 105. 137. and 142.

D   from

from the confifcated eftates of thofe who fupported Harold, or who were afterwards driven into rebellion by the tyranny of the conqueror.

But whatever might be the original value and extent of the landed property of the crown, and however great the acceffions which it might receive, and though the ftricteft laws were enacted to prevent its alienation, and to check encroachments, yet the royal domains of England have fhared the fame fate with thofe of other countries, and hardly a veftige now remains of the extenfive property which William I. and his fucceffors were poffeffed of. Nor is this to be wondered at; for when great eftates are with difficulty kept for any length of time in the families, of private individuals, it cannot be expected, that property much more valuable and extenfive can be long preferved from the artful rapacity of needy favourites, the natural profufion of courts, or the negligence and treachery of their officers.

2. Forefts.   The royal forefts yielded no direct or certain revenue to the crown : an income could not be expected from wafte lands fet apart for deer and other animals of the chace, and deftined not for the king's profit, but for his recreation and amufement. However, as many laws were paffed, and particular courts and officers were appointed, for preferving the royal game, and as thofe who trefpaffed upon the royal forefts, were liable to heavy fines and amerciaments, profufe and needy monarchs were thence enabled to raife confiderable fums from fuch of their fubjects as lived in their neighbourhood [1]. This mode of raifing money was often complained of as oppreffive. It fell into difufe about the time of Charles I. and indeed was totally incompatible with the nature and principles of a free conftitution.

3. Mines.   The only remaining fpecies of property which the crown of England was intitled to, was a right to all the mines of gold and filver difcovered in the kingdom : nay, it was contended, that if the fmalleft quantity whatever of thefe precious metals was difcovered in a mine, it inftantly became the property of the monarch. This harfh and im-

[1] The king poffeffed fixty-eight forefts, thirteen chafes, and feven hundred and eighty-one parks in different parts of England, which, confidering the extreme paffion of the Englifh and Normans for hunting, were fo many fnares laid for the people, by which they were allured into trefpaffes, and brought within the reach of arbitrary and rigdrous laws. Hume, Appendix ii. vol. 2. p. 136.

politic

politic idea, was not completely effaced, until it was enacted foon after the Revolution, that the crown fhould only be intitled to purchafe the ore at a certain fixed price [1]; and even that provifion was of too unpopular a nature to be carried into practice.

2. Lucrative Prerogatives.

The prerogatives of a fovereign are certain rights annexed to the royal dignity with which he is invefted [2]. They are privileges entrufted to him for the common benefit of the public ; and, as they are properly confined to the fovereign, and ought not to be fhared by any of his fubjects, they are fometimes attended with lucrative advantages, and have yielded, when at their greateft height, no inconfiderable revenue.

The king, in particular, by the laws of England, was accounted **Right of Seigniory.** the fovereign lord, and original proprietor of all the lands in his kingdom. It was fuppofed that every portion of the foil was at firft granted by the crown, and was holden of it, fubject to military fervices. " The " intention of this fiction was, to enable the king, by his royal prero- " gative, to put the kingdom in a ftate of defence, whenever it might " be neceffary ; and every holder of land was thus obliged to maintain " the king's title, and to defend his territories with equal vigour and " fealty, as if he had received his eftate upon that exprefs condition [4]." But this fyftem, originally intended for the public protection and fecurity, was afterwards made a pretext to introduce a plan of tyranny and oppreffion hardly to be equalled in hiftory.

For, in the firft place, the proprietor of every eftate in the kingdom, **Efcuage.** in proportion to its extent, was burdened with military fervices ; for which, in procefs of time, a certain fum of money was taken, by way of fine or commutation, called *efcuage* [5]. 2. He was alfo fubject to **Quit rents.**

---

[1] 1 Will. and M. feff. i. c. 30. 5 Will. and M. c. 6.

[3] Black. Comm. on the Laws of England, book i. chap. vii. vol. i. p. 239, 7th edit.

[4] Ibid. vol. ii. p. 51. 53, &c.

[5] Efcuage is derived from *efcu* (French) a fhield ; and *efcuage* was a certain fum of money paid in lieu of the fervice of the fhield.

certain

certain annual payments or *rents* in money, laid on as a mark of the lord's pre-eminence, and in order to keep the vaſſal in perpetual remembrance of his feudal ſubordination.   3. He was obliged, under the name of *aids*, to give pecuniary aſſiſtance when neceſſary, to ranſom the king's perſon if taken priſoner, to furniſh a portion to his daughter, and to contribute to the expence incurred on making his eldeſt ſon a knight.   4. It was ſuppoſed, upon the death of the feudal poſſeſſor, that the eſtate ought to revert into the hands of the ſuperior lord, and under that pretence it was contended, that the new vaſſal ought to make him a preſent of a ſuit of armour (which, in ancient times, was reckoned peculiarly valuable), or to pay a fine under the name of *relief*; to which, in proceſs of time, an addition was made called *primer ſeiſin*, intitling the king to demand from the heir of any of his tenants *in capite*, who died ſeized of a knight's-fee, one year's profit, upon his being put in poſſeſſion of the eſtate.   5. If the heir was under age at the death of his predeceſſor, the king was intruſted with the *wardſhip*, or the cuſtody both of his perſon and eſtate, and enjoyed the income which it yielded, till he arrived at the age of twenty-one years, and conſequently was able to perform the ſervices ſtipulated for his feud.   If the heir was a female, ſhe came of age at ſixteen years, being then ſuppoſed capable of marrying a huſband who might act in her ſtead.   6. If the poſſeſſors of feudal eſtates had the power of entering into matrimonial connections during their minority, according to their own fancy and humour, they might introduce into the joint poſſeſſion of the *fief*, an enemy of the lord ; perhaps one deſcended from a family with whom he had an hereditary variance[c]. Upon this ground, the feudal ſuperior was inveſted with ſome degree of control over the ward's marriage, and at length the right of ſelling the ward in marriage, or of receiving the price or value of the match, was confirmed by an expreſs act of the legiſlature.   7. It was aſſerted by the feudal lawyers, that when the king gave an eſtate to be holden of himſelf and his ſucceſſors, it was a gift to a choſen and ſelected individual, which no other perſon ought to be put in poſſeſſion of, without his privity and conſent ; and that any attempt to infringe upon this eſſential ſtipulation, by alienating the lands to a ſtranger, ought to be

Side notes: Aids. / Relief. / Wardſhip. / Marriage. / Fine of alienation.

[c] Dalrymple on Feud. Prop. chap. ii. ſect. 2. 4th edit. p. 38.

2   attended

attended with the forfeiture of the grant[7]. This right was exercifed with great feverity, during feveral reigns in the earlier part of the Englifh hiftory, until at laft it was determined by ftat. Edward III. c. 12. that one third of the yearly value of the lands fhould be paid by way of *fine*, for a licence *of alienation*; but if the tenants prefumed to aliene without a licence, that they fhould be liable to a full year's rent of the eftate. 8. *Efcheat* was the laft fruit or incident refulting from the feudal fyftem. It was a fpecies of confifcation[8], by which the feud reverted to the fovereign, either from the delinquency of the vaffal (who held it under the implied condition that he fhould not prove guilty of any act of felony or treafon), or in confequence of his dying without an heir either fit to perform the ftipulated fervices, or intitled by the original grant to fucceed to the feud.

Efcheat.

Such was the heavy and complicated fyftem of perfonal flavery, and of financial oppreffion, to which this country was fubject, from the invafion of William the Norman, until the reftoration of the regal government in the year 1660. Fortunately, by 12 Car. 2. chap. 24. the whole fabric was demolifhed at one blow, and it is now a matter of juft aftonifhment how a nation who gloried in its freedom, and boafted of the mildnefs and benignity of its laws, could fuffer itfelf to be loaded for fo many centuries with a burden, which, notwithftanding fome partial mitigations, feems to have been almoft infupportable. This, among many other examples which might be produced from hiftory, clearly evinces how ftrongly men are rivetted to ancient ufages, and how difficult it is to bring about any material innovation, however falutary it may prove.

But thefe were not the only advantages attending the right of feigniory: for, as lord paramount of the kingdom, the fovereign claimed all *bona vacantia*, or goods to the property of which no other perfon had any legal pretenfion. Upon this principle chiefly, the king of England was intitled, 1. To all *treafures* of money, gold, filver, plate, or bullion, found hidden in the earth. 2. To *waifs*, or goods ftolen and waived, or thrown away by the thief in his flight, for fear of being

Treafure-trove.
Waifs.

---

[7] Bacon's Works, folio edit. vol. iii. p. 551.

[8] Lawyers make a diftinction between efcheats and forfeitures. See Wright on Tenures, p. 117. note x.

apprehended,

apprehended, provided the party injured did not exert himself in the *Eftrays.* purfuit or conviction of the offender.   3. To *eftrays,* or valuable animals found wandering without an owner, which, it is faid, belonged to the king, not only as *bona vacantia,* but alfo to recompenfe the damage done by them to the foil, of which he is the general proprietor. *Royal fifh.* 4. To certain fifh called royal on account of their fize and value, if they were either thrown afhore upon the coaft, or caught fo near it, as *Goods* to require little dexterity to kill them.   5. To *goods wrecked,* if no *wrecked.* proof could be made within a certain fpace of time who were the legal proprietors; a privilege perhaps given to the fovereign with a view of inciting him to check the inhuman practices too common upon fuch occafions, when fuch goods are fuffered to be pillaged by the inhabit-*Cuftody of* ants of the coaft.   6. To the annual profits arifing from the eftates *idiots.* of idiots, or natural fools, after defraying the expence of their main-tenance. For an idiot was accounted nobody by the law : his effects, therefore, during his life, were confidered as a fpecies of *bona vacantia,* and confequently belonged to the fovereign ; but after his death, they *Goods unin-* again reverted to their natural owners. Laftly, To the perfonal, as *herited.* well as landed property of every individual, to whofe inheritance no juft and legal claim could be produced.

However trifling any advantages arifing from fuch rights may appear in modern times, yet anciently they were accounted of confiderable value and importance. Nor was it reckoned at all beneath the dignity of the crown to exercife any of its rights, even the moft obnoxious, provided it yielded profit to the exchequer.

The remaining prerogatives of the crown attended with any lucra-tive advantages, were either of a military—judicial—political—inquifi-torial—commercial, or ecclefiaftical nature.

1. Military The right of declaring war, and of making peace, is a very import-*prerogatives.* ant prerogative, of old vefted in the fovereigns of this country. It was originally given to the monarch, in confequence of his having ufually acted as the general of the community ; and it was fuppofed, with fome degree of juftice, that none was fo capable of judging when the nation was in a condition to carry on war, or required a peace, as the commander of its forces. This prerogative was attended with fome profit. For, in confequence of it, the crown was intitled to a fhare of
the

the plunder taken in war, and it received into its exchequer, fuch tributes as the enemies of the State were compelled to pay, in order to purchafe, either a continuation of peace, or a ceffation from hoftilities.

The power of diftributing juftice, either perfonally, or through the medium of courts inftituted for that purpofe, was another royal privilege, acquired at an early period of fociety, and productive of fome revenue. As the adminiftrator of the laws, and guardian of the public peace, all fines and pecuniary punifhments were appropriated to the ufe of the fovereign ; nay, under the pretence of giving a recompence to the king and his officers for their trouble in adminiftering juftice, they were permitted to exact fees in the courfe of a great variety of legal proceedings, the profits of which were originally intended for the royal maintenance, though fince diverted to lefs ufeful or effential purpofes. *2. Judicial.*

The fovereign of England was accounted the fole fountain of honour—of office, and of privilege. It will appear, in the progrefs of this work, that this prerogative yielded fome profit to the exchequer; fome monarchs difpofing of offices for money; others making a fale of titles and honours; and in general, all of them demanding pecuniary returns for any privileges they beftowed, either on corporate bodies or individuals. *3. Political.*

It was imagined, that the king would often find it neceffary, with a view of examining into the real ftate and circumftances of the country, to make a perfonal progrefs throughout his dominions; and, as the removal of the court would occafion an unufual demand, at the places to which it went, for every fpecies of provifions, it was thought requifite to give the crown a right of purchafing neceffaries for the maintenance of the royal houfehold, at an appraifed valuation, in preference to all other perfons, and even to force the fale or the hire of any thing peculiarly wanted, without the owner's confent [9]. This prerogative, which obtained the names of *purveyance* and *pre-emption*, was afterwards extended to every fpot where the royal family refided. But the powers vefted in the purveyors, or officers appointed for that purpofe, being greatly abufed, and indeed becoming every day lefs requifite, *4. Inquifitorial.*

[9] Hume's Hiftory, vol. v. p. 365. 490. 547.

in confequence of the great increafe of cultivation and improvement, and of the abundance which neceffarily followed, the whole right was abolifhed, at the fame time with the harfh and obnoxious fyftem of military tenures; and, by 12 Car. II. chap. 24. the hereditary excife, and a duty on wine licences, were fettled on the crown in their ftead.

5. Commercial.

The king was alfo accounted the arbiter of commerce.   In that capacity, he had the direction and government of the internal trade of the country.   He alone eftablifhed public marts; and he might appropriate to his own ufe, the tolls and other profits arifing from them.   He had the entire regulation of the weights and meafures of the kingdom, a right that was attended with fome profit, until by ftatute 11 and 12 W. III. chap. 20. the office of aulnager (who received certain fees for meafuring cloths for fale) was taken away; and, as money is.the medium of commerce, it was in confequence of the fame prerogative, that the crown enjoyed the right of coining money, and the gain attending it [10].   Nor were thefe the only advantages refulting from this right; for, in virtue of acting as the arbiter of commerce, the king claimed the lucrative privilege of granting patents and monopolies, which, in the reigns of the firft monarchs of the Stuart race, was particularly abufed : nay, the poft-office is properly a mercantile monopoly, which is ftill retained for the benefit of the public, yielding no inconfiderable revenue.

6. Ecclefiftical prerogatives.

Since the reign of Henry VIII. the monarchs of England have been accounted the head of their people, not only in civil, but in ecclefiaftical matters; and, even before the Reformation, they enjoyed fome privileges and revenues from the church, not, however, attended with much real profit, as they were held under the implied truft of being alone made ufe of for the advantage of the clergy.   Without examining the propriety of that reftriction, it is fufficient to remark, that either

---

[10] The profit of coinage was five fhillings in every pound weight of gold; out of which a fhilling, and fometimes eighteen pence, was given to the mafter of the Mint, for his work and trouble; and a fhilling for every pound weight of filver, of which the king referved only a fourth part to himfelf.   Afterwards, in the reign of Henry V. the feignorage on filver was raifed to fifteen pence.   Sir M. Hales's Sher. Accounts, p. 6.

as head of the church, or before the Reformation, as poffeffing royal authority, the King claimed a right, 1. To the profits of all archbifhoprics and bifhoprics during a vacancy. 2. To a corody, or a right of compelling any of his bifhops to maintain one of his chaplains, or to give him a benefice. 3. To the tythes of all extra-parochial diftricts; and laftly, to the firft fruits and tenths of the livings of the clergy, which they originally paid to the pope; but which, upon the deftruction of his authority in England, were demanded by the King, as his fucceffor in clerical fupremacy.

Such were the lucrative prerogatives annexed to the fovereignty of England, of which it was thought neceffary to give this brief account, principally extracted from the works of that learned commentator on the laws of England, Sir William Blackftone, who had collected almoft every thing that either has been, or could be faid upon the fubject. The author flatters himfelf, that from this fhort ftatement and explanation of the feudal terms, any obfcurity in the following chapters will be prevented. With regard to thefe prerogatives, it may in general be remarked, that they were of too harfh and individious a nature, to be productive of much income, without occafioning the loudeft complaints: and hence it was found neceffary, by other means, to provide a revenue.

III.   Voluntary Contributions.

When the income of the public is found inadequate to the national expences, it is natural for a Monarch poffeffed of any degree of popularity, in the firft place to truft to the voluntary contributions of his fubjects; and in the financial hiftory of England, it will be found, that various benevolences or free gifts, were at different times paid by the people. But fupplies of fo precarious and uncertain a nature could not be much depended on; and it was neceffary at laft to have recourfe to taxes or contributions, exacted by the government of the country, without particularly confulting the inclinations of the people, in their individual capacity; a fyftem of revenue, which, though, when abufed, it has given birth to much difcontent, and indeed has occafioned many revolutions, yet has hardly ever been accompanied either with much
E   difguft

difguft, or with great oppreffion, where this rule has been invariably adhered to, *never to exact from any individual a fum of money, which, confiftently with his circumftances and the fituation of the public, he ought not, on every principle of juftice,* SPONTANEOUSLY *to have given.*

IV. Taxes.

Taxes are the laft legal expedient for procuring a public revenue, to which a financier can apply. They were not unknown in England prior to the Revolution ; but as they bore no refemblance, either in refpect to their weight, or the variety and number of their branches, to the immenfe farrago of heavy burdens with which we are now loaded, it is hoped that the following general view of this part of the fubject will fuffice.

1. Taxes in
kind.

The fcarcity of money in England, as well as in other kingdoms of Europe, prior to the difcovery of America, rendered it occafionally neceffary to levy taxes in kind. Of this, fome inftances occur in the Englifh hiftory, particularly in the time of Edward III. who, without either money or fome valuable commodity, could not have carried on his bold attempt of wrefting the crown of France from the houfe of Valois. In the twelfth year of his reign, *anno* 1338, he procured the enormous grant of half the wool in England, amounting to 20,000 packs, which was then worth, according to fome authors, 40 *l.* a pack, and confequently muft have brought in the immenfe fum of 800,000 *l.* Other hiftorians, however, deny that wool was at that time fo valuable.

2. Perfonal
Taxes.

Poll taxes, by which a man is compelled to pay for his perfonal exiftence, have always been accounted peculiarly hateful and oppreffive. It is well known, that an attempt to levy fuch a tax in the reign of Richard II. occafioned an infurrection under the command of Tyler, Straw, and others, which had nearly ended in a revolution[14]; and almoft in every inftance, when attempted in England, they have either proved obnoxious or unproductive. One exception, however, it is neceffary to take notice of.

3. Taxes on
the Jews.

From the period of the Norman invafion, to the eftablifhment of the Hanfeatic league, the commerce of the northern parts of Europe

[14] Stevens's Hiftory of Taxes, p. 118.

was

was principally carried on by the Jews; and as, in addition to the profits of trade, they enjoyed the more lucrative gains of ufury, it is eafy to perceive that they muſt in time have engroſſed a great proportion of the wealth of the country. But ſuch as were ſettled in England, did not long eſcape the fatal notice of the ſovereign and his miniſters; and as in conſequence of the method in which their riches were acquired, and the peculiarity of their dreſs and manners, joined to religious prejudices, they were deteſted by the people at large, the king met with no oppoſition in oppreſſing and pillaging them, in any way he thought proper. A court denominated the Exchequer of the Jews, was inſtituted for the ſole purpoſe of managing the revenue of Judaiſm, as it was called, which remained unaboliſhed until the year 1290, when the Jews were expelled from England by Edward I [12].

The ſpecies of houſe tax, called Hearthmoney, is among the moſt ancient in the kingdom. It is even mentioned in Doomſday Book, under the name of Fumage, or Fuage, and conſequently muſt have exiſted before the Conqueſt [13]. By Stat. 13 and 14 Car. II. ch. 10. an hereditary revenue of two ſhillings for every hearth, in all houſes paying to church and poor, was granted to the crown for ever. But as the duty could not be regularly collected, unleſs the revenue officers were empowered to view the infide of every houſe, it was thought contrary to the principles on which the Engliſh government is founded; and upon that ground, by 1 W. & M. ſeſſ. 1. ch. 10. it was utterly taken away, in order (it is ſaid in the preamble of the bill) " to erect a " laſting monument of their Majeſties goodneſs, in every houſe in the " kingdom."

But however neceſſary it might be, in conſequence of the politics of the times, to enact ſo popular a law, yet the real juſtice and propriety of ſuch an alteration may now be queſtioned. The tax might ſurely be levied without much hardſhip to the poor, or any great encroachment upon the nice feelings of the wealthy; and as the tax upon coals, carried by water, is a great diſcouragement to the manufactures and agriculture of the country, checks the increaſe of our naval ſtrength, and is in every reſpect abſurd and unequal, it is hoped that the time will come

4. Hearth-money.

---

[12] See Maddox's Hiſt. Excheq. c. 7. and Tovey's Anglia Judaica.
[13] Du Cange, v;;; Focagium. — Spelman, v;;; Fuage.

when

when fo impolitic a duty will be abrogated, and the more equal and falutary tax of Hearth-money eftablifhed in its room.

Before this part of the fubject is concluded, it may be proper to remark, that for fome years pofterior to the Conqueft, there exifted in England, a particular kind of Hearth-money, called *Moneyage*, or Mintage money, originally levied in Normandy, and thence imported into this ifland. It was a tax of a fhilling for each Hearth, payable every three years, by way of bounty or recompence to the king, not to alter or debafe the coin, which he was entitled to do by his prerogative. This branch of the revenue " was abolifhed by the charter of Henry I. and it was fo particularly obnoxious to the Englifh nation, on account of its Normanic original, and its repugnance to the laws of the Confeffor, that none of that monarch's fucceffors attempted to revive it.

5. Land tax. The origin of land taxes, in this country, may be traced to the duty called Efcuage, or Scutage, which has been aiready taken notice of, as refulting from the feudal fyftem. At firft, it was levied on the proprietors of land by the royal authority; but in confequence of this right being abufed, it was at laft declared by Magna Charta, and afterwards repeatedly confirmed by acts of parliament, that no Scutage fhould be impofed without the confent of the great men and commons, in parliament affembled. This tax was fometimes exacted, under the name of Hydage, or Carrucage. But taxes on land came, at laft, to be included under the general name of fubfidies, and of monthly affeffments.

6. Taxes on perfonal property. Nor was perfonal property exempted from incidental burdens. It will be feen, in the courfe of this work, that a tenth or fifteenth part of the moveables, or perfonal eftates of the people, was occafionally given to the king for carrying on his government. Tenths were firft granted in the reign of Henry II. to enable him to defray the expences of a pious expedition he had projected, in order to check the progrefs of Saladine, who threatened to drive the Chriftians from their poffeffions in Afia "; and hence it obtained the name of the Saladine Tythe. In the eighth year of the reign of Edward III. this tax was brought to a certainty. A tenth and fifteenth was then raifed, to the fum of 29,000l..

" Hume, Append. II. p. 132. Mort. vol. i. p. 206.

" Hume, vol. i. p. 458. Black. Comm. vol. i. p. 308.

equal

equal to 58,000l. of our prefent money [16]; and, ever after, it was affelfed according to that ftandard over the whole kingdom, without any alteration in the proportion of each diftrict.

A fubfidy was properly neither a tax upon perfonal or landed pro- 7. Subfidies. perty, but upon *income*. Every defcription of perfons, in proportion to their reputed eftates, paid after the nominal rate of four fhillings in the pound for lands, and two fhillings and fixpence for goods, whilft aliens paid in a double proportion. This tax was originally introduced in the reign of Richard II. and was calculated at fo low a valuation, that one lay fubfidy, at the above rates, did not exceed 70,000l. which, in the fhape of a modern land tax, would now produce two millions. But it is to be remarked, that the eftates of the clergy were not included in this fum ; for their fubfidies (until the 15th of Charles II.) were granted, not by parliament, but by their own convocation ; and a fubfidy from the church, at the rate of four fhillings in the pound, produced about 20,000l. The laft tax, by this mode of fubfidy, was levied *anno* 1670; fince which period, it was laid afide, and what is now called the Land Tax, though it alfo impofes a burden upon perfonal property, was eftablifhed in its room.

The cuftoms were an old branch of the royal revenue. It is faid, 6. Cuftoms. that they were, at firft, fmall fums paid by the merchants for the ufe of the king's warehoufes, weights, meafures [17], &c. Afterwards, a tax, known under the name of *Prifage*, took place, which was in fact nothing but a branch of purveyance ; in virtue of which, the king's officers feized two tuns of wine from every fhip belonging to England, importing twenty tuns, or more, in order to fupply the king's houfehold with that valuable article ; and for which they paid at the moderate rate of only twenty fhillings *per* tun. Merchant ftrangers were exempted from the tax of Prifage, but in lieu thereof, paid a duty of two fhillings for every tun they imported, which was called *Butlerage*, becaufe it was paid to the king's butler. The fubfidy called Tunnage and Poundage, or a tax upon every *tun* of wine, and every *pound* of merchandife, imported into this country, firft took place in the reign of Edward I. But the hiftory of that important branch of the revenue,

[16] Hume, vol. iii. p. 178, Note Z, vol. vi. p. 193.
[17] Gilb. Excheq. p. 214. Hume, vol. ii. p. 177.

and

and the income which it produced, will more fully appear, in the farther progrefs of this work.

The excife was firft eftablifhed in England by the long parliament, *anno* 1643. It is fuppofed, that the plan was firft adopted, in confequence of its fuccefs in the neighbouring commonwealth of Holland. It is not to be wondered at, that fo efficacious a mode of raifing money, when once it found admittance, fhould be perpetually increafing. Its prefent fize and magnitude, and the variety of its branches are well known; and, unfortunately, it is more likely to receive fome additions, than to fuffer any diminution.

Thus it appears, that there is hardly any produdtive tax to which we are now fubjedt, which may not be traced to a period earlier than the Revolution, though the duties which then exifted, were neither fo heavy in their amount, nor extended into fo many various branches.

The prefent fituation of England, however, in regard to financial burdens, cannot juftly be compared with the paft, without taking into our confideration, the illegal exadtions of the fovereign, and the wealth drawn from this country, by the extortions of the church of Rome.

5: Regal Exactions.

Hume juftly remarks, " That the ancient kings of England, feem to " have put themfelves on the footing of thofe barbarous eaftern princes, " whom no one durft approach without a prefent; who fell all their " good offices; and who intrude themfelves into every bufinefs, that " they may have a pretence for extortion"." And it is certain, that if the difgraceful means they adopted to procure money, had refted folely on the authority of hiftorians, inftead of remaining in our public records, the ftanding monuments, and indifputable evidence of their fhameful venality, they would have been rejedted as incredible. The exadtions to which I allude, are known under the names of Oblations—Queen-Gold —Amerciaments—Talliages—and Farms of Counties; to which might be added, extorted Benevolences, and compulfive Loans, if they required any particular explanation.

) Hift. vol. ii. p. 131.

Oblations,

Oblations, or Fines, as they were alfo called, are defcribed to be voluntary proffers of money, or of any other article, or commodity, to procure the favour of the crown, or to deprecate its refentment. It is hardly poffible to enumerate the various fpecies of them, which appear upon the ancient rolls of the revenue ; but it may not be improper to give a fhort view of the moft fingular and important.

1. The Kings of England were, in the firft place, accuftomed to receive confiderable fums of money for granting, or confirming rights and franchifes of every kind. A few inftances are fufficient to fhow the general nature of thefe payments. Robert de Cardinan gave ten marks, that he might have a market at the ancient borough of Leftwithiel [18]; the burgeffes of York, 200 marks for a confirmation of their liberties : the burgeffes of Bedford paid forty marks, to have the fame liberties as the burgeffes of Oxford : the vintners of Hereford paid forty fhillings, to have the king's grant, that a fextercium of wine might be fold for ten pence, in Hereford, for the fpace of a year [19].

2. A confiderable revenue alfo accrued to the Crown, by the fines which were paid on account of proceedings at law. The fame Sovereign who pretended to be the fountain of juftice, became too often the fource of iniquity and of oppreffion. Even in the reign of Henry II. who was undoubtedly the beft of the Norman Princes, there are inftances of money being given to the King by feveral of his fubjects, for ftopping or fufpending pleas, trials, and judgments, or for expediting them as fpeedily as poffible ; for procuring reftitution of lands, or chattels, or that they might not be diffeifed ; for obtaining an acquittal of certain crimes, and certain modes of trial, or a difcharge from imprifonment; and for infuring the king's protection, or his mediation in their affairs [20]. Nor was it unufual for a creditor, to offer the fovereign a certain portion of the debt, which he, as guardian of the laws, and the executor of juftice, would affift him in recovering [21]. To guard againft fuch fhameful abufes, was the object of the famous claufe in

---

[18] 6 Ric. I. Madox, p. 274.
[19] For a variety of other inftances ; fee Madox's Hift. Excheq; ch. 11.
[20] Lytt. Hift. vol. iii. p. 261.
[21] Madox, p. 311. Hume's Hift. vol. ii. p. 132.

Magna

Magna Charta : " *Nulli vendemus, nulli negabimus, aut differemus rectum,* " *aut justitiam* ["]."

3. A variety of inftances might alfo be produced, of oblations of fo mifcellaneous a nature, that it is impoffible to reduce them under particular heads. Many fines were paid, for leave either to hold or to quit certain offices. The tenants of the crown, who held *in capite,* frequently proffered confiderable fums of money, that they might not be compelled to marry, or at leaft, might be permitted to marry whom they chofe. None were fuffered to exercife commerce, or induftry of any kind, unlefs they furnifhed the crown with money. Thus merchandife, in all its various branches, became a fruitful fource of revenue. Some inftances likewife occur, of what were called, *concurrent fines,* and *counter fines :* The firft, when both parties concerned in any matter, fined to obtain the fame thing : The laft, when their requefts to the crown were directly oppofite. But it is to be remarked, that though the money was paid by each fuitor, yet, that the party who was unfuccefsful in the fuit, had his money returned to him ".

4. Nor was there any profit, however fmall, or any bufinefs, however ftrange, unimportant, or even difhonourable, in which the king would not interfere, when an oblation was proffered. Roger, fon of Nicholas, gave twenty lampreys, and twenty fhads, for an inqueft to find, whether Gilbert, fon of Alured, gave to Roger two hundred muttons, to obtain his confirmation for certain lands, or whether Roger took them from him by violence ". The wife of Hugh de Nevile (who was probably a prifoner under clofe confinement) gave the king two hundred hens, that fhe might fleep with her hufband one night ; and not being able to provide them immediately, her hufband, and Thomas de Sanford, pledged themfelves, that they fhould be delivered within a limited time ". Peter de Perariis gave twenty marks for leave to falt fifhes, as Peter Chevalier ufed to do. The Abbot of Rucford gave ten marks for leave to erect houfes, and place men upon his lands, near

---

²² Art. 47.   ²³ Lytt. Hift. vol. iii. p. 262.   ²⁴ Madox, 305.
²⁵ Ditto, p. 326. This fingular Oblation was proffered, in the fixth year of the reign of John. Lord Lyttelton, however, properly remarks, that the ludicrous kind of tyranny which the King exercifed over his fubjects, muft rather be imputed to the character of the man, than to the law, or cuftom of the times. Hift. of Hen. II. vol. iii. p. 263.

2   Welhang,

Welhang, to fecure his wood there from being ftolen. Ralf Bardolf was fined five marks, for leave to rife from his infirmity: and to the difgrace of the laws and juftice of England in thofe days, the rich and powerful county of Norfolk thought it neceffary to proffer an oblation of forty marks, in order that it might be fairly dealt with: the burgeffes of Yarmouth, twenty-five marks, that they might be dealt with according to the king's charters, which they have for their liberties; and feveral hundreds of Northamptonfhire, fixty marks, that they might be heard without impeachment [16].

When an oblation was proffered to the king in money, the Queen-confort at the time was entitled to demand from the party, a certain addition to it, founded on the fuppofition, that when the king granted any fpecial favour to any of his fubjects, or mitigated any burden or penalty to which they were liable, that fhe had interpofed her good offices in behalf of the fuitor. This ancient perquifite was called Queen Gold, or *Aurum Reginæ*, becaufe the queen received an ounce of gold, for every hundred marks of filver promifed to the king [17].

The pecuniary punifhments impofed by the fovereigns of England, for crimes and trefpaffes committed by their fubjects, formed another lucrative and difgraceful branch of their revenue; and as no limit whatever was put to thefe amerciaments, until they were fortunately brought within fome reafonable bounds by *Magna Charta*, many were obliged to pay great fums of money, and were brought to the brink of ruin, for trivial, and fometimes imaginary offences. Among the various inftances which may be found in Madox's Hiftory of the Exchequer [18], the following will fufficiently explain the nature of thefe exactions. The men of Northumberland were ammerced, for not cutting off the feet of their dogs [19]: Harvey, the clerk, for impleading the abbefs of Winton, contrary to the king's command [20]: Ralph Fitz-Roger, for faying a thing which he afterwards contradicted [21]: Stephen de Merefict, *pro fulto refponfo*. Gilbert de Henley, *pro falfo dicto*: Nicholas, fon of

2. Queen-Gold.

3. Amerciaments.

---

[16] Madox, Hift. Excheq. p. 295, 296. Thefe infamous tranfactions took place in the reigns of John, and of Henry III.
[17] Dial. de Scaccario, lib. ii. c. 26. Blackft. Comm. vol. i. p. 219. Lytt. Hift. vol. iii. p. 263. Henry's Hift. vol. iii. p. 351. [18] Chap. 14.
[19] Madox, p. 388.   [20] Ibid. p. 390.   [21] Ibid. p. 388.

F   Liulf,

Liulf, *pro ſtulto diƐto :* Henry, the dean, and many others, *pro ſtulti-loquio*[31]: The hundred of Boƈtone, for the default of a certain maid-fervant, who was prefent when a horfe ftruck a man, and killed him[33]. The amerciaments for the forefts were particularly oppreffive; and by trefpaffes, defaults, purpreftures, and otherwife, a great revenue was an-nually raifed from the diftriƈts in their neighbourhood[34].

4. Talliages.   The tenants in the royal demefnes (in which, originally, all the great towns in the kingdom were comprehended) were alfo fubjeƈt to certain arbitrary exaƈtions, called *talliages,* or *cuttings,* becaufe a certain pro-portion of their perfonal property was under this name taken from them, and appropriated to the ufe of the fovereign[35]. In the king's manors and landed eftates, fuch exaƈtions were totally arbitrary; but in towns, it was a kind of free-gift from all the inhabitants, as a body corporate, who were affembled together by the juftices itinerant in the courfe of their circuits, in order to be made acquainted with the king's neceffities, and the fum which he expeƈted. If any town, or borough, however, in confequence of this requifition, did not give, according to the wants or expeƈtations of the crown, the jufticiar enquired into their behaviour, and into the manner in which their privileges were made ufe of, and any plaufible pretence was embraced, of iffuing out *Quo Warranto's,* and of confifcating the charters they had received[36]. Thofe who held their land in *Frank Almoigne,* or were fubjeƈt to military fervices, and to the commutation known by the name of *Efcuage,* were exempted from this exaƈtion[37]. But in procefs of time, when the profits of Efcuage (for reafons which will be afterwards mentioned) were greatly reduced in value and amount; and when it was perceived, that in confequence of the great wealth acquired by thofe towns which were liable to be tal-liaged, that they were capable of being made a great and produƈtive fource of revenue; it was then that Edward I. faw the propriety of colleƈting the military and commercial tenants of the crown into one body, and of procuring, by means of fuch an union, not partial aids, but fubfidies from the kingdom in general. The happy effeƈts refulting from this judicious meafure are well known. The public revenue was

[31] Madox, p. 392.   [33] Ibid. p. 393.   [34] Ibid. p. 272.
[35] Talliage is derived from the French verb *Tailler*, to cut. See Du Cange Gloff. *voce* Tallagium.   [36] Gilb. Excheq. p. 20. 21. 33. 34. & 192.
[37] Lytt. Hift. vol. iii. p. 256.

increafed,

increafed, and the lower houfe of parliament thus acquired that weight
and confequence in the ftate, which enabled it to eftablifh the rights and
liberties of the people upon the firmeft foundations.

But the ancient kings of England, not contented with thefe exactions, were alfo accuftomed to let the different counties in the kingdom, in farm, to certain officers, called Sheriffs, who, in confideration
of fums annually paid to the exchequer, were entrufted with powers,
too often attended with the greateft oppreffion of the people.   Such officers would not exercife much caution in their mode of proceeding,
when they were accounted " *the deputies of the Lord, of the great Seig-*
" *neurie of the realm.*"   And as the leafes which they received were
only annual, that circumftance would not tend to diminifh the various
abufes, which fuch petty tyrants would naturally be inclined, either
to countenance, or to commit, in their refpective diftricts [18].

5. Papal Exactions.

Whilft the authority of the Pope was acknowledged in this country,
England was defervedly accounted one of the richeft jewels in the papal
crown.   Without entering minutely into the various exactions of the
Roman pontiffs, which may be found, at full length, in a volume confined to that particular fubject [19], it is fufficient for our prefent purpofe
to remark, that, during the reign of King John, an annual tribute of
700 marks was paid for England, and 300 for Ireland; and that every
houfe in the kingdom, in which there was twenty penny worth of
goods, paid a penny yearly to the Pontiff, or his legate.   This tax
was levied with fuch ftrictnefs, that it was held to be a *confuetudo quafi
apoftolica* [20].   The firft fruits, and tenths, of all the fpiritual livings

[18] Maddox. Excheq. p. 223.   The particulars of the *proficium commitatis*, may be feen
in Hales's Sheriff's Accounts, p. 30, 31, 32.   The Crown alfo exacted yearly farms,
or rents, from towns, burghs, and gilds.   Madox, p. 226.

[19] See the Romifh *Horfe Leech*, or an impartial account of the intolerable charge of
Popery to this nation, by Thomas Staveley, Efq; The firft edition was publifhed *anno* 1664,
the fecond in 1769.   Alfo Egane's Book of Rates, now ufed in the Sin Cuftom-houfe
of the Church of Rome, printed *Anno* 1673.

[20] Sleiden fays, that when Peter's pence was abolifhed by Henry VIII. it
amounted to the fum of 7500l. *per annum.*   See Lawfon's Mite into the Treafury,
chap. xi. p. 81.   If this fum arofe from a penny a houfe, there muft have been
1,800,000 houfes in England alone, which is hardly to be credited.

in the kingdom were alſo exacted, and, beſides regular taxes, there were a variety of occaſional exactions, as " penſions, cenſes, procura- " tions, ſuits for proviſions, and expeditions of bulls, for archbiſhoprics " and biſhoprics, and for delegacies ; and the reſcripts in cauſes of con- " tentions and appeals, juriſdictions legatine, diſpenſations, licences, " faculties, grants, relaxations, abolitions, and infinite ſorts of bulls, " brieves, and inſtruments of ſundry natures, names, and kinds, to " the great decay and impoveriſhment of the kingdom ".". It is in- credible, what ſums of money are ſuppoſed to have been extracted out of this kingdom under theſe pretences ; and how much they contri- buted, to render it difficult for the crown, to raiſe a revenue adequate to the exigencies of the ſtate.

Concluſion. Such were the burdens to which the inhabitants of England were formerly ſubject. It is certain, that they did not exiſt at once ; and that ſometimes one mode of exaction prevailed, which, in proceſs of time, was abandoned in favour of another. But, whatever the *lauda- tores temporis acti* may ſay, it muſt be evident to every impartial perſon, that our anceſtors had great reaſon to be diſſatisfied with their political ſituation, even in the article of taxation ; and perhaps the preſent æra, is, in that, as well as in many other reſpects, as deſirable a period to live in, as any that can be pointed out in the hiſtory of this country ; our additional weight of taxes being fully compenſated, by a more extended commerce, by improvements in every branch of ſcience and of art, and by great acceſſions to our wealth, our ſecurity, and our freedom.

4' 25 Henry VIII. cap. 1.

CHAP. V.

Of the Revenue of England under the Government of the Norman Line.

IT is natural at the firſt glance to imagine, that an inſular dominion is peculiarly inacceſſible, and eaſy to be defended ; that the expence of a maritime expedition, the hazards of the ſea, the difficulty attending the landing of troops, and the riſk of famine, joined to the oppoſition of the natives, would place almoſt unſurmountable obſtacles in the way of an invader ; and though, by chooſing a happy moment, one attempt might perhaps be proſperous, yet that many ages would elapſe, before another opportunity, equally fortunate, could poſſibly occur. It is ſingular, however, that Britain has hardly ever been invaded, without having produced an important revolution ; and it may not be improper, briefly to ſtate, whence this has proceeded, and what peculiar circumſtances contributed to render the Norman invaſion ſucceſsful.

The more ſecure a nation is, or conſiders itſelf to be, the leſs precaution it will take for its ſafety and defence. Deriding the idea of invaſion, and laughing at the efforts of an enemy, it is unprepared to reſiſt an attack when it actually takes place. If the firſt difficulties, therefore, are ſurmounted, and more eſpecially if the invader is fortunate enough to conquer in the firſt engagement, he afterwards finds no fortreſs to check his progreſs, or to obſtruct his march to any place of which he wiſhes to be maſter. The whole country becomes a ſcene of tumult, anarchy, and confuſion ; and every diſtrict ſtrives which of them ſhall manifeſt the greateſt readineſs to ſubmit to his yoke.

An invader, qualified for any bold enterprize, on the other hand, is thoroughly appriſed of all the difficulties he has to encounter ; and is ſenſible, that his only proſpect of ſucceſs depends upon his power and dexterity to overcome them. He makes, therefore, every neceſſary preparation—he proceeds upon a ſettled plan—he cautiouſly weighs every adverſe and untoward circumſtance ; and never ventures to ſet

out,

out, without a ftrong probability in his favour, and a full affurance, if fuccefsful, of being amply rewarded.

The being pent up in an ifland, and that ifland poffeffed by an enemy, without any place of refuge, or hopes of efcape, is a ftrong fpur to the greateft exertions. An ancient general, who was determined to conquer, placed his army, with a deep river behind them, and informed his troops, that they muft either vanquifh.the foe, or perifh in the flood. An enemy, by whom an ifland is invaded, is uniformly in that defperate predicament; and has no alternative, but either to conquer, or be deftroyed.

Peculiar circumftances alfo contributed to the fuccefs of the Duke of Normandy. When he made his attempt, the Englifh nation confifted of a motley mixture of Danes and Saxons, who detefted each other, and many of whom had a predilection for the Norman manners, language, and government. Edward the Confeffor indulged himfelf in this attachment to the greateft excefs; and his example was followed by all the retainers and fervants of the court.

Though Harold poffeffed perfonal courage and abilities, yet he was not the legal, hereditary fovereign of the country. The Englifh admired his valour, and they had recently feen all the qualities of a great commander fuccefsfully difplayed againft a formidable army of Norwegians; but they knew, that he fat upon a throne, to which another was entitled. They fought under his banners therefore, as if they contended rather to fupport their own character, and to defend their own rights, than to fecure his crown from the pretenfions of a rival. Indeed, if Harold had not been confidered as an ufurper, they would not have murmured becaufe the Norwegian booty was withheld, nor would they have abandoned his colours, in confequence of that difappointment, or difregarded the orders of their general, when the fate of England depended upon their difcipline and obedience.

To crown the whole, Edgar Ætheling, the reprefentative of the Saxon monarchs, and confequently the legitimate fovereign of the country, to whom, after the death of Harold, the Englifh naturally looked up, had neither experience nor abilities calculated to act with vigour in fo critical a juncture. He neither knew how to curb the foe, how to conciliate the affections of his fubjects, or how to animate troops

4   difpirited

difpirited by the overthrow they had received; and being better fitted for the calm fcenes of private life, than for the tempeft of war or the intrigues of a cabinet, he relied on his infignificance, for at leaft perfonal fafety; and throwing himfelf at the feet of the Norman, was one of the firft who furnifhed an example of fubmiffion to the Conqueror.

In confequence of thefe fortunate circumftances, joined to the countenance of the Pope, the affiftance of the Englifh clergy, the pretended will and deftination of the Confeffor, but above all to the prudence of his own conduct, and the ftrong affurances he gave his new fubjects, that every attention would be paid to the prefervation of their public liberties, and private rights; William of Normandy, after having vanquifhed the army of England, and flain its monarch, at the decifive battle of Haftings, was acknowledged the fovereign of the country, and crowned at Weftminfter, with all the forms ufual at fuch folemnities. His pofterity have ever fince fat upon the throne of England. But as Henry the Second was likewife defcended from the old Saxon line, to whom, in the opinion of the Englifh nation, the crown belonged; and as, in the perfon of that Prince, the former royal race was faid to have been re-eftablifhed, and a new æra to have been introduced into the Englifh hiftory, the prefent Chapter is therefore reftricted to the reigns of the four firft Kings after the Norman invafion.

Revenue of WILLIAM the Conqueror.

It has been much controverted, whether William ought to be accounted the Conqueror of England, in the plain and literal fenfe of that word; antiquarians having difcovered, that *conqueftus* may be applied not only to an acquifition by force of arms, but alfo by purchafe, or by donation. They have thence contended, that by the Norman Conqueft, ancient hiftorians meant the acquifition of England by the Duke of Normandy, in confequence of the pretended will of the Confeffor, and the voluntary fubmiffion of the Englifh. It is certain, that William conducted his meafures with the greateft art, prudence and dexterity; that he foothed the inhabitants of the country, until they were completely in his power: and, perhaps, he would have trufted them,

them, if he could have depended on their fidelity and attachment. But both parties were jealous of each other, and it is impoffible, confiftently with hiftorical evidence, to confider the firft of the Norman monarchs in any other light, than as *a conqueror who, partly by force, and partly by ftratagem, fubdued a country, to the government of which he had no juft pretenfion, and a majority of whofe inhabitants detefted the tyrant they were fubject to, and would gladly have thrown off his yoke.*

Among the other means purfued by William I. to fecure his acquifition, the following are more particularly connected with the object of this work: namely, the complete eftablifhment of the feudal fyftem— the furvey made of the kingdom in general, and in particular, of the value and extent of the royal domains; and the inftitution of a court of exchequer, after the model of a fimilar court in Normandy.

1. Eftablifh-ment of the feudal fyf-tem.

The enjoyment of landed property, fubject to military fervice, is not an unufual mode of holding an eftate. It was cuftomary in ancient, as well as in modern times: it exifted in the Roman, as well as other empires. But what diftinguifhed fiefs from every other military fyftem was this, that in the firft place, they were not hereditary : and fecond-ly, that in order to remedy this original defect, a thoufand fubtilties were invented, to fecure the advantages of fucceffion to the heirs of the original proprietors. Hence arofe wardfhips, reliefs, and other in-cidents, or peculiar characteriftics of the feudal tenure. Even under the Saxon monarchs, every proprietor of land was bound to affift his fovereign in war, without pay or recompence ; and he was alfo fubject to a relief, or acknowledgment to his immediate fuperior, when he firft entered into the poffeffion of his eftate. But the various burdens of the feudal fyftem were not completely eftablifhed until after the conqueft. The whole kingdom was then divided into 60,215 knights fees; the holder of each of which, was not only bound to furnifh a knight, or armed horfeman, for the public defence, but he was likewife liable to a variety of impofitions, at firft light and eafy, and apparently for the benefit of the vaffal, but afterwards converted, by the fubtile dexterity of the feudal lawyers, into a fyftem fraught with every fpecies of oppreffion.

2. Dooms-day Book.

The monarchy of England was originally compofed of feven inde-pendent kingdoms, the fovereign of each of which, was poffeffed of a

6

confider-

confiderable domain in all the various diftricts of the heptarchy: and as, in confequence of that circumftance, the eftates belonging to the crown of England, when the heptarchy was deftroyed, were not only extenfive in themfelves, but difperfed and fcattered over the whole face of the country, they were expofed to great diminution, and could hardly be preferved entire, unlefs frequently furveyed and diftinguifhed from the property of individuals. It is certain, that Alfred completed a furvey of that nature, which, for a long time, was carefully preferved at Winchefter[1]. In imitation of fo laudable an example, and, as fome imagine, with a view of extending his feudal prerogatives over every diftrict in the country, William began, and actually finifhed a furvey, not only of the royal domains, but alfo of all the landed property of the kingdom, fome of the northern counties only excepted[2]. Six years were employed in this laborious undertaking. The fruit of it was, that ancient record, lately engraven at the public expence, called *Dom-boc*, on account of its being the *book* which contained the final *doom*, or fentence, in what manner each eftate was to be held, and afterwards Doomfday Book (in allufion to the day of judgment), becaufe no man was fpared, but every perfon was obliged to give in a particular account of his eftate[3]. Its authority was held to be fo final and conclufive, that all controverfies in regard to tenure were decided by it, even in cafes where its evidence proved unfavourable to the crown.

The extent of the royal domains, and the number of diftricts into which they fpread, joined to the great variety of the feudal fources of revenue, rendered it neceffary, foon after the Conqueft, to erect a new court, called the Court of Exchequer, for the better management of the royal income. Some antiquaries have contended, that an inftitution of a fimilar nature exifted under the Saxon government; a point which it is unneceffary to enter into, as it is acknowledged, that the

3. Court of Exchequer.

[1] Hearne's Life of Alfred, p. 115.

[2] This furvey, however, is not fo complete as fome authors pretend. Some cities and towns of note are not mentioned in it, and the greater part of the villages are omitted. It was principally intended to give the king a true account of his own lands, and demefnes, and thofe held by his tenants *in capite.* Rapin, vol. i. p. 177. Note 4.

[3] Dial. de Scaccario, lib. i. cap. 16. But fome imagine, that *Domefday* is a corruption of *Domus Dei*, from this book being at firft kept in a church. Hearne's Alfred, p. 115. Note 4.

G name

name is of Norman extraction, and that it imitated, in a great meafure, the Norman forms and manner of proceeding *. It was founded on principles perfectly confonant to thofe on which the Conqueror acted; whofe great object, at leaft in the latter part of his reign, certainly was, to opprefs a nation of whom he was jealous, and whofe fpirit he wifhed to crufh, under the appearance of law, and femblance of juftice.

The revenue of William I. may be confidered under four heads— The income of the Royal Domains—Voluntary Gifts—Legal Taxes— Tyrannical Exactions.

1. Landed Eftate.

Notwithftanding William's liberality to thofe who affifted him in the conqueft of England, and the immenfe eftates which he beftowed upon his particular favourites, yet fpecial care was taken, to referve a domain amply fufficient to fupport the dignity of the crown, and to maintain that rude hofpitality for which feudal courts were diftinguifhed. Indeed, without that immenfe fupply of provifions, that was furnifhed by the tenants of their demefnes, it would have been impoffible for the firft of the Norman monarchs, to have celebrated the feftivals of Chriftmas, Eafter, and Whitfuntide (when all the great barons of the kingdom, with their principal followers, were entertained by their fovereign), with the plenty and abundance to be expected at a royal table. It is to be remarked, that this practice continued until the middle of Henry the Second's reign, by whom, on account of the expence which it occafioned, it was finally abolifhed.

2. Voluntary Gifts.

William began his reign, in a manner which tended fo much to conciliate the affections of his new fubjects, that they were prevailed upon, foon after his coronation, to make him voluntary gifts and prefents to a confiderable amount. The Englifh fondly imagined, that by fuch means they would not only ingratiate themfelves with their fovereign, but would alfo enable him amply to reward his Norman followers, without requiring any tax or addition to his revenue. But, notwithftanding the large fums of money, which he thus found means to obtain ; and though he had got poffeffion of the treafures which Harold had amaffed, which were not inconfiderable, yet he foon difcovered, that with money alone, it was impoffible for him to fatisfy a rapacious

* Dial. de Scaccario, lib. i. cap. 4. Madox, p. 120.

3   foldiery,

foldiery, who had joined his ftandard in hopes of durable eftablifhments in land, and not of a temporary bounty; and hence it is faid, that he was reduced to the neceffity, of exafperating the Englifh, and driving them to rebellion, in order that he might have a pretence for diftributing their forfeited eftates, among his friends and followers.

The income received by the firft of the Norman monarchs, as Lord Paramount, or Feudal Superior of all the lands in England, depended upon fo many contingencies, that it is impoffible to form any eftimate of its value or amount. But in addition to the great but uncertain revenue which he thus received, and the other fources above-mentioned, he joined the odious tax of Danegeld; at firft, under the ufual pretence of guarding the fea from pirates; but afterwards, in confequence of an attack he apprehended from Sueno King of Denmark, who intended, it was faid, to vindicate his claim to the throne of England, with all the ftrength and forces of which he was poffeffed. During the reign of William, Danegeld varied from one to fix fhillings *per* hide [5], according to the exigencies of the crown. But the revival of fo obnoxious an impofition, however plaufible the grounds might be, on which it proceeded, gave much difcontent, and greatly contributed to the frequent infurrections, by which his government was difturbed.

3. Taxes.

It is afferted alfo, by fome ancient hiftorians, that William extorted confiderable fums of money from his fubjects, without any legal pretence: and finding that many of the Englifh, in terror of his exactions, had depofited their wealth in monafteries, he ordered them to be fearched; and not only appropriated to his own ufe, all the money, jewels, plate, and other valuable effects, belonging to individuals, which were difcovered there, but alfo feized the very fhrines and chalices of the churches [6]: articles which were accounted fo facred and inviolable, in that fuperftitious age, that it is difficult to conceive how a prince, who affected fo much zeal for religion, could hazard fuch an attempt.

4. Tyrannical exactions.

The amount of the Conqueror's income has been much difputed. *Ordericus Vitalis* fays, that, befides all the cafual profits of his feudal

Amount.

---

5 Matthew Paris fays, that Danegeld was raifed to fix fhillings *per* hide, *anno* 1083. He calls it *graviffima pecuniarum exactio*, p. 10.

6 Matthew Paris, Hift. Angl. Folio edit. 1606, p. 10.

preroga-

prerogatives, he enjoyed a revenue of about 400,000*l. per annum*[7]. This, in the opinion of two celebrated modern historians, is perfectly incredible. Hume remarks, that a pound of silver in that age contained three times the weight that it does at present; consequently 400,000*l*. then was equal to 1,200,000*l*. of our specie; and as any given sum of money, would then purchase about ten times more of the necessaries of life, than at present, the Conqueror, according to this calculation, must have enjoyed an unencumbered annual income, equal to nine or ten millions of the present currency. His military tenures, likewise, furnished him with a formidable army without any expence; so that he must have exceeded, in real power and opulence, any monarch recorded in history[8]. Voltaire, though he converts the Conqueror's income only into five millions of modern money, also contends, that ancient writers must have been greatly mistaken in their account of his wealth. For the revenue of England, he says, including Scotland and Ireland, does not yield so much, if we deduct what is levied for payment of the national debt[9]. The subtraction of any thing on account of the interest paid to the public creditors, is a very inaccurate and unjustifiable position, because it arises from taxes levied on the subject, as much as any other part of the national income. But these two great authors seem to have carried their scepticism too far in this, as they have done in many other instances. It is probable, that both of them would have been equally incredulous, had they been told thirty years ago, that Great Britain and Ireland could have raised in the year 1784, a revenue of above fourteen millions *per annum*. After all, it is impossible totally to discredit the accounts of *Vitalis*, an historian who was born only nine years after the conquest, and consequently must have enjoyed better access to information, than any modern can pretend to. Indeed, without such an income, it would have been impossible for the kings of England to have lived with such splendour and magnificence; to have bestowed such li-

---

[7] Or 1061 *l*. 10*s*. 0 ½*d*. a day. The words of Vitalis are—" Ipsi vero regi (ut fertur), " mille et sexaginta libræ sterilensis monetæ, solidique triginta, et tres oboli ex justis redditi- " bus Angliæ, per singulos dies redduntur, exceptis muneribus regiis, et reatuum redemp- " tionibus, aliisque multiplicibus negotiis, quæ regis ærarium quotidie adaugent." L. 4. p. 523. apud Duchef.

[8] Hume's History, vol. i. p. 277.   [9] Gen. Hist. vol. i. p. 166.

beral

beral donations on the church; to have carried on fo many public works; to have engaged in fo many expenfive wars; and after all, to have left behind them fuch confiderable treafures. Sixty thoufand pounds in filver, equal to 900,000 *l.* of modern money[10], was found in the Royal Treafury at Winchefter, after the death of the Conqueror; befides gold, jewels, veftments, and other articles of great value: and as he died in Normandy, where he had alfo large fums of money hoarded up (indeed it was his ufual practice to carry a treafure about with him), there is lefs reafon to believe that the accounts given of his wealth and annual income, could be greatly exaggerated. Befides, *Vitalis* is fo particular in the fum he mentions, ftating not only the pounds, but even the number of farthings which William received; namely, one thoufand and fixty pounds and thirty fhillings and three farthings a day (which is the mode of counting ftill ufed in the exchequer, inftead of one thoufand and fixtyone pounds ten fhillings, &c.), that one would fuppofe his information was derived from authentic records, and was not founded on vague or hafty computations.

As to the amount of this income in modern money, authors greatly differ. Dr. Henry computes it, as equal in efficacy to 5,808,975 *l.*[11]; Lord Lyttleton, to 5,369,925 *l.*[12]; and as they both differ fo much from Hume and indeed from other hiftorians, it is eafy to perceive what latitude there is in fuch computations for prejudice and fancy; and, perhaps, on the whole, there is more reafon to conclude, that a modern may err in making fuch calculations, than to fuppofe that an ancient writer could be grofsly miftaken in a plain matter of fact[13].

WILLIAM RUFUS.

The fecond fon of William the Conqueror, called Rufus, or the Red, on account of the colour of his hair, fucceeded to the throne of Eng-

[10] Henry's hift. vol. iii. p. 28.   [11] Ibid. vol. iii. p. 352.   [12] Hift. vol. iii. p. 454.
[13] The Conqueror's income muft have arifen, firft, from the tax of Danegeld, which at fix fhillings per hide would produce 73,080 *l.*; and fecondly, from the rents of his domains, which, it is more than probable, would make up the deficiency. This is a point, however, which muft foon be afcertained, as our antiquaries will now be able, from the publication of *Domefday-book*, fully to explain the value of the Royal Domains, and the income which they produced.

land,

land, in confequence of his father's deftination, the remiffnefs of his brother Robert, his own activity, and the attachment of Lanfranc Archbifhop of Canterbury, by whom he had been educated, and who poffeffed great weight and authority with the Englifh. The thirteen years during which this tyrant governed England, was a perpetual feries of extortions, of which the church in particular had great reafon to complain. It was an ufual practice with him, when any Bifhopric or Abbey became vacant, to feize all its temporalties, and to farm them out to his favourites, or to thofe who made him the higheft offer; and when any circumftance induced him to fill the vacancy, he exacted confiderable fums from thofe who were appointed. The plunder he collected from the church muft have been very great, when it is confidered that, at his death, he held in his own hands the Archbifhopric of Canterbury, the Bifhoprics of Winchefter and of Salifbury, and twelve of the richeft Abbacies in England[14].

Nor were the laity lefs haraffed by his extortions[15]. A tax of four fhillings for every hyde of land in the kingdom, was levied, to enable him to acquire the poffeffion of Normandy. Great fums were extorted, under the name of *benevolences* or free gifts, though, in fact, they were compulfatory; for it was well known that the king would punifh thofe who refufed to contribute. In the fixth year of his reign, he enlifted troops for an expedition into Normandy; and when they were affembled, in order to be embarked, either finding their affiftance unneceffary, or imagining that a fum of money would anfwer his purpofe better, he exacted ten fhillings from each man, under the pretence of defraying the expence he had been put to in furnifhing them with provifions[16]. In fhort, he was unqueftionably well entitled to the name of *the Red Dragon*, by which appellation his miferable fubjects attempted briefly to defcribe his violence and rapacity.

The hiftory of this monarch furnifhes an ufeful leffon on the vanity of human ambition. He fucceeded to the throne of England, contrary to the hereditary pretenfions of an elder brother, diftinguifhed for valour and military fkill. He found means to acquire, from that very brother, the poffeffion of the dutchy of Normandy, in confideration of ten thou-

Anno 1096.

---

[14] Matt. Paris, p. 52.   [15] Ibid. p. 42.   [16] Ibid. p. 16.

fand marks, advanced to him by way of mortgage; a fum which, though very inadequate to its value, yet enabled Robert to undertake his favourite enterprize (an expedition for the recovery of Jerufalem) in a manner fuitable to his dignity and ftation. Rufus had entered into an agreement with William Duke of Aquitaine, who was feized with the fame phrenzy of devotion; and, had not his death prevented it, he would foon have been mafter of that important dutchy for a fimilar confideration: nay, it was commonly fuppofed, that he intended to embrace any favourable opportunity that might occur, of attempting the acquifition or the conqueft of France, either by corruption or force. But, in the midft of his ambitious projects, whilft engaged in his favourite diverfion of hunting, he was pierced by an arrow, which foon put a period to his days; and it has never been clearly afcertained by whofe hand he fell, or whether his death was occafioned by any fortuitious accident, or was purpofely effected.

HENRY I.

The abfence of the Duke of Normandy, who had not yet returned from his crufade, furnifhed Henry, the Conqueror's third fon, with an opportunity of mounting the throne fo unexpectedly vacant by the death of Rufus. Not an inftant was loft in taking every ftep neceffary for that purpofe. The regalia, and the royal treafures, kept at Winchefter, were firft taken poffeffion of. A council was haftily affembled at London, by whom his title to the crown was recognized; and, in lefs than three days after his brother's death, the ceremony of his coronation was performed at Weftminfter, by Maurice Bifhop of London. The whole was conducted in a manner, which impreffes us with a favourable idea, of his vigour and abilities.

As Henry's title to the throne was highly queftionable, he found it neceffary, in order to conciliate the affections of his fubjects, to purfue a fyftem of government very different from that of his brother: according- Anno 1100. ly, foon after his coronation, he granted a charter, which contained many articles highly favourable to the liberties of the people. It was the bafis on which *Magna Charta* itfelf was founded; and it fully proves at what an

early

early period the Englifh were attentive to the prefervation of their rights and privileges, and that no fit opportunity was loft to have them afcertained.

Though this king is, in general, reprefented by our hiftorians in a very advantageous light, yet he is accufed of having occafionally forgotten his engagements to the public. Contrary to an exprefs claufe of the charter he had granted, he feized the temporalties of the archbifhopric of Canterbury, fold the woods belonging to it, plundered the tenants, and kept poffeffion of its revenues for above five years. His levying three fhillings on every hyde of land, when his daughter Matilda was married to Henry IV. Emperor of Germany, may be juftified upon feudal principles; but the fpecific fum he demanded (amounting, it is fuppofed, to about 800,000*l.* of modern currency) was to the greateft degree oppreffive[17]. The exactions of this monarch, however, are to be attributed, principally to his great anxiety, at firft to acquire, and afterwards to preferve the dutchy of Normandy; a re-union with which, many of his Englifh fubjects confidered to be effential. In the fifth year of his reign, they were particularly oppreffed, to raife a fum of money for defraying the charges of an expedition to the continent, upon which the poffeffion of that dutchy depended. A tax was laid even upon churches; and every incumbent was made anfwerable for the rate at which his parifh-church was affeffed[18]. Many heavy taxes were alfo laid on, in the feventeenth year of his reign, in confequence of a war he was obliged to carry on againft the King of France, for the fecurity of Normandy[19].

The reign of Henry is diftinguifhed by a very important alteration in regard to his revenue. We are informed by *Gervas of Tilbury*, in his famous Dialogue on the Exchequer[20], that the rents of the Royal Domains, for many years after the Norman Conqueft, were principally paid in kind; and that, in the reign of this monarch, they were converted

---

[17] Brady, vol. ii. p. 270.

[18] During the rage of this oppreffion, Henry was met, in his road to London, by two hundred parifh priefts in their furplices, who, on their bare knees, petitioned for fome mitigation of fo oppreffive an impofition; but their entreaties were ineffectual: for Henry never fuffered pity, to get the better of intereft. Mort. vol. i. p. 212. Note.

[19] Stevens, p. 18.   [20] Lib. i. ch. 7.

into

into money". As Henry lived much in Normandy, and was engaged in many foreign expeditions, money was particularly convenient to him; and in confequence of the fcarcity of fpecie at that time, the converfion was made on terms highly favourable to the vaffal, an ox being only valued at one fhilling, and a fheep at four pence. Both parties were then fatisfied; but it is certain that Henry's fuccefsors had much reafon to complain of the inadequate compofition he had accepted of: for it not a little diminifhed, at an after-period, the relative value and amount of the royal income; and greatly contributed to the future poverty and ne-ceffities of the crown.

S T E P H E N.

The attempt of Stephen to feat himfelf upon the throne of England, is one of the boldeft enterprizes recorded in hiftory. He was the grand-fon, it is true, of William the Conqueror, whofe daughter Adela had been married to his father the Earl of Blois, but he was the third fon of that marriage; and, as both his elder brothers were living, he had no he-reditary claim to the fucceffion. He oppofed the daughter of a fove-reign who had long reigned over the Englifh; and whofe government, though fometimes harfh and oppreffive, was in general popular. His rival, the Emprefs Matilda, indifputably reprefented the Norman, and had fome pretenfions to the inheritance of the Saxon fovereigns of Eng-land. Nor could he truft to the effects of his lavifh promifes to the Englifh nation, of maintaining a ftrict regard to the prefervation of their rights and privileges; for having abandoned the folemn engagements he had contracted to fupport the emprefs in her fucceffion to her father, it was natural to fuppofe that he could not be depended on to fulfil any other obligation. But fuch was the unfettled ftate of fucceffion to the crown; fo much were the people of that age delighted with bold and daring enterprizes, and fo attached to men of gallantry and fpirit, that Stephen found his attempt fuccefsful beyond his moft fanguine expectations. He was anointed King of

²¹ Madox Excheq. p. 186. Carte's Hift. of England, vol. i. p. 518. Hales's Sher. Accounts, p. 22. Dalrymp. of Feudal Prop. p. 27.

England

England foon after his arrival, and aſſumed the exercife of the royal authority with hardly any oppoſition.

The reign of this monarch paſſed in perpetual war and civil bloodſhed. During the whole period, the nation is reprefented to have been
in a ſtate the moſt deplorable. Some forfook their native country, to
avoid the miferies under which it groaned. A multitude of foreign
mercenaries brought over by Stephen to aſſiſt him in his uſurpation,
and to fupport his authority, fpread horror and devaſtation wherever
they went. Many who had lived in opulence were glad to ſhelter themfelves in the meaneſt cottages, and to feed upon dogs and carrion—the
fields lay fallow and negleɗed—commerce and induſtry were abandoned—towns of confiderable note were deferted by their inhabitants :
nor was any place, however facred or remote, exempted from the general
calamity [22]. Such is the defcription given us of the ſtate of England
during the reign of this ufurper, who at the fame time was a prince
(if we may judge from fome traits of his charaɗer) well qualified to
have promoted the happinefs and profperity of his fubjeɗs, had he fucceeded by a juſt title, or had he enjoyed the undiſturbed poſſeſſion and
government of the country [23].

Stephen had promifed on his coronation day, for ever to remit the
odious tax of Danegeld ; but the neceſſity of his affairs compelled him
to exaɗ it, notwithſtanding his oath, and a charter which he had granted.
It was the only regular tax he impofed. For during the greateſt part
of his reign, the only means he had of fupporting his troops, and maintaining his dignity, was by plunder and extortion. He is also accufed
of having alienated the demefnes of the crown, of having debafed the
coin, and of felling to the higheſt bidder, honours, offices, dignities,
and benefices in the church, the laſt pitiful refource of a profufe and
indigent monarch.

Conclufion.   It appears from this chapter, what little progrefs had been made in
the knowledge of finance, from the Norman invafion to the death of
Stephen. During the whole period, it was underſtood, that the king
ſhould live upon his own domains, and the profits of the feudal prero-

<hr>

[22] Lytt. vol. i. p. 328. and vol. ii. p. 133.   Stevens, p. 21.
[23] Hume, vol. i. p. 369.

2   gatives ;

gatives; and every fpecies of taxation (military fervices only excepted) was the object of averfion and difguft. Danegeld, the only regular tax that exifted at the time, though perhaps neceffary for the protection of the commerce of the nation, was confidered as fo peculiarly fevere, that every monarch who attempted to levy it, was accounted a tyrant and an oppreffor, and that fingle tax occafioned as many complaints, and as great an outcry, as the whole load of multifarious imposts, to which this country is at prefent fubject.

C H A P. VI.

Of the Revenue of England, during the Saxon Line, or Houfe of Plantagenet.

THE hiftory of England, and indeed of every other country fubject to a monarchical form of government, clearly demonftrates the manifold advantages refulting from a ftrict hereditary fucceffion. Whenever any doubt exifts to whom the crown legally belongs, difputes will arife; and turbulent and ambitious men, will embrace the party, which feems the moft likely to be of the greateft advantage to themfelves, without regarding the welfare or fafety of the State. The country is thus ruined by a competition between rivals, perhaps equally worthlefs; and, after all, the conteft is determined, not in favour of him who has the beft title, or who will govern beft, but of him who makes the moft lavifh promifes, or who is able to command the greateft number of bold and defperate adherents. It was by means of fuch promifes, and fuch fupport, that Stephen vindicated his pretenfions to the crown of England, to which another was legally intitled; at leaft, if the immediate defcendants of William the Norman had a right to the fovereignty.

H 2   But

But Henry II. not only claimed the crown, as lineally defcended from the Conqueror, but alfo as in fome meafure ' reprefenting the Saxon monarchs of England. His mother, the Emprefs Matilda, was defcended from Edmund Ironfide, the laft of the Saxon race who left any pofterity. Edmund's fon, known by the name of Edward the Out-law, had two children, Edgar Etheling, who died without iffue, and Margaret, in whom the Saxon hereditary right confequently refided. By her hufband, Malcolm king of Scotland, fhe had feveral children, and among the reft, Matilda, the wife of Henry I. who by him had the Emprefs Maud, mother of Henry II.—At the fame time, it muft be acknowledged, that he could not claim an hereditary right to the king-dom, by a regular courfe of fucceffion from the royal Saxon family; for the fons of Margaret unqueftionably inherited her rights in pre-ference to her daughter, and confequently her title to the crown de-volved on her grandfon David King of Scotland: however, Henry's connexion with the Royal Saxon family was fuch, that it endeared him not a little to the Englifh nation; and they fondly imagined, that they faw another Alfred feated upon the throne.

In conformity therefore to a very ancient prejudice, we fhall confider Henry's acceffion, as the reftoration of the old Saxon line, though that event did not, ftrictly fpeaking, take place, until James I., the lineal heir and reprefentative of Margaret, fucceeded to the crown.

Revenue of Henry II.

Among the various meafures taken by this monarch after his acceffion, perhaps the boldeft and moft important was, the refumption of fuch of the crown-lands as had been granted by his predeceffor Stephen, and even by his mother, the emprefs Matilda. And here it is neceffary to take notice of a very material diftinction in regard to the royal demefnes. The ancient patrimony of the crown, called in Doomfday-book *Terra Regis*, was held to be fo unalienable, that if any portion of it was given away, either the king by whom it was granted, or any

---

' Black. vol. i. p.,201. Lytt. vol. i. p. 223. Matthew Paris traces his Saxon genea-logy from the Flood, p. 90.

OF THE BRITISH EMPIRE.

of his fucceffors, could at any time refume the donation. Whereas lands which efcheated to the crown, in confcquence of a default of heirs, or any feudal delinquency, it was in the power of the fovereign to difpofe of, in any manner he thought proper. This diftinction was, at different periods of the English hiftory, productive of very oppofite effects. At firft, when a prejudice ran in favour of the unalienability of the public domains, it was difficult to fupport any grant, even of lands which the crown had acquired by any mode of confifcation or efcheat. But when the popular cry took an oppofite direction, it was held impoffible to diftinguifh between the two kinds of domain : the one became gradually confounded with the other ; and hence the king acquired the right of alienating both. The crown was thus enabled to diffipate the immenfe landed property which it originally poffeffed, and which, had it remained undiminifhed, muft have rendered our kings perfectly independent, and almoft uncontroulable.

The refumption, by Henry, was unqueftionably juftifiable. In the treaty with Stephen, that monarch became bound to refume what had been alienated to the nobles, or ufurped by them of the royal demefnes [2]: and though Stephen had neglected to carry this article of the treaty of Winchefter into execution, yet it was neceffary for Henry to enforce it, in confequence of the exorbitant grants which had been made by his predeceffor, and the confequent poverty of the crown. He therefore fummoned a parliament, and having laid before it his diftreffed fituation, the illegality of the grants in queftion, and the neceffity of an immediate refumption, he obtained the concurrence and authority of that affembly for fo effential a purpofe. Little difficulty was found in refuming the grants made by Stephen, whofe neceffities had compelled him to alienate the royal domains in a manner not to be defended. But thofe which had been given by the Emprefs, and with which fhe had recompenfed the greateft and moft meritorious fervices to herfelf and family, her adherents fcrupled to reftore. Henry, however, was determined to make no diftinction ; and, after fome oppofition, actually recovered the poffeffion of all the landed property which Henry I. had enjoyed ; thofe lands only excepted, that had been granted to the church, which that

[2] Lytt. Hift. vol. ii. p. 256. 290.

powerful

powerful and politic body, in the original treaty of Winchefter, had
taken care to fecure.

Defects of the feudal fyftem.

" The military force, eftablifhed by the feudal inftitutions (it is re-
" marked by a great hiftorian), was extremely burthenfome to the
" fubject, yet rendered very little fervice to the fovereign. The
" barons, or military tenants, came late into the field; they were
" obliged to ferve only forty days; they were unfkilful and diforderly
" in all their operations; and they were apt to carry into the camp,
" the fame refractory and independent fpirit, to which they were
" accuftomed in their civil government[1]." Such a military eftablifhment might, by great attention and by frequent exercife, prove a fafe
and adequate defence to dominions entirely infular, but was ill calculated
for the exigencies of thofe foreign wars which the crown of England
was fo frequently engaged in at that time, in confequence of its
continental poffeffions[*].

Origin of fcutages.

Henry, it is probable, had the merit of firft difcovering a remedy
for this defect. It was originally attempted in the fecond year of his
reign, when, in order to carry on a war againft the Welfh, he laid a
duty, or *fcutage*, as it was called, of twenty fhillings for each knight's
fee, upon the eftates of thofe prelates who were bound to military
fervices[1]. Many fcutages were afterwards levied in the courfe of his
reign. In particular, one for carrying on the war of Touloufe, which
amounted to the fum of 180,000 *l.* equal to 2,700,000 *l.* of modern
money[6]. This commutation, though heavy, was, on the whole, lefs
burdenfome to the vaffals of the crown, than to perform their fervices
in perfon. For, befides the expence of going to war in a diftant
country, and returning from it at their own charges when the campaign
was over, their affairs at home were neglected, their eftates were
fuffered to lie wafte, and thus, in addition to the hazards of war, they
were fubject to a thoufand domeftic incoveniences. It was a plan, at
the fame time, attended with much advantage to the crown; as inftead
of troops, though brave, yet diforderly and untractable, it was thus

---

³ Hume's Hift. vol. i. p. 468.   See alfo Carte, vol. i. p. 570. 731.
⁴ Lytt. Hift. vol. ii. p. 429.   ⁵ Maddox's Hift. of Excheq. p. 435.
⁶ Lytt. Hift. vol. ii. p. 429.

enabled

enabled to purchafe the fervices of real foldiers, equally martial and difciplined[7].

But the religious zeal, fo prevalent at that time, gave rife to a new impofition, with which England had been hitherto unacquainted[8]. It was a tax on perfonal property, and it was levied in a very fingular manner. A cheft was erected in the different churches, into which every man, after having taken an oath, and juftly fummed up the value of his effects, and the debts of which he had a certainty of being paid, was obliged to put in two pence in the pound for the firft year, and a penny in the pound for the four following years, under the penalty of his breaking his oath, and incurring the fentence of excommuication denounced againft thofe who acted fraudulently[9]. This was the firft tax on perfonal property known in England; and though it amounted to fix pence in the pound only, it would not probably have been eafily fubmitted to, had it not been appropriated for fo popular a purpofe as that of affifting the chriftians in the eaft, who were then threatened with expulfion.

First tax on perfonal property.

This contribution, however, did not much avail. At leaft, *anno* 1188, more powerful affiftance became neceffary[10]. For in that year, intelligence arrived from Palestine, that Jerufalem, the darling conqueft of the chriftian world, had been taken by Saladine, the fultan of Egypt, and that he was preparing to drive the worfhippers of the crofs from their remaining poffeffions in Afia. The greateft potentates in Europe, alarmed at the news, confederated together to check the progrefs of fo formidable a conqueror, and, if poffible, to recover the holy city from the hands of the infidels. Not only Henry, but the emperor Frederic I. and Philip, king of France, determined, with their united forces, to engage in this crufade. A council of the bifhops and nobility of England was foon after held, to confider of the beft means to raife the neceffary fupplies; and at laft it was determined, to levy a tax of a tenth part of all the perfonal property of thofe, who, remaining at home, took no fhare in fo pious an enterprife. This, which is the firft inftance

Saladine tithe.

---

[7] Hume, vol. ii. p. 265.   [8] Anno 1166. 12 Henry II.
[9] Stevens's Hift. p. 28, 29, 30. Carte's Hift. vol. i. p. 599.   M. Paris, p. 101. on the other hand, fays, that four pence was collected from every ploughland.
[10] 35 Hen. 2. See Hoveden, p. 366.

of

of a tenth being exacted, was called the *Saladine Tithe*, from the
name of the gallant Muſſulman, whoſe valour gave riſe to this impoſition ". It is ſaid, that the Engliſh paid above 70,000 *l.* and the Jews
in England, about 60,000 *l.* as their reſpective proportions of the tax,
which, when joined together, was equal to about two millions of
modern money. The diſproportion was very great: but it is to be
conſidered, that none of the Jews were exempted; whereas many of
the wealthieſt of the Engliſh, in conſequence of their having taken the
croſs, pleaded immunity from the impoſt. Nay, the greater part of
the regular clergy were freed from the burden, having contended that
they were obliged by their prayers only to aſſiſt the cruſade, their
lands being held in *frank almoigne*, a tenure which exempted them
from all duties but religious exerciſes.

**Feudal aid
pur fille
marier.**
In the thirteeenth year of his reign, Henry having married his
daughter Matilda to the Duke of Saxony, levied an aid from his ſubjects, to enable him to give her a portion adequate to her rank, and that
of her huſband. This tax amounted to one mark for each knight's-
fee. It was paid by the ſeveral knights and barons holding of the crown
in capite, according to the number of their reſpective fees. Nor were
the biſhops or abbots exempted from this impoſition ".

Danegeld.
The odious tax of Danegeld, though levied in the beginning of
Henry's reign, was either totally remitted by this monarch, or fell into
diſuſe. There is much uncertainty in our public records, as to the final
extinction of this tax, which *Madox*, with all his knowledge and induſtry, has not been able clearly to develope". After the ſecond year of
Henry II. he conjectures, that it was not a ſettled part of the public
revenue. Perhaps it was difficult, however, at once, totally to abandon
ſo conſiderable a branch of the royal income; and there is reaſon to
believe, that it was occaſionally levied, particularly in the thirteenth and
twentieth years of Henry's reign, and probably in the twenty-firſt,
when writs of ſummons, for that purpoſe, were iſſued out of the exchequer.

Some authors have accuſed this monarch of pillaging the poſſeſſions
of the church; of executing, with the greateſt rigour, the harſh regula-

tions

tions of the foreft laws; and of reviving the old Saxon taxes of *Burg-bote, Brig-bote, Heregeld* and *Horngeld*". But, on the whole, there feems to have been little reafon to complain of the general tenor of his government; and it is recorded, much to his honour, that having been for fome time abfent from England, and finding, upon his return, that great abufes had taken place in the collection of his revenues, and indeed in the adminiftration of juftice, he appointed a commiffion of fome of the moft refpectable of his fubjects, to enquire fully into the grievances that were complained of; and, in confequences of their report, many of the fheriffs, and other officers of the crown, were removed, and obliged to give fatisfaction, not only to the king, but to any private individuals who were injured ".

The amount of the treafure which Henry left behind him, is a point Treafure. about which hiftorians differ. Hume ftates it only at an hundred thoufand marks ". But Matthew Paris, and other authors, affirm, that it amounted to 900,000 l. in gold and filver, befides plate, jewels, and precious ftones ". The former account, however, is the more probable: for, with fo great a treafure as Matthew Paris fuppofes this monarch to have been mafter of, he muft have carried on the war, in the latter part of his reign, with more fpirit, and with more fuccefs; and would not have been reduced, a few days before he died, to the hard neceffity of ratifying a treaty, which impofed terms equally ruinous and difgraceful, and which tarnifhed all the glory and renown he had formerly acquired.

RICHARD I.

The reigns of heroes, or of martial monarchs, however advantageous to the military character, yet are uniformly deftructive to the property, and baneful to the commercial interefts of a nation. The fubjects of fuch monarchs, though uninterefted in the fuccefs of the wars in which they are engaged; and though, if fuccefsful, the glory wholly centers in the fovereign, yet are under the neceffity of defraying the heavy load of expence, which the wildnefs of their ambition occafions; and thus the folid interefts of a nation are facrificed, to gratify the pride, to in-

" Stevens, p. 34. " Lytt. Hift. vol. iv. p. 292. " Vol. ii. p. 5.
" Matth. Paris, p. 147. Carte, vol. i. p. 738.

I dulge

dulge the paffions, and to promote the aggrandizement, of one arro-
gant or vain-glorious individual. Notwithftanding thefe circumftances,
the reign of *Richard Cœur de Lion*, or the Lion-hearted, is a favourite
one with the Englifh reader, who fondly fancies, that, by his valour,
the fame of England was eftablifhed in the moft diftant corners of the
Eaft.

The Crufade.   The preparations made by Richard for his expedition, are a full proof
of that monarch's zeal for the enterprife he had undertaken; and indeed, if his fubje&ts had not entered into it with the fame alacrity, they
could hardly have fuffered him to take fteps of fo oppreffive and dangerous a nature. Every means that could be invented for raifing money,
was adopted without hefitation. The crown lands, and offices of the
greateft truft and power, were difpofed of, almoft at any price. The
feudal fuperiority of Scotland was fold for ten thoufand marks. Arbitrary
fines were levied from the officers of the crown, under the pretence of
delinquency. The rich, who had efcaped other modes of extortion,
were compelled to fupply the king with money by way of loan, without
any hope of being repaid. Nay, under colour that the great feal was
loft, former grants were held to be invalid. A new feal was made, and
every perfon was obliged to purchafe a renewal and confirmation of his
grant. It is faid, that, by thefe and other means of exactions equally
odious, fo much money was raifed, and carried out of the kingdom,
that a genuine coin, of this monarch's ftamp, is hardly to be met with,
in the moft valuable and curious collections ".

Richard's   The confequence of this monarch's expedition to the eaft, the re-
ranfom.   nown he acquired in the courfe of the war, and his difgraceful captivity
on his return home, are circumftances well known to every perfon in
the leaft converfant with the Englifh hiftory. Leopold, duke of Auftria,
and Henry, emperor of Germany, by whom Richard was imprifoned,
having demanded the exorbitant fum of a hundred and fifty thoufand
marks for his releafe, a heavy tax was laid upon his fubjects, in aid of
the king's ranfom, to which the vaffals of the crown were bound by
the nature of their tenures. England had not yet recovered the lofs of
fpecie, which it had fuftained by Richard's former extortions, and the

treafure

treafure that he carried with him to Afia. At a time when money was fcarce in Europe, and the commerce of England was inconfiderable, a frefh fupply of fpecie was not eafily procured : it was, therefore, with the utmoft.difficulty, that the firft payment of 100,000 marks was made, though his fubjects, notwithftanding the variety of taxes impofed upon them at that time, vied with each other, which of them fhould pay in the greateft voluntary contributions for the ranfom of their fovereign ".

From the return of Richard to his death, his reign was a perpetual feries of war abroad, and of extortion at home ; principally, however, occafioned by the attempts of Philip Auguftus, king of France, to conquer the dominions of England on the continent. In confequence of the enterprifes of that formidable enemy, joined to the heavy ranfom he had been obliged to pay, he was reduced to the neceffity of cancelling all the contracts he had entered into, previous to his Afiatic expedition ; and of refuming all the offices, together with fuch of the crown lands as were purchafed at that time. The whole body of the clergy alfo, but more particularly the Ciftercian monks, were obliged to pay confiderable fums of money to fupply the king's neceffities ; and at this period we firft hear of wool being taken in kind for the purpofes of revenue. In the tenth year of his reign, Danegeld likewife, under the lefs obnoxious name of Hydage, was levied at the rate of five fhillings *per* hyde ".

It is not a little fingular, that the reign of this monarch fhould furnifh an example of raifing a revenue by means of licences ; a mode which, in modern times, has become fo prevalent. Neceffity, however, is the parent of invention ; and, confidering the difficulties to which Richard and his minifters were reduced, it is not to be wondered at, that they fhould make this important difcovery. At the period we are now writing of, it is well known, that, for the better exercifing of the people in the arts of war, jufts and tournaments were encouraged, and they naturally became fafhionable in fo martial an age. But, with

Extortions.

Licences.

19 Carte, vol. i. p. 759. Authors differ much as to the amount of this monarch's ranfom   Diceto calls it 100,000l. of filver. Jervafe of Canterbury, 150,000 marks. M. Paris, p. 167, 140,000 marks of filver. The MS. Chronicle at Chefter, 160,000 marks. But Hoveden, p. 415, gives us a copy of the agreement, from which it appears, that 100,000 marks were paid down, and that, for the remaining 50,000, hoftages were to be given, but the payment was conditional. 100,000 marks was equal to 194,000 l. of modern money. Folkes on Coins, p. 6. Note.   20 Stevens, p. 40.

a view

a view of rendering that practice profitable to the exchequer alfo, it was enacted, by Richard, that every perfon fhould pay for a licence before he engaged in fuch exercifes, according to the following rates : every earl, twenty marks of filver ; every baron, ten marks; every knight, having lands, four marks ; and fuch as had no lands, two marks. No perfon under the rank of a knight was permitted to enter the lifts[21].

Amount.

It is related by Hoveden, a very refpectable ancient hiftorian, that, in the fpace of two years, 1,100,000 marks, equal to 753,332 l. fterling, or 376,666 l. *per annum*, had been collected for public fervices[22]. This fum, Hume fuppofes to be totally incredible[23]. But it is ftated upon the authority of Hubert, archbifhop of Canterbury, who had infpected the records, and examined the public accounts, to difcover the real amount ; and it is to be obferved, that this was not the annual income of the crown, but comprifed the various fums which had been extorted to carry on the war againft Philip, and perhaps the money which the Englifh had paid, either in the fhape of taxes, or of voluntary contri-butions, for the redemption of their captive fovereign.

J O H N.

This defpicable and odious tyrant, whofe hiftory it is impoffible to contemplate without a mixture of difguft, indignation, and horror, claimed the crown, as next of kin to the deceafed king, of whom he was the only furviving brother. But the Englifh had foon reafon to regret the fupport they gave him, in oppofition to the pretenfions of Arthur, and of his fifter Eleanor, the children of Geoffrey, who was next brother to Richard, and whofe defcendants, therefore, by the right of reprefentation, were entitled to the throne. To remove fo danger-ous a rival as Arthur, who had difplayed, at an early period of life, fpirit and abilities beyond his years, every art that treachery could invent, or barbarity could execute, was put in practice by his inhuman uncle ; and it is fuppofed, that this obftacle to his ambition, which no

---

[21] Carte, vol. i. p. 764.   [22] Hoveden, folio edit. p. 437, *anno* 1196.

[23] Vol. ii. p. 38.   See alfo Carte, vol. i. p. 769; and Davenant, vol. iii. p. 74, who fuppofes the fum equal to eleven millions of modern money.

other

other perfon had the cruelty to remove, was murdered by his own hands [14]. By the death of this unfortunate prince, and Eleanor's captivity and imprifonment, he flattered himfelf, that his government was eftablifhed on a rock, which could not eafily be fhaken. Inftead of which, abroad, he loft the ancient patrimony of his family on the Continent; and, at home, paffed a life of mifery, turbulence, and difgrace.

His extortions.

Neither the clergy nor the laity were exempted from his rapacity. In the twelfth year of his reign, he is faid to have exacted 140,000*l.* from the church. In his thirteenth year, 400,000 marks were alfo demanded; and in the courfe of a reign of feventeen years, only three are diftinguifhed as being freed from one fpecies of impofitions or another. But the Jews in particular felt the weight and violence of his extortion. *An.* 1210, 66,000 marks were demanded from them; and perfons of both fexes were feized, imprifoned, and tortured, in order that they might deliver up all they were worth [15]. One of them, a Jew of Briftol, having refufed to pay 10,000 marks affeffed upon him, the tyrant ordered a tooth to be pulled or beat out every day, until this exorbitant fum was paid, which the unhappy Ifraelite was at laft compelled to do on the eighth day, after feven of his teeth had been ftruck out [16].

Magna Charta.

The only circumftance which can prove in any refpect agreeable to the reader during the whole courfe of his reign, is the confirmation, extorted from this monarch with confiderable difficulty, of the rights and liberties of the people of this country, in the deed fo emphatically named, The Great Charter of the Liberties of England [17]. By this important inftrument, a variety of regulations were enacted, favourable to the vaffals of the crown, by which the pecuniary burdens of the feudal law were confiderably diminifhed; and by the 14th, 15th, and 16th articles it was declared, that no fcutage or aid fhould be impofed on the kingdom in general, and in particular on the city of London, or any of the other cities, towns, or boroughs of the kingdom, unlefs with the confent of the common council of the realm, excepting for ranfoming

[14] Hume, vol. ii. p. 48.   [15] Stevens, p. 44.
[16] M. Paris, p. 220. Tovey's Anglia Judaica, p. 70. Madox Excheq. p. 151.
[17] See the famous Petition of Right, claufe 3.

the

the king's perfon, making his eldeft fon a knight, or marrying his eldeft
daughter; and even then, only a reafonable aid was to be demanded:
and by another claufe, fines and amerciaments, which had formerly
been very grievous and oppreffive, were reftricted within proper
bounds. On the whole, this charter, though it does not contain a
complete fyftem of civil liberty, is, at the fame time, without doubt,
the moft important, extenfive, and valuable compact entered into
between a reigning monarch and his fubjects, to be met with in the
hiftory of almoft any age or country.

Cuftoms. ▪ It appears from the forty-eighth article of Magna Charta, that fome
duties were paid on goods at that time, and had been formerly exacted.
The merchants were to trade, "*fine omnibus malis toltis.*" But, at the
fame time, the articles in which they dealt, were to pay cuftom "*per*
"*antiquas et rectas confuetudines.*" What thofe *ancient and equitable
duties* were, is now unknown; but they muft have been very inconfiderable, as they were let in farm, in the fourth year of John's reign,
for only 1000 marks ".

John continued the dangerous practice, begun by his brother Richard,
of felling the offices under the crown. Nay, he ventured to difpofe of
the high employment of chancellor, to one Gray, during his life, for
only 5000 marks.

H E N R Y   III.

At the age of nine years, Henry III. inherited the crown of England. He mounted the throne at a time when the greateft experience
and the moft fplendid abilities were neceffary to preferve the kingdom
from the ruinous confequences of inteftine wars and foreign invafion.
Fortunately, William Earl of Pembroke, the marifchal of England, and
confequently by his office, in times of fuch turbulence and confufion, at
the head of the government, was poffeffed of virtue and abilities adequate
to fo dangerous a crifis; and, by means of his prudence, vigour, and
exertions, and the return of many of thofe barons to their allegiance,

---

" An. 1202. See Madox, p. 529. It appears alfo from p. 530, that the cuftoms of
all England, and the profits, arifing from its principal fairs, amounted only to £ 4958 : 7 : 3½
from the faft of St. Margaret in the fourth, to the feaft of St. Andrew in the fixth year
of this monarch's reign.

who,

who, from hatred to their late monarch, had thrown themfelves into the arms of France, Henry at laft acquired the peaceable poffeflion of his dominions, both in England, and on the continent.

The reign of this monarch, which lafted upwards of fifty-fix years, is the longeft in the annals of this country. Unfortunately, it cannot boaft of fplendour equal to its duration : it was neither happy at home, nor refpectable abroad. His fubjects complained of the weaknefs of his government, of his rapacity and profufion ; whilft his enemies had no reafon to tremble at the vigour or abilities of their opponent. Henry's character, perfectly well adapted to the ftill life of a private citizen, was but ill fitted for the buftle and intrigues of a court, or the tumults of hoftility and war.

His attachment to unworthy favourites, and profufe liberality to the Revenue. minions who were about him, in a great meafure occafioned the miferies of his reign. By his inconfiderate bounties, he had reduced the income of the crown to 60,000 marks *per annum* [9], and he was not fcrupulous as to any means of making up the deficiency.

It would be trefpaffing upon the reader's patience, to attempt an enumeration of the number of fcutages, aids, talliages, carrucages, hydages, tenths, fifteenths, benevolences, &c. which this king, by different means, and under various appellations, obtained, or extorted from his fubjects, in the courfe of his long adminiftration. He is faid to have taken 400,000 marks from the Jews [10]. His expences in a vain attempt to conquer Sicily for his fecond fon, are faid by Matthew Paris to have amounted to 950,000 marks [11]. In the forty-third year of his reign, he was reduced to the greateft neceffity. And when Lewis king of France, who was not perfectly fatisfied with his right to Normandy and Anjou, offered him 300,000 livres Tournois, and lands to the value of 20,000 livres *per annum*, in full of his claim to the fovereignty of thofe two provinces, for that trifling confideration he renounced all his pretenfions to the ancient patrimony of his family, and ever after ftruck out from his other titles, thofe of Duke of Normandy, and Earl of Anjou. To this king and his minifters may be attributed a new device

---

[9] M. Paris, p. 647. [10] Steven's Hift. of Taxes, p. 48.
[11] M. Paris, p. 918. This is the probable meaning of a paffage which has puzzled many of our hiftorians.

to raife a revenue, of which his fucceffors afterwards availed themfelves. The mode was, to compel every one who poffeffed fifteen or twenty pounds a-year in landed property holden of the crown, either to take the order of knighthood, or to pay a certain fum of money in its ftead, by way of compofition. This was a fure mode of raifing money ; for thofe who did not compound, were obliged to pay confiderable fees at their creation, which all went into the exchequer.

Confe-quences of his profufion. The miferable ftate to which Henry was reduced, is fufficient, one fhould imagine, to deter any monarch from imitating his extravagance and profufion. He found the utmoft difficulty to pay his eldeft fon Edward, the fmall pittance of 15,000 marks *per annum*, for his fupport. His debts, amounting to about 300,000*l.*, he was totally unable to difcharge. In order to raife money, he was obliged to fell the very furniture of his palace; to pawn the jewels of the crown ; nay, the fhrine of St. Edward the Confeffor, for whom he had always expreffed the higheft veneration[32]. He is reprefented as wandering about the country, foliciting the charitable contributions of his fubjects[33] ; and his attendants were reduced to fuch ftraits and difficulties, that they were compelled to confederate with gangs of robbers, in order, by their fhare of the booty, to fecure a maintenance[34].

Cuftoms. In the reign of Henry, this branch of the revenue was increafed to 6000*l. per annum*[35]. But the exaction of fuch high cuftoms was complained of, as contrary to Magna Charta, and was faid to be attended with an apparent overthrow of trade[36] : a proof how much people are apt to complain of the flighteft burdens, and indeed how inconfiderable the commerce carried on by England at that time muft have been.

---

[32] Noy's Rights of the Crown, chap. viii. Stevens, p. 70.
[33] Stevens, Pref. p. 31.   [34] Hume, vol. ii. p. 228.
[35] Hume, vol. ii. p. 170. Note C.
[36] Noy's Rights of the Crown, p. 78.

E D W A R D

EDWARD I.

Edward the Firſt, the great reformer of our laws, and hence called the Engliſh *Juſtinian*, was one of the wiſeſt and moſt fortunate princes, that ever ſat upon the throne of England. In him were united the prudence and foreſight of the ſtateſman and legiſlator, with the valour and magnanimous ſpirit of the hero. The expenſive wars, and the variety of important enterpriſes in which he was engaged, occaſioned the levying of many taxes, and ſometimes gave riſe to oppreſſions, of which his ſubjects had ſome reaſon to complain: but the money he exacted from them, was uniformly expended for the honour and benefit of his kingdom ; and the laws which he propoſed, or to which he gave his conſent, firſt extended that commerce, confirmed thoſe liberties, and eſtabliſhed that conſtitution, on which the future happineſs of this country depended.

Among the other great tranſactions by which the reign of this monarch is diſtinguiſhed, the final eſtabliſhment of Magna Charta, together with ſome important additional articles, and a full and complete confirmation of the famous ſtatute " *de tallagio non concedendo,*" are intitled to particular attention. The former (Magna Charta) had already been frequently confirmed by the different monarchs, who, ſince the firſt paſſing of that important deed, had ſat upon the throne ; but it was ſtill thought requiſite, to have that ſolemnity again repeated. The latter was rendered neceſſary, in conſequence of ſome defects in the Great Charter, particularly as it had permitted the crown, by its own authority, to levy aids for ranſoming the king's perſon, making his eldeſt ſon a knight, or marrying his eldeſt daughter ; a prerogative liable to abuſe ; and, at the ſame time, it had laid the crown under no reſtraint, in regard to exacting arbitrary talliages, from its demeſnes. But by the ſtatute above-mentioned, *no aid or talliage whatſoever* could be demanded, without the conſent and approbation of Parliament ; and this important conceſſion, in the words of Hume, " the Engliſh nation had " the honour of extorting from the ableſt, the moſt warlike, and the " moſt ambitious of all their princes, who was thus bereaved of the

Confirmation of Magna Charta, and of the ſtatute de Tallagio non concedendo.

K power

" power which he and his predeceſſors had hitherto aſſumed, of impoſ-
" ing arbitrary taxes on the people ".." By this famous ſtatute, the
people of England, as Bodin well expreſſed it, defended themſelves, as
if with a ſhield, from the exactions of their ſovereign ".

Exactions
from the
Jews.

But whatever acquiſitions of liberty, or ſecurity for their perſons and
eſtates, were obtained by the people in general, yet ſome of his ſubjects,
who thought themſelves equally intitled to his protection, were treated
in a manner which impreſſes us with no very favourable idea of Edward's
humanity. It is his treatment of the Jews to which I allude. Beſides
large ſums of money extorted from them at his acceſſion to the throne,
in the third year of his reign, they were made ſubject to a poll-tax of
three-pence each, without any exception on account of poverty, ſex, or
age ". In the fourth year, the tax was raiſed to five-pence a head : but
in the eighteenth year, the whole nation was ſentenced to perpetual

Anno 1290.

exile by act of parliament. All their property was confiſcated for the
uſe of the crown ; many were hanged under various pretences ; in particular two hundred and eighty in one day, who were accuſed of having adulterated the coin ; and above fifteen thouſand were plundered of
all their wealth, and baniſhed the kingdom⁴⁰. So odious were the Jews
at that time to the nation in general, that the laity granted the king a
fifteenth, and the clergy a tenth of their perſonal eſtates, for conſenting
to, and perhaps encouraging their expulſion ".

Exactions
from the
Church.

But Edward's conduct to the clergy ſoon convinced them, that
attachment to the ſuperſtition prevalent at that time, had no ſhare in
rendering him ſo great an oppreſſor of the Jewiſh race. The church
from the beginning had ſome reaſon to be afraid, that a monarch ſo
high-ſpirited and ſo ambitious as Edward, would be frequently under the
neceſſity of applying to it for pecuniary aſſiſtance ; and the clergy
were not a little alarmed, when, in the ſixteenth year of his reign, he
gave orders to ſearch all the monaſteries in England, and to ſeize for his
own uſe the money and valuable effects depoſited in them. They flattered themſelves, however, that the authority of the Pope would ſhield
them from his rapacity ; and, in conſequence of an application from

³⁷ Hume, vol. ii. p. 292. 295.   ³⁸ De Repub. lib. i. cap. 8.   ³⁹ Stevens, p. 79.
⁴⁰ Tovey's Anglia Judaica, p. 232. Hume's hiſt. vol. ii. p. 236.
⁴¹ Stevens, p. 84.

the

the Archbithop of Canterbury, Boniface VIII. who then fat upon the Papal throne, iffued a bull, prohibiting all princes to levy any taxes upon the clergy, and all clergymen to pay any impofition without the authority of the Pope. Edward was determined, by the moft vigorous meafures, to punifh the clergy for making this application, and to compel them to renounce any benefit it could poffibly afford. He put the whole church out of his protection : he declared that thofe who refufed to fupport the civil government, were not intitled to receive any advantage from it. The judges were directed to fuffer any perfon to harafs or plunder them with impunity ; whilft, on the other hand, no court of law would give them any redrefs. The king at laft prevailed in the 'conteft : the Pope's bull was either contemned or evaded, and the clergy were glad, almoft on any terms, to be reinftated in the royal protection, and to enjoy again the benefit of the laws ".

Thus the church was made fubject to the civil power ; nor was it afterwards thought neceffary to have a bull from the Pope, previoufly to any clerical impofition.

Taxes on the exportation and importation of goods, became, in the reign of this monarch, an important branch of the revenue. It is probable that cuftoms were at firft only fmall duties, levied at ferries and bridges, and, perhaps, for the liberty of trafficking on the Thames, together with fees for weighing and warehoufing of goods, which the officers of the crown exacted for their labour and attendance. Thefe trifling exactions might gradually take place, without the fanction of parliament, in confequence of the king's (who was accounted the arbiter of commerce) having provided weights and beams, and erected warehoufes, where, fubject to certain cuftomary fees and duties, (thence called cuftoms) all goods and commodities might be fold ".

But Edward I. was not fatisfied with fuch petty advantages : for having feen, during the courfe of his expedition to Paleftine, with what facility confiderable fums of money were levied by way of cuftom in foreign countries, he thought it would be a happy expedient for raifing a revenue in his own kingdom. The firft duties laid on, however, were very moderate, amounting only to fix fhillings and eight-

Marginal notes: Cuftoms. The Antiqua Cuftuma.

" Carte, vol. ii. p. 265. 267. Hume, vol. ii. p. 286.
" Gilb. Hift. of the Exchequer, chap. xv.

pence

pence on every fack of wool exported; and the like fum for every
three hundred wood-fells; and a mark, or thirteen fhillings and four-
pence, for every laft of hides, at the rate of twelve dozen *per* laft [44].
Thefe duties, Lord Coke imagines, were granted by parliament in the
third year of his reign; and, though the record is now loft, it is evidently referred to in a fubfequent act (25 Edw. I. c. 7.); in which notice is taken of the cuftoms on wool, fkins, and leather, formerly granted
to that monarch, by the commonalty of the kingdom [45].

Origin of
tunnage and
poundage.   Edward's neceffities however demanded a more productive revenue; and he began with additional duties on aliens or foreign mer-
chants, wifely conjecturing that any taxes they were willing to pay,
might afterwards be extended with lefs difficulty to his own fubjects.
Feb. 1,
1304.   He granted, therefore, a charter (entitled *Charta Mercatoria*) to the
merchant ftrangers fettled in England, by which certain valuable privileges were beftowed on them, in confideration of their having agreed to
pay the following cuftoms. 1. In lieu of the duty called *Prifage*, the
fum of two fhillings for every tun of wine imported by them, over and
above the ancient cuftoms; a tax which afterwards obtained the name
of *Butlerage*, being paid to the king's butler. 2. Forty pence for every
fack of wool, and for every 300 wood-fells exported, in addition to the
half mark, or fix fhillings and eight pence, paid by the natives; together with fix fhillings and eight pence additional for every laft of hides.
3. Befides fome duties upon cloth and wax, a general *poundage*, or tax of
three-pence in the pound on all goods imported or foreign commodities
re-exported, after having been landed in England, exclufively of the ancient cuftoms to which they were formerly fubject. Thefe rates were
called *Nova Cuftuma*, and fometimes *Alien duties*; and were levied by the
authority of the crown, without the fanction of parliament, in confequence of the voluntary confent that was given by the foreign merchants [46]. In the third of Edward II. however, this charter was fuf-
pended; and it was totally repealed in the fifth of Edward II. by the
lords, who at that time were entrufted with the government of the
country: but it was again eftablifhed in the reign of Edward III. [47], and

---

[44] Madox, p. 536. Forfter on the Cuftoms, Introd. p. 14.
[45] Gilb. Excheq. p. 276.   [46] Forft. p. 26.   [47] 27 Edward III.

in

in fact it is the foundation of the duties of tunnage and poundage, so famous in the history of England.

Such were the cuftoms paid by aliens in the reign of this monarch. As to the native merchants of the country, it was always the policy of England to give them fuperior advantages for carrying on their commerce; and as the *Nova Cuftuma* above-mentioned, were founded upon an agreement between Edward and the foreign merchants, the legality of which the commons were much difpofed to queftion, there is every reafon to believe, that the natives of the country were not at all affected by thefe new impofitions. Here it may be proper to remark, that, *anno* 1298, the duty upon wool exported had been raifed by Edward to forty fhillings per fack, an increafe grievoufly complained of; not only as it was laid on by the authority of the crown alone, but was in itfelf too high[48]. The right of adding to the old, or of levying new cuftoms, came at length to be a matter of fuch public importance, that, for many years, it was warmly contefted between the crown and the people. But fince the forty-fifth of Edward III. and eleventh of Richard II. chap. 9, it has been generally held, that no impofition whatever can be levied, either on exports or imports, without the confent of parliament[49].

The difcovery of fome valuable mines in Devonfhire, alfo tended to enrich this monarch[50]. It is on record, that within three years from their being firft difcovered, about 1700 pounds weight of filver were extracted from them; and it is probable that, afterwards, they would produce more, in confequence of a greater number of workmen having been employed.

Mines.

From the conqueft to the æra we are now confidering, the ufual mode of levying money for the extraordinary expences of the crown, was by fcutages, or pecuniary commutations for perfonal fervice: but a variety of circumftances contributed to render fuch a fyftem no longer effectual. Scutages were levied in proportion to the number of knights fees which each perfon poffeffed. But, in confequence of the fluctuation of private property, and of many evafions which it was impoffible to forefee, and difficult to check, joined to the inaccurate manner in which the rolls of

New fyftem of taxation and government.

---

[48] Stevens, p. 96.   [49] Forft. Introd. p. 16.   [50] Stevens, p. 79.

knights

knights fees were kept, it became impracticable to afcertain the number of fees with which each perfon ought to be charged. And when a fmall number was once accepted of, it was confidered to be a binding precedent for the future". Thus the crown was deprived of the military fervices of its vaffals; was defrauded of the compenfation to which it was juftly entitled; and was reduced to the neceffity of providing fome other means for the public defence. Some fcutages, however, were levied during the reign of Edward: indeed fo prudent a monarch could never have entirely relinquifhed an old and eftablifhed mode of taxation, until he had known, by experience, that a more productive. fyftem of revenue could be carried into effect.

In the mean while, a new defcription of perfons, attracted the attention of the fovereign. For many years, pofterior to the conqueft, the poffeffors of lands were the only rich and powerful individuals in the community: but, in procefs of time, towns came to be emancipated from their former fubordination and dependence; their citizens became induftrious and opulent; they engroffed a confiderable fhare of the wealth and property of the country; the fmalleft portion of which they were unwilling to part with, unlefs with their own confent. Originally the principal towns in England were included in the royal domains, and the crown was entitled to impofe talliages or taxes upon them, whenever it thought proper. The city of London itfelf was in that predicament; and, after fome conteft, whether it was talliable or not, in the thirty-ninth of Henry III. was compelled to pay a talliage of 3000 marks affeffed upon it by the king and his council". But when the famous ftatute *de tallagio non concedendo*, paffed into a law, there was an end of that prerogative; and it was neceffary for the crown, if it wifhed to reap any pecuniary advantage from the opulence of the towns and boroughs, to affemble their deputies together, and to endeavour, through their medium, to obtain the fupplies neceffary for the exigencies of the State. Hence arofe the practice of regularly fummoning the reprefentatives of boroughs to parliament, which had occafionally taken place before the reign of Edward, but fince his time has never

---

[1] Hume, vol. ii. p. 278.

[2] Madox, p. 491. Authors differ as to the nature of this *council*, but it was evidently not a parliament. Lytt. vol. iii. p. 258.

been

been interrupted. Brady and Hume, confider the twenty-third year of the reign of Edward, as the epocha of this great revolution"; but it cannot, with ftrict propriety, be faid to have taken place until, in confequence of the ftatute above-mentioned, enacted in the twenty-fifth year of this reign, all other legal means of taxing cities and boroughs, excepting by their reprefentatives in parliament, were finally abolifhed.

Thofe who look upon themfelves as the warmeft friends of public liberty, cannot hear, with patience, that the commons houfe of parliament had not acquired, at an earlier æra, its full dignity and importance. The period of five hundred years, which has almoft elapfed fince the twenty-fifth of Edward I. does not alleviate their anxiety, or fatisfy their zeal. They wifh to trace the origin even of burgal reprefentation throughout all the dark labyrinths of Saxon and Norman antiquities. The natural prejudices of a free country, it is always difagreeable and often dangerous to oppofe: but it may furely be remarked, without giving the moft ardent friend to ancient liberty the fmalleft offence, that if taxation and reprefentation are fo infeparably connected, as fome political writers are defirous of inculcating, boroughs could have no reprefentatives in the earlier part of the Englifh hiftory; for this plain reafon, that they were not liable to parliamentary taxes. For, above a hundred years after the Norman invafion, no tax was laid upon perfonal effects, by which alone the boroughs could be materially affected. Indeed, before the reign of Edward I. or, at leaft, of Henry III. very few inftances occur of impofitions upon perfonal property. Whatever right therefore the towns and boroughs originally might have, in confequence of the free principles of the Saxon government, to partake in the legiflative power of the country, it is certain, that, for many years after the conqueft, it was unneceffary for them to be loaded with the burden and expence of fending reprefentatives. Inftead, therefore, of carrying on fo abftrufe, and, after the lapfe of fuch a number of years, fo unimportant a controverfy, it were better to contend, who fhould pay the fincereft tribute of gratitude, to thofe patriots, whofe exertions eftablifhed the rights and privileges of England. It ought ever to be remembered, that, to the zeal and prudence of Langton, Archbifhop of Canterbury, the great charter was principally owing; and that, to the undaunted fpirit and manly

---

" See Brady on boroughs, edit. 1777. p. 68. Hume, vol. ii. p. 272.

perfeverance

perfeverance of Humphry Bohun, earl of Hereford, the conftable, and of Roger Bigod, earl of Norfolk, the marifhal of England, the paffing of that ftatute ought to be attributed, which, by annihilating for ever the royal prerogative of impofing arbitrary taxes upon the fubject, laid the true foundation of a limited monarchy, without which every other right and privilege were in vain.

EDWARD II.

The reign of Edward II., comprizing a period of about twenty years, is remarkable for the inconfiderable taxes levied upon the fubject. The power of the crown to raife money, in virtue of its own prerogative, having been completely abandoned by his father, it is not to be fuppofed that it could poffibly be regained, under the adminiftration of a fon in every refpect his inferior: and, as Edward's mifconduct in government, and his attachment to unworthy favourites, did not entitle him to any great pecuniary affiftance from his people, they had fome little confolation in the lightnefs of their taxes, for the difgraceful calamities of his unfortunate reign.

Among the other events, which contributed to heap difhonour on the government of this monarch, the lofs of Scotland was unqueftionably the moft important. It is natural for a native of that part of the ifland to imagine, that Edward's character could not be materially tarnifhed, for failing in an attempt to fubdue that country, defended as it was by a gallant nation, renowned, both in ancient and in modern times, for its fortitude and valour. Their refiftance, however, would probably have been ineffectual, had Edward endeavoured to complete the conqueft of that country immediately after his acceffion, before the Scots had recovered their fpirit, or had received affiftance from their allies on the continent. But, though Edward fucceedtd to the crown on the 7th of July 1307, the battle of *Bannockburn*, on which the reduction of Scotland depended, was not fought till the 25th of June 1314: and thus Robert the Bruce and his fubjects enjoyed an interval of about feven years, and had time fufficient to acquire ftrength, difcipline, and experience. The fubfidies granted to this monarch were principally intended to carry on his wars againft the Scots, the fuccefs of which yielded no encourage-

ment

OF THE BRITISH EMPIRE. 73

ment to his fubjects to furnifh him with fupplies for any other purpofe
whatfoever.

The new mode which Edward I. had difcovered, of increafing his Cuftoms.
revenue by duties upon commerce, occafioned fo much jealoufy, that in
the famous ordinances, which were enacted *anno* 1311, for the better
government of the kingdom, they were entirely abolifhed. By one
article, the tax of Butlerage was prohibited to be collected; and by
another it was declared, that natives only fhould be employed in the
collection of the cuftoms; fome foreigners, to whom that branch of
the revenue was farmed, having been guilty of extortion.

It was alfo enacted, that the money which the remaining branches of
the cuftoms yielded, fhould be appropriated to the maintenance of the
houfehold, that the king might be enabled to live upon his own revenue, without being reduced to the neceffity of oppreffing his fubjects [54]. In the fecond year of his reign, he had impofed, after his
father's example, two fhillings a tun upon foreign merchants, in addition to what they had formerly paid; and as this tax was exacted
without the fanction of parliament, it gave rife to much fufpicion,
and, probably, was the reafon why the articles above-mentioned were
fo particularly infifted upon. For it was a principle in the law of England, that levying new cuftoms, or adding to the old, could only be
done either by parliament, or *confenfu mercatorum;* and impofts laid on
by the royal authority alone, were called *Maltoltes* [55], or evil duties,
by which trade was materially injured, and which it was neceffary,
therefore, to take the earlieft opportunity to abrogate and repeal [56].

The anxiety of the Englifh nation to atchieve the conqueft of Scot- New tax.
land, made them chearfully fubmit, in the reign of this monarch, to an
impofition of fo dangerous a nature, that it was exprefsly provided in
the grant, that it fhould not be made a precedent for any fimilar demand
in future. By this fingular grant, which took place *anno* 1316, every
village, town, and city in the kingdom, was ordered to furnifh a certain

54 Mort. Hift. vol. i. p. 498. Note.

55 Some writers have fuppofed, that *Maltoltes* were duties upon *malt;* and others, a
fpecies of excife, without confidering, that cuftom-houfe duties were then as much
dreaded as excifes are now.

56 Noy's Rights of the Crown, p. 77 & 80. Gilb. Excheq. p. 272. 275.

L number

number of ftout, and well-armed foldiers, in proportion to its wealth
and ability, provided with fubfiftence for fixty days ; after which, they
were to be maintained at the expence of the crown. In addition to
this tax, a fifteenth part of the moveables of the laity was granted, to
render the conqueft more fecure. But the feafon was paft : for the
battle of Bannockburn had previoufly eftablifhed the independence of
that country.

Forefts.   An attempt was made by Edward and his minifters, to increafe the
public revenue, by cultivating the forefts belonging to the crown. In
his fecond year, a commiffion was granted to farm out fuch wafte lands,
fi abfque injuria alterius fieri poteft ; and in his fifteenth year, a great
part of his woods were let for rent. The idea, however, was not then
purfued. But it is hoped, that a plan, of which it was faid of old,
" That it would increafe many thoufand families for the public fervice,
" would bring many thoufand pounds into the public coffers, and
" would convert much wafte land, to habitations of chriftians," will be
no longer neglected[57].

E D W A R D III.

The reign of Edward III. is, without doubt, the moft fplendid in
the Englifh hiftory, for warlike atchievements. Befides many important
victories obtained by himfelf, his fon the Prince of Wales, the general
whom he employed, and even his Queen Philippa, boafted of exploits,
which would have adorned any other æra, but which were all loft in the
fuperior luftre of thofe of Creffy, of Sluys, and of Poictiers. His
fubjects were fo dazzled by his valour and fuccefs, that they willingly
fubjected themfelves to the moft exorbitant taxes ; and with reafon
afferted, that they had gone beyond all the commons in the world, in
liberality to their fovereign[58].

Grants.   A variety of parliamentary grants, under the ufual denominations of
tenths, fifteenths and twentieths, were received by Edward ; and fome
taxes in kind were alfo granted him, as the ninth fheaf, the ninth lamb,
and fometimes a fubfidy in wool. But in the forty-fifth year of his
reign, there was a tax of a very particular nature, which is recorded alfo

[57] Noy's Rights of the Crown, p. 61.
[58] Rot. Parl. 50 Edward III. Num. ix. vol. ii. p. 322.

as the firſt inſtance of any ſpecific ſum of money having been voted by
Parliament. It was a grant of 50,000 l. for carrying on the war with   Anno, 1371.
France. To raiſe this ſum, every pariſh in England was aſſeſſed in the
payment of 1 l. 3s. 4d. each, the greater to aſſiſt the leſs; and it was
ſuppoſed, that there were pariſhes enough in the kingdom, to make up
the complete ſum that was required.   But ſo ignorant was the Parliament at that time of the ſtate of the country, and of the number of
parochial diſtricts into which it was divided, that, inſtead of 1 l. 3s. 4d.
every pariſh was obliged to pay 5 l. 16 s. each [19].

    The expences to which this monarch was put, appeared to be ſo   Cuſtoms.
much beyond the natural powers and reſources of his kingdom, that it
was currently reported, he had diſcovered the art of making gold from
Raymond Lully, or ſome other ſkilful alchymiſt [60]. But the only ſecret
which Edward made uſe of, was to encourage the commerce of his
ſubjects; for he knew well, that the neceſſary conſequence of an increaſe of trade muſt be an addition to his revenue. Nay, he found
means to raiſe the cuſtoms of the port of London alone to 12,000 marks
per annum, which was more than the whole cuſtoms of England had
yielded in the time of Henry III.[61]. In the twenty-firſt year of his
reign, many merchants having been robbed and murdered by pirates
on the coaſt of England, it was thought neceſſary to equip a fleet for
the protection of commerce; and in order to raiſe the money wanted
for that purpoſe, an ordinance was made by the king and peers for
levying two ſhillings upon every tun of wine, and ſix-pence upon all
goods imported, which was only an addition of three-pence in the
pound, to the duties formerly laid on by the *charta mercatoria*. But
the commons complained, that the manner in which this tax was impoſed, was a violation of their privileges, and contrary to law [62]. The
ſecond grant of theſe duties (46 Edward III.) was equally illegal; for it
was granted by the citizens and burgeſſes only, without the concurrence
of the knights of the ſhires, or the peers of the realm [63]. Perhaps they

---

[19] Stevens, p. 109. 111. Carte, vol. ii. p. 527, erroneouſly ſtates this tax at 1 l. 16s.
inſtead of 5 l. 16s. per pariſh. It appears from Hutchin's Dorſetſhire, Introd. p. 56, that
the miſtake was not ſo much in regard to the number of pariſhes, as to the number of
thoſe able to pay the ſum aſſeſſed.   [60] Gilb. Exchequer, p. 217.
    [61] Noy's Rights of the Crown, p 86.
    [62] Rot. Parl. 21 Edw. III. Num. xi. vol. ii. p. 166.
    [63] Ibid. 46 Edw. III. Num. xv. vol. ii. p. 310.

thought

thought themfelves juftified, from their reprefenting the .commercial intereft, to authorife the impofition of any tax by which trade alone was affected, without the additional fanction of the other branches of the legiflature. The firft complete legal grant, therefore, of tunnage and poundage, impofed by full parliament, and extending to natives, was *anno* 1373 [64], fince which period, thefe duties have exifted in this country with hardly any exception.

Poll Tax.   The firft poll tax upon the natives was granted to Edward. It was a duty of four-pence a-head for every man and woman beyond fourteen years of age, beggars only excepted [65]. The clergy alfo granted twelve-pence for every beneficed perfon ; and four-pence for all other religious perfons, excepting Mendicant Friars, who profeffing poverty, were not fuppofed able to furnifh fupplies. Either the laying on of this tax, or the oppreffive manner in which it was collected, occafioned much difcontent [66], and ought to have prevented a fecond attempt of the fame kind, and the fatal confequences which refulted from it in the following reign.

Exactions.   But Edward's great undertakings were of too expenfive a nature to be carried on, either by the ordinary revenues of the crown, or by the grants, however liberal, which he received from parliament. Accordingly, his exactions were loudly complained of. The famous ftatute, *De tallagio non concedendo*, was far from being ftrictly obferved. It is faid, that he impofed arbitrary talliages upon his domains ; that he feized the money and effects of the merchants or bankers of Lombardy, who, fince the expulfion of the Jews, had followed the fame ufurious practices, with the fame deteftation and obloquy. He is alfo accufed of having been the firft who attempted to raife money by the pernicious mode of erecting monopolies ; of having extorted loans ; of compelling fuch of his fubjects as poffeffed eftates to the value of forty pounds *per annum*, to take the order of knighthood ; nay, of feizing the goods of his fubjects, and felling them for his own behoof, giving the owners fecurity for payment at a diftant day, and at a price inferior to their value [67].

[64] Rot. Parl. 47 Edw. III. Num. xii. vol. ii. p. 317.
[65] Ibid. 51 Edward III. Num. xix. vol. ii. p. 364.   [66] Mort. vol. i. p. 614.
[67] Stevens, p. 105. 110. Hume, vol. ii. p. 490 ; and Noy's Rights of the Crown, p. 64. 66.

But

But England alone could not furnifh, at that time, an income Foreign plunder and refources. adequate to the expenfive enterprifes which Edward had undertaken ; and it muft be confeffed, that he endeavoured, as much as poffible, to make his wars feed themfelves, by plundering the countries through which his armies paffed, or forcing the miferable inhabitants to pay heavy military contributions. Having taken in battle the kings of France and Scotland, their ranfoms amounted to a fum which it was very convenient for Edward to receive. By the treaty of *Bretigny*, the king of France's ranfom was fixed at three millions of crowns of gold, equal to 1,500,000 *l.* of our prefent money, of which, however, only one-half was actually paid[61]. The king of Scotland's ranfom was only 100,000 marks fterling, which, though a fmaller fum, yet was equally exorbitant, confidering the inferior extent and opulence of his dominions. But the greater part, if not the whole of it, was difcharged[62]. Nor were other refources wanting : for he alfo received 50,000 *l.* fterling from the duke of Brabant, as the portion of his daughter Margaret, the intended bride of Edward the prince of Wales ; and, it is faid, 30,000*l.* *per annum* from Ireland, after defraying the eftablifhments neceffary for its government and protection[70].

Notwithftanding the wealth which, from fo many fources, poured it- D.bts and difficulties. felf into Edward's coffers, and the fplendour of the greater part of his reign ; yet, on the whole, the events of it will furnifh no inducement to any monarch to afpire to the character of a conqueror, who coolly confiders the difficulties to which this king was reduced, the debts with which he was encumbered, and the unfortunate conclufion of his reign. Though every means that could be devifed for raifing money, to carry on his various undertakings, was adopted without hefitation or remorfe, he ftill found himfelf in the greateft perplexity and diftrefs. His queen pawned her jewels, and he himfelf was reduced to the neceffity of giving the great crown of England in fecurity for the money which he borrowed ; a gage which remained unredeemed for the fpace of eight years. Nay, he is reprefented, as afking the permiffion of his foreign creditors, to pafs over to England, and of pledging his royal word, to return to the continent, if he was unable to procure the money

[61] Hume, vol. ii. p. 469, and note K. p. 510.   [62] Mort. vol. i. p. 605.

[70] Stevens, p. 124.

neceffary

neceſſary to ſatisfy their demands. But the concluſion of his reign, in particular, formed a miſerable contraſt to its former luſtre. Not only were all his conqueſts (Calais only excepted) torn from him, but the ancient patrimony of his family on the continent was confined to the narrow bounds of Bayonne and Bourdeaux; and he who had deſolated every province of France; who had taken its ſovereign priſoner, and who had filled Europe with his renown, was glad to accept of any terms that his enemies condeſcended to offer". Thus the ſame monarch, who, in the earlier part of his reign, had conquered the dominions of others, towards its cloſe, began to tremble for the ſafety of his own. Theſe public miſeries were aggravated by diſtreſſes of a private nature, which it does not come within the compaſs of this work to relate.

Conſequences
of extortion. It is impoſſible too frequently to inculcate the doctrine, that more revolutions have ariſen from the extortions of a ſovereign, than from any other political cauſe whatſoever; and the reign of Edward unfortunately furniſhes us with an important inſtance of the truth of that propoſition. His ſon, Edward the prince of Wales, had undertaken an expedition to Spain, for re-inſtating Peter, ſurnamed the Cruel, upon the throne of Caſtile; an enterpriſe which he ſpeedily accompliſhed with his uſual ſucceſs. But the ungrateful tyrant refuſed to defray the charges of the expedition; and Edward was reduced to the neceſſity of demanding, from his ſubjects in Aquitaine and Gaſcoigny, a ſum of money to diſcharge the debts which he had incurred. This he propoſed to do, by levying the tax called Fuage, or Hearth-money, which, at a livre per hearth, it was calculated would produce 1,200,000 livres. But the attempt was attended with the moſt fatal conſequences. It filled the whole dominions of England, on the continent, with a ſpirit of revolt; and the French, taking advantage of an alteration ſo greatly in their favour, flew to arms; and in a little time, by the conqueſts they acquired, made ample amends for their want of ſucceſs in their former hoſtilities againſt Edward". Thus England found then, what it has alſo lately experienced, the difficulty of long retaining diſtant acquiſitions; and thus the levying of a trifling impoſt, occaſioned of old a revolution of as much importance to this country, in its conſequences, as the independence of America. At the ſame time, it is to

" Hume, vol. ii. p. 482.   " Ibid. vol. ii. p. 478.

be

be remarked, that the fuccefs of the French, on this occafion, was owing, not only to the affiftance of thofe who were exafperated at the propofed impoft, but alfo to the lingering illnefs with which the prince of Wales was afflicted, and to the imprudent confidence of the Englifh, who thought themfelves invincible.

It is faid, by a very intelligent author, that the revenue of the crown, in the twentieth year of the reign of Edward, amounted to £. 154,139 : 17 : 5 *per annum*. He mentions it upon the authority of a Pell of that year, which it is probable he has feen[73]. But we are not told where it is to be met with, or what were the particular fources from which that income arofe.

Amount of the revenue.

RICHARD II.

This monarch fucceeded his grandfather, Edward III. at a very early period of life; and, as naturally might be expected, the feeds of future mifery were laid during the courfe of his long minority. For his fubjects grew turbulent and factious; nor did he receive an education to fit him for his high ftation, or the critical circumftances into which he was led, partly by his own imprudence, and perhaps ftill more from the temper of the times.

The tax, known by the name of *Subfidy*, was firft attempted in the fecond year of his reign. The object of the tax was to fave the poor, and to lay the principal burden upon the rich. It was levied partly by a poll, and partly by a tax upon income. The dukes of Lancafter and Brittany, paid ten marks each; every earl was charged four pounds; every Baron forty fhillings, &c. But the great body of the people, merchants, artificers and hufbandmen, were affeffed a greater or leffer fum, *according to the value of their eftates*[74]. This fyftem, however, was too favourable to the indigent, to be much relifhed by the wealthier part of the community.

The firft fubfidy.

Anno 1379.

Notwithftanding the difcontent which the poll tax, levied in the reign of Edward III. had occafioned, Richard's minifters did not profit by the experience that circumftance might have afforded; and the neceffities of the ftate requiring a greater fum (160,000 *l.*) than ever had

Poll tax.

[73] Forft. on Cuftoms, introd. p. 31.   [74] Rot. Parl. 2 Ric. II. Num. 14. vol. iii. p. 57.

4   been

been formerly demanded from an Englifh parliament, the rich became
defirous of throwing a part of fo heavy a load upon their poorer
neighbours; and it was at laft determined to levy a poll tax of twelve-
pence upon every perfon in the kingdom, of whatev* condition or
eftate, above fifteen years of age, mere beggars only excepted. Some
indulgence the indigent were to receive; but it could not be very confiderable, as no perfon was to be charged above fixty groats, including
the tax he was to pay both for himfelf and family[75].

Rebellion.

This mode of taxation had ever been odious to the Englifh nation;
and, in the prefent inftance, it was fo directly oppofite to the principles
on which the fubfidy above-mentioned had been founded, that it foon
excited the greateft difcontent. By the former tax, the great men of
the kingdom were affeffed in a fum which bore fome proportion to their
property and wealth. But by the new mode, the greateft peer of the
realm, however opulent, could not be charged with more than fixty groats
or twenty fhillings. Nor was this all; for the tax, inftead of being
collected by the King's officers, was farmed out to contractors in the
different counties, who levied it with equal infolence and feverity. The
patience of the people was at laft exhaufted. They flew to arms; and
having chofen Tyler, Straw, and others for their leaders, they feemed
determined to bring about a total revolution in the country. The
infurrection, however, was fortunately quelled when it was leaft expected, and without much bloodfhed; and the king, though at that
time only fixteen years of age, acted on the occafion with fuch judgment and fpirit, that he impreffed his fubjects with the moft favourable hopes of the future fplendour and happinefs of his reign[76]. Nor
were their fond expectations diminifhed, when, upon taking the government into his own hands, he voluntarily remitted fome fubfidies
which had been granted to him; an event of which the Englifh hiftory
does not furnifh another example for many years after[77].

Exactions.

The miferable end of this monarch's reign is well known; and
though more tyrannical fovereigns have fat upon the throne of England,
and have died in peace, yet it can hardly be difputed, that his fubjects
had fufficient grounds to be diffatisfied with his conduct. He pro-

[75] Rot. Parl. 4 Ric. II. num. 15. vol. iii. p. 90.
[76] Hume's Hift. vol. iii. p. 10.   [77] Ditto, p. 24.

cured

cured, from a garbled parliament, the fubfidy on wool, leather and woolfells exported, *for life* — the firft inftance of fuch a grant, and which was confidered as a baneful precedent for the future. He extorted confiderable fums from his wealthieft fubjects, by way of loan, which it was dangerous for them to refufe, and ruinous to pay ; and under the pretence, that feveral counties had engaged in rebellious practices (notwithftanding a general pardon had been granted by act of parliament), he threatened them with the fevereft marks of his difpleafure, if they did not compound for their offences : and they were actually compelled to fign blank bonds, in thofe days called *ragmen*, which the king filled up in any manner, and with any fum he thought proper[78]. After all, the money which he obtained, either from the bounty of his people, or by means of extortion, inftead of being laid out for the glory and advantage of his kingdom, was either thrown away upon the minions of his court, or wafted in maintaining an enormous houfehold, amounting, it is faid, to 10,000 perfons ; of whom 300 were employed in the very kitchens of the palace. But, notwithftanding all thefe circumftances, he would probably have continued upon the throne of England, had he not found in his kinfman, Henry duke of Lancafter, an enemy, whofe ambition nothing but a crown could gratify, and whofe character, fpirit, and abilities were fully equal to any attempt, however bold, defperate, or flagitious.

Under the government of the Saxon line, or houfe of Plantagenet, Concluſion. no inconfiderable progrefs was made in the knowledge of finance. The neceffity of converting military fervices into pecuniary aids was difcovered. Taxes began to be laid upon perfonal as well as real property. The cuftoms came to be accounted a confiderable and important branch of the revenue, and the clergy were compelled to furnifh contributions for the public fervice; nor was the fanction of the pope any longer accounted neceffary for that purpofe. New modes of taxation alfo were attempted ; and though fome of them were ill contrived and unproductive, yet it proves the ftrong anxiety of thofe who were entrufted with the government of the country, to provide an effective revenue, adequate to the fupport of that high and diftinguifhed rank, which England was entitled to hold among the kingdoms of Europe.

[78] Carte, vol. ii. p. 628. Mort. vol. i. p. 657.

M   C H A P.

C H A P. VII.

Of the Revenue of England during the Government of the Houſes of Lancaſter and York.

THE æra, to the inveſtigation of which this chapter is dedicated, con-ſidering its duration, is the moſt calàmitous period of the Engliſh hiſtory, from the Norman invaſion.   It includes a ſpace of about eighty-ſix years, the greater part of which was ſpent in a bloody and deſtructive conteſt for the government of the country, between the two rival houſes of Lancaſter and of York ; both of whom, at different periods, were ſuccefsful.   The firſt monarch of the Houſe of Lancaſter, (for that family came earlieſt to the throne) paved his way to it, by forcibly depoſing his legal ſovereign ; and endeavoured to render his crown ſecure, by the murder of that unfortunate prince ; but in vain; for his government was perpetually diſturbed by a ſeries of dangerous inſurrections.   His ſon, Henry V. though a ſuccefsful warrior, and though it is probable, had his life been prolonged, that he muſt have ſucceeded in his views of ſubjugating France, neverthelefs waſted the blood and treaſure of the nation, in purſuit of an enterprife, which, if ſuccefsful, might have proved deſtructive to the liberties and to the national importance of England as an independent kingdom.   With refpect to the remaining monarchs of the two rival houſes, their hiſtory is nothing but a conſtant ſeries of battles, bloodſhed, crimes, horror, anarchy, and confuſion, ſcarcely to be paralleled in hiſtory.

Events, however, which at firſt ſight appear ſo ruinous and deſtructive, were, notwithſtanding, attended with conſequences in ſome reſpects bene-ficial.   The conteſt for the crown, between rivals of the ſame rank and pretenſions, rendered it neceſſary for both to court the favour of the people, and, when poſſeſſed of the government, to pay every poſſible attention to their liberties and rights.   During the whole period, no attempts were made to infringe upon the articles of Magna Charta, or to impoſe any tax without the ſanction of Parliament; whereas, it is

3   probable,

probable, that a race of monarchs, whofe title to the crown was unqueftionable, and who had no competitors for the throne, might have eafily ftifled the liberties of this country in their earlieft infancy, before they had arrived at that maturity and vigour, which they have fince fortunately acquired.

In the courfe of this bloody conteft, it is impoffible to learn, without regret, that the greateft and nobleft families of England, whofe gallant actions we read of in the earlier part of our hiftory, with equal pleafure and refpect, were almoft totally annihilated: but, perhaps, this circumftance alfo materially contributed to produce that free and popular form of government which we now enjoy. For, if the ancient nobles had continued in their original affluence and fplendour, in vain would the commons have endeavoured to raife themfelves to any degree of importance in the State. They muft have funk under the fuperior luftre and opulence of the peerage, and could never have attained that independent power, and that extenfive weight and influence which they at prefent poffefs, and which has fo much contributed to the profperity and happinefs of the country.

The union of France and England, under the government of one fovereign, had it been effected by the efforts of Henry V., or his fucceffors, would have proved a fatal circumftance to this ifland. The one kingdom muft have become a dependent province on the other; and it is hardly poffible to fuppofe, that England would not have been rendered fubfervient to a country, in which, both from confiderations of policy and of pleafure, the fovereign would naturally have refided[1]. That event, the conteft between the two rival houfes probably prevented; and although the faying of *Abbot Suger*, minifter to Lewis le Gros King of France, has, as yet, been verified, " that it was neither agreeable to nature or " reafon, that the French fhould be fubject to the Englifh, or the Eng- " lifh to the French[2];" yet fuch was the hold which England at that time had over fome of the moft fertile provinces of France, and fo martial

[1] By the treaty of marriage between Elizabeth and the Duke of Anjou, if their defcendants fucceeded to the crowns of France and England, the fovereign was obliged to refide in England, only eight months every two years. Mort. vol. ii. p. 397.

[2] Lytt. Hift. vol. i. p. 123.

were

were the Englifh during the whole period which is now under our confideration, that a junction of the two kingdoms would probably have been effected, if the warlike fpirit of the Englifh had not been wafted in domeftic quarrels, and if their diffentions had not furnifhed the French with an eafy opportunity, not only of conquering the poffeffions of England on the continent, but alfo of fecuring the affection and fidelity of the inhabitants, before the Englifh were able to attempt the recovery of the provinces they had loft.

Perhaps, alfo, the inutility and uncertainty of foreign conquefts, and the miferies attending domeftic wars, fo vifible during this æra, might firft give the Englifh that attachment to commerce, and thofe habits of induftry for which the nation has been fo long confpicuous. At leaft, by fuch fpeculations as thefe, the mind is furnifhed with fome confolation, amidft the detail of the various calamities to which England was then fubject, whether they are furveyed as delineated in the philofophic pages of Hume, or as drawn from the life, in bold and unfading colours, by the mafterly pencil of Shakfpeare.

Revenue of HENRY IV.

This monarch was the fon of John of Gaunt or Ghent, Duke of Lancafter, fourth fon of Edward III.; and he would have enjoyed an hereditary title to the crown, after the death of Richard, if Lionel, Duke of Clarence, Edward's third fon, had not left defcendants behind him, whom the Houfe of York lineally reprefented. But no one dared to mention the pretenfions of that family, though their right had been folemnly recognifed by parliament: for Henry, at that time, enjoyed the favour of the nobles, and of the people, and the command of a formidable army. He mounted the throne, therefore, without oppofition, and filled the vacancy, which his own intrigues had effected, in a manner that proved him not unworthy of the crown, had it not been obtained by violence and ufurpation.

Cuftoms.   During this, as well as the former reign, the revenue of the Cuftoms became more and more productive, in confequence both of an increafe of trade, and of an addition to the duties. Richard had received a grant

of

of three fhillings upon every tun of wine, and one fhilling upon goods[3]. But Henry did not venture to demand more than a tunnage of two fhillings, and a poundage, firft at feven-pence, and afterwards at eight-pence, until the fourth year of his reign, when the duty of three fhillings *per* tun, and one fhilling *per* pound, was again revived: a circum-ftance with which the king was fo much delighted, that he gave both lords and commons a magnificent entertainment upon the occafion[4]. Special care, however, was taken, not to give this monarch a grant of the cuftoms for life; and one year was fuffered to elapfe without any grant of them at all, in order to prove that this branch of the revenue was not the property of the crown, but proceeded entirely from the good-will and bounty of the people.

A tax upon places and penfions, and grants from the crown, was alfo impofed in this monarch's reign. It was enacted by the famous *Par-liamentum indoctum*, or lack-learning parliament, into which no indi-vidual converfant in the law was admitted. By the ftatute, the king was empowered to take one year's profits of all annuities, fees, or wages, granted to any perfon fince the reign of Edward III. (certain minifters of ftate, the judges, and other officers in the courts of juftice, only ex-cepted), together with all revenues alienated from the crown, unlefs ei-ther granted to the royal family, or confirmed by act of parliament: and all patents of penfions, or annuities for life, fince the 40 Edward III., were ordered to be brought in and examined, that fuch as were unde-fervedly beftowed might be revoked[5].

Place tax.

Anno 1404.

In the courfe of Henry's reign, we have feveral inftances of the tax known by the name of Subfidy. It was properly a tax on income, whe-ther it arofe from real or perfonal property: and, as it comprehended, in one grant, the principal modes formerly practifed of raifing a re-venue, namely, by fcutage and by talliage, it was both more equal and more productive.

Subfidies.

The curiofity of our hiftorians has been not a little awakened, to know the particulars of an impofition of fo fingular and of fo danger-ous a nature, that it was granted upon this condition alone, that it

Singular fub-fidy.

---

[3] Gilb. p. 280. Forft. p. 38. N. B. Thefe authors differ as to the years.
[4] Stevens, p. 135.   [5] Rot. Parl. 6. Henry IV. num. 14. Vol. iii. p. 547.

fhould

fhould not be made a precedent of for the future. Nay, according to *Walfingham*, it was to be kept concealed from pofterity; no evidence of it was to be preferved in the treafury or in the exchequer; and every writing or memorial regarding it, was to be burnt[6]. This tax is farther reprefented to have been, " A monftrous birth fhewn to the world, to " let it know what could be done, and concealed by hiftorians, that the " world might not know what may not, or ought not to be done[7]." To difcover this hideous monfter, the public records were carefully examined by a judicious hiftorian; who informs us, that this unprecedented tax was nothing but a fubfidy upon real and perfonal property, amounting to twenty fhillings upon every knight's-fee: twenty pence upon every twenty pounds a year in lands; and one fhilling in the pound upon money and goods[8]. And, with regard to the claufe prohibiting it to be made an example of for the future, it was not unufual when any important grant was made at that time.

Attack on the church.   The doctrines of Wickliffe began in the reign of this monarch, as they had done in the time of his predeceffor Richard, to fpread a fpirit of reformation in the church, not only in England, but on the continent; and, as this fpirit gave rife to a plan for enriching the crown, by the plunder of the church, which had nearly taken effect in the reign of Henry, it may not be improper to give a connected view, of the origin and progrefs of an event, fo fingular and important.

The clergy, by their own proud and haughty behaviour, gave rife to the idea. It was firft openly declared in the year 1385, when Richard II., having affembled a parliament in order to procure a fupply, found the laity willing to grant one-fifteenth and a half, provided onetenth and a half were given by the clergy. This conditional offer they thought proper to refent; and *Courtney*, Archbifhop of Canterbury, declared, " That the clergy were free, and were only to be taxed by them- " felves; and that he would fooner lofe his head, than fuffer the holy " church of England to be reduced under the fervitude of laymen." So haughty an anfwer roufed the indignation and refentment not only

---

[6] Hift. Ang. p. 369, 370.

[7] Nat. Bacon's difcourfes, part ii. c. 13, p. 60. Month. Rev. vol. xiv. p. 43.

[8] See Carte's Hift. vol. i. p. 660. Parl. Hift. vol. ii. p. 82. It appears from Rot. Parl. 5 Henry I. num. 33. vol. iii. p. 529, that a fubfidy was granted.

of

of the commons, but of many of the peers, who affirmed, that it was neceffary to humble their pride, by feizing the temporalties of the clergy,
and that nothing would render them ufeful to the State but reducing them
to poverty. The king, however, interpofed: he declared himfelf the
champion of the church, and, by his influence, the project, for that time,
was totally defeated[9].

The next attempt originated, not in parliament, but in a military
council. It is well known, that Henry IV. had obtained an important
victory at Shrewfbury, in which the gallant Percy, known by the name
of Hotfpur, and all the other leaders of that dangerous infurrection,
were either killed or taken prifoners. Henry's finances were exhaufted
by the expences he had incurred in quelling this revolt; and he was totally unable to provide for the maintenance of fome troops neceffary to
ftop the progrefs of the Welfh, who had made an incurfion into England. In this emergency, his principal officers propofed that he fhould
feize the money, and the valuable equipages of thofe prelates who ferved
in the expedition. And the propofal would probably have been agreed
to, if *Arundel*, who was then Archbifhop of Canterbury, and a man of
fpirit and refolution, had not boldly declared, " that they fhould win
" with blood whatever they got from him:" and the times were too
critical to quarrel with fo high-fpirited and powerful a fubject[10].

But the moft dangerous attack was made by the *Parliamentum indoctum.* It was the fecond parliament that had been affembled that year,
and it was held under the pretence that the preceding parliament had not
been fufficiently liberal in its grants. The commons were ftung by the
reproach, and reprefented to the king that his neceffities might be provided for without burthening the laity, by feizing the temporalties of the
churchmen, and applying them to the public ufe: they added, that the
riches of the clergy made them inattentive to their duty, and that, diminifhing their exorbitant revenues, would prove equally ufeful both to
the church and State. But the nation was not yet ripe for fo important
an innovation; and the clergy were headed by the fame prelate who had
formerly withftood the commons, and who was determined not to fuffer
the rights of the church to be eafily infringed[11].

[9] Burn's Eccles. Law, *voce* Monafteries.   Stevens, p. 120.
[10] Mort. vol. i. p. 675.   [11] Parl. Hift. vol. ii. p. 88.

In

In the courfe of this difpute, it was ftated, that the church poffeffed 18,400 ploughs of land, and that its revenue amounted to 485,000 marks a year; and the commons propofed, in a parliament held at Weftminfter, *anno* 1410, to divide this property among fifteen new earls, fifteen hundred knights, fix thoufand efquires, and a hundred hofpitals, fubject to 20,000*l.* a year, for the ufe of the king[12]. Perhaps the inconfiderable portion which it was intended the crown fhould receive, was the principal obftacle to its fuccefs.

But the dangers with which the church was environed, were not yet brought to a crifis: for, in the fecond year of the reign of Henry V., the fame project was renewed: the commons again propofed to feize all the revenues of the church, and to appropriate them to the ufe of the crown[13]. The clergy, however, efcaped, by giving up all the alien priories, and by diverting the attention of the king and of the people, from the internal government of the country, to thofe plans of conqueft and of empire which were afterwards purfued. Thus the wealth of the clergy was referved for the plunder of Henry VIII., and proved a material inducement with that monarch to bring about the reformation, or, at leaft, to put an end to the authority of the pope in England, and to make a confiderable reduction in the opulence of the church.

Houfehold.

The expenfive houfehold which Richard had maintained, was a circumftance peculiarly obnoxious to his fubjects; and indeed had principally given rife to the oppreffions of his reign. Henry was determined to give, on this head, every poffible fatisfaction: and, accordingly, he at firft reftricted the eftablifhment of his houfehold to 10,000*l.* But, in Anno 1404. the eleventh year of his reign, he found it neceffary to increafe it to 16,000*l. per annum*[14].

Jealoufy of the parliament.

The jealoufy which the commons entertained of the crown at this time, in regard to its revenue, is worthy of particular attention. In two different inftances, they allowed Henry only 6000*l.* for his own ufe, appropriated the remainder of their grant to public fervices, and appointed their own treafurers, who were anfwerable for the money they received, and were obliged to give in an account of their difburfe-

---

[12] Hume, vol. iii. p. 81. Parl. Hift. vol. ii. p. 114.
[13] Hume, vol. iii. p. 91. Parl. Hift. vol. ii. p. 136. [14] Noy's Rights of the Crown, p. 5.

ments

ments to parliament: and when Henry propofed, *anno* 1410, that a grant fhould be given him of a tenth from the clergy, and a fifteenth from the laity, *for his life*, under the pretence of faving them the trouble of meeting annually for that purpofe, the artful and infidious propofal was indignantly rejected[15].

Henry IV.'s income, in the twelfth year of his reign, is faid to have amounted only to the fum of 48,000*l. per annum*, including the fubfidy of wool, and the tenths of the clergy[16]. But this is a point which it will be proper to difcufs in a fubfequent part of this chapter.

Amount of his revenue.

H E N R Y V.

It is natural to indulge a confiderable degree of curiofity, to afcertain what refources a monarch was poffeffed of, who attempted the conqueft of France, and had almoft accomplifhed an enterprife of fuch difficulty and moment: for, although many circumftances had taken place favourably to his views, and he had reaped very important advantages from diffentions among the French, and from his alliance with the royal family, yet he could never have accomplifhed what he did perform, without funds of great pecuniary value: and as hiftorians have rather depreciated the extent of his revenue, it is the more neceffary to confider, firft, what temporary grants he received from parliament; and fecondly, what was the probable amount of his annual income.

Hume, who feems to be defirous of increafing the admiration which his readers muft naturally entertain of Henry's atchievements, by placing his finances in the loweft and moft contemptible point of view, has ftated that all the extraordinary supplies, granted by parliament during the courfe of Henry's reign, amounted only to feven-tenths and fifteenths (about 203,000*l.*); and he mentions, at the fame time, that Henry's army amounted to fix thoufand horfe, whofe pay was two fhillings a day; and twenty-four thoufand archers, who received fixpence *per* day each[17]. The expences of fuch an army, therefore, muft

Grants.

N   have

[15] Mort. vol. i. p. 706.   [16] Noy's Rights of the Crown, p. 4. Stevens, p. 140.
[17] Hift. vol. iii. p. 120. But it appears, from the authority quoted, Parl. Hift. vol. ii. p. 174, and 175, that the parliamentary grants amounted to nine-tenths and a third, and nine-

have amounted to 430,000*l.* *per annum*; and confequently, all Henry's grants, joined together, would have been exhaufted in lefs than fix months. But, in the firft place, the grants given to Henry were greater than this hiftorian ftates; and, in addition to them, he received confiderable affiftance from the clergy, and the entire revenues of 110 monafteries in England, dependent on certain abbies in Normandy, which the Englifh clergy had facrificed for the fecurity of their own poffeffions.

Amount of his revenue. There is alfo reafon to believe, that hiftorians have fallen into an error with regard to Henry's annual income, which is faid to have amounted only to 55,754*l.* 10*s.* 10½*d.*[18] ; " and with this weak fupply " (according to Voltaire), he undertook the conqueft of France."

The record on which this idea of Henry's revenue is founded, may be feen in Rymer[19]. It is not a little defective ; but its omiffions may be fupplied, from the full and particular account of the income of the crown, which was laid before parliament *anno* 1433[20]. From a comparifon of the two records the following ftatement is drawn up.

Amount of HENRY V.'s annual Income.

1. To the parva cuftuma on wool - -	£ 3,976	1 2
2. To the magna cuftuma on ditto -	26,035	18 8¼
3. To the parva cuftuma on goods - -	2,438	9 1¼
4. To the fubfidy of tunnage and poundage -	8,237	10 9¼
	£ 40,687	19 9¼
5. To the cafual revenue, arifing from efcheats, the court of wards, &c. - -	15,066	11 1
Total, according to Rymer,	£ 55,754	10 10½

nine-fifteenths and a third, which would, at leaft, amount to 270,000 *l.*: nay, it is faid, by an old hiftorian, that 300,000 marks, or 200,000*l.* fterling, were given by the clergy and laity, to enable the king to begin his enterprife. Parl. Hift. vol. ii. p. 147.

[18] Hume, vol. iii. p. 120. Volt. Gen. Hift. vol. ii. part iii. c. 8. Mort. vol. ii. p. 192. Noy's Rights of the Crown, p. 5 and 6. Davenant, vol. iii. p. 100.

[19] Fœdera, vol. x. p. 113.   [20] Rot. Parl. vol. iv. p. 433.

To

Brought over £ 55,754 10 10½

To be added [11] :

1. Fee farm rents	-	£ 3612	11	3
2. Alien priories	-	277	5	0
3. Dutchy of Cornwall	-	2788	13	3
4. South Wales	-	1139	13	11
5. North Wales	-	1097	17	3
6. County of Chefter	-	764	10	2
7. Manor of Shotfwick	-	33	6	8
8. Ireland	-	2339	18	6
9. Dutchy of Lancafter	-	4952	13	3
10. Dutchy of Aquitaine	-	808	2	2
11. Profits of Calais	-	2866	1	0½
12. Revenue of Windfor	-	207	18	5

20,888 10 10½

£ 76,643 1 8¼

Many of thefe articles muft have yielded more in the reign of Henry V. For it appears, that in his fon's minority, the management of revenue, and of public affairs in general, was miferably neglected [12]; and, on the whole, it is probable, that this monarch's income might amount to about 80,000 l. per annum, equal to 160,000 pound weight

[11] Thefe articles were liable to various deductions in the reign of Henry VI. as fpecified in the record ; but it is probable that fuch encumbrances did not exift in the reign of Henry V.

[12] The following articles, in the account of Henry VI.'s revenue, are fuppofed to include thofe which are called cafual, in the record which Rymer has publifhed.

The farms of counties, green wax, &c.	-	-	£ 5,676	10	8
Efcheats	-	-	-	500	0	0
Rents of lands in wardfhip	-	-	-	1,604	19	11
Rents of the Dutchy of Norfolk	-	-	-	1,333	6	8
Other eftates in the hands of the crown	-	-	983	7	5
The Hanaper office, and a variety of other articles	-	3,237	15	2

£ 13,335 19 10

As the cuftoms had fallen in their produce about 10,000 l. in the reign of Henry VI. it is not to be wondered at, that thefe cafual revenues fhould alfo diminifh in their amount.

of

of filver, which, by the cheapnefs of provifions at that time, would be equivalent to 500,000*l.* of our prefent fpecie.

Cuftoms.

It is faid, that Henry V. was the firft monarch, who had the fub-fidies on the exportation of wool and leather, and the duties of tunnage and poundage, joined together, granted him *for life*[23]. But Forfter remarks, though the fact is true, yet that Coke, and other eminent lawyers, are miftaken in the roll, which is commonly adduced in proof of that affertion[24].

HENRY VI.

There is hardly any inftance in the hiftory of England, or indeed of any ftate, the government of which has not acquired an uncommon degree of firmnefs and ftability, of a prince's fucceeding to the throne in his infancy, in which his reign did not prove the fource of infinite mifery both to himfelf and his fubjects. It is therefore the lefs furprifing, that though Henry VI. was born with the moft fplendid profpects of any prince in Europe, they fhould all be blafted by the immaturity of his age. He was fcarcely nine months old when he loft his father; and though he was crowned the fovereign both of France and England, he lived to fee himfelf without a crown, a fubject, or a home.

Grants.

The beginning of this monarch's reign was not burdenfome to his Englifh fubjects. It is faid, that only one fubfidy was granted during the courfe of feven years, from 1437 to 1444, and that the lofs of France was greatly owing to the fcantinefs of the fupplies[25]. The parliament was probably apprehenfive, that England might be made fubfervient to France, if the conqueft of that country was completed, and perhaps might alfo be defirous of rendering themfelves popular by their public frugality.

Cuftoms.

After fome temporary grants of tunnage and poundage, thefe duties were at laft given for Henry's life[26]. They were continued at the fame rate as formerly to natives, with this diftinction in their favour,

[23] Hume, vol. iii. p. 111.
[24] Introd. p. 39. It is granted by 3 Hen. V. Rot. 5. Vol. iv. p. 63.
[25] Hume, vol. iii. p. 167. Note [Y].   [26] 31 Hen. VI. An. 1454.

that

that aliens were to pay as much again as natural born fubjects : " The " law juftly keeping (fays a writer upon that fubject) a watchful eye " over perfons that had not that fame kind of natural inftinct, if I may " fo fay, to a country, which all fubjects are fuppofed to have [27]."

Several fubfidies, or pound rates, were granted to Henry, particular- **Subfidies.** ly in the tenth, fourteenth, and twenty-feventh years of his reign. In the latter fubfidy, there was a judicious gradation in the tax. For every perfon poffeffed of only twenty fhillings *per annum*, and from thence to twenty pounds, was charged but fix pence in the pound; but from twenty to two hundred pounds yearly, one fhilling in the pound; and all eftates above two hundred pounds *per annum*, were to pay two fhillings [28].

During the whole courfe of this reign, not only ftrangers who oc- **Poll-tax on** cafionally came for the purpofes of trade, but alfo fuch as took up their **aliens.** refidence in the country, were the objects of general odium; and the confequence was, that poll taxes were laid upon them, from which the natives of the country were exempted. This plan was firft carried into execution in the eighteenth year of Henry, when a tax was impofed on aliens, who were not denizens, of fixteen pence each, if they were houfeholders; but if otherwife, only fix pence. The fame tax was renewed in the twenty-feventh year, with an additional tax of fix fhillings and eight pence on merchant ftrangers, and twenty pence on each of their clerks [29]. But the heavieft duty took place in the thirty-firft year of his reign, when a poll-tax of two pounds each was laid upon foreigners, not denizens, *during the king's life*; merchants who landed in the realm, and who had refided there fix weeks, were charged twenty fhillings; denizen houfeholders, ten marks, or 6 *l.* 13 *s.* 4 *d.* each [30].

Henry, and his minifters alfo, found means to raife money from foreigners by other meafures befides parliamentary taxes. Firft, by permitting James I. of Scotland to return to his own kingdom; and, fecondly, by ranfoming the Duke of Orleans, who had then been detained in captivity, ever fince the battle of *Agincourt*, and was at laft releafed, upon paying 54,000 nobles, equal to 36,000 *l.* fterling of our money [31]." With regard to the king of Scotland, as he was not a

[27] Forft. Introd. p. 40.   [28] Rot. Parl. 28 Hen. VI. Num. 12. vol. v. p. 172.
[29] Ibid. 27 Henry VI. Num. 14. vol. v. p. 144.
[30] Ibid. 31 Henry VI. Num. 10. p. 230.   [31] Hume, vol. iii. p. 178.

prifoner

prifoner of war, it was impoffible to demand a ranfom from him: but 40,000 *l.* was exacted by way of equivalent for the entertainment he had received in England; of which fum, it is probable that 10,000 marks remitted were in confequence of the fecond article of the treaty, and as much more abated by way of portion with a relation of Henry's, to whom James was afterwards married. The remaining 40,000 marks were exacted; and thus a prince who, in time of profound peace, was driven into the port of a neighbour by diftrefs of weather, was detained in his dominions for many years, and after all was compelled to pay a confiderable fum of money for his maintenance, previoufly to his releafe.

Benevolence.   In the twentieth, or, according to fome authors, in the twenty-fecond year of his reign, the king required *a benevolence* for the purpofe of defending Calais, at that time in imminent danger. Thefe contributions were originally accounted perfectly free and voluntary; they were called *liberalitas populi* by Richard I. *curialitas* by fuch of his fucceffors as attempted to raife them; and proceeded according to Henry the Fifth's confeffion, *ex fpontanea voluntate, ac de jure vindicari non poffunt.* But the inftructions given by this monarch to his commiffioners for procuring the benevolence, contained a very different doctrine. It is there ftated, that by law he could compel all his fubjects, at their own charges, to attend his wars; but that he was willing to fpare fuch as would contribute as much as two days perfonal fervice would ftand them in, according to their rank and quality. Thus he publicly declared, that if they did not tax themfelves, money would be exacted from them, by other means much lefs pleafing[22].

Amount.   There is extant in the rolls of parliament, a very particular account of this monarch's revenue[23], from which it appears, that the annual produce, in confequence of the decreafe of the cuftoms, and mifmanagement in the collection, had fallen to 64,946*l.* 16*s.* 4*d.*; and fuch were the deductions from it, and the expences of government, that the charges exceeded the receipts 35,000 *l. per annum.* Nay, it was afterwards declared in parliament, that the income of the crown was reduced, by grants, penfions, and otherwife, to only 5000 *l.*[24].

[22] Stevens, p. 157. Cotton, p. 177. Noy's Rights of the Crown, p. 48.
[23] Rot. Parl. vol. iv. p. 433.   [24] Ibid. 28 Henry VI. Num. 53. vol. v. p. 183.

During

During Henry's minority, the revenues of the crown had been Diftreffes. greatly diminifhed by the arts and negligence of thofe who were in power, and in confequence of the expences incurred in carrying on the war againft France, which were principally defrayed from the income of the crown, the parliament furnifhing very little affiftance. Nor were matters much amended when the king took the government into his own hands : for he fuffered himfelf to be defrauded by his minifters, who devoured the greateft part of his revenues, and who, in the words of an ancient record, gave away the rights, poffeffions, and profits of the crown, *in the manner of a fpoil*". Different fteps were taken by parliament, and by his council, to improve the king's fitua-tion. In the parliament held *anno* 1450, a full refumption was made, of all the grants which had taken place fince the death of Henry V. To prevent the king from wafting his revenues, his council advifed him to convey to the archbifhop of Canterbury, in truft, all the profits of wards, marriages, relief, efcheat, and forfeitures, to defray the expences of the houfehold [16]; and in the twenty-ninth year of his reign, thofe expences were reduced by parliament to 12,000 *l. per annum* ; whereof 2000 *l.* was paid out of the queen's jointure, or feparate eftate [17]. His debts, at the fame time, amounted to the enormous fum of 372,000 *l.* ; towards the payment of which, the parliament was obliged to give fome affiftance ; and his reign furnifhes one of the firft examples in the Eng-lifh hiftory, of a debt being contracted on that fpecies of fecurity [18].

EDWARD IV.

This prince (the firft of the houfe of York that afcended the throne) was at laft fortunate enough to recover the rights of his family, after a long, fevere, and bloody conteft. And, perhaps, it is the only ex-ample in hiftory, of one family driving another from the throne, who had poffeffed it fixty years ; after having been for that fpace of time in

[15] See Noy's Rights of the Crown, p. 23. The duke of Suffolk, was accufed by the Commons, of having embezzled 60,000 *l.* which had been left by his predeceffor, in the office of treafurer. Rot. Parl. vol. v. p. 181.

[16] Noy's Rights of the Crown, p. 23.   [17] Ibid. p. 16.

[18] Hume, vol. iii. p. 215. See part ii. chap. iii. where it will appear, that the prac-tice may be traced to a ftill more ancient period.

3   the

the power of its rival, and having often fwore allegiance to it. But, as on the one hand, nothing could exceed the fimplicity and weaknefs of Henry's character ; fo on the other, Edward's valour, fpirit, and activity, were fcarcely to be equalled.

Refumption. The difgraceful poverty to which the crown had been reduced, rendered a refumption of the crown lands a natural mode for Edward to purfue, in order to increafe his revenue; and, in fact, the plan (which was infinuated by Edward himfelf, in a fpeech from the **Anno 1648.** throne) was readily agreed to by his parliament. Edward's domains had been previoufly increafed by the forfeited eftates of no lefs a number than one hundred and forty of the principal nobility and gentry of England, who had fupported the houfe of Lancafter. It is probable, however, that what was feized from the adherents of that family, he was often under the neceffity of beftowing on his own friends, as a reward for their fervices and attachment.

Grants. Six tenths, and as many fifteenths, with three quarters additional of each, were obtained by this monarch from his parliament, together with different fpecific fums from the maintenance of a body of archers ; and a yearly fubfidy upon foreigners, whether denizens or aliens. But the fums which he received were very inadequate to the various expences he was put to, and which a young and gallant monarch, like Edward, would naturally be inclined to incur [39].

Benevolence. In the firft year of his reign, he had received from the clergy *a benevolence*, or, in the words of the record, *a voluntary fubfidy* [40] : but a partial contribution of that nature was infufficient when he engaged in a war with France; and accordingly, in the twelfth year of his reign, he endeavoured to procure a general benevolence, or free gift; and fending for all the wealthieft perfons in his dominions, he laid his neceffities before them, and earneftly entreated their affiftance. This meafure is faid to have produced a very confiderable fum. Many contributed to avoid being fuppofed parfimonious, and others, that they might not feem difaffected, and confequently bring upon themfelves the king's difpleafure and refentment. Some did it out of affection to his perfon and family, whilft others could not refift the obliging manner in which their aid was requefted. A ludicrous incident, which took place with

---

[39] Stevens, p. 160 and 161.   [40] Ibid. p. 161.

regard

regard to this benevolence, has been often related. A rich widow, advanced in years, was perfonally applied to by Edward for her benevolence. She was fo much pleafed with the manner in which the requeft was made, and the gracefulnefs of Edward's perfon, who was fuppofed to be the handfomeft man in his time, that fhe immediately anfwered, " *By my troth, for thy lovely countenance, thou* " *fhalt have even twenty pounds.*" The fum was fo very confiderable, that the king thought himfelf bound to give the old lady a kifs, in token of his fatisfaction, who was fo much delighted with that unexpected mark of the royal attention, that fhe added twenty pounds to her former donation [41].

The confequence of Edward's expedition to the continent, was a peace with Lewis XI. by which that monarch became bound to pay Edward 75,000 crowns (to indemnify him for the expences he had been put to), and an annuity of 50,000 crowns, for their joint lives. It has been much difputed, whether this annual payment fhould be called a tribute, or a penfion. The firft would imply the fubjection of France to this country, which it is impoffible to fuppofe could be really meant by the agreement; and the name of penfion, would infer bounty on the part of France, and dependance on the part of England, which was equally abfurd and ridiculous. In the acquittances given for this annuity, it is called *cenfus*: and, in fact, it was an infamous bargain, which none but fuch a king as Lewis would have agreed to, and which, confidering Edward's mighty boafts and preparations, did him very little credit [42].

Annuity from France.

This difgraceful end of the expedition to France, had filled the nation with fo much difcontent, that the king did not think proper to apply to parliament for any pecuniary affiftance, and was reduced to the neceffity of having recourfe to other means for fupplying his exchequer. It is faid, that he adopted fome very oppreffive expedients for that purpofe, which the hiftorians of this reign have not thought proper to communicate. But it is known, that thofe whofe titles were in any refpect defective, which might be expected in confequence of fo much internal confufion, were obliged to pay confiderable fums of money for a confirmation of their grants; and the church complained of the exorbitant

Extortions.

[41] Parl. Hift. vol. ii. p. 364.   [42] Hume, vol. iii. p. 257. Stevens, p. 163.

fines

fines he demanded for the reſtitution of temporalitics, and of his diſpoſing of the profits of ſuch biſhoprics as happened to become vacant [43].

Merchandiſe. Edward had twice ſolemnly pledged himſelf, firſt, in the ſeventh, and ſecondly, in the twelfth year of his reign, to live upon his own revenues, and not to burden his people [44]. Among the various plans he purſued to preſerve that pledge inviolate, may be conſidered his engaging in commerce, and carrying on merchandiſe to a conſiderable extent [45]. Such a ſyſtem other ſovereigns have purſued ; and a monarch who has the abſolute government of his kingdom, and who, in conſequence thereof, can ſecure a monopoly of any commodity he chuſes to deal in, may trade to advantage ; but, in general, this circumſtance may be conſidered as the certain mark of an indigent prince, and of an oppreſſed and barbarous people.

Houſehold. During the whole of this reign, the expences of the king's houſehold were a perpetual ſource of complaint. Edward had promiſed to reſtrain ſuch charges within proper bounds [46]. But the hoſpitable manner in which the kings of England lived at that time, rendered any material reformation very difficult to be effected ; and after all the promiſes which he had made, of living upon his own income, parliament was obliged to allow 11,000 *l. per annum* out of the cuſtoms, and other public revenues of the kingdom, to aſſiſt him in defraying theſe expences [47].

EDWARD V.

This unfortunate prince ſucceeded his father, when only about twelve years old ; and though he has a place in the catalogue of our kings, it can hardly be ſaid, that he actually reigned. The government of the country, it is true, was carried on in his name, for the ſpace of about two months ; but, during that period, no parliament was held, nor did any material tranſaction take place. His uncle, Richard duke of

---

[43] Carte, vol. ii. p. 796.　　[44] Noy's Rights of the Crown, p. 13. 32, & 33.

[45] Mort. vol. ii. p. 116. Carte, vol. ii. p. 796.

[46] Noy's Rights of the Crown, p. 13.

[47] Rot. Parl. 22 Edward IV. Num. 2. vol. vi. p. 199.

Glouceſter,

Gloucefter, employed the whole time in carrying on machinations for his own aggrandifement; and being proclaimed king, vainly endeavoured to fecure the power he had acquired, by the murder of this helplefs monarch, and of his brother the duke of York, the only males of that family, who ftood between him and the throne.

RICHARD III.

A tyrant, who paves his way to the throne by deceit, treachery and murder, cannot expect to enjoy much happinefs from the power which he has acquired, and foon finds that he has immerfed himfelf in an endlefs feries of crimes, for the poffeffion of very precarious and fhort-lived authority. Of this, Richard's reign, which continued for the fpace only of two years and two months, furnifhes us with a memorable inftance; as it proves, that valour and ability, though united, are not fufficient to preferve a crown on the head of an ufurper.

Richard's title to the crown, was grounded upon principles fo contrary to the conftitution of England, and fo fubverfive of every tie by which both private and public focieties are linked together, that he feduloufly endeavoured, by every popular art, to ingratiate himfelf with the people, and with that view having affembled a parliament, he procured an act to abolifh, for ever, that mode of exaction, called Benevolence, which had not a little alarmed the public, on account of the illegality of the practice, and the great extortion which it had occafioned [48]. *Abolition of benevolences*

The only grant which Richard received, during the fhort courfe of his reign, was that of tunnage and poundage for life [49]. Indeed the cuftoms had become fo important a branch of the revenue, that no monarch, however frugal, or however anxious to acquire popularity, could carry on the government without the additional income which they afforded. *Grants.*

To Richard, it is probable may be afcribed the firft attempt to eftablifh pofts in England. The plan was originally formed in the reign of his *Pofts.*

---

[48] See act 1 Rich. III. cap. 2. Yet this tyrant afterwards exacted a benevolence himfelf. Parl. Hift. vol. ii. p. 410.
[49] Rot. Parl. 1 Ric. III. vol. vi. p. 238.

brother

brother Edward, when ſtages were placed at the diſtance of twenty miles from each other, in order to procure Edward the earlieſt intelligence of the events that paſſed in the courſe of a war, which had ariſen with the Scots. But Richard commanded in the expedition; and as it was a projeċt which ſeems more likely to have occurred to a man of his ſagacity and talents than to his brother, the merit of it ought probably to be given to Richard, in whoſe reign the practice was extended over the greater part of the kingdom [10]. But his abilities and his valour were equally fruitleſs. For after a ſhort reign he was ſlain, fighting gallantly at the deciſive battle of Boſworth.

Concluſion. It is hardly neceſſary to ſum up, at the concluſion of this chapter, the little progreſs that had been made in the ſcience of revenue during the period to which it relates. It was a time too full of bloodſhed and confuſion for any advancement whatever to take place in any branch of the civil department. It is remarked, however, by a great hiſtorian, that during the courſe of the conteſt between the two rival houſes, not an inſtance can be produced of any tax being impoſed without the ſanction of parliament. That important law in the conſtitution came thus to be unalterably fixed, and could not afterwards be ſafely broken through by any monarch, however bold or daring, or whatever authority he might have acquired in other matters [11].

C H A P. VIII.

Of the Revenue of England under the Government of the Houſe of Tudor.

A Variety of circumſtances contributed to mark out the acceſſion of the Houſe of Tudor, as one of the.moſt important æras in the hiſtory of England. By the marriage of Henry VII. who was acknowledged to be the reprefentative of the royal branch of Lancafter to Elizabeth, daughter of Edward IV. and heirefs of the line of York, the fatal conteft between the two houfes was brought to a conclufion. The Englifh, no longer diftracted by domeftic ftrife and difcord, were enabled to turn their eyes towards the continent; and inftead of confining themfelves to the narrow tranfactions of their own ifland, began to take an active concern in the general politics of Europe. Henry's encouragement of commerce, and his plans' for reducing the power and opulence of the ancient nobles, and for exalting the Commons on their fall, proved the means of introducing internal changes of the greateft and moft effential importance. The fame æra boafted the difcovery of the Eaft and Weft Indies, and America, by which a total revolution was effected in the ideas of individuals, and in the views of ftates. In a word, to this period may be traced the feeds of that political fyftem, which has ever fince engaged the attention, and occupied the thoughts of the principal powers of Europe. Nor is it of lefs importance with refpect to the general object of this work; for, in proportion as the fcene became more extenfive, greater pecuniary aids were required, than England had been accuftomed to fupply; and new fources of revenue confequently became neceffary.

Revenue of Henry VII.

It is remarked, by a great hiftorian, that in the reign of Henry VII. the Englifh were confiderable lofers by their ancient privilege, which fecured them from all taxations, except fuch as were impofed by their reprefentatives in parliament '. But the juftice of this obfervation there is great reafon to doubt; for if Henry's avarice was fuch, that it broke through every reftraint of law, to what height would it not probably have been carried, had it been fubject to no limitation whatfoever? His appetite, like his power, would have known no bounds, and not only the rich, and thofe who were immediately under the eye of the fovereign and his agents, would have been pillaged, but every

' Hume, vol. iii. p. 389.

creek

creek would have been ranfacked, nor would the pooreft cottage in the remoteft corner of the kingdom, have been exempted from his rapacity.

Cuftoms. Henry, like his predeceffor Richard, obtained a grant of tunnage and poundage for life [2], and the cuftoms became ever after, a permanent branch of the royal income. The tunnage was at the rate of three fhillings to natives, and fix fhillings to merchant ftrangers; and the poundage at the rate of a fhilling on all merchandife exported and imported, tin only excepted, for which aliens were to pay two fhillings. No alteration was made during Henry's reign, except an additional duty of eighteen fhillings per butt laid upon malmfey, imported by merchant ftrangers, in confequence of a tax impofed by the Venetians upon the fhipping or commodities of this country [3].

Grants. Henry received confiderable grants from the different parliaments he affembled in the courfe of his reign; and he always found them obfequious. Even the people paid any moderate tax, or any impofition to which they had been formerly accuftomed, or which the exigencies of the ftate required, without murmur or complaint. But the king was fometimes fo exorbitant in his demands, and his parliaments were fo prodigal of the public money, that it gave rife to very dangerous infurrections.

Northern infurrection. A parliament had met, *anno* 1487, to furnifh the king with a fupply, for the purpofe of enabling him to give effectual affiftance to the dutchefs of Brittany; and a grant (about the nature of which hiftorians differ) was accordingly voted. But the amount and weight of the fubfidy, joined to the general harfhnefs and unpopularity of Henry's government, excited fuch difcontent among the inhabitants of Yorkfhire and Durham, that a rebellion fuddenly broke out. The earl of Northumberland, who refufed to countenance the infurrection, was flain by the infurgents, and they feemed determined to carry on their daring enterprife with the greateft ardor and perfeverance: but an engagement having taken place with the king's forces, in which they were unfuccefsful, the rebellion was fuppreffed [4].

---

[2] Rot. Parl. 1 Hen. VII. vol. vi. p. 268.   [3] 7 Hen. VII. cap. 7.
[4] Bacon's Hift. of Henry VII. Edit. 1666. p. 40.

A more

A more ferious revolt took place in the year 1497. In a parliament held that year, a fubfidy amounting to 120,000 l. and two fifteenths, had been voted, under the pretence of fome incurfions of the Scots[s]. The inhabitants of the Weft, who thought themfelves fecure from any attack on that quarter, and who confidered the northern barons as bound, by the tenure of their poffeffions, to repel fuch inroads, murmured not a little at the impofition, and the inhabitants of Cornwall, in particular, flew to arms. Their numbers were fo formidable (amounting to above 16,000 men), that until they ventured to approach the capital, they met with no refiftance. But in a battle fought near Blackheath, the king's troops gained a complete victory; and 2000 of the infurgents expiated their rebellion with their blood[6].

Cornifh rebellion.

Though by an act in the reign of Richard III. Benevolences had been for ever abolifhed, yet as he was deemed an ufurper, his laws, it was afferted, were confequently invalid; and Henry ventured, on two different occafions, to have recourfe to this unpopular mode of levying money, though, according to Lord Bacon, he did not venture to revive it, until he had procured the confent of parliament[7]. It is generally fuppofed that archbifhop Morton was the author of the propofal; and a claufe inferted in the inftructions given by him to the commiffioners for levying the tax, which is commonly known by the name of Morton's fork or crutch, has been often quoted. All defcriptions of men (he told the commiffioners) muft contribute largely to the king's fupply: for fuch as are fparing muft be enriched by their frugality, and cannot therefore have any excufe; whilft thofe who live in a fplendid and hofpitable manner, fhould pay in proportion to their expences. Confiderable fums of money were levied by thefe means. The city of London alone paid 9,688 l. 17 s. 4 d. and Henry was artful enough to have the exaction legally authorifed by an act of parliament, which empowered him to demand any fum that had been offered, by way of compofition, for the Benevolence, and had not yet been paid[8]. *Anno*

B.nevolence.

---

[s] Bacon, p. 92.   [6] Parl. Hift. vol. ii. p. 452.

[7] Hift. of Henry VII. p. 58. Hume (vol. iii. p. 350. note U.) fuppofes that Bacon was miftaken, but the contrary appears from 11 Henry VII. cap. 10. intitled, A remedy or means to levy a fubfidy or benevolence *before* granted to the king.

[8] See act 11 Henry VII. cap. 10.

1504, the second benevolence was levied, which, however, was not so productive: for the people were diffatisfied with such repeated exactions, and knew well that he had no occasion for money at that time, being at peace with all his neighbours, and having his coffers full[9].

Feudal aids.

The parliament 1504, was principally affembled to raife an equivalent for two well-known feudal aids, which Henry was entitled to demand, in confequence of the marriage of his eldest daughter to James IV. king of Scotland, and his eldest son Arthur (who died foon after) having been made a knight. Thefe were the two greateft and moft expenfive folemnities to which feudal lords were liable, when that fyftem was at its height; and hence, by an ancient cuftom, their vaffals were bound to furnish them with fome pecuniary affiftance, though, in ftrict propriety, it ought never to exceed the real charges they were put to. But Henry was refolved to take advantage of any pretence to fill his exchequer, and therefore obtained from parliament 31,006*l.* 4*s.* 7*d.* as an equivalent for thefe aids; and this fum, inftead of being furnished by the immediate vaffals of the crown, who alone were legally liable, was levied upon the whole community, whether poffeffed of perfonal or of real property, and was thus rendered particularly obnoxious[10].

Merchandife.

Henry, who thought no gain, however inconfidcrable, beneath his notice, made fome profit alfo by letting out ships for hire, and even by lending money, upon intereft, to merchants, whofe flocks were not adequate to the enterprifes they had in view[11]. Nay, fo ftrong was his defire to promote the commerce of his fubjects, that he is faid to have lent money without intereft when it was really neceffary[12].

Money from foreigners.

Among the other means which this monarch made ufe of to increafe his wealth, may be included the fums of money which he drew from foreign nations; the great object of the French, at that time, was the acquifition of the province of Brittany; and it was at laft effected, greatly owing to Henry's avarice and neglect. For the dutchefs of Brittany, unfupported by the king of England, was compelled, how-

---

9 Hume, vol. iii. p. 389.   10 See Rot. Parl. 19 Hen.VII. Num. 11. vol. vi. p. 532. In p. 535, there is a particular account of thofe who were to pay thefe aids in each town and county.

11 Noy's Rights of the Crown, p. 176.   12 Hume, vol. iii. p. 401.

ever,

ever reluctantly, to marry Charles VIII. of France, to whom she had an aversion; and thus her dominions were again annexed to that powerful monarchy. Henry was desirous of receiving, at least, some consolation by the money which the king of France would pay to secure so valuable a possession; and he actually obtained 745,000 crowns, equal to 186,450 *l.* sterling, in lieu of certain claims he had boldly urged, though they were far from being well founded[13]. Two hundred thousand ducats were also given by Ferdinand king of Spain, with his daughter Catherine, married first to Arthur, the king of England's eldest son, and after his death, to Henry his second. The king's principal inducement to celebrate the second marriage (an event productive of infinite misery both to his posterity, and to his subjects), was, to avoid refunding the considerable portion he had received from Ferdinand.

Henry renewed the old mode of extorting money, by compelling persons possessed of forty pounds a year in land, either to receive knighthood, or to compound in its stead. And the rights which he enjoyed as the feudal lord, and superior of the kingdom, proved, under his government, an endless source of exaction, to which every proprietor of land was exposed. But in the latter part of his reign, a general system of oppression was not only begun, but resolutely persevered in. Every penal law, however ancient, or however injurious to the public interest, was rigorously enforced; and Empson and Dudley, two able, but rapacious judges, employed by Henry, as ministers to fleece the people, thought no expedient that yielded money, however bold, mean, or fraudulent, too infamous to be pursued. In the strong words of Bacon, " *they converted law and justice, into wormwood and rapine*[14]."

As Henry received more money, and spent less than any of his predecessors on the throne of England, it is natural to expect, that he must have left him behind a very considerable treasure; and in fact, it amounted to 1,800,000*l.* equal to 2,750,000*l.* of modern money. Indeed, considering the increased price of commodities since that time, and the great augmentation of specie, this sum was equivalent to, at least, eight millions[15]

Extortions

Treasure.

---

[13] See Parl. Hist. vol. ii. p. 447. He also received an annual tribute, or pension, of 25,000 crowns. [14] Hist. of Hen. VII. p. 119.

[15] Bacon, p. 132. Hume, vol. iii. p. 389.

at

at prefent.   Some authots have magnified his treafure to four millions and a half in bullion, befides plate and jewels [16]; but that calculaticn is totally incredible.

Remorfe.   Henry found, however, that his immenfe treafures could not adminifter to him, either confolation or affiftance, in the hour of ficknefs, and on the bed of death.   His arts, and his extortions, then appeared in their real colours.   All the means that could be devifed, to allay the terrors of a guilty confcience, were tried in vain ; and yet his contrition was either fo weak, or his avarice ftill fo predominant, that he could not be prevailed upon, during his own life, to make any reparation to thofe whom he had injured ; and his fon, notwithftanding the ftrict injunctions which he received, was equally loath to part with any fhare of the plunder that had been amaffed.   Empfon and Dudley, indeed, the inftruments of his father's oppreffion, were publickly executed to gratify the people.   But that was a poor recompence for the many exactions to which the nation had been fubjected, in the courfe of their adminiftration [17].

H E N R Y VIII.

Whilft the hiftory of the reign of Henry VIII. remains unexpunged from the annals of this country, it is impoffible for the people of England, to undervalue the happinefs and fecurity, which neceffarily refults, from a free conftitution.   They may perceive, by a review of his imperious and arbitrary fway, to what miferies they would have been fubject, had the fame tyrannical fyftem been continued ; and they may thence learn to encounter any danger, however great, in order to preferve that limited form of government which fhields them from a thoufand oppreffions, and from which fo many important advantages are derived.   In particular, they will find, from Henry's hiftory, that abfolute governments are neceffarily accompanied with the moft intolerable financial exactions, and that the wealth of the people is often wantonly facrificed, to gratify the paffions of the fovereign, or the caprices of his minifters.

[16] *Reftauranda*, by Fabian Philips, p. 24, who fays, that Lord Salifbury fpecified that fum to king James.   See alfo Stevens, p. 171.   [17] Hume, vol. iii. p. 411.

As Henry had fo great a treafure left him by his father, he had no **Grants.**
immediate occafion to apply to parliament for pecuniary affiftance. But,
no fooner was it fquandered, than many confiderable grants were
obtained under various denominations; the particulars of which, are
not fufficiently interefting to the prefent times to require being enumerated. But the circumftances attending one grant are of fo very
fingular a nature, that it is proper to mention them. A parliament was
affembled in the year 1523, to raife fupplies for carrying on a war
with France, into which Henry, at the inftigation, and indeed to ferve
the purpofes of Wolfey, had rafhly entered. The Cardinal had pledged
himfelf for the obfequioufnefs of the Houfe of Commons; and, fully
impreffed with ideas of his own dignity and importance, he came perfonally to the Houfe, and after making a long harangue to prove the
urgency of the king's neceffities, concluded with requiring a grant of
800,000 *l.* payable at the rate of 200,000 *l. per annum*, for the fpace of
four years[18]. So exorbitant a demand had never been heard before
within the walls of that houfe; and the court met with a firmer and
ftronger oppofition than was expected. Only one half of the fum was
voted, to which, afterwards, a fmall addition was made, in confequence
of a circumftance which evinces the manner in which Henry treated
his parliaments. Finding that the bill of fupply had met with fuch
unexpected obftructions, he fent for Edward Montague, a lawyer of
diftinguifhed eminence, and one of the greateft leaders of the Houfe,
and briefly told him, that if the fupply did not pafs, his head fhould
anfwer for it in the morning[19].

In a fpeech which Wolfey made to parliament, the increafe of the **Cuftoms.**
cuftoms is mentioned as a ftrong proof of the increafing wealth and opulence of the kingdom; and it is certain, that tunnage and poundage were
paid during the whole of Henry's reign. There is fome difference of
opinion in regard to the manner in which thefe duties were granted.
Hume ftates, that Henry had levied them for fix years by his own authority, without any fanction from parliament[20]. But Gilbert afferts, that

[18] Hume, vol. iv. p. 47.
[19] Parl. Hift. vol. iii. p. 35. This anecdote, however, is only traditional.
[20] Hift. vol. iv. p. 272.

they

they were exprefsly given by parliament in the firft year of his reign".

Poll-tax.

In the fourth of Henry, a poll-tax was granted in addition to other impofitions. A duke was charged ten marks; an earl four pounds; a baron two pounds; a knight thirty fhillings; and befides other rates every perfon of fifteen years of age, and upwards, was charged four pence ". This tax, which was impofed with fome degree of attention to the wealth and ftation of the different ranks of the people, was paid without much oppofition.

Feudal prerogatives.

The feudal prerogatives of the Crown, were becoming every day lefs profitable. A perpetual ftruggle was maintained between the fuperior and the vaffal, in which the latter was generally the moft fuccefsful; and, among other artifices, it became, at laft, a common practice entirely to evade the payment of any feudal incident, by making a truft fettlement of an eftate. For, on the one hand, it was faid, that the Lord Paramount could not attack the truftee, who held it for the behoof of another; and on the other, it appeared, that the real proprietor was not in poffeffion of the property, and confequently could not be made liable. In fome degree, to remedy what was then confidered as a very dangerous abufe, Henry propofed, that every man fhould be permitted to difpofe of one half of his landed property in truft, and that the other half fhould be fubject to the former incidents of the feudal tenures. This compromife, though agreed to by the Lords, was rejected by the Commons. But fuch was the fubjection under which parliament was held by the daring and imperious Henry, that it never ventured to oppofe his will without having reafon to regret it. On this occafion, he procured a decifion of the judges in his favour, and not long afterwards, the Commons were reluctantly compelled to agree to an act, by which it was declared, that the perfon who reaped the ufe, or enjoyed the profits of the eftate, fhould be deemed the proprietor ". Thus, inftead of the half, the whole of their lands were again made fubject to thefe feudal burdens.

" Treatife on the Exchequer. Appendix, p. 286. He fays, the roll is not printed. At any rate, the act 1 Hen. VIII. cap. 5. is fufficient.

" Lords Journal, vol. i. p. 25.

" Hume, vol. iv. p. 108 and 151, 27 Hen. VIII. cap. 10. See alfo 32 Hen. VIII. cap. 1.

At the time of which we are now writing, England was unqueftion- Firft-fruits and tenths. ably the richeft jewel in the papal crown. Befides the uncertain income arifing from indulgences, difpenfations, &c. the pope was thought entitled to the duty called Peter's pence, and to the firft fruits and tenths of all the benefices in the kingdom. The annates, or firft-fruits, was a tax which the pope received as an equivalent for the firft year's profits of every fpiritual preferment, originally introduced into the kingdom in the reign of king John, whofe mifconduct had reduced him to a total fubferviency to the church of Rome. It is calculated, that in the fpace of about fifty years, no lefs than 160,000 l. had been fent from England on account of that claim alone [24]. Upon Henry's quarrel with the pope, and his being invefted with the title of head of the church of England, the firft-fruits and tenths were annexed to the revenue of the Crown [25]. With regard to Peter's pence, and the various modes which had been invented by the church of Rome, of fleecing the people under religious pretences, they had been previoufly abolifhed [26].

Henry imitated his father's example, in endeavouring to reap pecu- Money from foreign princes. niary advantages from the treaties he entered into with foreign powers. Tournay having been taken by the Englifh, 600,000 crowns was demanded previoufly to its reftitution [27]; and Henry availed himfelf of the fituation to which France was reduced, by the captivity of its fovereign, Francis I. to obtain very lucrative ftipulations. But the moft fingular article of that nature, was contained in a treaty, concluded at London, *anno* 1527, by which Henry agreed to renounce all claim to the crown of France; in return for which, Francis became bound to pay, *for ever*, 50,000 crowns a year, to Henry and his fucceffors [28].

Under Wolfey's adminiftration, an attempt was made, which, had Wolfey's fyftem of extortion. it fucceeded, would have proved the entire ruin of the liberties of England. It was to raife money by royal proclamation. Commiffions were iffued for that purpofe; and it was intended to exact four fhillings in the pound from the clergy, and three fhillings and four-pence from the laity. So illegal and exorbitant an impofion, occafioned the greateft clamour and difcontent in every corner of the kingdom; and a dangerous rebellion would have followed, if the king had not denied having

[24] Black. vol. i. p. 284.   [25] 26 Hen. VIII. cap. 3.
[26] By 25 Hen. VIII. cap. 21.   [27] Hume, vol. iv. p. 14.   [28] Ibid. p. 72.
any

any knowledge of the impofition; and publickly declared, that his neceffities, however great, fhould never make him attempt to raife money by any other means than by the voluntary confent of his people, or the fanction of parliament [29]; a declaration, however, to which he did not ftrictly adhere, during the middle and latter part of his reign.

Debafing the coin.

There is no mode, by which a needy and tyrannical fovereign, may acquire inconfiderable fums of money, with greater detriment to his fubjects, than by tampering with the coin. From the Conqueft, to the reign of Henry VIII., the old ftandard of finenefs had been generally preferved; and, although fome bafe metal had been mixed in our coin, yet the adulterations were gradual, and confequently lefs pernicious. But Henry, befides enhancing the price of gold and filver to a confiderable degree, difgraced himfelf fo far, as to coin bafe money, and to order it to be current by proclamation [30].

Loans.

It was natural for a prince like Henry, reduced to confiderable difficulties by his own extravagance, to imitate the example of fome of his predeceffors, in extorting compulfive loans from his fubjects. He began with demanding particular fums from fome wealthy individuals; but

Anno 1523.

foon afterwards he impofed a general tax, under the pretended name of a loan, amounting to five fhillings in the pound on the clergy, and two fhillings on the laity [31]. It is faid, that the plan was propofed by Wolfey, who was then in the height of his power; and whofe friends, to prove their attachment to him, largely contributed. But they had foon reafon to repent of their zeal; for an act was paffed, abolifhing all the debts which the king had incurred fince his acceffion, in which this loan was included. From various motives, this meafure met with a very general concurrence. The friends of the court rejoiced, that the king's debts were annihilated, and the friends of the people, that a mode of fupply, fo dangerous to public liberty, fhould be difcredited. Nor were either the court, or the nation difpleafed, that Wolfey's attached friends, who had enriched themfelves by their connection with that haughty minifter, fhould thus be impoverifhed. Notwithftanding

[29] Hume, vol. iv. p. 61. Parl. Hift. vol. p. 38. Godwin's annals, p. 40.
[30] Harris on money and coin, part ii. p. 3. Stevens, p. 209.
[31] Hume, vol. iv. p. 46.

this

this abolition, another loan was exacted ; and Henry had even begun to repay fome part of the money that he had borrowed ; but his exchequer was not adequate to fo great an undertaking ; and he found it neceffary to procure another act, which not only freed him from his incumbrances, but by which thofe who had been paid either in whole, or in part, were obliged to refund any fum they had received[22]. What rendered the loans in the reign of this king particularly obnoxious, was, that the people were compelled to reveal the extent of their fortune upon oath, and were charged accordingly[23].

Of all the plans which he purfued for raifing money, that which Benevolence. paffed under the name of a Benevolence, was unqueftionably the moft tyrannical. To extort money from his fubjects, illegally, was not fufficient ; but Henry had the infolence to compel them to give that as a free gift, which was actually forced from them by compulfion. To the firft benevolence that was exacted, he himfelf gave the name of the *Amicable Graunte*[24] ; yet fuch as refufed to pay the fum that was expected from them, were threatened with punifhment. In the thirty-fifth year of his reign, he extorted 70,000 *l.* under the fame pretence; and meeting·with much oppofition from the citizens of London, on whom fuch exactions were particularly fevere, he took care to make an example of two of the moft refractory aldermen ; the one, by fine and imprifonment ; and the other, by compelling him to ferve in perfon againft the Scots, by whom he was taken prifoner[25].

But Henry's extravagance was fuch, that all ordinary expedients for Attack on the raifing money, and every mode of extortion, that had ever been church. formerly practifed in England, were inadequate to his expences ; and a variety of circumftances concurred to make the wealth and property of the church, a defirable object of his rapacity. The rifk which it had run in the reigns of Henry IV. and of Henry V., has already been taken notice of ; and the principles of reformation which Wickliffe preached up at that time, had fince met with more encouragement, and been carried to greater lengths under the banners of Luther and of Calvin. Wolfey himfelf, though a cardinal of the church of Rome, and a candidate for the papal throne, had fet the firft example of an

---

[22] 35 Henry VIII. cap. 12.

[23] Stevens, p. 181.

[24] Stevens, p. 180. Noy, p. 49.

[25] Godwin's Annals, p. 111.

encroach-

encroachment upon ecclefiaftical property, by procuring a bull to diffolve forty of the leffer monafteries, in order to endow two colleges he propofed to erect at Oxford and Ipfwich [16]; and Cranmer, who fucceeded Wolfey in the confidence of the king with regard to ecclefiaftical affairs, detefting the luxurious manner in which the monks lived ; and convinced, that they were addicted to many vices incompatible with the ftrict and auftere life they profeffed, was eafily perfuaded, that their wealth could be better employed than in miniftering to their voluptuoufnefs [17].

Means pur-
fued by
Henry.

The means purfued by Henry were highly politic. He firft procured, both from his church and parliament, a recognition of his right of fupremacy ; and then, as head of the church, he appointed Cromwell his vicar-general, and directed him to employ commiffioners on whom he could depend, for the purpofe of vifiting the different monafteries, and of making the ftricteft enquiry into the lives, morals, and behaviour of thofe by whom they were inhabited. It is faid, that difcoveries were made, fo unfavourable to the character of thefe religious hypocrites, as to render their fuppreffion popular with the people, as well as profitable to the crown [18].

Suppreffion
of the leffer
monafteries.

The firft attack upon the patrimony of the church, was by an act of parliament paffed *anno* 1536 ; by which, under the pretence, that no reformation of the vices of the monks in the leffer monafteries could be effected, but by their diffolution, all fuch inftitutions, poffeffed of revenues under 200 *l.* a year, were given to the crown [19]. Three hundred and feventy-fix monafteries were fuppreffed by this act ; whofe landed property produced above 32,000 *l. per annum*, and whofe perfonal effects yielded above 100,000 *l.* though difpofed of greatly under their value [40].

Suppreffion
of the greater
monafteries.

The wealth which Henry had thus procured was however foon exhaufted ; and his neceffities impelled him to carry ftill farther a plan at-

---

[36] Godwin, p. 41.

[37] Cranmer was convinced, that the reformation could not be carried on, unlefs the monafteries were fuppreffed. Burn's Ecclef. Law, *voce* Monafteries.

[38] Hume, vol. iv. p. 150.   [39] 27 Henry VIII. cap. 28.

[40] Hume, vol. iv. p. 150. Stevens, p. 211.

tended

tended with fo much gain. Accordingly, two years afterwards, in Anno 1533. confequence of a fecond vifitation, the greater monafteries were fupprefled.; and fix hundred and five great abbies, together with ninety ,colleges, and a hundred and ten hofpitals for the relief of the poor, were ,by one act annihilated ". The monks, dreading the king's refentment, had, in general, previoufly delivered up their property into his hands; and all doubts were removed by this act, in regard to the legality of fuch furrenders.

But Henry was not yet fatisfied with the pillage of the church. Under the pretence, therefore, of *regulating the clergy*, many of the bifhops were compelled to furrender the landed property of their fees into his hands". No lefs than feventy manors were taken from the archbifhopric of York, and other diocefes fuffered proportionably ". The monafteries in Ireland, and the knights of St. John of Jerufalem, were alfo fupprefled ; and, to crown the whole, an act was pafled, by which parliament granted to the king the revenues of the two univerfities ; and of all the chantries, free chapels, and hofpitals in the kingdom".

Other clerical extortions.
Anno 1542.

Anno 1542.

It was imagined, that the great value of the religious houfes,which were thus fupprefled, would have furnifhed the crown with fuch an addition to its income, as to render any farther application to parliament for new grants unneceffary. In the reign of Henry IV. the income of the church had been computed at 485,000 marks.; and it was fuppofed, that its revenues muft have greatly increafed fo many years after. But the clergy had been prepared for the blow. With a view of rendering themfelves popular, their eftates were let at very moderate rates ; and, inftead of an addition of rent, they were accuftomed to exact fmall fines when the leafes were renewed. Befides ", the commiffioners who were appointed to vifit the monafteries, expecting either to procure a grant of fome of the lands they furveyed, or to purchafe them at low prices, undervalued them as much as poffible ; and the income of the whole was only given in at 152,517 l. 18 s. 10 d. per annum, grofs-rent, and was ftated at no more than 131,607 l. 6 s. 4 d. net produce, after all deductions". The real value of thefe poffeffions, however, was

Value.

41 31 Hen. VIII. cap. 13.   42 37 Hen. VIII. cap. 16.
43 Stevens, p. 193.   44 37 Hen. VIII. cap. 4.
45 Hume, vol. iv. p. 182.   46 See a particular account of them, Stevens, p. 213.

Q   incon-

inconceivably great. It appears from an account drawn up *anno* 1717; that the annual income of the houfes fuppreffed by Henry, muſt have amounted to about 273,000 *l.*; and at a moderate computation, would now yield at leaſt fix millions *per annum* [47]. The abbey of St. Albans, which was valued only at 2500 *l. per annum*, poffeffed eſtates, which, a century after the fuppreffion, brought in 200,000 *l.* a year [48].

Henry's pro-fuſion. Many fuggeſtions had been thrown out by zealous and public fpirited men, to render the revenues of the church ufeful to the public. Among other plans of a beneficial nature, it was propofed to found feminaries for the ſtudy of law; for the acquiſition of ufeful languages; and for the education of thoſe intended for foreign embaſſies, or to fill the high offices of the ſtate. But Henry's prodigality rendered all fuch fchemes abortive. Inſtead of fixteen, as he had originally propofed, he was only able to erect fix new biſhoprics. The immenſe property he had acquired was foon waſted; in a ſhort time, the crown became as neceſſitous as ever; and, in conſequence of its poverty, again dependent on parliament for fupport.

Poor's rates. The fuppreffion of the monaſteries, inſtead of proving, as was expected at the time, a means of freeing the people from the weight of taxes, was the fource of one of the heavieſt burdens to which this country is at prefent fubject. The monaſteries, previous to their diſſolution, had been the great afylum of the poor; and it was much apprehended, that the latter would become a load upon the public, in confequence of the fuppreffion of the former. Large quantities of the church lands, therefore, had been fold at eafy rates, that the purchafers might be enabled to keep up the hoſpitality, and charitable donations, which had been practiſed by their predeceſſors; and a penalty of 6 *l.* 13 *s.* 4 *d. per* month was impofed upon fuch as failed in the obligation [49]. An attempt was made in the year 1536, to lay this burden upon the fecular clergy; the incumbent of every pariſh being ordered to fet apart a confiderable portion of his revenue for repairing the church, and for fupporting the poor [50]. It is not known how long this regulation continued in force;

[47] Summary of all the religious houfes in England and Wales, at the time of their diffolurion, p. 63.   [48] Stevens, p. 188. 216.
[49] See 27 Hen. VIII. cap. 28. § 9, 10. Repealed by 21 Jac. c. 28. § 11.
[50] Hume, vol. iv. p. 170.

5   but

but it is certain, that after many other ineffectual endeavours, it was at laft thought neceffary, to compel the parifh where the poor were born, or where they acquired a fettlement, to provide for their maintenance: a grievous burden, which, it is fuppofed, amounts at prefent to at leaft three millions *per annum.*

In the reign of Henry, a general furvey was made of the whole kingdom; of the number of the inhabitants, their age, profeffions, wealth, income, and every other important particular that a ftatefman could wifh to be acquainted with. The furvey is unfortunately loft; and the only information which it contained, at prefent known, is, that the income of the whole kingdom was eftimated at four millions *per annum*[51]. It is remarked, therefore, by Hume, that the landed property of the different monafteries, that were fuppreffed, was only equal to about a twentieth part of that fum[52]. But it has been already obferved, that the real value of thefe lands was greatly fuperior.

Survey of the kingdom.

E D W A R D VI.

This young prince fucceeded to the crown at the age of about nine years. As his reign lafted during the fpace only of fix years and a half, the government muft have been in a great meafure conducted by the advice of his minifters. Yet, unlefs the accounts given us by hiftorians are greatly exaggerated, he himfelf enjoyed no inconfiderable fhare in the adminiftration. It is at leaft certain, that he was educated in habits of induftry, and of attention to bufinefs, which, had his life been prolonged, would probably have made him one of the beft and greateft monarchs that ever fat upon the throne of England.

During the greater part of his reign, Seymour duke of Somerfet, Edward's maternal uncle, governed the kingdom under the name of Protector. Notwithftanding the endeavours of this minifter to acquire popularity, he found it was impoffible to carry on the public bufinefs without fupplies from parliament; particularly, after he had engaged in wars with France and Scotland, which the revenues of the crown, impaired by Henry's prodigality, were by no means able to fupport.

Grants.

---

[51] Hume, vol. iv. p. 47. Parl. Hift. vol. iii. p. 26. [52] Vol. iv. p. 182.

In

In addition, therefore, to tunnage and poundage, fome tenths, fifteenths, and fubfidies, were applied for, and chearfully granted.

Tax on fheep. The reign of Edward is remarkable for an attempt to lay a poll-tax upon fheep " : Every ewe, kept in a feparate pafture, was charged three-pence ; every wether, two-pence ; and all fheep kept on commons, three halfpence. But the tax was found fo difficult to collect, or fo oppreffive, that it was repealed in the next year ".

Tax on woollen cloth. England began about this time to make a diftinguifhed figure, as an induftrious and commercial nation ; and the manufacture of woollens, in particular, was raifed to fuch a height, that it was fuppofed able to bear an impofition. A tax of eight pence in the pound, therefore, was laid upon all cloth made for fale in England. But this, and the duty upon fheep joined together, were found fo oppreffive, upon an' article which had not arrived at its maturity, that they were both repealed after a fhort trial, though they had been granted for three years ".

French annuity. The kings of England, fince the reign of Edward IV. had conftantly endeavoured to procure fome pecuniary compenfation from the crown of France, for the right they claimed to that kingdom. Mention has been made already, of the treaties between the two crowns in regard to this demand. In the reign of Edward, the arrears of the annuity, amounted to two millions of crowns. But the king of France (Henry II.) abfolutely refufed to pay any part of the fum, declaring, that he would not fuffer himfelf, or his kingdom, to be tributary to any one ; and as a treaty was concluded, in which no notice was taken of this claim, it has ever fince been confidered as totally abandoned ".

Sale of Boulogne. The town of Boulogne was the only acquifition which Henry VIII. had made, in a war which is faid to have coft the fum of 1,340,000 *l.* fterling. It was a poffeffion which England could not hold without confiderable expence, and indeed greater charges than its revenues could at that time afford. As the French were defirous of acquiring it, the parties found little difficulty in coming to an agreement. Boulogne, **Anno 1550.** therefore, and its territories, were reftored, in confideration of 400,000 crowns, or 133,333 *l.* 6 *s.* 8 *d.* fterling ".

---

[1] 2 & 3 Edw. VI. cap. 36.   [14] 3 & 4 Edw. VI. cap. 23.
[13] Stevens, p. 225.   [15] Hume, vol. iv. p. 342. Mort. vol. ii. p. 306.
[17] Carte, vol. iii. p. 246.

The

The difficulties to which the protector was reduced, made him have Debafing the coin. recourfe to the dangerous expedient of debafing the coin. Nay, it is faid, that 20,000 pounds weight of bullion was ordered to be coined, fo as to yield the king a profit of 140,000 *l.* " The ufual confequences enfued from fo pernicious an attempt. " The good coin was hoarded or ex-" ported, bafe metal was coined at home, or imported from abroad in " great abundance; the common people, who received their wages in " it, could not purchafe commodities at the ufual rates; an univerfal " diffidence and ftagnation of commerce took place, and loud com-" plaints were heard in every part of the kingdom [58]." It is remarked by the fame hiftorian, that in confequence of the importation of fome bullion from Sweden, good fpecie was again coined, and fome of the bafe metal, formerly iffued, was recalled. The Swedes were tempted to fend what bullion they could fpare into England, in confequence of a treaty of commerce between the two kingdoms; by which they were permitted to export Englifh commodities duty free, provided the price was paid in bullion [59].

In Edward's reign, an alteration took place with regard to the Cuftoms. cuftoms, which was attended with the moft important confequences. A body of foreign merchants, called the Corporation of the Steel-yard, had been erected in the reign of Henry III. and had obtained, by patents from the crown, very valuable privileges. In particular, they were exempted from feveral duties paid by other aliens, and confequently, enjoyed all the advantages of the natives in England, whilft, at the fame time, by means of their connexions on the continent, they had a better opportunity of difpofing of their commodities at foreign markets. Edward's minifters were fortunately apprifed of all thefe circumftances; and being convinced how neceffary it was to encourage the commerce and navigation of England, they determined to annul the privileges of this foreign company, and perfevered in their refolution, notwithftanding the oppofition and remonftrances of the principal trading cities in Europe. Aliens duty being thus impofed upon all foreigners without diftinction, the natives of the country were led to engage in commer-

---

[57] Mort. vol. ii. p. 456.
[58] Hume, vol. iv. p. 328. Harris on Coins, part ii. p. 3.
[59] Hume, vol. iv. p. 349.

cial

cial undertakings with greater eagernefs than formerly, with more profit to themfelves, and more advantage to their country [60].

Church Lands.

In the latter end of the reign of Henry VIII. an act had paffed for the fuppreffion of all the chantries, free chapels and colleges in the kingdom ; and commiffioners had been actually appointed to take poffeffion of their revenues. But Henry died before the commiffion was carried into execution, and it was thought neceffary to pafs another act, by which no lefs than 2374 religious eftablifhments were at once abolifhed, and given to the crown [61]. It is declared in the act, that thefe foundations were thus annexed for purpofes of the greateft national utility. They were appropriated for erecting fchools ; for augmenting the feminaries of learning in the two univerfities; for the better provifion of the poor, and for difcharging the king's debts. But as minifters of ftate were then endowed with deaneries, prebends, and other fpiritual preferments, it was eafy to perceive into whofe hands they would fall. Nor was this the only ecclefiaftical plunder in the reign of Edward. For the bifhop of Winchefter and others were deprived of many of their manors, and obliged to change the property they had, for lands and rights of inferior value. The churches were alfo fearched, and the plate, jewels, and every other article of any value belonging to them (one chalice, and one covering for the communion table alone excepted), were appropriated to the ufe of the crown [62].

Poors rates.

The diftreffes of the poor were in the meanwhile daily increafing ; and it became more neceffary than ever for the legiflature to interfere in their behalf. Accordingly, *anno* 1552, an act was paffed, empowering the church wardens in every parifh to collect money for their relief; and if any refufed to give in charity, or diffuaded others from contributing, the bifhop of the diocefe was entrufted with difcretionary powers to proceed againft them [63].

Fines.

The loofe government which always takes place during a minority, had flattered many of the fervants of the crown with impunity, and encouraged them to commit crimes of a very dangerous nature. It was determined to punifh them by heavy pecuniary fines, not only as a chaftifement for their offences, but that fome advantage might be

---

[60] Hume, vol. iv. p. 348.

[61] Stevens, p. 220. 222.

[61] 1 Edward VI. cap. 14.

[62] 5 & 6 Edw. VI. cap. 2. Parl. Hift. vol. iii. p. 260.

reaped

reaped by the exchequer. Lord Paget, chancellor of the dutchy of Lancaster, confcious of his guilt, furrendered his office, and paid down 4000 l.; and Beaumont, Mafter of the Rolls, and Whalley, receiver of Yorkfhire, compounded for their offences by fimilar means [64].

The debts contracted by Edward, had been made ufe of as a ftrong argument in parliament, to beftow on him the remaining property of the regular clergy; and fome of the lands, thus obtained, were actually fold, and the purchafe-money applied to free the crown from thofe difagreeable incumbrances. But fuch was the rapacity of Edward's minifters, that they not only appropriated to their own private ufe the greater part of the property taken from the church, but alfo defrauded the crown of its domains, and left the king involved in a debt, amounting to above 240,000 l. *Debts.*

In the reign of Edward, it became an ufual practice to negociate loans on the continent; for which, it is faid, he paid an intereft of 14 per cent. Antwerp, and other cities in Flanders, were then fuppofed to be the only places where any confiderable fums of money could be borrowed. *Foreign loans.*

M A R Y.

The reign of Mary, who fucceeded her brother Edward, fufficiently accounts for the deteftation in which the Englifh nation has ever fince held every attempt to re-eftablifh the Roman Catholic religion in their country, and their dread of having another popifh prince feated upon the throne. For, during the whole period, we find nothing but difgrace abroad, and mifery at home; the moft folemn engagements abandoned; and the interefts of her kingdom facrificed, to gratify her pernicious attachment to the religion of Rome, and to the politics of the Spaniards. Fortunately, her reign fcarcely exceeded five years; and it may be confidered merely as a foil to difplay the happy and fplendid government of Elizabeth, in more lively, and more durable colours.

[64] Mort. vol. ii. p. 312. 456.

Mary

Grants.   Mary had the duties of tunnage and poundage granted to her for life, by an act which contains the following fingular preamble: " In their " moft humble wife fhewn, unto your moft excellent majeftie, your " poore and obedient fubjects and commons ", &c. " . The whole is drawn up in a ftyle which tends to juftify the right of the crown to tunnage and poundage, without any fanction from parliament, and indeed, if poffible, to render that affembly contemptible. As to other grants, fhe is faid to have received in all but five-fifteenths, and three fubfidies [65].

Demefnes.   The landed property of the crown was perpetually fuffering fome diminution; and an act, particularly fatal to it, was paffed *anno* 1588, by which all the grants or fales of the crown lands, which either had been made by the queen, or fhould be made during the fpace of feven years pofterior, were at once confirmed: a meafure which could not fail to produce, and indeed was intended to countenance, a very confiderable alienation.

Church lands.   A bigoted queen, like Mary, could not bear to reap any pecuniary advantage from that change in religion which had taken place during the reign of her father, and of her brother.   A bill was therefore paffed, not only reftoring to the church the firft fruits and tenths, and all the impropriations which remained in the hands of the crown, but alfo all the church lands that ftill continued in its poffeffion [67].   Nay, fome new convents and monafteries were founded, notwithftanding the low ftate of the exchequer.   The bifhopric of Durham alfo, which had been fuppreffed by Edward, was reftored to its former condition, and the reftitution confirmed by parliament,   She knew well how unpopular fuch meafures were ; but fhe declared to her council, " Albeit you may " object to me again, that confidering the ftate of my kingdom, the " dignity thereof, and my crown imperial, cannot be honourably main- " tained and furnifhed without the poffeffions aforefaid ; yet, notwith- " ftanding, I fet more by the falvation of my foul, than by ten king- " doms, and therefore the faid poffeffions I utterly refufe here to hold " after that fort and title [68]."

[65] 1 Mary, cap. 18.   [66] Stevens, p. 234.   [67] 2 & 3 Phil. and Mar. cap. 4.
[68] Stevens, p. 244.

The

The principles on which Mary acted in ecclefiaftical matters, were fo generally obnoxious to her fubjects, that when an application was made to parliament for a fubfidy, it was rejected; and many members declared, that it was in vain to beftow riches upon a monarch, whofe revenues were thus wafted[69]. She was therefore obliged to have recourfe to tyrannical extortions to replenifh her exchequer. *Anno* 1455, by means of embargoes, compulfive loans, and exactions of a fimilar nature, fhe raifed about 240,000 *l.*; and two years afterwards, contrived to fit out, by the fame methods, an armament for the affiftance of her hufband Philip II. king of Spain; but finding it impoffible to fupply it with provifions, fhe feized, for that purpofe, all the grain that the counties of Suffolk and Norfolk could furnifh, without making the owners any recompence. In fhort, fuch was her infatuation for the perfon and principles of Philip, notwithftanding his indifference and contempt of her, that in order to contribute to his aggrandizement, fhe made no fcruple to tarnifh her own character by the moft difgraceful rapacity, and facrifice the effential interefts of her crown and kingdom without hefitation or remorfe.

Extortions.

Mary imitated her brother's example, in endeavouring to borrow money on the continent. But her credit was fo very low, that though fhe offered 14 *per cent.* intereft to the town of Antwerp, for the loan of 30,000 *l.* fhe could not obtain it, until fhe had compelled the city of London to join in the fecurity[70].

Foreign loans.

We are told by Hume, that the revenues of England, in the reign of Mary, *exceeded* 300,000 *l.*[71]. It is queftionable, whether the permanent income of the crown amounted to fo much, particularly after the churchlands, the firft-fruits, and tenths, &c. were reftored: even in the twelfth year of the reign of Elizabeth, the profit of the kingdom, exclufive of the wards and the dutchy of Lancafter, amounted only to 188,197 *l. per ann.* The authority quoted by Hume alfo, is that of a foreign author[72], and confequently the lefs to be relied on.

Amount of her revenue.

There is only one circumftance, during Mary's reign, that can give us a favourable idea of her political character; and that is, the volun-

Remiffion of a fubfidy.

---

[69] Hume, vol. iv. p. 422.
[71] Hume, vol. iv. p. 433.
[70] Carte, vol. iii. p. 320.
[72] Roffi, Succeffi d'Inghilterra.

R

tary

tary remiffion of a fubfidy, which had been granted to her brother Edward, but which had not yet been paid. This was artfully done, with a view of ingratiating herfelf with the public, and of beginning the new government with a popular and acceptable act, to which the nation had not been accuftomed fince the reign of Richard II. The remiffion was originally contained in letters patent [73]; which, for the fake of greater fecurity, were afterwards confirmed by parliament. It is to be remarked, at the fame time, that the letters patent and the act, only remit the fubfidy of four fhillings in the pound on lands, and two fhillings and eight pence on goods and chattels; but exprefsly referve the grant of two-tenths and two-fifteenths [74]. And fo little able was Mary to afford this affected piece of generofity, that fhe was obliged to borrow 20,000 *l.* at the fame inftant from the city of London, for the expences of her coronation.

Advantages of the Union with Scotland. The reign of Mary furnifhes us with a ftrong proof of the beneficial confequences refulting to England from the union with Scotland. For in the acts by which fubfidies were granted, the whole counties of Northumberland, Cumberland, and Weftmoreland, and the towns of Berwick and Newcaftle, and the Bifhoprick of Durham, were entirely exempted, on account of their vicinity to the Scots, by whofe incurfions, notwithftanding the fuperior ftrength and refources of England, they were perpetually ravaged [75]. It is well known, that what was then called a fubfidy, was of the fame nature with the modern land-tax; had not the union therefore taken place, the land-tax at prefent paid by thefe towns and counties (which, at the rate of four fhillings in the pound, amounts to 31,900 *l.*) could not have been demanded upon any principles of juftice or equity.

ELIZABETH.

We are now to contemplate the reign of a fovereign, of whom England has reafon to be proud. For though it is certain, that neither

---

[73] Parl. Hift. vol. iii. p. 288.   [74] See 1 Mar. Seff. 2. cap. 17.
[75] Stevens, p. 241, 242.

her private conduct, nor all the principles of her public administration, were totally blamelefs and irreproachable; though her attachment to Leicefter, and to Effex, betrayed a confiderable portion of female weaknefs; though the imprifonment and death of the unfortunate Mary, will for ever prove an indelible ftain to her memory; and though the manner in which fhe treated her parliaments, and fupported the pretended prerogatives of the crown, fo contrary to the principles, and fo oppofite to the ideas and practices of thefe times, muft appear to us harfh and illegal; yet fuch was the general happinefs of her fubjects at home, and fuch the reputation fhe eftablifhed abroad with foreign powers, that her reign may be accounted the moft fplendid and fortunate of any female fovereign perhaps recorded in hiftory: nor can the annals of England produce a period, on the whole, more to be preferred. It is therefore propofed to ftate, with fome degree of minutenefs, firft, the general nature of the expences in which fhe was involved; and, fecondly, from what fources they were defrayed.

Expences.

Elizabeth was put to heavier charges in providing for the national protection and defence than any of her predeceffors; it was juftly remarked by Sir Thomas Egerton, keeper of the great feal, in a fpeech to parliament, " that the wars formerly waged in Europe, had com- " monly been conducted by the parties without any farther view than " to gain a few towns, or at moft a province, from each other; but " that the object of Spain, in the hoftilities which it carried on at that ' " time, was no other than utterly to bereave England of her religion, " her liberty, and her independence [76]." It was neceffary, therefore, to fpare no expence, when fuch objects were at ftake. Nor did the queen content herfelf with merely defending her own territories, fhe made her enemies feel the miferies of war at their own homes. Her fuccefsful enterprifes againft the Spaniards are well known; and it is faid that fhe expended no lefs a fum than 1,200,000, from the year 1589,

1. National Defence.

[76] Hume, vol. v. p. 385.

when

when the war with Spain began, to the year 1593, when she received a considerable supply from parliament for the same popular purpose [77].

2. Ireland. Ireland was a possession which had not as yet proved, in any respect, useful to this country. Its revenue was reduced to the trifling sum of 6000 *l. per annum*, and it required 20,000 *l.* a year additional, out of the exchequer of England, to defray the charges of the ordinary peace establishment [78]. This load was far from being relished by Elizabeth and her council; and their frugality proved the source of much expence to the one kingdom, and of infinite misery to the other. For such was the weak state of the Irish government, that it emboldened Tyrone to revolt, whose rebellion continued for the space of eight years, and is said to have cost at the rate of 400,000 *l.* a year, before it was totally suppressed. In the year 1599, 600,000 *l.* were spent there in the space of six months; and Sir Robert Cecil affirmed, that Ireland had cost, in ten years time, the sum of 3,400,000 *l.* [79]

3. Scotland. Elizabeth's critical situation at her accession to the crown, rendered it necessary for her to keep up a party in Scotland, attached to her interest, and ready to support her views; and however unwilling she was to engage in unnecessary expences, yet she found it requisite, until her rival, Mary, had fallen into her power, to furnish her Scottish friends with pecuniary, and, occasionally, with military assistance. Indeed she artfully contrived to render the politics of Scotland subservient to her own, during the greater part of her reign.

4. Holland. It was, during this æra, that Holland first attempted to render itself independent. As Elizabeth had every reason to be jealous of the power of Philip; and as her subjects had long been connected with the provinces of Flanders in traffic and correspondence, they naturally trusted to her assistance and protection; and, at one period, actually offered her the entire sovereignty of the country. This proposal she had the magnanimity, and perhaps the prudence, to refuse. But she spared nothing to enable them to throw off the Spanish yoke; demanding, instead of the sovereignty of the new states, only security for the reimbursement of her expences : in consequence of which three

---

[77] See an account of these extraordinary charges, Parl. Hist. vol. iv, p. 364.
[78] Hume, vol. v, p. 398.   [79] Hume, vol. iv. p. 474.

of

of the moſt valuable fortreſſes they were poſſeſſed of, were delivered
up to her, and garriſoned by the Engliſh.

The powerful monarchy of France was, for ſome time, no ſmall in- 5. France.
cumbrance on the finances of Elizabeth. The arts of the church of
Rome, and the wealth of the court of Spain, had rouſed ſuch a
ſpirit of oppoſition to Henry IV. the legal ſovereign of the country, that he could not poſſibly have withſtood the united efforts of
his enemies, ſupported by a conſiderable party of his own ſubjects, if
it had not been for Elizabeth's aſſiſtance, who advanced him to the
amount of 450,000 l. in his greateſt neceſſities[80]: a ſum which
he could never be prevailed upon to repay, notwithſtanding the
ſtrongeſt· repreſentations of her pecuniary diſtreſſes from the war in
Ireland, and although he had begun to amaſs a very conſiderable treaſure[81].

Her predeceſſors of the houſe of Tudor had frequently involved 6. Crown
themſelves in conſiderable debts. Her brother Edward owed the ſum debts.
of 240,000 l. and ſome of her father's and ſiſter's debts were yet unpaid. Elizabeth thought it incumbent upon her to diſcharge theſe
claims, and actually paid the debts of the crown, with their full intereſt, to the amount, it is ſaid, of four millions. This, Hume conſiders to be incredible[82]. But as this ſum probably includes both principal and intereſt, and alſo the money ſhe raiſed by loans, which (with
only one exception) ſhe punctually repaid, there is the leſs reaſon to
ſuſpect any great exaggeration.

Elizabeth had the credit and expence of bringing back the coin of the 7. Recover-
kingdom to a proper ſtandard. Its debaſement in the reigns of Henry VIII. ing the coin.
and of her brother Edward, was very great. Though ſome ſteps
had been taken to remedy this national diſgrace, yet the progreſs was
inconſiderable: and before that monſter, as ſhe called it, could be con-

80 Charles duke of Burgundy was wont to ſay, " That the neighbouring nations
" would be in a happy caſe, when France ſhould be ſubject, not to one ſceptre, but to
" twenty petty kings." But Elizabeth thought otherwiſe, and therefore ſupported·
Henry. Camden's Hiſt. of Elizabeth, Edit. 1675, p. 444, Had ſhe lived till theſe
times, ſhe would probably have altered her opinion.

81 Hume, vol. v. p. 473.   82 Ibid. Camden, p. 191, obſerves how much the
debt was increaſed by neglecting to pay the intereſt, then at 14 per cent.

queried,.

quered, the queen was obliged to borrow 200,000 *l.* from the city of
Antwerp, to enable her to complete her intentions[13]. But she did not
carry her ideas, with regard to the purity of the coin, to the extent
that might be wished; for, unfortunately, she was afterwards prevailed on, in the forty-third year of her reign, to divide the pound of
filver into fixty-two shillings inflead of fixty, the former flandard[14];
nay, she was perfuaded to give her fanction to the coinage of bafe
money for the ufe of Ireland. The pretence was, however, fpecious.
It was faid, that the great fums of money remitted to Ireland, found
their way, through the medium of circulation, into the hands of the
natives, who were thus enabled to purchafe thofe fupplies of arms and
of ammunition, without which they could not perfevere in their rebellion. And it was afferted, that an inferior fpecies of coin could
never be employed to procure ufeful commodities at foreign markets.
Her wifer counfellors, in vain, endeavoured to prove the weaknefs and
fallacy of fuch reafoning[15]. It is faid that Burleigh, whilft he lived,
would never give way to any project of that nature; nor was it
till after his death, that it was carried into execution[16]. Since the
reign of Elizabeth, no fovereign of England has attempted to debafe
the coin current in this country.

§ Bounties
to favourites.   The laft confiderable expence on the exchequer of Elizabeth, was
her bounty to her favourites. Her gifts to Dudley, earl of Leicefter,
were very great. At one time fhe gave to the earl of Effex a prefent of
30,000 *l.*; and is fuppofed to have beftowed pecuniary favours upon
that gallant nobleman, to the value of 300,000 *l.* in which a lucrative
monopoly he enjoyed, was probably included. To the great minifters
who were employed in the public fervice, fhe was not over bountiful:
fome of them died in poverty; and Burleigh's fortune was more owing
to his own frugality, than to her friendfhip. But to thofe courtiers
who ingratiated themfelves with her, by the charms of their perfons, or the
infinuation or flattery of their addrefs, no fovereign was more liberal. The
queen, it was faid, *pays bountifully*, though fhe *rewards fparingly*[17].

---

[13] Hume, vol. v. p. 476.   [14] Folkes on Coins, p. 58. Harris on Coins, part ii. p 9.
[15] Camden, p. 637.   [16] Ney, p. 105.

[17] Naunton, in his *Fragmenta Regalia*, gives a brief account of queen Elizabeth's
favourites, amounting to twenty-two in number. Many of them principally depended
upon the queen's bounty for their fupport. But among them Burleigh and other minifters are included.

Supporting the fplendor of the court, and defraying the charges to which Elizabeth's vanity fubjected her (who left, it is faid, above three thoufand fuits, of various fhapes and colours, in her wardrobe when fhe died) were the only other material expences during her reign. Let us next fee from what refources her income was derived.

Refources.

It is impoffible, at prefent, to afcertain the income which the royal do- Demefnes. mains produced in the time of Elizabeth. To James I. they only yielded the fum of 32,000 l. but they were fuppofed worth 96,000 l. *per annum*; when the leafes which then exifted would expire[18], and their value would have been ftill more confiderable, had it not been for the queen's fyftem of alienation, who preferred making an almoft continual dilapidation of the royal domains rather than to demand the moft moderate fupplies from her commons[19]. In the forty-fecond year of her reign, in order to procure money for carrying on the war in Ireland, commiffioners were appointed, with full powers to confirm the poffeffion of the crown lands, to fuch as held them by titles, liable to be controverted. And in the enfuing year an act was paffed, ratifying all the grants and alienations made by Elizabeth fince the 25th year of her reign, whether for value received, or in confideration of a difcharge being granted of any of the crown debts[90]. It is faid, however, that her grants in general contained this provifo, that in default of iffue male, they were to revert to the crown. A claufe, of which the public, at this time, might probably avail itfelf.

Elizabeth's attachment to what fhe fuppofed to be the inherent pre- Feudal prerogatives. rogatives of the crown, is too well known to require being dwelt on. It is faid that the income arifing from wardfhip (which, with other claims of a fimilar nature, were very rigoroufly enforced), joined to the revenue of the dutchy of Lancafter, amounted to the fum of 120,000 l. yearly[91]. Of all the feudal prerogatives, that of purveyance was the moft obnoxious. The queen at firft had victualled her navy under pretence of that right, but with a view of endearing herfelf to her

---

[18] Noy's Rights of the Crown, p. 51, 52.   [89] Hume, vol. v. p. 473.
[90] 43 Eliz. cap. 1.   [91] Hume, vol. v. p. 474. Note Y.

fubjects.

subjects. She had afterwards revoked all her warrants, and had given directions to pay for any provisions that had been furnished for that purpose. In the fixth and fifteenth years of her reign, however, she caufed confiderable quantities of beer to be purveyed, and fold it on the continent for her own behoof". Although it is impoffible to defcribe the vexation and diftrefs which the exercife of this prerogative occafioned, yet the haughty Elizabeth would neither fuffer its abufes to be redreffed by parliament, or rectify them herfelf.

Cuftoms.

The cuftoms had gradually become a ftanding part of the revenue of the crown. In the year 1590, they were raifed from 24,000 to 50,000 *l.* a year: and Sir Thomas Smith, by whom they had been farmed, was obliged to refund fome part of the profits he had received ". Tunnage and poundage were granted to Elizabeth for life : but it is remarked by Hume, that thefe duties were levied previous to the vote of parliament; and indeed it is afferted, in difpatches from her council to her ambaffador in France, " that it was as lawful for the queen of England, for her eafe " and relief, to take impofitions of her fubjects, of fuch wares as lyked " hir, as it was for other princes to fet impofitions of theyrs ". " Thus it appears that the fanction of parliament was accounted, by the queen's minifters, a mere matter of form; at leaft they were politic enough to hold that doctrine to foreign courts.

First fruits and tenths.

One of the firft fteps taken by parliament, after the acceffion of Elizabeth, was to reftore to the crown the firft-fruits and tenths which Mary had given up; and the members of both houfes (fome bifhops only excepted) fhewed, upon that occafion, fo ftrong a difpofition to fupport the principles of the reformation, that it greatly encouraged the queen and her council, to take further meafures for the abolition of popery.

51 Noy's Rights of the Crown, p. 66.

52 Authors greatly differ with regard to the fum which Smith originally paid. Philips (Reftauranda, p. 35.) fays, that they were raifed from thirteen thoufand, firft to forty-two, and afterwards to fifty thoufand pounds. Camden, p. 440, inftead of thirteen, makes it fourteen thoufand. Naunton, in his Fragmenta Regalia, p. 15, fays, that in the fpace of ten years the rent was doubled. But it appears from Brown's tranflation of Camden, (Appendix, note to p. 32 l. 16) that there are fome miftakes in the other tranflation, and I fuppofe that fourteen has been put down inftead of twenty-four thou- fand pounds.

53 Forbes's full view of the tranfactions of Elizabeth, vol. i. p. 133.

The

The authority of parliament was alfo procured, to re-annex to the Church
lands. crown, the lands which Mary had beftowed on religious houfes; and the Queen was empowered, when any bifhopric became vacant, to feize all the temporalities, and to beftow on the new bifhop an equivalent in church-lands, and impropriations belonging to the crown[95]. In confequence of this regulation, the church was often injured by unfair and difproportionable exchanges. Nor was this all: for after the example of fome of her moft detefted and tyrannical predeceffors, fhe retained the temporalities of the bifhoprick of Ely in her own hands for the fpace of nineteen years; and it was not unufual for her, when fhe promoted a bifhop, to pillage the fee of fome of its moft valuable manors, or to countenance injurious bargains between the new incumbent and fome favourite courtier[96].

It is difficult to know, with any degree of precifion, what was the Amount of
the queen's
permanent
income. amount of the permanent revenue of the crown at this time. We are told, from refpectable authority, that the profit of the kingdom, in the twelfth year of the reign of Elizabeth, exclufive of the wards and the dutchy of Lancafter (which yielded about 120,000l.), amounted to 188,197l. per annum[97], making in all the fum of 308,197l. Anno 1590, a confiderable addition was made to the cuftoms. The whole of her annual permanent income, however, could hardly amount to 350,000l.

Though the expences of Elizabeth's government were very confi- Grants. derable; and though her permanent revenue was far from being great, yet the earlier part of her reign is not diftinguifhed by numerous

[95] Hume, vol. v. p. 10. Stevens, p. 247.

[96] The poverty of the crown is a circumftance not a little aftonifhing, when one confiders the immenfe property of which the church was deprived, during the government of the houfe of Tudor. But the matter is fully explained in a paper prefented to Elizabeth, containing an account of the frauds and abufes that had been committed by the officers, to whofe charge this new branch of the revenue had been committed. For particulars, Stevens, p. 248, may be confulted. One fact, however, may be taken notice of. It is afferted in the paper he tranfcribes (which feems to have been drawn up by one of the commiffioners, or at leaft by a perfon perfectly acquainted with the whole tranfaction), that the plate, jewels, and moveable effects of the different abbeys were worth a million of money, though fold, by means of the artful contrivances of the commiffioners, greatly under their value. Nay, that a confiderable part of the low prices that were given, remained unpaid for many years.

[97] Noy's Rights of the Crown.

S

grants

grants from parliament. The queen's frugality was such, that expences, however trifling, even the charge of expreffes, on delicate and important tranfactions, were not reckoned beneath her notice. But, above all, her imperious fpirit, and her anxious defire to maintain her dignity and independence, made her feduloufly avoid afking fupplies from parliament, unlefs when abfolutely neceffary; nor would fhe ever liften to any plan of retrenching her prerogative, and of adding to the rights and privileges of the people, or of gratifying them even in regard to the appointment of a fucceffor, for the fake of any pecuniary recompence [91]. The following is a ftate of the parliamentary fubfidies and fifteenths received by Elizabeth, during the courfe of her reign, in which eighteen fubfidies from the clergy are not included.

A. D.	Year of her reign.	Subs.	Fift.
1558	1	1	2
1563	5	1	2
1566	8	1	1
1571	13	1	2
1575	18	1	3
1581	23	1	2
1584	27	1	2
1588	31	2	4
1593	35	3	6
1597	39	3	6
1601	43	4	8
		[59] 19	38

Amount of the grants.   The value of the grants beftowed by parliament upon this princefs, may be thus eftimated: Every fubfidy amounted to about 70,000 l. [100], and as there were nineteen fubfidies, they muft have produced 1,330,000 l. A fifteenth yielded 29,000 l.; and confequently, thirty-

[91] Parl. Hift. vol. iv. p. 73.

[59] After examining the Statute Book, the whole grants feem to have been but nineteen fubfidies, and thirty-eight fifteenths; and D'Ewes, p. 232, fays, that the grant anno 1575, was of one fubfidy, and only two fifteenths.

[100] See Black. vol. i. p. 310. Subfidies were at firft more productive.

eight

eight fifteenths, was about 1,103,000 *l.* Eighteen subsidies were granted by the clergy, valued at 20,000 *l.* each, consequently equal to 360,000*l.* The whole, therefore, might amount to about 2,800,000 *l.* which is the sum stated by Sir Robert Cotton [101]; and indeed by Lord Salisbury in parliament [102]. Hume very justly remarks, that if the supplies granted to Elizabeth, during a reign of forty-five years, amounted even to the sum of three millions, it would only make 66,666 *l.* a year [103].

But Elizabeth's resources did not depend entirely, either on the common revenue of her kingdom, or on the temporary and occasional aids of parliament. For the crown, at that time, claimed a right of granting exclusive privileges of trading, in any article it thought proper, to any person it chose to appoint. Such monopolies were sometimes sold, and it is probable, yielded considerable sums to the exchequer; and sometimes they were granted, as a reward to those who had distinguished themselves in civil and military employments; but they were much oftener given to the minions of the court, in recompence for their servility.

Monopolies.

The number and importance of the commodities which were thus monopolized, is almost incredible. Among many others, historians mention salt, iron, powder, cards, calf-skins, fells, pouldavies, ox-shin-bones, train oil, lists of cloth, pot-ashes, anniseeds, vinegar, sea-coals, steel, aquavitæ, brushes, pots, bottles, saltpetre, lead, accidences, oil, calamint-stone, oil of blubber, glasses, paper, starch, tin, sulphur, new drapery, dried pilchards; transportation of iron ordnance, of beer, of horn, of leather; importation of Spanish wools, of Irish yarn, &c. &c. We are told, that when this list was read over in the House of Commons, a member (Mr. Hackwell) loudly exclaimed, " *Is not bread in the number?*" " *Bread,*" said every one with astonishment! " *Yes, I assure you,*" replied he, " *if affairs go on at* " *this rate, we shall have bread reduced to a monopoly before next par-* " *liament* [104].

[101] See Stevens, p. 206,

[102] See Comm. Journ. vol. i. p. 395. Lord Salisbury however calculates, that there were twenty subsidies, and thirty-nine fifteenths, granted to Elizabeth.

[103] Hist. vol. v. p. 475.

[104] D'Ewes, p. 648. Hume, vol. v. p. 439. Parl. Hist. vol. iv. p. 462.

It

It is eafy to fee the confequences of fuch a fyftem. Trade was abandoned, and induftry almoft totally extinguifhed. " *It bringeth* " (faid a member in the Houfe) *general profit into private hands, and* " *the end is beggary and boudage.*" A fingle patent, contrived for the advantage of four rapacious courtiers, occafioned the utter ruin of feven or eight thoufand induftrious fubjects[105]. This abufe, and the manner in which fo deftructive a prerogative was exercifed by Elizabeth, is one of the greateft blots in her reign. In vain did parliament interfere. The haughty fovereign would not permit her prerogative to be called in queftion; and the more the Houfe endeavoured to procure a redrefs of the grievance, the more refolutely was it maintained. In a fpeech from the throne, at the diffolution of one of her parliaments, whofe conduct fhe particularly refented on that account; fhe told them, "That " with regard to the patents, fhe hoped that her dutiful and loving " fubjects, would not take away her prerogative, which is the chief " flower in her garden, and the principal and head pearl in her crown " and diadem, but that they would rather leave the matter to her " difpofal." However, not long after, fhe iffued a proclamation for repealing fome of the moft obnoxious monopolies; particularly on falt, oil, ftarch, &c. for which fhe received the folemn thanks of her Commons[106].

Extortions.　　　Nor is it poffible totally to acquit this high-fpirited princefs, of illegal extortions from her fubjects. She is faid to have exacted, every new-year's-day, above 60,000 crowns, in gifts from her dependants; and to have raifed 100,000 crowns yearly, by granting licences to Roman Catholics and Non-conformifts, exempting them from the penalties which the law impofed upon fuch as neglected to attend the public fervice of the eftablifhed church. She alfo made ufe of the prerogative which the crown enjoyed, of laying an embargo on merchandife, if not to extort money, like her predeceffor Mary, at leaft, to procure, at an eafy rate, the commodities fhe wanted[107].

Burleigh's fyftem of extortion.　　　The power of the crown during the reigns of the houfe of Tudor, was fuppofed to be fo abfolute and uncontrouled, that Burleigh, the

[105]　D'Ewes, p. 242.
[106]　See her famous fpeech upon that occafion, D'Ewes, p. 659.
[107]　Strype's Annals of the Reformation, vol. i. p. 28.

ableft

ableſt ſtateſman of his time, actually built upon that idea, a ſyſtem of
extortion, which it is hardly poſſible to credit. In a ſpeech he made to
the queen and council, he propoſed the erection of a new court, to be
entruſted with a general inquiſitorial power over the whole kingdom,
for the better correction of abuſes. By ſuch methods, he aſſerted,
Henry VII. had added greatly to his revenues; and he expreſſed his full
expectations, that ſuch an inſtitution would procure a greater acceſſion
to the royal treaſure, than Henry VIII. derived from the abolition of
the abbies, and the ſeizure of the property of the church [108]. The propoſition was wiſely rejected; but it is not a little ſingular, that ſuch a
plan ſhould ever meet with the ſmalleſt countenance from ſo reſpectable
a character.

Elizabeth continued the practice, of which ſo many examples had Compulſive
loans.
been ſhown by her predeceſſors, of extorting loans from her ſubjects,
and of impriſoning ſuch as ventured to refuſe, and although ſhe took care
to repay them when it was in her power (a very unuſual ſtep with the
former ſovereigns of England), yet the money that was borrowed, lay
in the hands of the crown, without intereſt, and conſequently, ſuch
loans were productive of conſiderable loſs to thoſe from whom they
were exacted. By an act in the ſecond year of Richard II., the prerogative of exacting loans had been recogniſed by parliament; at leaſt, a
clauſe was inſerted, exempting none who could not produce a *reaſonable*
excuſe; the juſtice of which, the king alone had the power of deter-
mining. Indeed, this right was ſuppoſed to be ſo firmly eſtabliſhed
in the crown, that Burleigh propoſed to demand a general loan from
the people, equivalent to a ſubſidy, which, if the money was not repaid,
was in fact impoſing taxes without the ſanction of parliament [109].

The ſovereign of a country, which has ſince borrowed ſo many mil- Foreign
loans.
lions, was then occaſionally obliged to apply to Hamburgh, Cologn,
Antwerp, and other wealthy cities on the continent, for ſmall loans.
The intereſt ſhe paid was generally from 10 to 12 *per cent.*; and ſhe
was farther obliged to furniſh the additional ſecurity of the city of London, and ſometimes the perſonal bonds of her principal miniſters,
before her wants could be ſupplied. But the wealth of her kingdom

[108] Strype's Annals, vol. iv. p. 234. Suppoſed to have been *anno* 1594.
[109] Hume, vol. v. p. 460.

increaſing,

increasing, and her credit being fully eftablished by her frugality, the
punctuality and fuccefs, fhe was at laft enabled to procure at home the
money fhe required, and was no longer dependent on foreigners for
pecuniary affiftance [112].

Plunder.

In the courfe of the war againft Spain, many important enterprifes
were undertaken at the expence of private adventurers, in which Elizabeth took a part, in common with her fubjects, and received her proportion of the plunder that was captured. On fome occafions, the
fpoil was very unequally divided; particularly *anno* 1592, a valuable
fhip having been taken by Raleigh and Frobifher, fuppofed to be worth
200,000 *l*., twenty thoufand pounds, a tenth of the prize, was all that
the queen was entitled to from her fhare of the veffel. But this fum
was far from being fatisfactory, and they were glad to give her 100,000 *l*.
in full of the claims, to which they would probably have been made
liable, in favour of fo potent a partner in the adventure [111].

It may be proper here, to mention her receipt of a fum of money,
which it is not known whether it ought to be placed under the head of
a foreign loan, or of foreign plunder. *Anno* 1571, fome merchants of
Genoa had contracted to tranfport 400,000 crowns, for the ufe of
Philip's forces in the Netherlands. The fhips, on board of which the
money was put, being attacked by fome French privateers, were glad
to take fhelter in the Englifh ports; and the money was feized by
Elizabeth, under the pretence that it was the property of the Genoefe
merchants, from whom fhe would borrow it herfelf, having occafion
for money. This circumftance not only greatly contributed to the war
that arofe between Spain and England, but was alfo attended with other
important confequences; for the want of this fupply, being likely to
occafion a mutiny in his troops, reduced the duke of Alva to the neceffity of raifing money, by methods of fo oppreffive and tyrannical a
nature, that it gave rife to the revolt of the Dutch, and the independence
of their republic [112].

Calais.

The poffeffions of England on the continent had been reduced, previous to the acceffion of the houfe of Tudor, to the town and inconfiderable territories of Calais; and even that laft remnant of the con-

---

[112] Stevens, p. 246.   [111] Camden, p. 466. Hume, vol. v. p. 466.
[111] Hume, vol. v. p. 194.

quefts made by the Henrys and the Edwards, had been recovered by the French, during the difgraceful adminiftration of Mary. It was a town which France was determined not to give up, and which England could not avowedly relinquifh. But as both parties were equally defirous of peace, it was at laft agreed upon, that the French fhould hold Calais for the fpace of eight years, at the end of which it was to be reftored, under the penalty of 500,000 crowns; the receipt of which was not to deftroy Elizabeth's title to that poffeffion. Five hoftages were given for the performance of this article, who were afterwards releafed for the fum of 220,000 crowns. Her claim, fuch as it was, fhe ftill retained; and at the end of the ftipulated period, care was taken to demand the reftitution. The French, however, found pretences fufficiently plaufible to evade their engagement; and the queen thought it better to fubmit to the lofs, than to profecute fo doubtful a title by a war, equally dangerous and expenfive, and at that time peculiarly unfeafonable [113].

Anno 1563.

It is evident, from this long enumeration of the various fources which contributed to fill the coffers of Elizabeth (many of which were of a very precarious and uncertain nature), that it is impoffible to eftimate what was the real value of her annual income. Voltaire imagines, that it exceeded 600,000 l. a year [114]. Hume, on the other hand, conjectures, that it fell much fhort of 500,000 l. [115], and there is every reafon to give full credit to the latter computation.

Amount of her income.

A particular account is ftill extant, of the fpecie coined during the reign of Elizabeth, to the value of 5,513,717 l. 11 s. 1½ d. of which 4,718,579 l. 2 s. 8½ d. was in filver, and only 795,138 l. 8 s. 4½ d. in gold. This includes filver to the amount of 85,646 l. 19 s. 5½ d. employed in coining the bafe money, iffued for the ufe of Ireland [116].

Specie coined.

We are told, that the office of poftmafter-general exifted in England during this reign [117]. Some poft-houfes confequently muft have been erected. But the poft-office was productive of expence, and not of revenue, until the time of the commonwealth.

Poft office.

The heavy burden of maintaining the poor, which it was imagined would have been provided for by voluntary contribution, or would have

Poors rates,

---

[113] Carte, vol. iii. p. 460. [114] Gen. Hift. vol. iii. p. 85. part v. c. 13.
[115] Hift. vol. v. p. 474. [115] Folkes on Coins, p. 65, Note.
[117] Camden, p. 261.

fallen,

fallen, either on the poffeffors of the church-lands, or on the fecular clergy [118], became in the reign of Elizabeth, a general tax upon the community. The fituation of the poor, before the acts were paffed for their relief, is reprefented as moft deplorable; and even after they had a legal title to fupport, the affeffments were fo low, that it is faid many perifhed for want [119]. Befides the taxes levied for the relief of their parochial poor, every parifh was alfo charged from two to eight fhillings a week, for the maintenance of fick and wounded foldiers and feamen, for whom there was then no regular provifion.

Debts.   Elizabeth left behind her debts to the amount of about 400,000 l. which were paid by her fucceffor [120]. But that fum was much more than compenfated by the claims to which, at her death, he was entitled. The king of France owed her 450,000 l. The ftates of Holland were indebted in no lefs a fum than 800,000 l. a confiderable part of which was paid; and the fubfidies due Elizabeth, when fhe died, amounted to about 350,000 l. which James received foon after his acceffion [121].

Subfidies re-mitted and refufed.   This reign is diftinguifhed for the laft example in the Englifh hiftory, of a fubfidy being rejected by the fovereign, when offered by the people; and Elizabeth publickly declared, on that occafion, that fhe confidered it to be the fame thing, whether the money they offered was in the pockets of her fubjects, or in her own exchequer. A fentiment equally expreffive of the ftrength of her judgment, and of her confidence in her fubjects; and *Anno* 1585, when the Commons offered her a *benevolence*, fhe nobly refufed it, declaring, that fhe had no occafion for money at that time [122].

Voluntary contribu-tions.   It is a pleafing circumftance to be able to relate, the grateful return which Elizabeth met with from her fubjects, for the general popularity of her government, and the great wifdom and fuccefs of her adminiftration. When her crown was in danger, in confequence of the warlike preparations of Philip king of Spain, who fitted out, what he called, an Invincible Armada, for the conqueft of England, and the capture of

---

[118] It appears from D'Ewes, p. 561, that a bill for relieving the poor out of impro-priations, and other church livings, was loft by twenty-nine votes. The Ayes were 117, the Noes 146.   [119] Stevens, p. 254, 255. 262.

[120] Reftauranda, p. 35. Frag. Reg. p. 12. Parl. Hift. vol. v, p. 147.

[121] Parl. Hift. vol. v. p. 219.   [122] D'Ewes, p. 494.

Elizabeth,

Elizabeth. The fpirit and loyalty of the people are hardly to be conceived. The nobility and gentry fitted out forty-three fhips at their own expence. London, and the other principal ports in England, voluntarily equipped double the number of veffels that was demanded. Formidable armies were collected without difficulty or murmur. Every direction given for the better fecurity of the coaft, met with a prompt and cheerful obedience; and each perfon, in proportion to his ability, furnifhed pecuniary affiftance, and gloried in an opportunity of difplaying his attachment to his fovereign, and his zeal to preferve the liberties and independence of his country.

Such were the different modes adopted under the government of the house of Tudor, for raifing a revenue. During this æra, fome progrefs was made in finance; the advantages of public credit, and of a ftrict adherence to public faith, were difcovered by the politic and fagacious minifters of Elizabeth; and the cuftoms, and other branches of the revenue, were rendered more productive. But the period is particularly remarkable, for laying the true foundation of the poverty of the crown, and of the confequent power and importance of the commons. When the emperor Charles V. was told, that Henry had fuppreffed the monafteries, he judicioufly remarked, that the king of England had killed the hen that laid him the golden eggs. In fact, the opulence of the church was always a fure refource for the crown to look up to. The clergy could hardly evade any burden the king thought proper to impofe. When, in addition therefore to the royal domains, the property of the church was fquandered, the fovereign had nothing to depend upon, but the affiftance of the nation at large, through the medium of its reprefentatives; and Elizabeth's fucceffors found, that fuch affiftance could not be procured, without redreffing the grievances of the people, and agreeing to fuch farther fecurity for their rights and privileges, as they thought proper to demand.

Conclufion of this chapter.

T   C H A P.

C H A P. IX.

Of the Revenue of England, from the Accession of the House of Stuart *to the Revolution* 1688.

THE accession of the house of Stuart to the throne of England, and the consequent union of the two crowns, it was imagined, would have been at once attended with the most beneficial consequences to both kingdoms. But, unfortunately, such happy prospects were blasted, first, by the imbecility of this monarch's character, and afterwards, by the infatuation and obstinacy of his successors. Whereas, if James had acted with vigour and prudence, and if his posterity had avoided the rocks of despotism, and of tyranny, on which they split, these kingdoms might have arrived at their full maturity and strength at a much earlier period. But the domestic quarrels of England, besides retarding her progress towards maturity and strength, enabled France to acquire a degree of power and influence which could not afterwards be checked without the utmost efforts; and the usual revenue of the country being inadequate to such exertions, the foundation was unfortunately, but almost necessarily laid, of that heavy load of debt with which we are now incumbered.

In addition to the weakness of this monarch's conduct, and the high notions which both he and his successors entertained of the inherent prerogatives of the crown, other circumstances concurred to retard the British monarchy in its progress towards its meridian strength and glory. The former jealousy and rancour between the English and the Scots still continued; and every plan of uniting the two countries encountered, particularly on the part of the English parliament, much obstruction. The attention of both kingdoms was also taken up by religious controversies; and, at last, a fatal contest arose with regard to the revenue of the crown, and the franchises of the people, and indeed, respecting every branch of the constitution, however important or minute; and the consequence was, a series of calamities, which even the history of England can hardly parallel.

. 3   The

The circumftances have already been pointed out, which had contributed to diminifh the income of the crown, arifing from the alienation of the royal domains, and the deftruction of that ancient fource of revenue, the great wealth and property of the church, which, after having been feized by the fovereign, was wafted, without leaving a remnant to enrich the exchequer. But the royal income rapidly diminifhed, not only in nominal amount, but alfo in real value. After the difcovery of America, fpecie became every day more plentiful in every part of Europe; and the confequence was, fuch an addition to the price of all commodities, as rendered the fame revenue much lefs efficient than formerly. Thus the crown was reduced to poverty, at a time when it was natural for the fovereign to afpire to an equality, in point of magnificence and expence, with the other monarchs of Europe; or, at leaft, to preferve the fame appearance when compared to his own fubjects, by which the rank and dignity of his predeceffors had been fupported. Whilft thefe circumftances led the crown to wifh for a great and independent revenue, the people reluctantly fubjected themfelves to every unufual burden; and were determined, unlefs in a legal manner, by the votes of their reprefentatives in parliament, not to part with any fhare of the property acquired by their own induftry and labour. Learning alfo began to flourifh, and to be very generally diffufed; the rights of mankind, both to civil and religious liberty, were every day more frequently difcuffed, and the more they were examined, appeared the clearer and better founded; and from natural differences of opinion, between the crown and the people, as to thofe important articles, difputes arofe, which, in the reign of this monarch's fucceffor, were attended with circumftances equally fingular and important [1].

Revenue of JAMES I.

It might naturally be expected, that a prince who had been fo long accuftomed to live upon the flender revenue which Scotland could then afford, would have carried with him to the throne of England fome inclination to frugality; but the contrary was vifible during his whole

[1] Hume, vol. vi. p. 47.

reign : and though, in confequence of his great care to avoid engaging in wars, his expences were almoſt entirely of a domeſtic and perſonal nature, yet they conſtantly exceeded his income; particularly in the year 1610, to the amount of 81,000 *l.* [2], though afterwards reduced in 1617, to 36,617*l.* a year [3]. The exceſs, he truſted, parliament would fometime or other fupply, and therefore could hardly be prevailed upon to make the neceſſary retrenchments, or to eſtabliſh any economical arrangement.

Expences.

1. Perſonal expences.

Though this monarch is reprefented, by a great hiſtorian, as but little addicted to luxurious expences [4], yet it is difficult to reconcile fuch an opinion with the events of his reign. He kept up three courts; one for himfelf, another for his queen, and a third for his eldeſt fon ; being at leaſt one more than had ever been maintained by any former king of England. His brother-in-law, the king of Denmark, twice viſited the court of London, and James was far from difcouraging the expences which fuch viſits neceſſarily occaſioned. The charges attending the marriage of the king's daughter to the Elector Palatine, including the portion of that princeſs, amounted to 93,278 *l.* a much larger fum than had been expended by any of his predeceſſors on a fimilar occaſion ; and this prince, who had not a fpark of avarice in his compoſition, but loved delicate and luxurious living, was far from being fparing in the expences of his table [5].

2. Bounty to favourites.

It was at firſt imagined, that the king's prodigality to thofe for whom he entertained a regard, originated from national attachments. His inconfiderate gifts and bounty to fome of the Scotch nobility and gentry who attended him to England ; and in particular, the unmerited favours which he conferred on the infamous Car, earl of Somerfet, were attributed

---

[2] Comm. Journ. vol. i. p. 395.

[3] See an Abſtract, or brief Declaration of the prefent State of his Majeſty's Revenue, London, printed for M. S. *anno* 1651, p. 9. Reprinted in Sommer's Collection of Tracts, 3 Coll. vol. ii.   [4] Hume, vol. vi. p. 172.

[5] In Macaulay's Hiſtory of England, we have many inſtances of this monarch's profuſion. See vol. i. p. 22. 34, note 39. 65. 88. 104. 114. 153, &c.

to a blind partiality for his countrymen. But James clearly demonstrated, that he could be as profuse to an English, as to a Scotch favourite. His bounty to Villiers duke of Buckingham was unlimited. This despicable minion, formed by nature, to be only the pageant of a court, was raised, at once, to the summit of power, of honour, and of wealth. The highest offices of the state were centered in his person; the most important transactions were conducted according to his humour and caprice; and, whilst his enemies were openly discountenanced, those who boasted of the most distant connection with himself, or his family, were enriched with the most unbounded profusion[6].

The king was not contented with giving his favourites all the lucrative employments of the state, and considerable grants from the royal domains, but gifts in money, of great value, were also lavished on them. In the first fourteen years of his reign, 424,469 l. were thus expended[7]. One of his minions, Rich, afterwards created earl of Holland, happened to whisper in the king's presence, how happy it would make him, to be master of a sum of money, amounting to 3000 l. which a porter was carrying to the treasury; and in consequence of so trivial a circumstance, the whole load was given to him by his generous sovereign[8]. It is said, by the English writers, that James did not make the proper distinction, between pounds Scots, and pounds English, and that lord Salisbury was unable to convince him of the immensity of one gift, until he had artfully brought a considerable part of the sum, in specie, into his royal presence, when it appeared so enormous, that the king, for once, ordered his bounty to be diminished[9].

It has already been observed, that in the reign of Henry III. his eldest son, afterwards Edward I. had an income of only 15,000 marks; but after the conquest of Wales, the revenues of that principality, together with the dutchy of Cornwall, and earldom of Chester, were given to the eldest son of the reigning monarch, to defray the charges of his court. These possessions yielded, in the time of Edward the Black Prince, 9982 l. 12 s. 7 d. which was then a very considerable income. But James exceeded all his predecessors, in his liberality to the heir

3. Prince of Wales.

---

[6] Hume, vol. vi. p. 79.   [7] Abstract, &c. p. 16.   [8] Hume, vol. vi. p. 173.

[9] Twelve pounds Scotch, make but one pound sterling. The story may be seen in the Historical Narration of the first fourteen years of King James, p. 11.

apparent:

apparent: for he beftowed on Henry prince of Wales, his eldeft fon, a clear revenue amounting to 51,415 *l.* equal to at leaft 150,000 *l.* of money at this time. Henry, whofe death is much regretted by all the hiftorians of that reign, had given early indications of great application, joined to the ftrongeft natural powers; and he feems to have been well entitled to every poffible mark of his father's attention and liberality. His premature death was therefore juftly confidered as a great national lofs, it being more than probable, that his talents, equally fplendid and popular, were better calculated than thofe of his brother Charles, to prevent the fatal diftractions by which the conftitution was overwhelmed.

4. Ireland.   During the reign of James, as well as of his predeceffor, Ireland continued to be a heavy load on the exchequer of this country. At one time, an army of 19,000 men was kept up there, whofe maintenance, from the high pay which even the common foldiers received, amounting to eight-pence a day, was not a little burthenfome. It was alfo neceffary to tranfmit the money from England, in confequence of the low ftate of the Irifh treafury [10].

5 Palatinate.   The Elector Palatine was induced, by his own ambition, and his reliance on the countenance and aid of the powerful monarchy of England, to engage in a plan of adding to his former territories, the kingdom of Bohemia ; and when he proved unfuccefsful in this attempt, and was even driven from his patrimonial poffeffions, he put the Englifh nation and its fovereign to very confiderable expences. James afferts in a fpeech to parliament, that befides the voluntary contributions of the Englifh remitted to the Palatine, he had expended a very confiderable fum in his caufe [11]. The king's pacific difpofition, and his confidence

[10] Hume, p. 59. 178.

[11] What the fum actually is, is very difficult to underftand from the obfcurity of the following paffage : " I permitted a voluntary contribution to preferve the Palatinate, which " came to a great fum ; for that purpofe, I borrowed alfo 75,000 *l.* of my brother of " Denmark, and now have fent to him to make it up 100,000 *l.* and all this have I done " with the charge of embaffadors and otherwife, which hath rifen to an infinite fum, " which I have borne myfelf, and hath coft me above 200,000 *l.* in preferving the Pa- " latinate from invading ; finding no hope of the reft, befides 300,000 *l.* and befides the " voluntary contributions." The King's Speech, 30th January, 1620. Franklyn's Annals, p. 350. See an abftract of the fpeech in Latin, Lords Journals, vol. iii. p. 8.

in

in his own skill in the arts of negotiation, had made him endeavour to procure a restoration of the Palatinate, by means of a treaty; but finding that mode ineffectual, he was obliged to have recourse to arms, in which he proved equally unfortunate.

Before the reign of Elizabeth, the navy, excepting in time of war, was not an expensive department. In her time it amounted to 30,000 *l*. [12] But James was at first particularly attentive to his fleet, and annually expended 50,000 *l*. in repairing and keeping up this bulwark of his kingdom, exclusively of timber from the royal forests, to the amount of 36,000 *l*. He afterwards abated 25,000 *l*. *per annum* in this important article [13].

6. Navy.

The only remaining material expence incurred by James, was, paying off the debts of Elizabeth, amounting to about 400,000 *l*. being money borrowed upon the credit of subsidies, the produce of which he received. Nothing can be more disgusting than to hear this sum, and the charges of her funeral, made use of as strong arguments with parliament, to augment their supplies. In return for such a crown as England, James ought surely to have defrayed, without notice or complaint, the small incumbrances of his generous predecessor, and the insignificant cost of her interment.

7. Elizabeth's debts.

Let us next consider from what sources his revenue was derived.

Resources.

Though almost every reign since William the Norman sat upon the throne, had been productive of some diminution of the landed property of the crown, yet it still continued to be of considerable value. The nominal rent was small (amounting at James's accession to the sum of only 32,000 *l. per annum* [14]) It was well known, however, to be worth more; and indeed it afterwards yielded about 80,000 *l*. a year. An attempt was made, in the beginning of this reign, to procure a strict entail of the crown lands on the king and his successors for ever: but a bill for that purpose, though passed by the lords, was rejected by the commons;

1. Demesnes.

---

[12] Noy's Rights of the Crown, p. 8. Stevens, p. 272.
[13] Parl. Hist. vol. v. p. 316. [14] Noy's Rights of the Crown, p. 52.

and

and James, finding no obftruction to the fale of thofe lands, continued the practice, and raifed by that means no lefs a fum than 775,000*l.* [15]

2. Feudal prerogatives. The rights which the king enjoyed as lord paramount, ftill remained a badge of the feudal flavery of the Englifh. Purveyance in particular was carried to fuch a height, that the officers of the crown compelled the people to take for their commodities, whatever price they chofe to offer [16]; and all the feudal prerogatives had become fo intolerable, that parliament propofed to fettle an independent revenue on the crown in their ftead. An agreement was likely to have been entered into, at the rate of 200,000*l.* a year [17]; when, in confequence of difputes between the king and his parliament as to other matters, the plan was rendered abortive.

3. Feudal aids. The reign of James furnifhes us with the laft example in the Englifh hiftory, of any aid being levied on the knighting of the king's eldeft fon, and the marriage of his eldeft daughter. The act on which the firft claim was founded, though of a very old date [18], had been frequently carried into execution by James's predeceffors; and Henry, the prince of Wales, was fuch a favourite with the people, and the whole was managed with fuch moderation, that it yielded a confiderable fum [19]. The other tax on the marriage of James's daughter to the elector Palatine, produced 20,500*l.* It is remarked, that a century had elapfed fince this aid had been demanded; no opportunity having occurred fince the reign of Henry VII. whofe eldeft daughter Margaret was married to James IV. of Scotland; in confequence of which alliance, James himfelf inherited the crown of England.

4. Cuftoms. The firft parliament that James affembled, granted him, according to former practice, the duties of tunnage and poundage for life. But the more productive this branch of the revenue became, the greater anxiety did the crown feel to enjoy it in its own right, without the neceffity of any application to parliament. Thence originated the difpute fo

[15] Brief Declaration, &c. p. 10.

[16] For inftance, in the beginning of the enfuing reign, it was complained of, that the purveyors would only give fix-pence for a dozen of pigeons, worth fix fhillings; and two-pence for a fowl, worth one fhilling and fix-pence in the market. Comm. Journals, 25th of May, 1626. vol. i. p. 864.

[17] Parl. Hift. vol. v. p. 264. 267.   [18] 25 Edw. III. c.

[19] £ 21,800. See Brief Declaration, &c. p. 10.

warmly

warmly contefted between James and his commons, with regard to the power of levying cuftoms, and of adding to the rates of the duties that were impofed [20]. The payment of cuftoms by natives, at leaft to any amount, certainly originated in the grants of parliament ; but the crown had fo long received thefe duties, that it began to confider the cuftoms as a permanent branch of its revenue. Both Mary and Elizabeth had fhown James the example of altering the rates on fome particular commodities. The fame practice he intended to purfue, and to carry to a confiderable height, though he was at firft cautious not to give umbrage by any important alteration. But the commons took fire at the principle, forefeeing to what lengths it might be extended ; and, indeed, paffed a bill, abolifhing thefe additional impofitions, which the houfe of lords thought proper to reject [21]. The next parliament was proceeding to take fimilar fteps, when it was fuddenly diffolved ; and thus the difpute remained undetermined in this monarch's reign.

Anno 1610.

Anno 1614.

The amount of the cuftoms was rapidly increafing. At James's acceffion they yielded only 127,000*l.* a year. The following is a ftate of their produce, *anno* 1613.

At the port of London	Outwards Inwards	— —	— —	£ 61,322 16 7 48,250 1 9
				£ 109,572 18 4
In all the out ports	Outwards Inwards	— —	£25,471 19 7 } 13,030 9 9 }	38,502 9 4
			Total £ 148,075 7 8	

And, towards the clofe of this reign, they amounted to about 190,000*l.*

[20] Among feveral treatifes publifhed upon this fubject, the beft in fupport of the prerogative of the crown, is, " The queftion concerning impofitions, fully ftated," by Sir John Davis, his Majefty's Attorney General. Printed *anno* 1656. And the beft defence of the rights of the people, " The Liberty of the Subject maintained againft the pre- " tended Power of Impofitions." By William Hackwell. Printed *anno* 1641.

[21] Hume, vol. vi. p. 51.

U

The

The difproportion between London and the out-ports is very great; and proves how confiderable a fhare of the commerce of this country has uniformly centered in the capital.

5. Grants.   It was afferted by the famous Lord Salifbury, in a fpeech to parliament, that there are but three inftances in the Englifh hiftory for 600 years, prior to James's acceffion, of a fupply being refufed by the commons when requefted by the fovereign[22]; and the firft parliament that James affembled was as frugal of the public money as any of its predeceffors, and would grant nothing but tunnage and poundage. The king, finding them determined, and being unwilling to have it fuppofed that his parliament and he were at variance, took the ftrange ftep of fending a meffage to the houfe, that he defired no fupply, and was refolved not even to accept of a fubfidy[23], when every perfon knew, there was nothing he fo anxioufly wifhed. The grants he received, during the whole courfe of his reign, were only as follows.

A. D.		Year of his reign.		Subs.		Fift.
1606	—	3	—	3	—	6
1610	—	7	—	1	—	1
1621	—	18	—	2	—	0
1624	—	22	—	3	—	3
				9		10

Thefe were all the fupplies granted by parliament; and of thefe, it is faid by Hume, that the three fubfidies and three fifteenths, granted *anno* 1624, amounting to about 300,000*l.*, being paid to parliamentary commiffioners, ought not to be ftated to the king's perfonal account[24]. But this idea has been fully refuted by the female hiftorian of this reign, who remarks that, though the commiffioners received the money, yet they were totally ignorant how it was

<hr>

[22] Comm. Journ. vol. i. p. 395.   Hume obferves, that Salifbury was miftaken in this affertion. Vol. vi. p. 72   Note R.

[23] Comm. Journ. vol. i. p. 246.   [24] Vol. vi. p. 172.

expended;

expended; and as they were obliged to anfwer all money draughts made upon them by the crown, their power was merely nominal. " One penny of this money (the king declared) fhall not be beftowed " but in fight of your committees: but whether I fhall fend two thou- " fand, or ten thoufand, whether by fea or land, Eaft or Weft, by di- " verfion or otherwife, by invafion upon the Bavarian, or the Empe- " ror, *you muft leave that to your king*[1]." It appears that a fubfidy produced about 70,000*l.*, and a fifteenth about 36,500*l.*[2]; confe- quently, the whole parliamentary grants received by James, amounted to about a million. To this, there are to be added about twelve fubfidies from the clergy, which, at 20,000*l.* each, would produce 240,000*l.*; and one of the clerical fubfidies was at the rate of fix, and not of four fhillings in the pound; and therefore yielded 10,000*l.* additional. One year with another, it is probable that he received, by parliamentary and clerical grants, about 60,000*l. per annum* during the courfe of his reign.

James had a price affixed to each rank of nobility, on the payment of which a grant was made out. The dignities of Baron, Vifcount, and Earl, might be bought at the rate of ten, fifteen, and twenty thoufand pounds: and we are told of four earls who purchafed their refpective patents, at the fum fixed upon, in one year[3]. But the moft complete inftance of this mode of raifing money, either in the reign of James, or, indeed, in the Englifh hiftory, is the creation of baronets. It is fuppofed, by our hiftorians, that this was a plan invented by Lord Sa- lifbury: but it is more probable that the idea originated with Sir Ro- bert Cotton, who drew up, *anno* 1609, an account of " the manner in " which the kings of England fupported and repaired their eftates." In this he remarks, that, " if his majefty would make a degree of " honour hereditary as baronets, next under barons, and grant them " in tail, taking of every one 1000*l.* in fine, it would raife, with eafe, " 100,000*l.*; and, by a judicious election, be a means to content thofe " worthy perfons in the commonwealth, that by the confufed admiffion

6. Sale of ho- nours.

[1] Macaulay's Hift. vol. i. p. 251.
[2] See Brief Declaration, &c. p. 70 and 71. Fifteenths formerly produced lefs, on account of the great deductions made for decayed towns.
[3] Franklyn's Annals, p. 33.

" of

" of many knights of the *Bath*, hold themfelves difgraced[28]." The plan was carried into execution *anno* 1611: each baronet, by way of purchafe for the honour, became bound to maintain thirty foot foldiers for three years, at eight-pence a day each, to affift the king's troops in the reduction of Ulfter in Ireland. The price confequently was 1095*l.* Ninety-three were created, the fale of whofe patents yielded 98,550*l.*[29]

7 Monopolies.   Among the other fources of diffention between James and his parliaments, that which refpected monopolies was of peculiar importance, being equally connected with the commerce and the revenue of the country. The king had annulled, of his own accord, all patents for monopolies by which any fpecies of domeftic induftry was fettered: but all foreign trade, that of France excepted, was poffeffed by exclufive companies; and hence the navigation and commerce of the kingdom, were every day fenfibly diminifhing. " Thus" (in the ftrong expreffions of Hume) " the trade of England was brought into the hands " of a few rapacious engroffers; and all profpect of future improve- " ment was for ever facrificed to a little temporary advantage to the " fovereign[30]." *Anno* 1621, a patent which had been granted to Sir Giles Montpeffon and Sir Thomas Michell for licenfing inns and alehoufes, and another to Sir Edward Villiers, for the fole making of gold and filver lace, came into difcuffion. The powers given to thefe patentees were fo very exorbitant, and fo rigoroufly carried into execution, that they naturally excited the indignation of parliament. Yelverton, the attorney-general, was fined 15,000*l.* for having drawn up the patents: Michell and Montpeffon were punifhed by fines, confifcation,

---

[28] This curious treatife is contained in a fmall volume, entitled, " Cottoni Pofthuma," printed *anno* 1672: and the very fame work, with fome trifling alterations and differences, is printed *anno* 1715, under the title of " A Treatife of the Rights of the Crown, by " William Noy, Efq. collected *anno* 1634." As Noy's work is printed feparately, I have, in general, referred to it. But the work was certainly compofed in the reign of James I., and moft probably by Sir Robert Cotton. Dr. Smith, in his Life of Sir Robert Cotton, fays, that it was drawn up at the defire of the Earl of Northampton, and that there are two copies of it in the Cotton library, one in Latin, and the other in Englifh, as publifhed in the Pofthuma. See Carte's full Vindication of the Anfwer to the Byftander, p. 38.

[29] Brief Declaration, &c. p. 11. Befides fome after creations.

[30] Hume, vol. vi. p. 23.

and

and imprifonment; and even Villiers, though fupported by all the credit of his brother the Duke of Buckingham, fuffered a fpecies of banifhment under the appearance of being employed in a foreign embaffy". At laft an act was paffed, by which all monopolies were *Anno 1624.* condemned as contrary to law, and the known liberties of the people" : An act which ought for ever to have put an end to fo deftructive a grievance.

As early as the year 1604, James had begun the dangerous practice *8. Loans,.* of compelling his fubjects to lend him money on the fecurity of the privy-feal: but it is not known how much he then procured, or whether any part of it was repaid". Two hundred thoufand pounds were afterwards extorted under the fame pretence. James's opinion on the fubject, he took no pains to conceal: for when the commons petitioned, that no man fhould be enforced to lend money, or to give a reafon why he would not, the king returned for anfwer, that in matters of loans, he would refufe no reafonable excufe; but that he did not wifh to have his conduct directed by precedents drawn from the reigns of ufurping princes, or a people too bold and wanton".

James exacted, *anno* 1613, a fum to the amount of 52,000l. under *9. Benevo-* the name of *a benevolence*; but fo fmall an advantage was certainly no *lences.* compenfation for the odium and unpopularity of the meafure. Nor was he much more fuccefsful in his fecond attempt: for though the cafe was faid to be fo urgent that it could not brook the delays that would attend affembling the parliament; and though it was collected to fupport the popular caufe of the Elector Palatine, yet the people, anxious to difcourage fo pernicious a practice, at firft very flowly and reluctantly contributed".

The neceffities to which this monarch was reduced, made him con- *10. Money* clude a treaty with the States of Holland on terms, in a pecuniary view, *from the Dutch.*

---

31 Parl. Hift. vol. v. p. 382.   Hume, vol. vi. p. 108.
32 21 Jac. cap. 3.   33 Stevens, p. 269.
34 Macaulay's Hift. vol. i. p. 60.
35 This benevolence became at laft more productive.   One Barnes, a citizen of London, who refufed to contribute, being ordered to prepare himfelf for carrying a difpatch to Ireland, had the meannefs to fubmit to pay his quota; and no one afterwards ventured to deny his proportion.   See Hume, vol. vi. p. 140.   Note G.

indeed,

indeed, rather beneficial to himfelf, though, on the whole, not a little favourable to the New Republic. It has already been ftated, that the Dutch were indebted to Elizabeth to the amount of 8co,ool. Of this fum 200,000l. had been paid to James, and he was to receive the remainder at the rate of 40,000l. *per annum*, until the whole was difcharged. But the payment depended upon a very uncertain contingency, namely, the continuation of a truce concluded between Spain and the United Provinces. The politic Elizabeth had been put in pof-feffion of the important fortreffes of Flufhing, the Brille and Ramme-kins, as a fecurity for her debt: but the expences of the garrifons (which England was obliged to fupport) amounted to 26,000l. a year: confequently 14,000l. was all the clear profit that accrued from the annual payment; and the whole fum which the king could poffibly receive, in the fpace of fifteen years, after defraying the neceffary charges, was only 210,000l. The Dutch, however, being anxious fully to eftablifh their independence, which remained infecure, whilft thefe important fortreffes, the very keys of their country, continued in the hands of England, offered to take the garrifons into their own pay, and to give James 250,000l. for the immediate poffeffion[26]. The

June 6, 1616. terms were accepted; and from the day on which thefe cautionary towns were evacuated, the complete eftablifhment of the Dutch republic may be dated. Nor was this the only money that James inherited from his predeceffor. He alfo received 60,000l. of the debt which Henry IV. of France owed to that princefs[27].

11. Licence for fifhing. *Anno* 1608, the Dutch were compelled to pay an acknowledgment for the liberty of fifhing on the Britifh coafts: a fource of revenue, which was attempted to be more fully enforced during the enfuing reign.

12. Fines. The laft fource of James's wealth arofe from the heavy fines which it was then cuftomary to inflict. Forty thoufand pounds were impofed upon the earl of Northumberland, and the lords Mordaunt and Stourton, who were fufpected of having fome knowledge of the famous gunpowder plot, and of concealing it from the king and his minifters. Sir John Bennet, judge of the Prerogative Court, was fined

---

[26] Hume, vol. vi. p. 80.   [27] Brief Declaration, &c. p. 11.

20,000l.

20,000 *l.* The celebrated chancellor Bacon was fentenced to pay 40,000 *l.* which however was remitted. The earl of Suffolk, who held the office of lord high treafurer, was fined 30,000 *l.* by the court of Star-chamber; and the earl of Middlefex, in confequence of a parlia-mentary impeachment, was condemned to pay 50,000 *l.* If thefe fines had been all exacted, they would have yielded the fum of 184,000 *l.* and would have proved no fmall addition to this monarch's impoverished exchequer ".

A particular account has been publifhed of James's revenue, during the firft fourteen years of his reign, from which it appears, that his ordinary income did not exceed 450,863 *l.*: that the extraordinary fums he had received during that time, amounted to 2,200,000 *l.* and that his ordinary difburfements exceeded his permanent income 36,617 *l.* a year ". *Anno* 1610 lord Salifbury declared in parliament, that the king was burdened with a great and urgent debt of 300,000 *l.* His income, from all the different fources above enumerated, was probably about 600,000 *l.* though his permanent revenue, including the grants of parliament, could not much exceed 500,000 *l.* a year; efpecially, as during the latter part of his reign, he had fome reafon to complain of the parfimony of his commons. But that fum was fufficient to carry on the government of England in thofe days, under a frugal monarch, and in peaceful times, though very inadequate to the fplendid manner in which James wifhed to live, and to thofe plans of hoftility againft the houfe of Auftria, into which the Commons would willingly have plunged him.

The fcheme afterwards profecuted by the long parliament, of raifing money, by abolifhing the order of bifhops, and felling the lands belonging to the church, was firft planned in the reign of James, and at one period was not a little encouraged by his favourite Buckingham ". But the views and politics of the court, upon Charles's acceffion, took a very oppofite direction.

Amount of his revenue.

Church lands.

Anno 1624.

" From the brief declaration of his majefty's revenue, p. 11. it appears, that many of thefe were compounded for fmall fums, making in all about 16,000 *l.* to which there is to be added 4000 *l.* of fines for new buildings in and about London.

" An Abftract, or brief Declaration of the prefent State of his Majefty's Revenue, p. 5, and 9. " Hume, vol. vi. p. 142. Macaulay, vol. i. p. 230.

The

Lottery.

The firſt lottery to any amount ever known in England, at leaſt drawn under the ſanction of public authority, was in this reign. The profit of it was principally dedicated to the expences attending the eſtabliſhment of our ſettlements in America[41], to retain the dominion of which, the produce of ſo many lotteries, loans and taxes, has of late been ineffectually expended.

Coin.

The quantity of ſpecie coined in the reign of James, was about 5,432,000 *l.* of which 3,666,000*l.* was in gold, and only 1,765,000 *l.* in ſilver[42]. It ſtill continued to be the practice to iſſue ſome baſe money for the uſe of Ireland.

It is impoſſible, in this place, not to regret the want of a performance which lord chancellor Bacon intended to compoſe upon the finances of England. In a letter to king James, dated 2d January 1618, he ſays, " God having done ſo great things for your majeſty, it reſteth that you " do ſo much for yourſelf, as to go through (according to your good " beginnings) with the rectifying and ſettling of your eſtate and means, " which only is wanting : *hoc rebus defuit unum.* I therefore, whom " only love and duty to your majeſty, and your royal line, hath made " a financier, do intend to preſent unto your majeſty, *a perfect book of* " *your eſtate,* like a perſpective-glaſs, to ſhew your eſtate nearer to " your ſight, beſeeching your majeſty to conceive, that if I have not " attained to that that I would do in this which is not proper for me " in my element, I ſhall make your majeſty amends in ſome other " thing in which I am better bred[43]." It does not appear that this promiſe was ever fulfilled ; and the only valuable work of this great author, connected with finance, at this time known, is an account of the lately erected office of Compoſition for Alienations, ſaid to have been compoſed in the reign of queen Elizabeth, about the end of the year 1598 ; which, though not written upon an important branch of revenue, yet fully proves what this great genius was capable of effecting, had he dedicated his time and his abilities to a full inveſtigation of the extenſive ſubject he had propoſed.

---

[41] Mort. vol. ii. p. 512.   [42] Folkes on Coins.

[43] Bacon's Works, fol. edit. vol. iv. p. 673. Perhaps, the " Brief Declaration of " the preſent State of his Majeſty's Revenue," was drawn up to aſſiſt this diſtinguiſhed author in the taſk he had undertaken.

CHARLES

CHARLES I.

It is difficult to judge impartially of the important events which took place during the reign of this unfortunate monarch.

On the one hand, when we contemplate Charles's private character and deportment, we are apt to confider the multiplied charges againft him as malicious and ill-founded, and can hardly be perfuaded, that an affectionate hufband, an indulgent parent, and a generous mafter, could by any means be converted, as his enemies are apt to reprefent him, into a rapacious tyrant, determined to pillage the property, and to trample on the rights and privileges of his fubjects. But on the other hand, if our attention is folely fixed upon public tranfactions, we naturally run into a very oppofite extreme. Even Hume, who has defended this prince's conduct with fubtlety, ability, and perfeverance, does not fcruple to confefs, that Charles affumed powers incompatible with the principles of a limited government; and that his difafters ought to be afcribed, neither to the rigours of deftiny, nor to the malignity of his enemies, but to his own precipitancy and indifcretion [44].

Thefe topics, however, are better fuited to a political, than to a financial hiftory of England; nor is it propofed to enter into the various important queftions agitated at that time, excepting fo far as they may be connected with the particular object of this work.

1. Expences.

Though Charles, at his acceffion, inherited a crown and kingdom apparently in the moft flourifhing fituation, and enriched, during the courfe of his father's peaceful, but inglorious adminiftration, yet he had many difficulties, both foreign and domeftic, to encounter.

The conqueft of the Palatinate, and the injurious manner in which it was pretended the court of Spain had acted, whilft Charles's marriage with the infanta was negotiating, had occafioned, not only a rupture with that powerful kingdom, but a war with Ferdinand II. emperor of

War with Spain.

[44] Hift. vol. vi. p. 472.

X   Germany,

Germany, one of the ableſt and moſt powerful monarchs that ever ſat upon the Imperial throne: and the king declared·to parliament, that it would require at leaſt 700,000 /. a year to carry on theſe hoſtilities. effeΔually [45].

2 War with France.Though Charles was baffled in all his attempts againſt the emperor and the Spaniards; though he had· found how unwilling his parliaments were to grant him ſupplies; and how difficult, if not dangerous, it was to raiſe money by other means; and though his connection with the Houſe of Bourbon ought to have rendered him cautious of raſhly entering into a conteſt with that powerful family, unleſs on grounds of great weight and moment, yet hurried on by the capricious Buckingham, he ventured to engage in a war with France, even before hoſtilities againſt Spain were concluded. This enterprize alone, was much beyond the impoveriſhed ſtate of Charles's finances. An expenſive expedition, however, was undertaken to the Iſle of Rhe; and five ſubſidies granted by parliament, anno 1628, were expended in an attempt·to relieve Rochelle, which, by the artifices of the Engliſh court, had been drawn into a rebellion. But Charles was unſucceſsful in every foreign enterprize he undertook: and when a peace was concluded, inſtead of ſecuring terms of oblivion and indemnity to the unhappy Huguenots whom he had pledged himſelf to ſupport, he abandoned them to the mercy of their ſovereign, after fruitleſsly, but it is probable, feebly attempting to procure ſome ſtipulation in their favour [46].

3 War with Scotland.The inglorious foreign wars into which Charles had entered, were terminated by ſeparate treaties of peace. The firſt was concluded with France, anno 1629; the ſecond with Spain, anno 1630; and for about ten years afterwards Charles governed his dominions in peace, and· managed his own revenue, together with the ſums which he exaΔed from his ſubjeΔs, with ſuch a rigid œconomy, that he not only paid off the debts

---

[45] Hume, vol. vi. p. 206.

[46] " Les Reformes de France n'y furent point compris. Une ſi grand infidelité après " des paroles authentiquement données, et ſouvent reiterées, ſera une fletriſſure eternelle " à la memoire de l'infortuné Charles I." Vaſſor Hiſtoire du Regne de Louis XIII. tom. vi. p. 110.

he·

he had contracted during the Spanish and French wars, but alſo contrived to amaſs treaſure to the amount of about 200,000 *l.* Perhaps this circumſtance gave him ſome encouragement to engage in an enterprize to which all his misfortunes may be aſcribed. Impelled by deference for his clergy, and perhaps by a real conviction of its importance, he reſolved to eſtabliſh a ſimilarity in eccleſiaſtical government and ceremonies throughout all his dominions; and in particular to introduce a liturgy into Scotland, however obnoxious to the natives of that country. The Scots, ſtrongly attached to the doctrines and diſcipline of Calvin, determined to oppoſe a ſyſtem which they conſidered as equally ſubverſive of ſound religion, and contrary to ſacred authority. No obſtacle, however, could alter the king's reſolution: and though very moderate conceſſions at firſt would have appeaſed the tumults in Scotland, yet conceſſions were never made until it was too late, and until time had ripened new demands, which were as reſolutely inſiſted on. Twice did Charles put himſelf at the head of formidable fleets and armies for the reduction of Scotland; but in vain: for the Scots acted with equal valour and prudence, and the Engliſh in general reluctantly ſupported his attempt, juſtly conjecturing, that the conqueſt of the Scots would prove a prelude to the utter ruin of their own liberties. The expence attending theſe hoſtilities, reduced the king to ſuch diſtreſs, that he found it neceſſary again to have recourſe to parliament; and conceſſions were extorted from him, which enabled the commons to trample upon the crown, and emboldened the army they had raiſed, to deſtroy both the king and the conſtitution.

To the credit of Charles it is to be remarked, that he ſpared no expence to render his navy formidable. At ſea, he had no rival in Europe. The Dutch were compelled to pay 30,000 *l.* for the liberty of fiſhing on the Britiſh coaſts; and Africa, for the firſt time, felt the maritime force of this country: Sallee, the principal receptacle of the Turkiſh pirates, being deſtroyed by an Engliſh ſquadron[47]. Even the mound which Richelieu erected acroſs the harbour of Rochelle, was a confeſſion that it could never be conquered by the arms of France,

4. Naval expences.

[47] Macaulay, vol. ii. p. 228.

X 2 whilſt

whilſt it remained acceſſible to the powerful fleets of which England
was then miſtreſs[48].

This monarch, with all his frugality, affected much the ſtate and
ſplendor of a king. He kept up twenty-four palaces, all of them ſo
completely furniſhed, that when he removed from one to another, he
was not obliged to tranſport any article of furniture along with him.
His collection of pictures was the moſt valuable in Europe, and he
ſpared no expence, nay he rivalled Philip IV. of Spain, the maſter of the
Indies, in endeavouring to engroſs the moſt valuable productions of
the ableſt artiſts[49].

It has been much controverted, to whom the odium ought to be
aſcribed of the fatal rupture between this monarch and his parliament.
Both parties had grounds ſufficiently plauſible at the commencement of
the diſpute, to juſtify their proceedings. The king had to plead the
arbitrary ſyſtem of government practiſed by his immediate predeceſſors;
whilſt the commons, with juſtice, urged more ancient precedents favourable to the liberties of the people, and indeed the unalienable rights of
natural freedom. In the progreſs of the conteſt, as might naturally be
expected, both were equally to blame. The commons cannot well be
defended, for not endeavouring, in the firſt place, to gain the king, by
ſoothing arts, rather than having recourſe to violence; and the propoſals which they made in the earlier part of the war, were too harſh
and rigorous. But it can hardly be denied, that the illegal means which
the king adopted for raiſing money; the dangerous and exorbitant
prerogatives which he claimed; and the tyrannical manner in which
both he and his miniſters acted, " rendered an oppoſition to the
" meaſures of the crown not only excuſable, but laudable in the
" people[50]."

Let us next conſider from what ſources his income was derived.

[48] The French had then no idea of rivalling England at ſea. It appears from *Le
Vaſſor's Hiſtoire du Regne de Louis XIII. Liv.* xxv. that the fleet of France, at the
ſiege of Rochelle, amounted only to about forty veſſels, and the Spaniſh ſquadron
to thirty-ſix more, but very ill equipped. The ſuperiority of the Engliſh fleet, when it
amounted only to ſeventy ſail, is acknowledged by the king's miniſters. Tom. v.part 2.
p. 763, 764. But it was afterwards increaſed to about 140 ſail; and then, ſays Vaſſor,
" C'étoit une des plus belles armées navales, qu'on eut vûe depuis long-tems." p. 833.

[49] Hume, vol. vii. p. 341.   [50] Ibid. vol. vi. p. 304.

2. Income.

It is probable that the crown lands yielded a greater revenue in the *1. Demefnes,* reign of Charles I. than under the government of his father. It is certain, that a ftrict enquiry was made into the rights by which individuals held fuch lands as originally compofed a part of the royal domain ; and, after the example of Elizabeth, fome money was raifed, by compounding with thofe whofe titles were defective. One of the means alfo by which the king was enabled to raife an army for the reduction of Scotland, was borrowing 300,000 *l.* on the fecurity of his demefnes.

The jealoufy which parliament entertained of the houfe of Stuart, *2. Grants,* rendered the commons very fparing of their grants to the monarchs of that race. Nor were they fo valuable as formerly. In the eighth year of Elizabeth, a fubfidy amounted to 120,000 *l.* ; in the fortieth, it fell to 78,000*l.*, and its produce *anno* 1640, had fallen to 50,000 *l.* ⁵¹ Subfidies were a tax upon income ; and as the wealth of the country was rapidly increafing, no reafon can be affigned for the decreafe of the produce of this tax, but the fraudulent practices of the affeffors, who wifhed to cultivate the favour of the people by moderate affeffments, or who countenanced every means of evafion, to diminifh the value of the grant, when the government happened to be unpopular ⁵².

The grants which Charles received may very eafily be enumerated. His firft parliament granted him two fubfidies from his Proteftant, and four from his Roman-catholic fubjects, which together are fuppofed to have yielded about 112,000 *l.* ; and the Commons were at that time fo very parfimonious, that they rejected a motion for adding twofifteenths to their former inconfiderable donation ⁵³. The next parliament that was affembled, voted four fubfidies, and three-fifteenths ; but

⁵¹ In the famous Remonftrance, 15th Dec. 1640, it is faid that fix fubfidies, and a poll-bill, equal to fix more, would yield 600,000 *l.* It is certain that parliament would not diminifh their value, and confequently a fubfidy cannot be accounted worth more than 50,000 *l.*
⁵² Davenant, vol. i. p. 33.　⁵³ Rufh. vol. i. p. 190.

It

it was haftily diffolved before the vote paffed into a law. His third parliament granted five fubfidies, in confideration of which, the famous petition of right received the royal affent. This grant did not exceed 250,000 *l.* But the manner in which this mark of the liberality of parliament was received, deferves to be commemorated. When fecretary Cook informed the king of the fum that was voted, his majefty was anxious to know by what majority it had been carried. "By One," the fecretary replied; and when the king feemed to be difturbed with the information, he added, " Your majefty has no caufe to be alarmed, " for the Houfe was fo unanimous in making the grant, that it feemed " to have but One voice." It is faid, that tears of affection ftarted in his eyes, when he was told of this conceffion [54].

These, amounting to feven fubfidies, and producing only about 372,000 *l.* were the only grants which Charles received from his Commons, prior to the meeting of the long parliament, by whom fix fubfidies and a poll-tax were voted before the commencement of the civil war. But the produce was appropriated to pay the Englifh and Scotch armies, and the money was given to commiffioners, appointed by parliament, and not to the treafury. It is worthy of obfervation, that the king demanded twelve fubfidies, about 600,000 *l.* in lieu of his claim to fhip-money; and he offered, in confideration of that fum, to confent to its being abolifhed, in any manner that was thought moft effectual. This propofal was, with the greateft propriety, rejected; as any bargain to procure the remiffion of that odious duty, would have been a kind of acknowledgment that it had been legally levied. It was propofed to raife the fum in the fpace of three years, and confequently at the rate of only 200,000 *l.* a year. It will appear, in the courfe of this chapter, what confiderable fums were foon afterwards collected in England; and yet to prove how ignorant men generally are to what extent taxes may be carried, it was afferted in

Anno 1640. parliament, by perfons who were fuppofed to underftand well the ftate of the nation, that twelve fubfidies in three years was a greater fum than could be raifed in all England [55].

Clerical grants. During the reign of this monarch, the fortunate confequences which refulted from the diffipation of the revenues of the church, were clearly

----

[54] Hume, vol. vi. p. 245.   [55] Clarend. vol. i. p. 136.

difcovered,

difcovered. Had that valuable property remained within the grafp of the crown, the king might eafily have defrayed all the expences which he could poffibly have incurred, without requiring the affift-ance of parliament; and all controul on the regal authority muft have been for ever at an end. Notwithftanding the great diminution of the property of the church, the affiftance which Charles drew from the clergy was confiderable. Befides voluntary contributions, he received, in the earlier part of his reign, eight fubfidies, which at 20,000 *l.* each, amounted to 160,000 *l.* ; and it fhould feem, that another fub-fidy was granted, *anno* 1640 ; for the long parliament loudly com-plain of a tax having been impofed by the Convocation, after the former parliament had been diffolved [5].

It has already been ftated, that Elizabeth had reaped fome pecuniary benefit, by difpenfing with the penal laws, enacted againft thofe who adhered to the Roman catholic religion. This expedient Charles had recourfe to; but inftead of fecret compofitions, a commiffion was openly granted, and the papifh religion became an avowed and regular fource, of revenue [17]: A ftep highly impolitic at a time when his fub-jects in general were fo ftrongly impreffed with the moft inveterate prejudices againft the profeffors of that religion.

4. Compofi-tion with Ro-man catho-lics.

James I. had conceived a ridiculous idea, that a king of England would be degraded if he fhould efpoufe any princefs not of royal ex-traction, and indeed that the daughters of France or Spain were the only females to whom his fon ought to be married. In confequence of this notion, he had entered into a tedious negotiation with the court of Spain, which was broken off through Buckingham's caprice and in-difcretion, much to the king's regret, who was to have received a dowry with the infanta, of two millions of pieces of eight, equal to 600,000 *l.* fterling. Upon the failure of that plan, James made pro-pofals to the court of France, the confequence of which was, the mar-riage of Charles to Henrietta, daughter of the famous Henry the Great. Her portion was greatly inferior, being only 400,000 crowns ; neither was it paid until fome years after the marriage was concluded ; but it came at laft very opportunely for Charles, in the midft of his greateft pecuniary diftreffes [18].

5. Queen's portion.

---

[5] Mort. vol. ii. p. 544. [17] Rufh. vol. i. p. 413. [18] Stevens, p. 276.

The

6. Fishing
licence.

The question how far the sea can be made the property of any particular nation, has been much controverted ; and two learned authors (Selden and Grotius) were employed by the respective governments under which they lived, the first to support, and the second to oppose this species of dominion.   But Charles knew that superior strength at sea was the only argument by which such pretensions could be supported ; and having, by means of the illegal imposition of ship-money, equipped a formidable fleet, he ordered the admiral, Algernon, earl of Northumberland, to sail to the northern coasts of his dominions, and to drive away all vessels fishing in their neighbourhood without licence. The Dutch, against whom this equipment was particularly aimed, were glad to pay 30,000 l. for the liberty of fishing that year ; and the king would have persevered in exacting an annual tribute for permitting them to fish on the British coasts, had not his attention been taken up by more important objects.

7. Customs.

One would imagine it was impossible for the warmest friend of the unfortunate house of Stuart to justify the steps which Charles pursued, in respect to exacting the revenue of the customs for so many years without legal authority, and in a manner so harsh and oppressive.   He

Anno 1629.

himself declared to parliament, that he did not mean to levy the duties of tunnage and poundage as belonging to him by hereditary right, but out of the full persuasion that the House of Commons would grant them by bill [59].   And it appears from the history of these taxes, the origin and progress of which have been traced in the preceding part of this work, that the Customs, instead of having originally been a permanent branch of the royal income, arose from a voluntary consent of the people by their representatives in parliament.

Though the law was clear, the practice was very irregular.   Ever since the accession of the House of Tudor, the duties of tunnage and poundage had been levied without intermission ; and though granted only for the life of the reigning sovereign, yet his successor continued to exact them, trusting to the future sanction of parliament.   Charles, at his accession, had continued a practice, on which so considerable a branch of his revenune depended ; and he would probably have received a grant for life, as had been given to his predecessors, had not

[59] Parl. Hist. vol. viii. p. 256.

the

the Commons required it as a preliminary, that he fhould, for once, entirely defift from levying thefe duties. He haftily diffolved the parliament rather than agree to their propofal. This important controverfy was at laft determined in a manner unfavourable to the crown. The exaction of the duties, was not totally abftained from, but they were granted only for two months; and the grant was renewed from time to time, for very fhort periods. Care alfo was taken, to affert, in the ftrongeft terms that could be conceived, the exclufive right of parliament to beftow the grant; and in the preamble to the bills that were paffed, all pretenfions that the crown could make, to levy the duties by its own authority, were for ever annulled [60].

An. 1640.

It is faid, that the cuftoms, previoufly to the civil wars, had been raifed to 500,000 *l*. a year in confequence of the increafe of commerce, and the additional impofitions which had been laid on by Mary, Elizabeth, and James [61]: an account [that feems, however, to have been exaggerated.

But Charles, not fatisfied with exacting impofitions, which, though in fome degree fanctioned by cuftom, yet were unqueftionably illegal, was imprudent enough to attempt to levy a new tax, to which the nation had not been accuftomed; and the illegality of which was, confequently, the more apparent. It is faid, that a fpecies of fhip-money was impofed by Elizabeth *anno* 1588: but, befides, that one precedent, particularly in fo arbitrary a reign, is not a fufficient juftification; it is farther to be remarked, that Elizabeth exacted fhips, and not money; that every exertion was neceffary to oppofe fo deftructive an invafion as that of the Spaniards; and that, notwithftanding the danger and urgency of the cafe, fo moderate were her demands, that many of the ports, London in particular, of their own accord, fent double the number of fhips that were required.

8. Ship-money.

This monarch's firft attempt to levy fhip-money, was *anno* 1626; and the precedent afforded in the reign of Elizabeth, was pretty ftrictly adhered to; for the maritime towns only were required to furnifh fhips, and the adjacent towns were ordered to affift in the equipment. Twenty fhips were the proportion of London, and the other towns were rated accordingly [62].

Firft exaction of Ship-money.

[60] 16 Car. I. cap. 8.　　[61] Hume, vol. vii. p. 340.　　[62] Ibid. vol. vi. p. 224.

Y

But

But this claim was afterwards carried to a much greater extent. It is aſſerted, that the ſituation of Europe in general, and the rapid increaſe of the Dutch republic, in commerce, and in maritime ſtrength, and the ſuccefsful piracies of the Barbary corſairs, who infeſted the very coaſts of the kingdom, had rendered it neceſſary for Charles to equip a fleet ſufficient to ſupport the naval dignity of his crown, and the commercial intereſts of his kingdom. The only obſtacle was the low ſtate of his exchequer.

In this emergency, he applied to Noy, then his attorney-general, a very able lawyer; whoſe advice was, to extend the impoſition of ſhip-money over the whole kingdom; the crown being entitled, he affirmed, to levy a naval aid for the public defence in time of neceſſity[c]. But Charles, not ſatisfied with this authority, or willing to have it ſtrengthened by every means in his power, and anxious to prevent, if poſſible, all oppoſition to ſo favourite a meaſure, required the opinion of the twelve judges on the caſe, who unanimouſly declared, " That when the good " and ſafety of the whole kingdom is concerned, the king might com- " mand all his ſubjects, at their own charge, to provide and furniſh " ſuch number of ſhips, with men, victual, and munition, for ſuch " time as he thought fit, for the defence of the kingdom, and that he " was the ſole judge both of the danger, and how the ſame is to be " prevented[4]." It is to be obſerved, that this opinion, though gene- rally accounted deciſive in favour of the crown, yet is very cautiouſly worded. It is not ſtated, that the king could legally levy money by his own authority: nothing could be raiſed but ſhips, men, victuals, and ammunition in kind, nor is any power of converſion inſinuated.

In oppoſition to this public declaration of the very judges before whom his cauſe muſt be tried, and undiſmayed by the power of the crown, which was then ſuppoſed to be uncontroulable, and which, he knew, would be ſtretched to the utmoſt, to wreck its vengeance on any one who firſt ventured to refiſt its authority, John Hambden, an Engliſhman, equal in zeal, courage, and integrity, to the moſt re-

[c] Noy is ſaid to have examined, at this time, all the precedents of levying money by regal authority; and hence, it is probable, aroſe the ſuppoſition of his being the author of Cotton's Treatiſe on the Rights and Revenues of the Crown. He died ſoon after that ſhip-money began to be levied.   [4] Stevens, p. 277.

nowned

nowned patriots of antiquity, refufed to pay the inconfiderable fum of twenty fhillings at which he was affeffed, and refolutely determined to hazard any confequences, rather than fubmit to the impofition. A fuit was inftituted by the crown to compel the payment, and the caufe was folemnly argued for twelve days before all the judges of England. Notwithftanding the convincing arguments urged in his defence [65], only four of the judges gave an opinion in his favour, whilft eight fupported the legality of the tax. This victory, however, was fo generally odious and unpopular, that it was equivalent to a defeat. It roufed the indignation of the people at large, and occafioned that firm and fteady oppofition to the meafures of the court, which it afterwards encountered.

Charles had propofed to the fourth parliament he had affembled, in confideration of twelve fubfidies, to agree to the abolition of fhip-money, in any manner it fhould think proper. But the Commons wifely refufed to give the flighteft countenance to fo illegal an impofition ; and one of the firft fteps which the Long Parliament took, was, to vote that fhip-money was arbitrary and illegal. The fentence againft Hambden, alfo, was declared contrary to law. The judges who had given their opinion in favour of fhip-money were impeached, the officers employed in collecting the duty were declared highly culpable, and a law was paffed, by which this obnoxious impoft was for ever abolifhed [66]. Abolition of fhip-money.

Ship-money was raifed, during the fpace of four years. It was computed to yield about 200,000l. a year: confequently, it muft have produced, altogether, the fum of 800,000 l. Its produce.

An attempt was made, during this monarch's reign, not only to maintain a fleet, but alfo to levy, and to fupport an army, without the fanction of parliament. Every county in England was ordered to raife a certain number of horfe and foot, and to furnifh a certain number of carriages, at their own charges, for profecuting the war againft the 9. Levying foldiers.

---

[65] Nothing can be drawn up with more ability, than the general view which Hume has given of the arguments againft fhip-money, vol. vi. p. 314. See alfo Macaulay, Appendix to vol. ii.

[66] 16 Car. I. cap. 14.

Y 2

Scots.

Scots[47]. Thefe military operations were carried on, through the medium of the lords lieutenants, in the different counties, and their conduct was juftified by fome ancient precedents, in times of danger and invafion; but no exprefs ftatute could be produced in fupport of the meafure. It was, therefore, voted illegal by the Long Parliament; and fuch as had exercifed any powers of that nature, were declared guilty of delinquency.

10. Monopolies.

Charles, not contented with the exercife of lucrative prerogatives, on very flender legal pretences, had alfo, rafhly, endeavoured to raife money in oppofition to the exprefs words, or at leaft, in evident contrariety to the fpirit of a recent ftatute. It has already been obferved, that a law was paffed *anno* 1624, by which all monopolies were prohibited: but an exception had been admitted in favour of new inventions; under which flight pretence, the former grievance was renewed, and the kingdom again filled with exclufive patents, to the ruin of induftry and commerce. Not only falt, foap, leather, and other ufeful articles were put under harfh reftrictions; but grants were made out for gauging redherrings, for marking butter cafks, and for gathering rags[48]. The king, afraid of the confequences, or afhamed of having adopted fuch ridiculous expedients for raifing money, abolifhed about thirty of thefe deftructive patents, when he undertook the firft expedition againft Scotland. But the people were not fatisfied with a partial diminution; and the long parliament had no fooner affembled, than it annulled all the remaining monopolies; and as a proof of how much they detefted fo illegal a meafure, expelled at once fuch of its members as were at all concerned in them[49]. It is faid, that Charles had raifed, by thefe patents, about 200,000 *l.* of which (according to Clarendon) fcarcely 1500 *l.* came into the king's coffers.

11. Loans.

It is natural to conjecture, that a prince, reduced to fuch neceffities as Charles experienced, would purfue the ancient practice of exacting compulfive loans from his fubjects; and, indeed, as early as the fecond year of his reign, letters, under the privy feal, were fent to the

[47] Hume, vol. vi. p. 372. In Stevens, p. 279, may be feen lifts of the troops, &c. which each county was ordered to furnifh. This author is much puzzled by the different lifts of horfes, not adverting, that one lift is, of horfes to mount the cavalry, the other, of horfes to draw the carriages with ammunition, &c.

[48] Stevens, p. 283, 284.   [49] Hume, vol. vi. p 374.

2   wealthieft

wealthieft perfons in the kingdom, demanding the loan of certain fums, in proportion to their fuppofed ability; and promifing to repay the money that was borrowed, in the fpace of eighteen months [12]. About 200,000 *l.* was raifed by this unpopular expedient. *Anno* 1626, the loan of 100,000 *l.* was demanded from the city of London, which it had the fpirit to refufe. Nor did the old plan of a benevolence, attempted at the fame time, prove more fuccefsful. But the boldeft meafure of that nature, was the exacting of a general loan. Four fubfidies, and three fifteenths, had been voted by Charles's fecond parliament. A fudden diffolution, however, prevented the grant from paffing into a law; and the king, inftead of calling a new parliament, refolved to demand thofe very fubfidies from the people under the name of a loan. The moft violent and arbitrary meafures were made ufe of to compel the payment. Such as refufed were imprifoned; were loaded with a number of foldiers illegally quartered upon them; and by various other oppreffions, were made fenfible of the king's anger and refentment [11].

The partiality of that able hiftorian Hume, in favour of the houfe of Stuart, is not a little confpicuous, in his calling the moft illegal extortions, by the fofter name of irregular levies of money [12]. But however acts of tyranny may be palliated by ingenious men, yet they will ftill appear to the impartial and the unprejudiced, in their real colours. Charles had ventured to threaten the Commons, if he was not furnifhed with fupplies in a legal manner, that he fhould be obliged to try *new councils* [13]; or, in other words, would raife money without their authority; and a commiffion was iffued accordingly, appointing thirty-three commiffioners to meet, and concert among themfelves, the methods of levying money by taxes, or by other means, " where" (in the words of the commiffion) " form muft be difpenfed with, rather than the " fubftance loft." The intention evidently was, to contrive the means of raifing money by prerogative alone [14]. In confequence of a fpirited

---

[10] Stevens, p. 274.

[11] Many of the lower people were compelled to enlift as foldiers, or feamen; and Glanville, an eminent lawyer, was forced to accept of an office in the navy, for having refufed to contribute. Hume, vol. vi. p. 230.

[12] Hume, vol. vi. p. 295.   [13] Ibid. p. 241, 248.   [14] Ibid. p. 218 and 257.

application

application from the Houfe of Commons, this commiffion was annulled : but it clearly proves in what manner the king would have reigned, had his power been equal to his inclination.

Though this commiffion was cancelled, yet it did not prevent Charles from purfuing many arbitrary meafures, in order to extort money from his fubjects. Large fees were annexed to new invented offices. Every county was obliged to maintain a mufter-mafter, appointed by the crown, for exercifing the militia. The vintners were driven, by the terrors of fines and profecutions, to fubmit to an illegal impofition upon all the wine they retailed. An ancient duty for furnifhing the foldiery with coat and conduct-money, which had long been abolifhed, was revived. It was intended to coin bafe money, and to circulate it by proclamation. Heavy fines were impofed in the ftar-chamber, and high commiffion courts. Sir David Fowles was fined 5000l. for diffuading a friend from compounding with the commiffioners of knighthood. Thirty thoufand pounds were exacted from thofe who had trefpaffed upon an obfolete law againft converting arable lands into pafture. Encroachments on the king's forefts were punifhed in a fimilar manner. Proclamations were iffued, commanding the nobility and gentry to retire to their country feats, and not to fpend their time idly in London. If convicted of trangreffing this arbitrary regulation, they were feverely mulcted by the ftar-chamber. It was contended, that proclamations had equal authority with laws ; and fuch as ventured to difobey them, were heavily fined, and in fome inftances, condemned to the pillory [75]. In fhort, more tyrannical fteps could hardly be taken by the greateft defpot on earth.

Of all the unpopular expedients adopted by Charles, to raife money without the confent of parliament, the only one that had any pretenfions to legality, was that by which, in imitation of precedents, taken notice of in the former part of this work, perfons poffeffed of a certain income, in land, were obliged to receive the order of knighthood. By a law, paffed in the reign of Edward II., a knight's fee was fixed at twenty pounds a year. In the reign of Henry VI., it was raifed to forty pounds. The law, though not repealed, had not been

[75] Hume, vol. vi. 296. Macaulay, vol. ii. p. 218.

enforced

enforced for many years, and was almoft forgotten [76]. But Charles was refolved to revive any act from which profit might be derived; and it is faid, that by compounding with fome, and fining others who re- fufed to appear in obedience to the king's mandate, about 100,000 *l.* was exacted [77]. It was thought, however, not a little oppreffive, that the great decreafe in the value of money fhould not be confidered, and that thofe poffeffed of fo fmall an income as forty pounds a year, fhould be obliged to accept of an honour they were unable to fupport. The letter of the law might be againft them, but its fpirit was evidently in their favour.

There is alfo the ftrongeft reafon to believe, that Charles was de- termined to take any ftep, that ambition or tyranny could dictate, rather than fubmit to the legal trammels of a limited government. It is known, that a commiffion was granted, and even money remitted to Germany, for the purpofe of raifing a thoufand horfe, to be tranf- ported into England. It is urged, in extenuation, that the number was too fmall for eftablifhing a defpotic government in this country. But though the force was apparently trifling, yet the king might eafily have added a formidable body of foot to thefe foreign mercenaries; and thus have been enabled to levy thofe excifes, and other taxes, which, it is faid, he intended to impofe by his own authority [78]. This dangerous meafure was prevented by the interpofition of parliament.

Syftem of military de- fpotifm.

It is hardly to be difputed, that Charles might have got over all his difficulties, if it had not been for the war he rafhly entered into with his fubjects in Scotland. It appears, that his revenue, from 1637, to 1641 inclufive, amounted, *communibus annis*, to 895,819 *l.* 5 *s.* of which, however, 210,493 *l.* 17 *s.* 4 *d.* arofe from fhip-money, and other illegal exactions [79]. But, on the whole, it was fully adequate to the ordinary expences of the crown, though it could not defray the charges of war, and other burthenfome contingencies.

Amount of his revenue

When the fatal conteft, between the king and his parliament, was at laft brought to the decifion of the fword, he found the utmoft difficulty in providing refources for the maintenance of his forces. The capital,

Supplies againft par- liament.

[76] Naunton's Fragmenta Regalia, p. 4.   [77] Stevens, p. 275.
[78] Rufh. vol. i. p. 612.   [79] Comm. Journ. vol. viii. p. 150.

and;

and the wealthieft part of the kingdom, fupported the parliament; and the only money that he could raife, was by pawning the jewels of the crown; by melting down the plate of the two univerfities, which they generoufly fent him; and afterwards, by imitating the example of his opponents in levying affeffments, and even excifes, in thofe diftricts where his authority was acknowledged. But the voluntary contributions of thofe who adhered to the crown were his principal refource. It is faid, that the marquis of Worcefter alone, fupplied the king with 100,000 *l.*; and the exertions of the marquis of Newcaftle, who devoted his whcle fortune to the fupport of the royal caufe, were no lefs remarkable [19].

Tax on cards.   Among the other taxes contrived by this monarch, one deferves to be mentioned on account of its fingularity, namely, a tax upon cards. Every pack was ordered to be *fealed*, by an officer appointed for that purpofe, previoufly to its being fold. The tax was far from being high, nor was it in itfelf exceptionable; but it met with fome oppofition on account of its illegality [20].

Coin.   The additional quantity of fpecie coined during the reign of Charles, when compared to that of his immediate predeceffors, is a ftrong proof how rapidly the wealth and commerce of England were increafing. It is computed by Folkes, that during his reign, 12,096,220*l.* fterling was coined in gold and filver; a greater fum than during the two reigns of James and of Elizabeth. But authors have, in general, omitted to remark, that Spain fent confiderable quantities of bullion to be coined in our mint, which was afterwards carried to Flanders; and the property of which did not belong to the natives of this country. They had only the profit of the coinage, and the benefit of the tranfportation [21].

Petition of right.   This reign is diftinguifhed by the famous petition of rights having paffed into a law; the object of which was to procure a full confirmation of the moft important privileges of the nation. Among the other articles which it contained, fome of which are of fuch moment, as to have produced almoft a total revolution in the nature of our government; there is one claufe by which it is particularly declared, " that no gift,

---

[19] Stevens, p. 288.   [21] Rufh. vol. ii. p. 103.

[20] Walker's Hift. Independ. part ii. p. 193.

" loan,

" loan, benevolence, tax, or such like charge, shall be exacted without " common consent, by act of parliament[1]." Since this valuable statute was enacted, these ancient modes of extortion have never been revived.

The fatal cataftrophe of this monarch's reign, is too well known to require being mentioned. In justice, however, to Charles, it may be remarked, that it was natural for a prince, like him, educated with high notions of the inherent prerogatives of the crown, supported by the example of his predecessors, and ignorant that a monarchy could exist under such limitations as parliament wished to establish, should gradually be led into that train of conduct which he unfortunately pursued. Indeed, when once suspicions and jealousies arise, it is impossible to say, to what lengths the most respectable characters may be hurried, amidst the heat of party, and the ardour of inteftine violence. On the other hand, it is equally necessary to observe, in behalf of those illustrious patriots, who first resisted the exorbitant claims of the crown, that whilst a Pym, a Hambden, and an Essex, conducted the opposition in parliament, though they demanded rather harsh concessions, yet that they still had the establishment of a limited monarchy in view. The side to which they leaned, that of liberty, was founded on the most noble, and the most generous principles. They knew well, that advantage must be taken of the existing circumstances in their favour; that such another opportunity might never again recur; and that the crown flood a better chance of adding to its prerogative, than the people to their privileges. As to the violences of an after period, the trial of the king, his condemnation and death, and the establishment of military despotism under Cromwell, they took place when these patriots were no more; when civil government was at an end, and when England lay at the mercy of an ignorant, fanatical, and desperate soldiery, headed by a daring, artful, and profligate usurper.

Reflection.

The Commonwealth.

Under this general name, it is proposed to comprehend the various republican and military systems of government, which took place from

[1] 17 Car. I. cap. 41.

the

the commencement of the civil war to the reftoration : An æra, during
which the public expences were very great, and indifputably fuperior
to thofe of any former period in our hiftory. Even before the war
broke out, parliament found it neceffary to provide a confiderable fupply
for difbanding the troops which the king had raifed for the reduction
of Scotland ; and to vote 850 *l.* a day, for the fubfiftence of the Scotch
army, to prevent its plundering the northern counties of England, of
which it was then in poffeffion. Three hundred thoufand pounds alfo
were granted to the Scots, as a reward for their brotherly affiftance [14].
But thefe were inconfiderable fums, when compared to the heavy
charges which were afterwards incurred.

Expences.

It is a faying attributed to Milton, that, as a republic was the leaft
expenfive, it was confequently the beft of governments ; nay, that the
trappings of monarchy would defray all the charges of an ordinary commonwealth. The hiftory of the republic of England does by no means
juftify this obfervation.

It is not propofed, however, minutely to inveftigate the expences incurred during the time of the commonwealth : for, it is impoffible now
to make up an accurate ftatement of them, in confequence of the great
fluctuation and inftability of government, and of the frauds practifed
by thofe to whom the cuftody of the public money was committed. It
will be fufficient to remark, in general, that the tedious and bloody
conteft which parliament carried on againft the crown, was attended
with charges, perpetually increafing, in proportion as the armies became
more numerous, and hoftilities · were more extended : That confiderable expences were incurred by the republic, before the reduction of
Ireland was accomplifhed, and before Scotland (where, after the death
of his father, Charles II. was proclaimed king), could be finally fubdued :
That fuccefsful wars were carried on againft the Dutch, who were
obliged to crouch under the fuperior ftrength and vigour of the new
republic ; and againft the enfeebled monarchy of Spain, from whom

[14] Macaulay, vol. iii. p. 22.

two

two important poffeffions, Jamaica and Dunkirk, were conquered during the adminiftration of Cromwell : And that, even in time of peace, a formidable fleet, and a numerous army, were maintained, to fupport the authority of the new government at home, and to render it more refpectable abroad. But all thefe fervices, however extenfive and important, could not have exhaufted the immenfe treafures, which, from various fources, flowed into the coffers of the republic.

Refources.

When the long parliament affembled, no idea was entertained of the bloody and deftructive difturbances which afterwards took place. It proceeded, therefore, to levy money conformably to ancient ufage ; and, inftead of affeffments, and other modes of exaction afterwards practifed, fix fubfidies, and a poll-tax equal to as many more, were granted, for difbanding the Englifh and Scotch armies, who then raged in the very bowels of the kingdom. The produce of thefe grants, however (for they were given at different times), was not confided to the treafury, but was ordered to be paid to parliamentary commiffioners appointed for that fpecial purpofe.

It was foon difcovered, that the difputes between the crown and parliament had been carried to fuch a height, that they muft unavoidably proceed to fome fatal extremities ; and at the commencement of the civil war, the conduct of the parliament was fo popular, and it was held in fuch high eftimation by the public, that incredible fums of money were raifed by voluntary contribution. The plate of almoft every inhabitant in London was brought in, to be coined for its fupport : no article, however mean, no ornament, however valuable, was fpared. The very thimbles and bodkins of the women were not withheld : every one was anxious to maintain the caufe of the godly againft the king and the malignants [s]. *(marginal note: Voluntary contributions.)*

But it was impoffible, that an expenfive war could be long fupported upon fo flender a foundation, as the temporary fervour of the people. *(marginal note: Land tax.)*

[s] Hume, vol. vi. p. 539, 540.

Z 2   The

The parliament therefore refolved, in order to provide for the better fuftenance of their forces, to levy affeffiments on the perfonal and landed property of the people. Thefe affeffiments varied, according to the exigencies of the times, from 35,000 *l*. to 120,000 *l*. a month. They were found fo productive, and in every refpect fo much fuperior to the ancient mode of fubfidies, that under the denomination of a land-tax, they have fince formed a very confiderable branch of the public revenue.

Weekly meal.

But armies muft be recruited as well as raifed; and for that purpofe, a very fingular impoft, fuited to the fpirit of the times, was laid on by the parliament. Every perfon was obliged to retrench a meal a week, and to pay the money thereby faved into the public treafury. This whimfical tax produced 608,400 *l*. in the fix years during which it was impofed[15].

Excife.

To the long parliament we owe the firft eftablifhment of excifes in this country. It is fuppofed, that the famous Pym was the perfon by whom the plan was originally propofed. It was at firft laid upon liquors only; and it was folemnly declared, that, at the end of the war, all excifes fhould be abolifhed. But the conteft continuing longer than was expected, this obnoxious mode of levying money was extended to bread, meat, falt, and many other neceffary articles. The excife on bread and meat was afterwards repealed[17].

Cuftoms.

In the time of the commonwealth, confiderable additions were made to the revenue of the cuftoms, by duties upon coals and currants. Four fhillings a chaldron upon coals, levied at Newcaftle, brought in about 50,000 *l*.[19] The cuftoms and excife, notwithftanding the deftruction with which civil wars are neceffarily accompanied, had become fo productive, that Cromwell, *anno* 1657, was offered 1,100,000 *l*. a year for a leafe of both the branches.

aft office.

The eftablifhment of a poft office, upon a productive and permanent footing, was principally owing to the long parliament. By their attention, and the wifdom of their regulations, it not only yielded 10,000 *l*. *per annum*, but alfo faved an annual expence of 7000 *l*. which the public

[15] Stevens, p. 290.
[17] Walker's Hift. Prof. p. 8. part ii. p. 193. 247.   Black. vol. i. p. 318, 319, 320.
[19] Walker's Hift. Part ii. p. 150.

was

was obliged to pay for the maintenance of poſtmaſters. It is ſingular, that the ſucceſs with which this mercantile project has been attended, ſhould not have encouraged the public to engage in other plans of a ſimilar nature.

When the parliament took the entire government of the country into their own hands, care was taken to ſequeſter the revenue of the crown, and to appropriate it to their own purpoſes: nay, the profits of ward-ſhip, fines of alienation, and other feudal prerogatives, though ſuppoſed to be inſeparably annexed to the crown, were rigorouſly exacted. Purveyance alone was given up, a uſeleſs privilege for a republic, and. ſo generally obnoxious, that Charles II. was obliged to abandon it, after the reſtoration.

Feudal pre-rogatives.

· In the reign of James I. a patent had been granted by the crown for the ſole licenſing of inns and alehouſes. But in conſequence of the ſpirited interpoſition of parliament, this monopoly had been annulled. It was not, however, the propriety of the tax, but the legality of the impoſition, with which the Commons were diſſatisfied. Accordingly, it was one of the new duties with which it reſolved to impoſe. The tax, it was imagined, would not only prove productive in reſpect to income; but would alſo operate as a neceſſary regulation of the police ; by preventing improper perſons from keeping houſes open for the reception of the public.

Wine licences.

The moſt popular of all the modes which parliament purſued for raiſing money, was that of ſequeſtrating the income of certain lucrative offices, and applying the produce for the ſervice of the public. It is not known what particular offices were thus appropriated ; but it appears, that in the ſpace of fifteen years, they yielded 850,000*l.*: conſequently, their value muſt have amounted to about 56,666*l. per annum.*

Public of-fices.

The value of the royal domains, as well as of the eſtates of individuals, was not a little diminiſhed, by ſo long and deſtructive a conteſt : and yet parliament, either driven to it by its neceſſities, or deſirous of aboliſhing every veſtige of monarchy, and in hopes that it would never be re-eſtabliſhed, diſpoſed of all the crown-lands and eſtates belonging to the principality of Wales, at the rate of ten years purchaſe. Nay, the houſes, furniture, and other perſonal effects belonging to the king,. were·

Crown lands,.

were fold at very moderate prices. But the reftoration of the royal family made thefe bargains dearer than was expected.

Church lands. The active part which the bifhops, and the clergy in general took in fupport of the royal caufe, naturally drew upon them the indignation of the oppofite party, and rendered their property not a little infecure when the parliament became fuccefsful [17]. But the fyftem of diminifhing the opulence of the church, was carried to much greater lengths than had ever been apprehended. Not only the lands of the bifhops, and of the deans and chapters, but even the rectory and glebe lands were fold, fome at ten, and others at twelve years purchafe. The tythes alfo were fequeftrated for the ufe of the ftate [18]; and, inftead of fettled minifters, fome wild enthufiafts propofed to have lecturers wandering about the country, in the primitive manner of the apoftolic times whofe falaries would prove but little burthenfome to the public exchequer.

Plunder of the royalifts. The victorious party, as is ufual in civil wars, adopted every means in their power to diminifh the wealth, and to punifh the fuppofed guilt and offences of their adverfaries. The prifoners they took, if particularly obnoxious, were put to death; if otherwife, were obliged to pay heavy ranfoms for obtaining their liberty. It is faid, that under colour of malignancy, about one-half of the perfonal, as well as landed property of the kingdom was fequeftrated, and either fold at low prices to the friends of thofe who were in power, or heavy compofitions were demanded, if reftored to the original proprietors [19]. Compulfive loans were alfo exacted from *heart malignants*, or perfons fufpected of fecretly favouring the royal caufe. Indeed, the miferable individuals who were comprehended in that defcription, were compelled to furnifh fuch fums of money, by way of loan, as were often attended with utter ruin to themfelves and their families.

Extortions. Under fo military and tyrannical a government, a variety of oppreffive exactions muft neceffarily have taken place. Among many others,

[17] On the 3d of April 1650, a commiffion was iffued, to enquire upon oath, into the number and yearly value of all rectories, vicarages, &c. purfuant to an act made June 8, 1649. The originals are faid to have been burned; but there is one copy in the Rolls chapel, and another at the archbifhop's library at Lambeth, in eighteen thick folio volumes. Hutchins's Dorfetfhire, Introd. p. 39.

[18] Walker's Hift. part ii. p. 198.　　　[19] Hume, vol. vii. p. 93.

　　　　　　　　　　　　　　　　　　　　　　　　　　　　that

that of free quarter was particularly complained of. The foldiers were billeted upon private houfes; paid nothing for their maintenance; were fpies upon the actions of thofe upon whom they were quartered; and though guilty of the moft fhocking abufes, their crimes were only fubject to the cognizance of their own officers; no civil court, or magiftrate, daring to interfere[90]. But when Cromwell affumed the government of the ftate, a general fyftem of oppreffion was for fome time put in practice[91]. The whole kingdom was divided into twelve diftricts, each of which was entrufted to the care of a major general, who was empowered to levy any tax the Protector thought proper to impofe. An edict was iffued, commanding the exaction of the tenth penny from all the royal party; and this oppreffive tax, known by the name of *decimation*[92], Cromwell's military fubftitutes very rigoroufly enforced. The whole country was expofed to their extortions; hardly any diftinction was made; nor were the firmeft friends to the exifting government always exempted.

The regular and permanent income of England, during the adminiftration of Cromwell, was about 1,517,274 *l*. 17 *s*. 1 *d*. Scotland, then fubject to the fame government, yielded 143,652 *l*. 11 *s*. 11 *d*.; and Ireland 207,790 *l*. making, in all, the fum of 1,868,719 *l*. 9 *s*.[91] But if all the exactions which were extorted from the people at that time are accumulated, they amount to a fum almoft incredible. It is afferted, in a treatife, printed *anno* 1647, that in four years, 17,512,400 *l*. or about 4,378,100 *l. per annum* were raifed[94]. Walker afferts, that in five years, forty millions had been collected[95]; but this feems to be a confiderable exaggeration[96]. The following account contains as full a ftatement of the money levied, during this whole period, as can now be procured.

Amount of the permanent income.

---

90 Walker's Hift. part i. p. 65, 66, 67.　　91 Hume, vol. vii. p. 244.

91 Walker's Hift. part iv. p. 27.　　92 Comm. Journ. vol. vii. p. 627, &c.

94 London's account, or a calculation of the arbitrary taxations within the lines of communication, during four years of the war, printed *anno* 1647.　　95 Hift. p. 8.

96 It is a ftrong proof of Walker's exaggeration, that the author of the treatife abovementioned (called London's Account), who makes out his calculations in the moft unfavourable manner to the parliament, fhould ftate the firft four years at only feventeen millions.

ABSTRACT

ABSTRACT of the Money raifed in England from Nov. 3, 1640,
to Nov. 5, 1659.

Six fubfidies, at 50,000 _l._ cach	£ 300,000
Poll money and aſſeſſments, to diſband the Scots and Engliſh armies	800,000
Voluntary contributions for the fupport of the good cauſe againſt malignants	300,000
Ditto, for the relief of the Iriſh proteſtants	180,000
Land-tax, or various aſſeſſments, for the maintenance of the army	32,172,321
Exciſe for fixteen years, at 500,000 _l. per annum_	8,000,000
Tunnage and poundage for 19 years, at 400,000 _l._ a year	7,600,000
Duty on coals	850,000
Ditto, on currants	51,000
Poftage of letters	301,000
Weekly meal for fix years	608,400
Court of wards, and other feudal prerogatives	1,400,000
Wine licences	312,200
Vintners delinquency	4,000
Offices fequeftered for the public fervice	850,000
Sequeftrations of the lands of biſhops, deans, and inferior clergy, for four years	3,528,632
Tenths of all the clergy, and other exactions from the church	1,600,320
Sale of church lands	10,035,663
Fee farm rents for twelve years	2,963,176
Other rents belonging to the crown, and the principality of Wales	376,000
Sale of the crown lands and principality (120,000 _l. per annum_)	1,200,000
Ditto of foreft lands and houfes, &c. belonging to the king	656,000
Sequeftrations of the eftates and compofitions with private individuals in England	4,564,986
Compofitions with delinquents in Ireland	1,000,000
Sale of the eftates of delinquents in England	2,245,000
Ditto of Iriſh lands	1,322,500
Ranfom of captives	102,000
New River water	8,000
	£ 83,331,198

In the account which Stevens gives us of the money raiſed during this period, there feems to
be a variety of miftakes. He ftates the fix fubfidies at 600,000 _l._, though they only produced
300,000 _l._ See Walker, p. 7. Tunnage and poundage he calculates only at the rate of
300,000 _l_ a year, though it often exceeded 500,000 _l_, and, at a medium, muft have been
400,00 _l._; and in the whole account, there is a ftrange confufion between income and expences. Thus there is ftated, in the account of the money raiſed, the charge of juftice, and
the fums voted to the members of the houfe, and given them by way of free-gift. The firft
voluntary contribution (omitted by Stevens) is put down only at 300,000 _l._, though probably
more productive.

This

This is the beft information which it is at prefent poffible to obtain with regard to the money levied in the time of the commonwealth: from which it appears, that during the fhort period of nineteen years, above eighty millions muft have been raifed, and confequently, one year with another, about 4,385,850*l. per annum:* but a confiderable part of that immenfe treafure was either lavifhed by parliament upon its own members, or was fraudulently embezzled.

By the old law of parliament, every member was entitled to receive wages, from the place he reprefented, to defray the charges of his journey, and the expences incurred during his refidence in the capital. But the members of the long parliament, when it affumed the government of the country, inftead of applying to their refpective conftituents, voted to each member, for his own private ufe, at firft four pounds a week, and afterwards, it is faid, diftributed among themfelves, out of the public treafury, about 300,000*l.* a year". Nay, under the pretence of rewarding the godly for their fervices in the good caufe, unbounded largeffes were beftowed. Lenthal, the fpeaker, received 6000*l.* at once, befides offices to the amount of 7,730*l.* a year. Bradfhaw, prefident of the high court of juftice, by whom the king was condemned, had the prefent of an eftate worth 1000*l.* a year, and the king's houfe at Eltham, for the active part he took in that memorable tranfaction; and in free gifts to the faints, the fum of 679,800*l.* was publickly expended". *[marginal note: Penfions and gifts.]*

The parliament is alfo accufed of fuffering the moft enormous frauds to be perpetrated with impunity. Inftead of the public accounts being examined at the Exchequer, where peculation could with difficulty efcape detection, every branch of the revenue, and every article of expence, was intrufted to committees of the houfe, who appropriated whatever fum they thought proper to their own private ufe". By thefe frauds, the parliament was difabled from paying the army regularly. Its arrears amounted to 331,000*l.*, and that mutiny, which proved the principal fource of Cromwell's exaltation, was owing to the *[marginal note: Public frauds.]*

97 Walker's Hift. Pref. p. 3.
98 Ibid. part ii. p. 151. 252. Part i. p. 143. 149. 166, 167, 168, 169, 170, &c. and part ii. p. 192, 206. 209. 248. Stevens, p. 294.
99 Hume, vol. vii. p. 92.

A a   indignation

indignation with which the troops faw the members of the houfe of commons rioting in wealth, procured by public plunder, whilft they, who had fought their battles, could hardly provide themfelves with fub-fiftence. They loudly complained, " that parliament beftowed upon " its own members 1000*l.* a week out of the public treafury, whilft " the foldiers wants were great, and the people in the utmoft ne-" ceffity [100]."

Secret intel-ligence.   It is faid that Cromwell expended 60,000*l.* a year in procuring intel-ligence; a circumftance which has been greatly celebrated, and contri-buted much to the charaĉter he has obtained for political ability: but it is highly probable that he fpent more in procuring perfonal than pub-lic intelligence. Indeed, .furrounded as he was with many powerful and defperate enemies, fuch arts were the only means by which his fafety could in any degree be fecured.

Debts of the republic.   It is faid, that the parliament left about 500,000*l.* in the treafury, and ftores to the value of 700,000*l.*, when its authority was abolifhed by Cromwell; and yet fuch was the expence of his adminiftration, that he died indebted to the amount of 2,474,290*l.* · It principally, how-ever, confifted in arrears to the army and navy, and therefore was paid even after the reftoration.

General fur-vey.   It was propofed, during Cromwell's adminiftration, to take a gene-ral furvey of the whole kingdom, in imitation of that taken in the reign of Henry VIII. It was begun in London, and the neighbour-hood, and certain committees were appointed, *to enquire upon oath, and certify the improved value of every man's eflate, both real and perfonal* [101]. But the attempt was, after all, given up: indeed, when thofe who were in power exaĉted what money they thought proper under any pretence, however frivolous, as delinquency, malignancy, &c. it was unneceffary to be at the trouble of inveftigating the wealth and ability of indivi-duals, for the fake of any regular fyftem of taxation.

[100] Walker's Hift. part ii. p. 109.   [101] Ibid. part ii. p. 185.

CHARLES

CHARLES II.

The reftoration, however paffionately defired by the people, and though, on the whole, attended with confiderable advantages to the public, from the re-eftablifhment of the ancient conftitution, and the deftruction of anarchy and military ufurpation, was neverthelefs far from being accompanied with all thofe beneficial confequences that might naturally have been expected. The diffolute character of Charles II., the bigotry of his brother James, by whofe advice public affairs were principally conducted, and the jealoufy of fuch as were ftill tinctured with republican principles, which led them to view every meafure of the court with fufpicion and difguft, rendered the greater part of his reign neither happy at home nor honourable abroad. But the conclufion of it, when he fubmitted to be the tool of Lewis XIV., when he determined to govern without affembling any parliament, and when it became the doctrine of the court that it was better for a king of England to be the penfioner of France than to be controlled by five hundred of his own infolent fubjects, bore but little refemblance indeed, to the legal adminiftration of the limited fovereign of a free people.

The materials with which we are furnifhed by hiftorians, and by the public records, with refpect to this monarch's income and expenditure, are fo numerous, that it is difficult to give a concife view of the fubject.

Expences.

The expences he incurred were either permanent or incidental.

During the reign of Charles, we firft perceive what may be called a peace-eftablifhment. Ever fince the reftoration, it has been thought neceffary to provide, even in time of peace, for the national protection and defence; and hence have arifen permanent, naval, military, and ordnance expences. *1. Permanent expences.*

The navy, at this period, required about 500,000l. a year, exclufively of the fums laid out in time of war, and occafional grants from parliament. But this, though a confiderable part of Charles's revenue, was *The Navy.*

A a 2

hardly

hardly fufficient to preferve that fuperiority in maritime power, which Britain ought ever to maintain. The ftrength of Holland, at fea, was nearly equal; and that ambitious monarch Lewis XIV. exerted all the abilities of his ftatefmen, and all the wealth of his fubjects, in attempting to raife a navy adequate to the fupport of his proud and lofty pretenfions to the univerfal monarchy of Europe.

Army. Charles was the firft king of England who kept up any body of troops in time of peace. Before his reign, the fovereigns of this country, confiding in the affections and native valour of their people, maintained no ftanding forces, and neither had guards to attend them in their progrefs, nor to ftand as centinels at their gates. This alteration in our domeftic œconomy has often been condemned; and yet the conduct of other powers, in keeping up formidable bodies of experienced veterans, rendered it to a certain degree indifpenfably neceffary. The annual expence of this monarch, for guards and garrifons, amounted to about 202,000*l.* and the number of his troops varied from four to eight thoufand men. Even that fmall body excited the fufpicion and jealoufy of the public; and, by a vote of the houfe of commons, *anno* 1679, was declared contrary to law[1].

Ordnance. The ordnance, including ordinary and extraordinary expences, amounted only to about 40,000*l.* a year: a very moderate charge, when compared to modern eftimates: but it was then imagined, that fortifications were unneceffary in England; nor had the artillery become fo important a branch of the military department.

Civil lift. The nature and amount of the civil lift, and of the other expences of the crown, during this reign, are fo clearly illuftrated by the following ftate of its propofed expenditure for the year 1676, that any farther explanation feems to be unneceffary.

[1] Hume, vol. viii. p. 106.

Expences

Expences of the Crown for one year, as allotted by the Council, January 26, 1675-6.

Houſehold	£ 52,247
Buildings and repairs	10,000
Privy purſe	36,000
For the queen	23,000
Public intelligence	5,000
Treaſurer of the chamber	20,000
Great wardrobe	16,000
Band of penſioners	3,000
Robes	4,000
Jewel office	4,000
Penſions, including the queen's mother, Duke of York, &c.	87,000
Ambaſſadors	40,000
Judges, maſters in Chancery, &c.	49,000
Maſter of the horſe	10,000
Caſual diſburſements	10,000
Hawks, harriers tents, tails, &c.	1,500
Secret ſervice money	20,000
New years gifts	3,600
Tower expences for priſoners	768
Management of exciſe and cuſtoms	63,500
Angel gold for healing medals	2,000
Liberates out of the Exchequer	1,500
	£ 462,115

Peace Eſtabliſhment.

Navy	£ 300,000	
Army	212,000	552,000
Ordnance	40,000	
		£ 1014,115

Miſcellaneous Expences.

Garriſon of Tangier	57,200
Intereſt of the king's debts	100,000
	£ 1,171,315

It is probable, however, that the permanent expences of government were in general more conſiderable; for previous allotments, ſtrict computations,

computations, and plaufible eftimates, can hardly ever be rigidly adhered to.

2. Incidental expences.
The parliament, foon after the reftoration, had voted the king a revenue of 1,200,000*l.* a year[101]. But that fum, which would have defrayed the ordinary expences of the crown, was never fully made up: nor were its deficiencies compenfated by new and additional fupplies. The king, at the fame time, incurred many temporary and incidental expences of fo heavy a nature that he was kept in perpetual diftrefs.

Expences on the reftoration.
At the conclufion of the civil war, every veftige of royalty had been annihilated. The king's palaces and furniture had been fold; the jewels of the crown had been difpofed of; and every meafure had been taken, as if monarchy were never again to be the eftablifhed government of England. Parliament, therefore, was obliged to grant confiderable fums to defray the expences of the coronation, and to make up for thofe heavy loffes which the crown had fuftained. By two different acts, 140,000*l.* were raifed and appropriated to thefe purpofes[104]: and afterwards, a free and voluntary prefent was given to his majefty, the produce of which is unknown.[105]

Debts of the crown.
Debts to a large amount were certainly contracted by the king, during his refidence on the continent, and by his father, during the courfe of the civil war; both of which it was incumbent on this monarch to difcharge. But, above all, Charles owed a debt of gratitude to the unhappy cavaliers who had ruined themfelves by their exertions in the royal caufe, which it was hardly poffible, with a fmall revenue, fully to difcharge. But he ought furely to have fubjected himfelf to any pecuniary difficulties, rather than to have fuffered fo many zealous friends to continue in fuch diftrefs. Parliament voted 60,000*l.* to be diftributed among that unfortunate defcription of men[106]; and this was the principal recompence they received for their loyalty and fervices. Some attention alfo was paid to thofe who had materially contributed to the king's prefervation after the battle of Worcefter; and Charles fometimes could not refift the accounts he received of their calamitous fituation, but occafionally fupplied them with what money he could poffibly fpare, from the rapacity of his courtiers.

101 Comm. Journ. vol. viii. p. 150.   104 12 Car. II. c. 21. 29.
105 13 Car. II. c. 13.   105 Ibid. c. 13, 14.

One

One of the firſt and moſt neceſſary ſteps after the reſtoration, was Diſbanding the army. the diſbanding of the republican army, which had occaſioned ſo many revolutions, and had been ſo much inured to rapine and ſlaughter. The expence of this meaſure was conſiderable; for it was requiſite to pay up their arrears, and other legal demands, previouſly to their diſmiſſion. It is ſaid that the king, when he reviewed this formidable body, before it was diſbanded, could not avoid expreſſing his wiſhes to retain them in his pay; and nothing but Clarendon's weight and influence could have prevented his attempting, by ſome evaſion or other, to have continued them in his ſervice.

The fortreſs of Tangiers in Africa, was included in the dowry which Tangiers,. Charles received with Catharine of Portugal: and the poſſeſſion of it was ſuppoſed to be of conſiderable uſe in protecting our trade to the Mediteranean. Great ſums of money, therefore, had been expended in the improvement of the harbour, and in adding to the fortifications; and the garriſon maintained there coſt from 50,000 l. to 60,000 l. per annum. But this expence did not continue throughout the whole of Charles's reign: for when he found that it was impoſſible for him to depend upon regular ſupplies from parliament, he ordered the town to be abandoned, the mole to be entirely deſtroyed, and the garriſon to be brought over to England.

· The war which Charles entered into with the Dutch, was unjuſt in Firſt Dutch war. its commencement, and impolitic in its continuance. They were willing to have given him every ſatisfaction he could reaſonably deſire; and in conſequence of the injuſtice of his conduct, he had not only to contend with the republic of Holland, then in the zenith of its power, but alſo with France and Denmark, by whom that ſtate was at laſt ſupported: and however keenly his ſubjects might at firſt engage in ſo unjuſtifiable a quarrel, from commercial jealouſy of their neighbours, yet he had every reaſon to expect that they would ſoon grow weary of furniſhing him with ſupplies, unleſs encouraged by the moſt ſignal ſucceſſes. Parliament voted the ſum of 5,483,845 l. for carrying on the war. But the funds appropriated to the purpoſe were not ſufficiently productive. The war coſt the Dutch forty millions of livres a year, above three millions ſterling [107]. The only advantage which England received from it was the

[107] Hume, vol. vii. p. 419. Note.

acquiſition

acquifition of New York: a poor recompence for the difgrace at Chatham, and the blood and treafure wafted in fo iniquitous a conteft! *.

Second Dutch war.

Of all the combinations which modern Europe can produce for the deftruction of any particular ftate, perhaps that between France and England, for the annihilation of the Dutch republic, is the leaft to be defended. Louis had fome reafon to be diffatisfied with Holland, for having deferted his alliance; and it might be expected that a defpótic monarch, impelled by political ambition, and religious bigotry, would rejoice in an opportunity of difplaying his ftrength, even if he did not add to his dominion; and would willingly contribute to humble the pride, and to crufh the power of a proteftant republic. But in Charles were united, upon this occafion, the meaneft treachery, the moft infatiable appetite for plunder, and a total difregard for the public interefts of his own kingdoms. His people, afhamed of the attempt, and dreading the confequences of its fuccefs, refufed to give him any confiderable affiftance; and by this negative fuccour to the Dutch, greatly contributed to their fafety. During the war, the fum of 1,238,750l. was voted by parliament; but the object of it was to procure the recall of the declaration of indulgence: and it was finally granted to recompenfe the king for agréeing to its being annulled.

Preparations againft France.

The only other material warlike expence, during this reign[101], was the making preparations for a rupture with France, to which the king was ftrongly urged by his parliament. Some fupplies were granted for that purpofe, which were faithfully applied: and it is alfo fuppofed that Charles added confiderable fums out of his own perfonal revenue. But the king and his parliament had become fo jealous of each other, that the affair ended in nothing; and in confequence of thefe unfortunate differences, the allies of England were left at the mercy of France, and obliged, at the congrefs of Nimequen, to accept of any terms that Louis thought proper to prefcribe.

Profufenefs.

Anno 1675.

The difgraces of this monarch's reign were greatly owing to his prodigality. In one of his fpeeches to parliament, he confeffed that he had not been altogether fo frugal as he might have been, and refolved to be for the future. With a narrow revenue, he endeavoured, during the

---

[101] Some affiftance was given to Portugal; an expedition fent againft Algiers; and fome difturbances quelled in Virginia. But the expence could not be very great.

4   greater

greater part of his reign, to support a splendid court, profuse mistresses, and rapacious favourites: but when he found that it was necessary, in consequence of disputes with his commons, to alter the former tenor of his life, he displayed a firmness and strength of mind, of which he was supposed incapable. He became as much distinguished for œconomy as he had been for profusion; and, greatly retrenching his expenditure, he was able to carry on the usual routine of government, for the space of about three years, upon his own revenue, without the assistance of any supply from parliament: and it is said that he had determined to alter the whole system of his public and private conduct, and to throw himself upon the affections of his people, when death interposed, and proved how dangerous it is to procrastinate such resolutions [109].

Resources.

Such were the expences which Charles incurred. His power and ability to defray these heavy charges arose from a permanent income—from parliamentary grants—and from miscellaneous resources.

When the commons took into confideration the settlement of the king's revenue, they found that his father's income had amounted to about 900,000*l.* a year; and they came to a resolution, that the permanent income of the crown should be made up 1,200,000*l.* The following are the principal branches of which it was intended to be composed.

One of the first acts, passed after the restoration, contained a grant of the subsidy of tunnage and poundage for the king's life. This act is, by persons conversant in that branch of the revenue, commonly known by the name of *the great statute* [110], on account of its being the foundation of our modern custom-house duties; and the rates thereby laid on are called *the old subsidy* [111], being a complete legal confirmation of all the ancient duties which had been formerly imposed. It is also remarkable from the rates varying according to different circumstances. Aliens were to pay 6*l. per* tun on wine imported: natives 4*l.* 10*s.* in London,

1. Permanent income.

Customs.

[109] Hume, vol. viii. p. 209. [110] Forster, introd. p. 40.
[111] 12 Car. II. c. 4. Smith's Wealth of Nations, vol. ii. p. 495.

and

and only 3 *l.* in other parts. Thus the higheſt duty was exacted in the capital, where the people were the moſt wealthy, and conſequently the beſt able to afford it.

Feudal pre-rogatives. The only ſtipulation that was made at this time, with the crown, in any reſpect beneficial to the people, was the abolition of the feudal rights, and incidents of wardſhip, marriage, livery, and purveyance, which, ſince the reign of William the Norman, had proved ſo grievous a load upon the inhabitants of this country. One would naturally have imagined that a ſcheme ſo generally uſeful could hardly have met with an opponent: yet a well-meaning and intelligent author has written a voluminous quarto, to prove the fatal conſequences that would neceſſarily reſult from the alteration[112]. Fortunately the event has fully diſproved his gloomy predictions.

Origin of the heredi-tary exciſe. Though the propriety of annihilating ſo obnoxious a branch of the revenue as the feudal prerogatives was pretty generally acknowledged, yet it was a matter of conſiderable difficulty to determine how to make up the deficiency. In ſtrict juſtice, thoſe ought to have been loaded with the payment of the commutation who were liable to the former burden; and in the reign of James, when the ſame plan was in agitation, it was propoſed that, in exchange, an annual fee farm rent ſhould be ſettled, and inſeparably annexed to the crown[113]. But exciſes having been introduced by the long parliament, and paid without much oppoſition or complaint, inſtead of a land-tax, an exciſeable duty of fifteen pence *per* barrel upon all beer and ale, and a proportionable ſum upon other liquors ſold in the kingdom, was eſtabliſhed; which, together with the profits of wine licences, it was calculated would produce from 200,000 *l.* to 300,000 *l.* a year, and was conſidered to be an ample compenſation.

Hearthmo-ney. But the income which parliament had voted as neceſſary for the public ſervice could not be raiſed without the aid of ſome new additional impoſition; and the duty of hearthmoney was at laſt granted to the

---

[112] The antiquity, legality, reaſon, duty, and *neceſſity,* of pre-emption and purveyance for the King; by Fabian Philips. London, printed *anno* 1663. 4to. in 495 pages.

[113] Blackſt. Comm. vol. ii. p. 77.

king

king and his fucceffors[114]. This was a tax of two fhillings for every hearth in all houfes paying to church and poor; and notwithftanding the popular objections which have been urged againft it, there is no well-founded reafon to call it either burdenfome or unequal, and it is ftill paid in Ireland without inconvenience or complaint.

The income which was in general collected from the various branches of the crown revenue, during this reign, will appear fufficiently evident from the following ftatement:

Account of the permanent Income of the Crown, *anno* 1663.

Cuftoms	—	—	—	—	£ 400,000 0
Royal domains	—	—	—	—	100,000 0
Dean Foreft	—	—	—	—	5,000 0
Poft office	—	—	—	—	26,000 0
Hereditary excife	—	—	—	—	274,950 0
Hearthmoney	—	—	—	—	170,603 12
Firft fruits and tenths	—	—	—	—	18,800 0
Coinage and pre-emption of tin	—	—	—	12,000 0
Wine licences	—	—	—	—	20,000 0
Mifcellaneous branches	—	—	—	—	54,356 14

[115] £ 1,081,710 6

It appears, from this ftatement, that the parliament did not make up the full income which it had voted. When the firft fervor of the reftoration was over, they probably repented of the rafh vote they had haftily come to, and perceived the neceffity of preferving the crown dependent upon the people. They confidered that they had beftowed a fceptre upon Charles, when his fituation was accounted to be the moft defperate; and they thought it unneceffary to accompany fo fplendid a gift with advantages greatly fuperior to what his anceftors had enjoyed.

[114] Hume (vol. vii. p. 377.) ftates, that it was only granted *during the king's life.* This, and fome other trifling miftakes of that excellent hiftorian, fhould be attended to in the future editions of his works. The firft act by which hearthmoney was granted was 13 Car. II. c. 10. [115] Comm. Journ. vol. viii. p. 498.

Hiftorians

Hiftorians differ greatly, whether the parliaments which Charles
affembled were fufficiently liberal to that monarch. Thofe who compare their grants with the profufenefs of their fucceffors, condemn them
as too parfimonious, and attribute to that circumftance a confiderable
fhare of the difgraces of his reign. Whereas others, who compare
their amount with thofe of preceding parliaments, accufe them of
prodigality; and contend that none but a penfionary houfe of commons could be fo lavifh. The fact feems to have been, that when parliament difcovered the king's tendency to profufion, and the inftability
of his natural character, they were afraid of trufting him with large
fupplies, and were determined, unlefs he purfued meafures for the
general good, totally to refufe their affiftance.—   —

The modes adopted to raife the money thus occafionally granted were
by poll taxes; by an addition to the excife and cuftoms by fubfidies;
by a land-tax; by a tax on perfonal property; and by a fpecies of
ftamp duty on legal proceedings.   ·   .

, Three different poll taxes were granted during Charles's reign; one
in particular *anno* 1660, for difbanding the army, which was intended
to raife 400,000*l.* But though every perfon in the kingdom, above
fixteen years of age, not receiving alms, was charged fixpence, and
heavy rates were impofed upon men of property and rank, yet it was fo
negligently collected that it produced, on the 24th of November 1660,
only 252,167*l.*[116]: nor does it appear that there was afterwards any
addition.

By different acts, additional duties were laid upon the importation of
wine and on the fale of excifable liquors. The firft, it was fuppofed,
would bring in 57,000 *l.* a year, and was granted for the fpace of eight
years[117]. The additional excife continued for nine years from the 24th
of June 1761[118]. Its produce was fuppofed to be 300,000*l.* Both
thefe grants were fuffered to expire in confequence of the difputes
which arofe between the king and his parliament.

[116] Comm. Journ. vol. viii. p. 196.   [117] 20 Car. II. cap. 1.
[118] The additional excife was firft granted for fix years, by 22 Car. II. cap. 5, and
afterwards continued for three years, by 29 Car. II. cap. 2.

The

The laſt example of money being raiſed under the name of ſubſidy *Subſidies.*
took place in this monarch's reign. Four entire ſubſidies were granted *Anno 1673.*
by the temporality, and an act was paſſed confirming a ſimilar grant
from the clergy[119]. It produced only 282,000 *l.* It was full time to
give up a ſyſtem of taxation which had become ſo very unproductive,
that the king ſtated in a ſpeech to parliament, that eſtates from 3000 *l.* to
4000 *l.* a year, did not pay above 16 *l.* for all the four ſubſidies.

Various land-taxes, then known under the name of aſſeſſments, were *Land-tax.*
granted by parliament. As the acts by which theſe taxes were impoſed are not among the printed ſtatutes, and as conſulting the original
record is attended with ſome difficulty, it is hoped that the note ſub-
joined, containing an account of the proportions of each diſtrict will
not be unacceptable[120].

[119] 15 Car. II. cap. 9. & 10.

[120] ASSESSMENT of 70,000 *l.* a month, as impoſed *anno* 1660.

	£		
Bedford	933	6	8
Berks	1,088	17	10
Bucks	1,283	6	8
Cambridge	1,102	10	0
Iſle of Ely	367	10	0
County of Cheſter	770	0	0
City of Cheſter	85	11	2
Cornwall	1,633	6	8
Cumberland	108	0	0
Derby	933	6	8
Devon	3,003	15	6
Oxford	107	6	8
Dorſet	1,311	10	6
Poole	10	14	0
Durham	153	14	4
Yorkſhire and York	3,043	8	10
Hull	67	13	0
Eſſex	3,500	0	0
Glouceſterſhire	1,626	6	8
Glouceſter	162	11	2
Hereford	1,166	13	4
Hertford	1,400	0	0
Huntingdon	622	4	6
Kent	3,655	11	2
Lancaſter	933	6	8
Carried over	£ 29,070	12	4

There was a grant in 1670, amounting to 800,000 *l.*; and the duties impofed upon the public to raife that fum, were a tax of fifteen fhillings on

	Brought over		£ 29,070	12	4
Leicefter			1,088	17	8
Lincoln			2,722	4	10
London			4,666	13	4
Middlefex and Weftminfter			1,788	17	10
Monmouth			466	13	4
Northampton			1,400	0	0
Nottinghamfhire			903	4	4
Nottingham			30	2	4
Norfolk			3,624	8	10
Norwich			186	13	4
Northumberland			179	19	10
Newcaftle			35	11	8
County of Oxcn			1,127	15	6
Rutland			272	4	6
Salop			1,322	4	4
Stafford			919	6	8
Litchfield			14	0	0
Somerfet			2,722	4	6
Briftol			171	2	2
Southampton			2,022	4	4
Suffolk			3,655	11	2
Surrey			1,565	5	6
Southwark			184	14	6
Suffex			1,905	11	2
Warwick			1,244	8	10
Worcefterfhire			1,182	4	4
Worcefter			62	4	6
Wilts			1,944	8	10
Weftmoreland			73	19	4
Wales			3,227	3	6
Berwick			5	16	8
			£ 69,786	10	0

One of the bills of affeffment in the time of the Commonwealth, for the year 1656 may be feen in Scobell's Collection, p. 400. But the above ftate is taken from a copy of the Ordnance of the lords and commons for levying the affeffment 1660, which I was fo fortunate as to meet with. Davenant, vol. i. p. 32, obferves, that the affeffment was on every hundred pounds belonging to bankers; the fame fum on every hundred pounds lent to the king at above 6 *per cent.* intereft; fix fhillings *per cent.* on all perfonal eftates; two fhillings in the pound on the falaries of all offices and places, to which was added a fhilling in the pound on lands and mines '''. This was principally aimed at perfonal property; and it is the only example, in the hiftory of our finance, of a tax on bankers, and on fuch of the creditors of the crown as received beyond the legal intereft, which at that time was 6 *per cent.*

The revenue arifing from ftamps was firft introduced into England anno 1671. It was impofed by a ftatute entitled, " An act for laying " impofitions on proceedings at law '''." The rates are various, and the particulars fo very numerous, that it would be improper to enter into the detail. The duty was at firft granted for nine years from the firft of May 1671. It was afterwards continued for three years longer, when, in confequence of the unfortunate jealoufies between the crown and parliament it was fuffered to expire.

It will now be proper to give as full an account as it is poffible to draw up at this time, of the money granted by parliament during Charles's reign, in addition to his permanent revenue.

was very favourable to the northern and weftern parts of England. He has formed a curious table of the taxes raifed in England by various modes, and what proportion was affeffed on each particular county; but the affeffment of 1660 was omitted, which was an additional reafon to infert it in this work.

''' 22 Car. II. c. 3.   ''' Ibid. c. 9.

Parliamentary

Parliamentary Grants.

1. For the Debts of the Republic, and difbanding the Army.

1661.			£	
	1. Three months affeffment, at 70,000 l. per month	-	£	210,000
	2. The firft poll tax	- - - -		252,167
	3. Two months affeffment, at 70,000 l. each	- -		140,000
	4. Six months affeffment, at 70,000 l. each	- -		420,000

Total   1,022,167

2. Temporary Grants.

1660.	1. For a fpeedy fupply to his majefty	- - - £	70,000
	2. Ditto for the expences of the coronation	- -	70,000
	3. Forfeited eftates of traitors [1]	- - -	75,000
1662.	4. Grant for paying the king's debts	- - -	1,260,000
	5. To be diftributed among the loyal cavaliers	-	60,000
1663.	6. Four entire fubfidies from temporality and clergy	-	282,000
1664.	7. Firft aid for the Dutch war	- - -	2,477,502
1665.	8. Second aid for ditto	- - - -	1,250,000
1666.	9. Third aid for ditto	- - - -	1,256,345
	10. Second poll tax for ditto	- - -	500,000
1668.	11. Grant for fitting out a fleet	- - -	310,000
1670.	12. Perfonal tax on bankers, and for the king's debts	-	800,000
1673.	13. Grant during the Dutch war, voted in order to procure the repeal of the declaration of indulgence	- -	1,238,750
1677.	14. Grant for building thirty fhips of war	- -	584,978
	15. Third poll tax for preparations againft France	-	150,000
	16. Grant for difbanding the army, &c.	- - -	414,000
	17. Grant for ditto	- - - -	206,462

3. Permanent Grants.

1670.	1. Additional tax on wine for eight years	- -	456,000
	2. Additional excife for nine years, about	- -	300,000
	3. Stamp duty for twelve years	- - -	266,666

13,014,868

Arrears of excife, voluntary prefents from parliament to the king, and the duke of York, and money in the hands of receivers at the reftoration, fuppofed   -   400,000

£ 13,414,868

[1] It appears from Comm. Jour. vol. viii. p. 498. that the clear annual value of thefe eftates amounted only to 5000l. They were not probably worth more than 15 years purchafe.

Befides

Befides thefe grants, feveral others, to the amount of about a million more, were loft by the difputes which fo frequently arofe, during this reign, between the crown and parliament [124].

But, in addition to the king's permanent revenue, and the grants of parliament, his exchequer was enriched by other means, which it will be neceffary briefly to explain.

3. Mifcella-
neous refour-
ces.

The dowry which the king was to have received with Catherine of Portugal, befides Tangiers in Africa, and Bombay in the Eaft-Indies, was 500,000*l.* Such engagements, however, are not always fulfilled with honour and punctuality; and it is faid, that only 250,000 *l.* was actually paid [125]. The expences which he incurred in defending Portugal from the Spaniards, foon exhaufted this fupply.

Queen's por-
tion.

The frugality of parliament during this reign, of which fo much has been faid, was perhaps in a great meafure owing to the impatience with which the people paid even very moderate burdens. When an affeffment for fix months was granted in 1660 to raife the fum of 420,000*l.*, it was thought neceffary, by a claufe in the act itfelf, to affure the public, that it was not intended to continue that mode of impofition, though it was the only productive one at the time. And the neceffities of the crown, *anno* 1670, being much greater than the Houfe was either willing, or perhaps could venture to fupply, the king, with little difficulty, procured an act to difpofe of the fee-farm rents, the principal part that ftill remained of the royal domains [126]. The produce of this fale is very uncertain; fome authors calculating it at 1,800,000 *l.* and

Sale of the
domains.

---

[124] The amount of Charles II.'s revenue has been a fubject of great difpute between the Whigs and Tories. It originated from a well-known Whig tract, intitled, " A Letter " from a By-ftander to a Member of Parliament;" in which the author dwelt much on the profufion of the Tory parliaments, which that monarch affembled. It was foon animadverted upon, in a paper printed *anno* 1742, called, "A *proper* Anfwer to the By-ftander." Mr. Carte, the hiftorian, foon afterwards entered the lifts, and publifhed a *full* anfwer to the fame work, which was attacked in a Letter to the reverend Mr. Thomas Carte, by a Gentleman of Cambridge, printed *anno* 1743. This produced an elaborate performance, by Mr. Carte, intitled, " A full and clear Vindication of the full Anfwer to a Letter from " a By-ftander," which clofed the controverfy. But the beft work upon the fubject is, " The prefent taxes compared to the payments made to the public, within the memory of " man, in a Letter to a Member of Parliament," printed for J. Marfhall, *anno* 1749.

[125] Hume, vol. vii. p. 385, note.   [126] 22 Car. II. cap. 6.

C c   others

others at only 100,000 *l.* The exact sum it is impossible at present to ascertain; but it probably must have amounted to 500,000 *l.*

Sale of Dunkirk.

The policy of acquiring a possession on the continent like Dunkirk, has been much disputed. Many great and respectable characters have contended, that such possessions are expensive; occasion disgust and enmity, in those to whom they naturally belong; and give rise to an interference in continental concerns, with which England has no immediate relation. These objections are weighty; but their force is considerably diminished by this important advantage. The keeping up of any considerable and collected body of forces, it is well known, is thought dangerous to the liberties of the people. If it were not, therefore, by means of remote foreign garrisons, it would be difficult for this country either to attain or to preserve that full and complete experience and skill in arms, and that knowledge of discipline, and the arts of war, which every nation ought to possess; and of all the places on the Continent, Dunkirk, naturally strong, easily defended, lying between the French and Imperial territories, and consequently less obnoxious and offensive to either of those two powers, was decidedly the most eligible. It was therefore not a little unfortunate that an acquisition which might have been so serviceable to this country, should have been disposed of merely in consequence of a fatal jealousy between the crown and parliament. The latter were afraid of trusting the king with the money necessary to defray the expence of maintaining the garrison, whilst the king, on the other hand, would not agree to transfer the possession of Dunkirk to the parliament (who were willing to bear any charges it might amount to), lest they should acquire a separate dominion and independent authority[17].

The famous Clarendon was the person by whom the sale was conducted on the part of England; and after much negotiation, a bargain was at last concluded for the sum of 400,000 *l.* A part of the price (amounting to 1,500,000 French crowns) was sent over in specie; and when coined into English money, yielded 338,773 *l.* Clarendon was afterwards impeached by the house of commons, for having advised this measure; and it was the most specious charge that could be urged against that virtuous and able minister.

[17] D'Estrades, August 21, 1661.

There

Penſion from France.

There is no circumſtance of Charles's reign ſo peculiarly diſgraceful as his acceptance of a ſecret penſion from the court of France. To whatever difficulties a ſovereign may be reduced, it is ſurely beneath the royal dignity to become a voluntary dependant on another. It was particularly infamous in Charles, who had it in his power, by vigorous meaſures abroad, and by cultivating a good underſtanding with his people at home, to become the arbiter of Europe. But to pretend to be the friend of Spain, of Holland, and of Auſtria, when in fact he was bound, by the moſt ſolemn engagements to the court of France, is a degree of treachery much beyond the common fineſſe and artifices of a court, or the utmoſt juſtifiable ſtretch of political manœuvre. It is im- poſſible to ſay what money Charles actually received in conſequence of this ſhameful connexion. It appears that he demanded 18,000,000 of livres (about 750,000l. ſterling), for ſecretly favouring Lewis, at the congreſs of Nimeguen. Various other ſums he alſo received at diffe- rent times[11]. The whole may be eſtimated at 950,000l.

The wars which this king entered into againſt the Dutch were princi- pally with a view of plundering a wealthy, and, as he imagined, an al- moſt defenceleſs neighbour; at leaſt one greatly inferior, in point of ſtrength and reſources, to the dominions which he governed. But in theſe ſelfiſh and intereſted deſigns, he was generally diſappointed. In the firſt Dutch war, an Eaſt Indian fleet, very richly laden, was pre- vented from falling into his hands by the aſſiſtance of the Danes, who protected it in the harbour of Bergen: and in the ſecond war, another fleet, coming from the Mediterranean, valued at a million and a half, eſcaped, though with conſiderable difficulty. Charles, notwithſtanding, found means to reap ſome pecuniary advantages from theſe wars. His ſhare of prize-money, during the firſt war, amounted to 340,000l.; and, in conſideration of his agreeing to conclude the ſecond peace, he received 800,000 patacoons, about 300,000l. ſterling.

Plunder.

Charles was reduced to ſuch difficulties, *anno* 1672, that he declared, whoever diſcovered a mode to ſupply his neceſſities ſhould be rewarded with the office of treaſurer. Clifford, created Lord Clifford, as well as entruſted with the care of the treaſury, for the expedient he ſug-

Shutting up the Exche- quer.

[11] Hume, vol. viii. p. 206, note T. 207, note U.

geſted,

gefted, propofed to fhut up the Exchequer; and inftead of repaying any principal fums that had been advanced upon its fecurity, to iffue only the legal annual intereft of 6 *per cent.* The nature of this infamous tranfaction will be more fully explained in another part of this work: at prefent it is only neceffary to ftate the pecuniary profit which Charles reaped from it. Hume calculates the advantage only at 1,200,000*l.* [119]; but it appears from the journals of parliament, that the intereft, at 6 *per cent.*, amounted to 79,566*l.* [120]; confequently the principal muft have been 1,328,526*l.*

Extortions.

The principles of the Englifh conftitution, in regard to taxation, were at this time fo fully underftood, and the power of the crown to levy arbitrary impofitions fo totally abolifhed, that during the greater part of Charles's reign, his fubjects had little reafon to complain of illegal exactions. An arbitrary duty, however, was laid on coals during the war with Holland, under the pretence of providing convoys, which the parliament very properly complained of. And when the king, in confequence of the imprudence and mifconduct of thofe who demanded the exclufion of his brother from the crown, had obtained a complete victory over that formidable party, and, indeed, had become almoft fully mafter of the liberties of the people, he compelled the different corporations to furrender their charters into his hands, and exacted confiderable fums previoufly to their reftitution [121]. But this did not take place till near the conclufion of his reign.

It will now be proper to give a general view of this monarch's income and refources.

[119] Hume, vol. viii. p. 326. [120] Comm. Journ. vol. x. p. 109.
[121] Ibid. vol. viii. p. 181.

GENERAL

GENERAL VIEW of the Money received by Charles II. during the whole courfe of his reign.

1. Miscellaneous Resources.

	£
1. Queen's portion — — —	250,000
2. Sale of the Domains — — —	500,000
3. Price of Dunkirk — — — —	400,000
4. Penfion from France — — —	950,000
5. Plunder — — — —	640,000
6. Shutting up the Exchequer — — —	1,328,526
7. Extortions — — — —	100,000
	£ 4,168,526

2. Parliamentary Grants.

The various fums granted by parliament for public fervices —	13,414,868
	£ 17,583,394

3. The Permanent Revenue.

The permanent income of the crown, at the rate of 1,100,000 l. a year, for the fpace of twenty-four years —	26,400,000
	[13] £ 43,983,394

Thus it would appear that Charles received, in all, about 43,983,394 l. in the courfe of his reign, which would make above 1,800,000 l. a year; a fum adequate to the national expences, had it been managed with frugality; at leaft equal to every neceffary charge in times of

[13] Authors differ much with regard to the total amount of this monarch's income. Hume, vol. viii. p. 326, calculates the ordinary revenue at about 1,200,000 l.; the grants of parliament at 476,808 l. a year: and to this he adds 1,200,000 l. for fhutting up the Exchequer; but he omits feveral of the other fources above ftated. The author of a tract, printed 1749, entitled, " The prefent Taxes compared to the Payments made to the " Public within the memory of Man," fuppofes the ordinary revenues, on an average, to be a million and a half yearly. Carte has drawn up an account in many refpects errone- ous, from which he contends, that only 32,474,265 l. was raifed upon the people of Eng- land in the twenty-four years of Charles's actual poffeffion of the government, making only 1,353,095 l. a year. See Full Anfwer, p. 161. Another author (Letter to Carte, p. 101) makes the whole fum received by this monarch 54,842,449 . or 2.300,000 l. per annum. I have endeavoured to ftate a juft and proper medium.

peace

peace and tranquillity; though in time of war it might have required
fome addition.

Coinage.

If we may judge from the ftate of the coinage during this monarch's
reign, no confiderable addition was made to the metallic wealth of the
country.   Only 4,177,253*l.* 12*s.* 5*d.* was coined in gold, and
3,722,180*l.* 2*s.* 8½*d.* in filver, making in all 7,899,433*l.* 15*s.* 1½*d.*

Fifhing Li-
cence.

The attempt was not abandoned, during this reign, of compelling the
Dutch to pay for the liberty of fifhing on the Britifh coafts.   Charles
demanded 10,000*l.* a year for granting them this privilege.   Whatever
juftice there might be in the claim, the bad fuccefs of his warlike enterprifes againft that nation, could not furnifh him with any flattering expectations of his demand being complied with.

The financial hiftory of this period is diftinguifhed by two important
alterations; in regard to the manner of impofing taxes on the clergy,
and the mode of granting public fupplies.

Alteration in
the mode of
taxing the
clergy.

Among the many valuable privileges which the church had acquired
in the dark and fuperftitious ages of modern Europe, that of an exemp-
tion of taxes was not the leaft confiderable.   Under the pretence that their
power was derived from Heaven; and that their eftates were the property of the Deity, and confequently facred and inviolable, they denied
all fubjection to temporal authority, and refufed to contribute in common, with the public at large, to the neceffities of the State.   The fubfidies they paid, were either in confequence of bulls from the Pope, whom
they confidered as their fpiritual, and, indeed, real fovereign, or impofed
by the authority of their own ecclefiaftical fuperiors, to whom they profeffed, in a fubordinate degree, canonical obedience.

Edward I. it has been already obferved, was the firft monarch of England who compelled the clergy to pay taxes, not only without the authority, but in avowed contradiction to a bull from Rome; and for
many years after, the convocation was regularly affembled at the fame
time with the parliament, for the purpofe of granting fupplies[113].   This
practice continued until the long parliament affumed the government of
the country: their religious principles were fo adverfe to all diftinct or

[113] Gilb. Excheq. p. 48.

independant

independant eccleſiaſtical authority, that no convocation was ſuffered to meet; and the income and poſſeſſions of the church were included in thoſe monthly aſſeſſments or taxes on real and perſonal property, which were levied during the exiſtence of the commonwealth.

After the reſtoration, the hierarchy and the rights of the convocation were again re-eſtabliſhed. But the clergy were afraid that the privilege of taxing themſelves would prove a burden inſtead of being a benefit. They remembered that during the reigns of the former monarchs of the houſe of Stuart, conſiderable grants were perpetually expected from them; and that ſuch was the influence attending the clerical patronage of the crown, that much heavier taxes were impoſed upon the property of the church, than on the eſtates of the laity. They were not a little anxious, therefore, to be put upon the ſame footing as to taxation and repreſentation, that they were in the time of the long parliament; and accordingly it was agreed upon, that the revenues and property of the church ſhould continue to be included in the monthly aſſeſſments which were impoſed [124]; and that the parochial clergy ſhould be allowed to vote at elections, though incapable of being elected [125]. Theſe terms the parliament aſſented to, as they proved the means of acquiring a con-ſiderable acceſſion to its power of taxation; and rendered the crown ſtill more dependant upon the only body of men by whom its wants could in any degree be ſupplied: nay, as an additional boon, two cleri-cal ſubſidies which had been granted by the convocation were re-mitted.

The grants of parliament were originally conſidered, merely as tem-porary aids to aſſiſt the ſovereign in defraying the expences he was ſub-ject to, for the benefit of the public; and unleſs the commons hap-pened to entertain at the time any particular jealouſy of the crown and its miniſters, the ſum granted was commonly left entirely to their diſpoſal. But after the reſtoration, not only more frequent grants were demanded, but, in conſequence of the poverty to which the crown was reduced, parliamentary grants had become really neceſ-

Alteration in the mode of granting ſup-plies.

[124] It was finally ſettled, *anno* 1664, in conſequence of a private agreement between Sheldon, archbiſhop of Canterbury, and Lord Clarendon, in conjunction with the other miniſters. See Burn's Eccleſ. Law; *vces*, Convocation, and Firſt Fruits.
[125] 13 Car. II. c. 4.

3 ſary

fary almoſt every year. It was impoſſible, however, for parliament, diſtruſting not only Charles's œconomy, but his regard for the intereſt of his kingdoms, to veſt conſiderable ſums of money in ſuch unſafe and improvident hands: it was, therefore, thought requiſite to ſpecify the purpoſes for which each ſum was voted. Thus appropriating clauſes came to be introduced. At one time, the jealouſy of the commons was car-

ried to ſuch a height, that they ſent a bill to the houſe of lords, containing a clauſe by which the money thereby granted was ordered to be paid into the chamber of London. But the peers would not ſuffer ſo great a ſtigma on the king and his miniſters to paſs into a law[134]. The mode of appropriation, though in the main right, was neverthelefs attended with unfortunate confequences. It abated the jealouſy of the commons. It was natural for them to imagine that grants, thus ſtrictly appropriated, could not be diverted to other purpoſes; and they became negligent in making the moſt effential of all enquiries, namely, how the public money was actually expended. At one time, committees of the houſe of commons, and at another, commiſſioners have been appointed to examine into the public accounts: but the wound has never been probed to the bottom; and public profuſion will never be fully checked, until not only eſtimates, which are too often fallacious and unintelligible, but alſo accounts of the manner in which the ſupplies granted were really ſpent, are regularly laid before parliament.

JAMES II.

There was no department of government in which this raſh and odious bigot did not betray the deſpotic and arbitrary principles on which he intended that his adminiſtration ſhould be conducted: but they were firſt exhibited to their full extent in the article of his reve- nue. Though the greater part of his brother's income had been granted only for the life of that monarch, and confequently expired with him, yet, contrary to the opinion of his council, who adviſed him to fufpend levying the duties until the payment was authorifed by par-

[134] Hume, vol. viii. p. 85.

liament,

liament, he iffued a proclamation, commanding the cuftoms and other taxes to be paid as formerly: and, in his firft fpeech from the throne, after declaring that he expected his revenue fhould be fettled on the fame footing with his brother's, which was no unreafonable requeft, he very plainly intimated, that any attempt to fecure the frequent meetings of parliament, by granting moderate fupplies, would be refented. " I muft plainly tell you, that fuch an expedient would be " very improper to employ with me; and that the beft way to engage " me to meet you often, is always to ufe me well'"." Thus he gave them to underftand, that he would only have recourfe to them, if they complied with his demands. His fpeeches furnifh the laft example in our hiftory of an Englifh monarch attempting to intimidate his people by the arrogance of his language.

The only public virtues which James poffeffed, were frugality in his expences, and a ftrong defire to increafe the naval ftrength of his kingdoms. In the latter article he difplayed fuch zeal and judgment as reflects a confiderable degree of luftre on that part of his adminiftration. But the army was by no means neglected. Under pretence that the militia were found very unferviceable during Monmouth's rebellion, he demanded a fupply from parliament to maintain thofe additional forces which he thought proper to levy at that time'"; and he actually had in pay 30,000 regular troops in England alone, when invaded by his fucceffor. E\pences.

The only temporary grant during James's reign, which was carried into effect, was a fupply of 400,000l. for the purpofe of fuppreffing Monmouth's rebellion'". Anno 1685, 700,000 pounds were alfo voted; but the king, as a mark of his difpleafure, and to prevent the houfe from interfering with his pretended prerogative, of difpenfing with the tefts impofed by law, for the exclufion of Catholics, from offices of truft and emolument, prorogued the parliament, before the grant paffed into a law'"°. Grants.

The propriety of granting a permanent income to the king for life, was one of the many important points which James's parliament had Permanent income.

'" Collection of King's Speeches, p. 177.   '" Hume, vol. viii. p. 180.
'" Hume, vol. viii. p. 226.   '") Mort. vol. ii. p 658.

D d to

to determine foon after his acceſſion; and ſuch was then the great authority of the crown, that a larger revenue was given to James for his life, than any monarch of England had ever enjoyed[141]. It appears from the following account, which was laid before parliament at the revolution, that it amounted to above two millions *per annum.*

ACCOUNT of the principal Branches of the Revenue, *anno* 1688, clear of all DeduＣtions.

	£.
Tonnage and poundage, including the wood, coal, and ſalt farm —	600,000
Exciſe on beer and ale	666,383
Hearth-money	245,000
Poſt office	65,000
Wine licences	10,000
New impoſitions on wine and vinegar	172,901
Duties on tobacco and ſugar	148,861
Duty on French linen, brandy, ſilk, &c.	93,710
	[142] £ 2,001,855

This account does not include ſome of the ſmaller articles of revenue.

Coinage. During this monarch's reign, which laſted only four years, there was coined, in gold, the ſum of 2,113,638*l.* 18*s.* 8¼*d.*, and, in ſilver, 518,316*l.* 9*s.* 5¼*d.*; making, in all, 2,631,955*l.* 8*s.* 1½*d.*

Reflexion. It is the peculiar happineſs of the people of England that every attempt to diminiſh their rights, or to encroach upon their liberties, has

[141] See the arguments on both ſides, ſtated by Hume with his uſual ability, vol. viii. p. 221. 222. 223. 224. Here we muſt take leave of this excellent hiſtorian, from whom much advantage has been derived in the courſe of this inveſtigation. Indeed, it is impoſſible to give a juſt diſplay of any branch of the hiſtory of England, without making a conſiderable uſe of his remarks. His work, however, is far from being equal. The firſt part and the concluſion of his hiſtory, is not excelled by any compoſition either modern or ancient: but the middle, which he firſt publiſhed, being composed with leſs experience in writing, is not only more prolix, but alſo ſeems to have been drawn up rather as a defence of the unfortunate race of Stuart, than as a candid and impartial hiſtory.

[142] Comm. Journ. vol. x. p. 37.

been

been attended with confequences diametrically oppofite to thofe which were defigned at the time; and that every king who has governed ill, has given the public fome compenfation for the offences or errors he committed, by proving the fource of beneficial laws, and of additional checks upon tyranny and oppreffion. The crimes and mifgovernment of John gave rife to *Magna Charta*, and all the important privileges which that charter tended to confirm. The extortions which that able and high-fpirited prince, Edward I. was led into, in confequence of the expenfive foreign wars in which he was engaged, occafioned the famous ftatute, *De Tallagio non concedendo*; the paffing of which is unqueftionably one of the moft important events in the hiftory of this country. And the exactions attempted to be enforced by the firft princes of the houfe of Stuart, joined to James's obftinacy, bigotry, and infatuation, were productive of a revolution equally favourable to our civil and religious liberties, and of the eftablifhment of a form of government " the moft perfect in theory, and the happieft in " practice, that has ever exifted among mankind:" a conftitution which, it is proper to obferve, was not the offspring of hafte, or projected by one man; but was gradually formed in the courfe of a long and important ftruggle, which lafted from the death of Elizabeth, to the acceffion of William III., and employed the powers of as able men as ever exifted in any country whatfoever. It was from the collifion of fuch abilities alone that fo valuable and well conftructed a fabric could have been erected; and its blemifhes (for, like all other works of human invention, it is, in fome refpects, defective) we truft will be removed, without pulling the edifice to pieces, without injuring its beauty, or impairing its vigour and its ftrength.

These were the moft important financial tranfactions which took place under the government of the houfe of Stuart, during whofe adminiftration many new branches of revenue were introduced, fuch as excifes, ftamps, the poft office, monthly affeffments, &c.; and many old refources were either abandoned, as unproductive, or abolifhed, on account of their oppreffion. Hence fubfidies were given up, and the whole fabric of feudal exaction, of wardfhip, marriage, &c., together with benevolences, free gifts, and compulfive loans, were for ever annihilated.

Conclufion.

But

But the period is particularly remarkable for enabling us to form fome kind of judgment of the full extent of that heavy burden which the funding fyflem introduced into this kingdom.

The revenue, of England, at the acceffion of the houfe of Stuart, *anno* 1602, was 500,000*l.* a year. Eighty-fix years afterwards, when James II. was expelled, it was raifed to about two millions: the annual increment confequently was near 17,441 *l.* At the fame rate of increafe, the revenue, *anno* 1774, eighty-fix years after the revolution, fhould only have been 3,500,000*l.*; and ten years afterwards, *anno* 1784, ought not to have exceeded 3,674,418*l.*, or, perhaps, with the addition of Scotland, rather more than four millions a year. If the prefent income of the State, therefore, is about fourteen millions, ten millions of that fum may be attributed to the funding fyflem; and would not have exifted, if the extraordinary expences of the public had been defrayed by money exacted at the time, without leaving any burden upon pofterity. Indeed, four millions would be amply fufficient, at this time, to defray the charges of the civil lift, and of our peace eftablifhment, if the load of taxes impofed to provide for the intereft of our public debts, did not raife the price of every commodity to fuch a height, as to render money much lefs efficient than it would otherwife be.

But, on the whole, though our circumftances might have been better, let us not too haftily either envy the fituation, or inveigh againft the conduct of our predeceffors. Lightly as we may imagine they were burdened, yet they complained as loudly as we do, of the intolerable weight of taxes, and of the diftrefs and poverty which they occafioned: and though, inftead of adding to their own burdens, they thought themfelves juftifiable in bequeathing to their pofterity a confiderable part of that grievous load of public debt, under the preffure of which we now ftagger, let it alfo be remembered, that they delivered into our hands a well cultivated ifland; dependencies of great value and importance; an extenfive commerce; flourifhing manufactures; a fuperior fyftem of agriculture; a high character for ability and valour; and, joined to all thefe advantages, a fyftem of government, unequalled in the annals of mankind for the bleffings which it affords.

END OF PART I.

THE

HISTORY

OF THE

PUBLIC REVENUE

OF THE

BRITISH EMPIRE.

PART II.

PART II.

CHAP. I.

Of the various Modes of providing for the extraordinary Expences of a Nation.

THE charges incurred by a nation in times of peace, feldom exceed its ordinary income, or what it may be made to produce. It requires no great revenue, to maintain the magiftrates entrufted with the general government of the country; to fupport fuch as are employed in expounding the laws, and in diftributing juftice; and to defray the expences of fuch public works as are effentially neceffary for the benefit of the community. Indeed, if nations were always at peace, fupplying a revenue for public purpofes, could never prove burdenfome to fociety.

But the neceffity there is, from the turbulent difpofition of the human fpecies, and the ambition of thofe individuals, who govern the affairs of States, to be perpetually providing for the expences of war, is uniformly attended with the heavieft charges. Maxims of frugality, however proper and defirable at other times, are found incompatible with a ftate of hoftility. When the fate of a nation is at ftake, or even when any of its important interefts are endangered, exertions muft be made, without regarding the expences they may occafion. The troops and armaments of the foe muft be oppofed, whatever coft fuch oppofition may require; and every citizen muft facrifice a part of his

fortune,

fortune, either to increafe the property and maintain the interefts of the community to which he belongs, or to preferve the wealth, which it has already acquired from the plunder of its enemies.

It is evident therefore, that a material difference neceffarily exifts between the revenue fufficient for times of peace, and the refources which are requifite to defray the various heavy charges which a war muft occafion.

The ingenuity of mankind, particularly in modern times, has been much engaged in attempts to difcover, what is the beft mode of providing for thefe extraordinary expences; and four fyftems have been fuggefted for that purpofe. It has been propofed, 1. To accumulate a treafure in time of peace, adequate to the exigencies of war.—2. To levy the neceffary fupplies within the year, by means of extraordinary additional taxes.—3. To exact compulfive loans from the wealthieft individuals of the community.—4. To borrow money from fuch as are willing to advance it, upon the fecurity of the public faith.

Each of thefe modes it is propofed briefly to examine.

I. Accumulating a Treafure.

At the commencement of political focieties, a confiderable fhare of the territory they poffefs, is uniformly dedicated to national purpofes. In the infancy of States, however, there is neither inclination nor opportunity to be prodigal; and confequently, when there happens to be any furplus, after defraying the neceffary expences, it is in general accumulated into a public treafure, and referved for any unforefeen emergency. In ancient times, the practice was very prevalent; and, in England, the monarchs who lived after the conqueft, were provided with fuch treafures, owing as much to their inability to expend their revenue, as to any parfimonious difpofition, or any forecaft for the future.

Sometimes, however, the fyftem of accumulation has arifen from real forefight; and among the various acts for which the political wifdom of the Romans has been celebrated, fome authors have included their levying a tax for the exprefs purpofe of preparing a fund for public emergencies. The commonwealth, we are told, had hardly been eftablifhed by the expulfion of Tarquin, before they began to collect colleæt the *Aurum Vicefimarium*, or impoft of the twentieth penny, upon the fale of flaves; the amount of which was depofited in the temple of Saturn, there to be kept facred for the moft preffing exigencies of the State[1]. It continued accumulating for many years, and remained untouched as long as the free government of Rome exifted, excepting during the fecond Punic war, when it was thought excufable, after Han-nibal had ravifhed Italy for ten years, to take four thoufand pounds weight of gold out of this treafure, to affift in defraying the various enormous expences to which the commonwealth was then fubjeæt.

But this mode of employing the furplus revenue of the public, is attended with one material difadvantage. If the precious metals at all contribute to the happinefs of political fociety (which cannot be doubted, at leaft by thofe who confider with how much greater facility commerce is carried on in confequence of fo ufeful a medium), every plan that tends to diminifh their abundance, muft be prejudicial. A fyftem of that nature may be lefs hurtful, before induftry and commerce flourifh; and at fuch a period may perhaps be neceffary, from the difficulty with which any confiderable fum of money is collected in critical emergencies. But, in general, it would be better to employ the furplus of the national revenue in works of public advantage, or even in the conftruction of ufelefs pyramids, as was done by the fovereigns of Egypt, than in ac-cumulating a hoard to lie dormant, without intereft and without cir-culation.

A well-known and eminent author has notwithftanding vehemently contended for continuing the practice of the ancients; and in particular grounds himfelf upon this idea, " That the opening of fuch a treafure " neceffarily produces an uncommon affluence of gold and filver, ferves " as a temporary encouragement to induftry, and atones, in fome degree, " for the inevitable calamities of war[2]." Unfortunately for this author's hypothefis, the fame circumftance, namely the abundance of gold and filver, which alleviates the calamities of war, augments alfo the bleffings of peace; and thofe bleffings are neceffarily diminifhed where treafures are accumulated : indeed, a public hoard can hardly be collected, without reducing a nation, in point of commerce and circulation, to much the

[1] See a beautiful poetical defcription of this treafure, Lucan's Pharfalia, l. iii. v. 155.
[2] Hume's Effays, vol. i. p. 365

fame

fame fituation in times of tranquillity, as in the midft of war. Befides, it is proper to remark, that the Romans always endeavoured, in the firft place, to procure money by loans, and never applied to their treafure, but when their credit was exhaufted.

There are other unfurmountable objections to the amaffing of public treafures ; fuch as, the dangers with which they are accompanied ; of ufurpation in monarchial governments ; of defpotifin in free ftates; and, under every form of government, of being improvidently expended. It appears from the Hiftory of England, that the ufurpations of the three monarchs who reigned after William the Norman, were greatly owing to their having fecured the treafures of their predeceffors. We learn alfo from the Hiftory of the Roman Commonwealth, that if no public treafure had exifted at the time, Cæfar could hardly have fuc- ceeded in his daring attempt upon the liberties of his country: and it is well known, that the immenfe treafure which the republic of Athens had been accumulating for the fpace of fifty years, and which at laft amounted to above ten thoufand talents, was diffipated in rafh and im- prudent enterprifes, to the ruin of the State[3]. Indeed, if nations are tempted, when their credit is high and flourifhing, to engage in deftruc- tive plans of hoftility and conqueft, how much more may not this be apprehended, if a treafure is already amaffed, which may eafily be ap- plied to gratify the ambition of an impetuous and inconfiderate mo- narch, or to carry into effect the political projects of an artful dema- gogue?

II. Raifing the Supplies within the Year.

When a nation finds, that its expences exceed its revenue, and that either no treafure has been accumulated, or that it is inadequate to the charges which are likely to be incurred, it naturally endeavours to raife extraordinary fupplies, by additions to its ordinary income. It was upon this principle, that aids were originally granted by Parliament to the Kings of England: nay, at the Revolution it was imagined, that a general excife, in addition to the ufual revenue, would have furnifhed money fufficient to defray the expences of the war[4]. Various circum-

---

[3] Hume's Effays, vol. i. p. 335.   [4] Davenant's Works, vol. i. p. 18.

ſtances, however, unfortunately contributed to render ſuch a plan at that time impracticable. The inſtant of a revolution is an improper period for increaſing, in any great degree, the burdens of a nation. Many would have rejoiced at ſuch an opportunity of ſpreading diſaffection to the new government. Taxes were at that time peculiarly unpopular in England; inſomuch, that it was thought neceſſary, in order to ingratiate the new ſovereign with his people, to diminiſh inſtead of increaſing the revenue, and to repeal the productive duty of hearth-money, by one of the firſt acts to which William III. gave the royal aſſent after his acceſſion.

The mode of raiſing the extraordinary expences of the nation, by ſupplies within the year, has often been recommended by different authors ſince the Revolution.

Sir Matthew Decker, in his famous plan for levying the whole revenue by a ſingle duty upon houſes, which he publiſhed *anno* 1744, expreſsly mentions the poſſibility of raiſing the current ſervices within the year; " a thing (he obſerves) greatly deſirable by every body, and " the want of which has been the cauſe of our preſent national debt[1]."

Poſtlethwayt (a laborious and intelligent writer), in a work publiſhed *anno* 1757[6], endeavours to convince his countrymen, both of the neceſſity and the practicability of that meaſure. But his idea was to raiſe only three millions *per annum* additional, and the war had become ſo enormouſly expenſive (requiring more than double that ſum), that it was evident, it could not prove, on ſo narrow a ſcale, of any material benefit, and no one ventured to ſtate the poſſibility of its being farther extended[7].

An able and public ſpirited ſenator, however, recently recommended the ſame plan to the public attention[8]. He ſuppoſes, that the whole property of the nation amounts to *one thouſand millions* in real value, a duty of one and a half per cent. therefore on every man's capital, paid by inſtal-

---

[1] SeriousConſiderations on the ſeveral high Duties which the Nation labours under, p. 20.

[6] Great Britain's true Syſtem, particularly, Let. ii. and xiii.

[7] Poſtlethwayt himſelf, in his dictionary, voce FUND, *in fine*, acknowledges, that when he recommended raiſing the ſupplies within the year, he never imagined that they would have riſen to ſo high a pitch.

[8] Conſiderations on the preſent State of Public Affairs, by William Pulteney, Eſq; 3d edit. p. 31. anno 1779.

I

ments,

ments, would raife, in the courfe of two years, fifteen millions; and he calculated, might, without much œconomy, fupport a vigorous war for that fpace of time. The fame ideas were alfo enforced by the ingenious Mr. Arthur Young; but he contends, that the additional taxes fhould be levied, not upon capital, but upon income. The permanent income of the nation, he imagines to be one hundred millions *per annum*, which could eafily bear a permanent burden of thirteen millions, and would yield befides, without much oppreffion, a temporary aid of eight millions more[9].

The advantages that would have refulted from this mode of raifing the fupplies, are difplayed by the authors above-mentioned in the moft flattering colours. Land, it was faid, inftead of felling from 20 to 25 years purchafe, would foon reach from 27 to 32. The three per cents would rife from 60 to 88 ; and obtaining money upon mortgage, would no longer be attended with difficulty. The alarming prophecies concerning a national bankruptcy, would vanifh ; and more would be done towards procuring an advantageous peace, than could be effected by many victories. Nay, the Chancellor of the Exchequer (Frederick, Lord North) in the opening of the budget 24th February 1779, declared in parliament, " That fuch a plan, he conceived, would not be " difficult, if there was a full confidence in government. Great facri- " fices, it was true, muft be made, and many gratifications given up ; " but if the meafure fhould become neceffary, that confideration ought, " and he believed would give way. The honour, the glory, nay the " very exiftence of the country, might require it[10]."

To carry fuch a plan into effect, two things are requifite ; firft, power and refources in a State ; fecondly, inclination in the Public at large.

The ability of a nation to make a great addition to its revenue, amidft all the horrors and calamities of war, more particularly in modern times, when hoftilities are prolonged to fuch a length, and are carried on in fo extenfive a manner, is at beft problematical. The Dutch, whofe example is commonly adduced upon this occafion, were contending for their own liberties at their own doors. Whereas, when Bri-

---

[9] Polit. Arithmet. Part II. By Arthur Young, Efq; p. 44. 37.
[10] Debates of the Houfe of Commons, publifhed by Almon, vol. xii. p. 8.

tain

tain engages in a war, it muſt employ fleets and armies to protect remote poſſeſſions almoſt in every quarter of the globe. Though ſufficient
property therefore actually exiſted in the country, yet ſtill the difficulty
of collecting it from the diſtant provinces of the kingdom, ſo as to
anſwer the critical moments of an extenſive war, muſt be very great.

Beſides, in a country like England, the wealth of which depends
ſo much upon the ſecurity and proſperity of its commerce, ſuch a plan
would be attended with peculiar difficulties. The following is Mr.
Young's calculation of the annual income of the nation :

Income from Land - - - - -	£. 63,000,000
——— from Manufactures . - - - -	20,000,000
——— from Commerce, and the profits of our Co-⎱ lonial Poſſeſſions - - - - ⎰	17,000,000
	£. 100,000,000

Thus it is ſuppoſed, that thirty-ſeven millions of the national income ariſes from property, liable, in time of war, to great hazard,
and much diminution in point of value, and conſequently unable to
bear any heavy additional burden.

Or, if inſtead of income, the capital of a country, according to Mr.
Pulteney's idea, is to be taxed ; without dwelling upon this objection,
that people may have great property, without having much money at
command, it will be eaſy to perceive the difficulty of collecting the tax,
and the great uncertainty of its produce, when it is conſidered, that
the ſuppoſed capital of *one thouſand millions*, comprehends the value of
the land ; the value of houſes ; the value of ſtock of all kinds ; of
materials for manufacture ; ſhipping ; caſh ; money in the funds due
to natives ; and, in ſhort, every thing that can be denominated wealth
or property [11].

But in nations where the ability exiſts, the inclination is often wanting. The reſpectable author above-mentioned very juſtly remarks,
" That it is in a free country only that mankind feel themſelves ſo con-
" nected with public proſperity, as willingly to ſacrifice, in ſupport of
" it, a part of their fortune, in great emergencies [12]." But free States
are in general ſo divided into parties, that hardly any adminiſtration

[B]   can

can expect the univerfal, or even the general confidence of the people. In luxurious and commercial ages alfo, which are the beft calculated in point of ability for executing fuch a plan, individuals are fo felfifh and interefted, and fo fond of pleafure, and the frivolous joys of diffi-pation, that zeal and public fpirit are rare, and few would curtail them-felves even in the moft .infignificant gratifications, for the purpofe of contributing, to equip an armament, for the defence of Madras, or the protection of Jamaica. Nay, it is queftionable, whether war at their own doors would raife them from their filken lethargy.

The plan of raifing its fupplies within the year, however, is a circumftance which every nation ought to have in view, as it may poffibly prove abfolutely neceffary for its prefervation and exiftence; and perhaps it might be rendered lefs oppreffive, and more practicable, if, inftead of fpecie, a part of the new additional fupplies were exacted in kind; and if the furnifhing of a certain number of recruits; the providing of a certain number of feamen, or a certain quantity of naval ftores, &c. &c. were confidered as a fufficient equivalent for the new taxes, at a certain reafonable converfion. For there may be property in a country amply fufficient to carry fuch a plan into effect, and yet, where money is demanded, it may be rendered impracticable, from the want of a fufficient quantity of circulating fpecie. Such a plan might perhaps be attempted, if the real ftrength and refources of the kingdom were fully known; and if it were afcertained, what each diftrict could afford for the public fervice, on any important emergency, not only in money, but in other articles ufeful to the State.

III. Compulfive Loans.'

Voltaire has defcribed in his ufual fprightly manner, the loans which were extorted from their fubjects, by the ancient Kings of England. " Thofe who lent their money.(he fays) generally loft it, and thofe who " did not lend, were fent to jail "." And it is evident, from what has been faid in the preceding part of this work, that fuch loans were highly oppreffive upon the fubject, without being of much advantage to the crown. Indeed, fo little were they entitled to the name of loan,

---

¹⁹ General Hiftory, vol. iii. part vi. c. 3.

that

that no intereſt was allowed for the money, nor was there any certainty of its being repaid.

The practice, however, of compelling wealthy individuals to contribute to the relief of the crown, may be traced to a very ancient period of our hiſtory[14]. Foreign merchants, who, in the words of the record, " had rights and privileges conferred upon them, by the grace " and ſufferance of the King, *reportant grand lucre*," were made ſubject to this exaction, during the diſgraceful and neceſſitous reign of Henry III."[15]. The practice was afterwards extended to the natives of the kingdom; but it was accounted ſo peculiarly obnoxious, that, among the articles for which Richard II. was depoſed, his having borrowed (or rather extorted, under the pretence of borrowing) great ſums of money, which were never repaid, is particularly infiſted upon[16].

In the reign of Henry VIII. Acts of Parliament were paſſed, diſcharging all his debts founded on loans, whether voluntary or compulſive; and the credit of the crown of England, in conſequence of theſe harſh and rigorous meaſures, continued at the loweſt ebb, until it was revived by the prudent meaſures taken by Elizabeth, and the punctuality which ſhe maintained. In general, ſhe found little difficulty in borrowing money, without being obliged to have recourſe to compulſion. But ſhe was ſometimes reduced to the neceſſity of imitating, in this reſpect, the example of her predeceſſors; and occaſionally iſſued letters under the privy ſeal, demanding the loan of a ſpecific ſum of money, from the wealthieſt of her ſubjects. This (according to an old writer) was, " an enforced piece of ſtate, to lay the burthen on " that horſe that was beſt able to bear it at the dead lift, when neither " her receipts could yield her relief at the pinch, nor the urgency of " her affairs endure the delays of a parliamentary aſſiſtance"[17]."

By the famous petition of right, compulſive loans were totally aboliſhed: but it is a curious ſubject of political ſpeculation, whether ſuch a plan might not be improved, ſo as to anſwer many beneficial

[14] Stevens (Pref. p. 15.) ſtates, upon the authority of a manuſcript in the Cottonian library, that compulſive loans began in the reign of Henry II.

[15] Cotton's Poſt. Work, p. 177. Noy's Rights of the Crown, p. 45. who ſays it was Henry V.

[16] Rot. Parl. vol. iii. p. 419.   [17] Naunton's Fragmenta Re galia, p. 12.

public purpofes ; and whether fuch a fyftem ought not to be kept in view, if another war fhould unfortunately foon break out. If every wealthy perfon in the kingdom were obliged, when called upon by the legiflature, to furnifh a certain fum of money, at a reafonable intereft, upon the faith and fecurity of Parliament, loans would be raifed upon moderate terms, and probably without much murmur or oppreffion. By fuch means, the enormous profits, which are exacted by ufurious money-lenders, who combine together, and take every unfair advantage of the public neceffities, would be prevented ; nor would the nation, to gratify their rapacity, be loaded with burdens almoft unfupportable.

IV. Voluntary Loans.

But of all the modes of providing money for defraying the extra-ordinary expences of a nation, that of borrowing from fuch as are will-ing to lend their property upon the public fecurity, is undoubtedly the moft efficacious ; and it may not be improper, briefly to ftate the progrefs of the fyftem.

1. On valu-ablePledges.
The moft ancient, and indeed the moft natural mode of borrowing any confiderable fum of money, is that of giving to the lender, in pledge, fome article, the value of which is well known, or can eafily be afcertained. It was a long time before other modes of fecurity were invented, or ufually practifed. Nay, after bonds and written obliga-tions had become more frequent, recourfe was occafionally had to pledges ; and many of the Kings of England were reduced to the ne-ceffity of pawning their jewels, crown, and other valuable effects, in critical emergencies.

2. On Perfo-nal Security.
John, King of France, we are told, nobly declared, that if good faith were banifhed out of the reft of the world, yet that it ought ftill to be found in the breafts of princes ; and fuch in general is the con-fidence placed in the Royal Diadem, that there are few monarchs who are not able to raife fome money upon their perfonal obligations. But the amount of fuch fums is feldom very confiderable. Indeed, the additional fecurity of the City of London, and fometimes of the prin-cipal Minifters of State, was required, before fome of the Sovereigns of England could in this manner obtain the money which their neceffities demanded.

In

In almoſt every country, the laws have fruitlefsly endeavoured to prevent the diſſipation of the Royal Domains ; and in England, it was held impious to alienate them. Nay, as an additional check, every King was entitled to refume his own grants, or thoſe of his predeceſſors. Mortgaging the Domains, however, is in general permitted, as a lefs pernicious meaſure, though often attended with more ruinous conſequences. For, after any individual has been long in poſſeſſion of lands as a mortgagee, the ſpecific nature of his right is forgotten ; and he is not a little apt to conſider himſelf, and to be conſidered by others, as the real proprietor.

The mode, by which a nation firſt raiſes a conſiderable ſum of money, is generally by mortgaging ſome particular tax or branch of its revenue, and anticipating its produce. This is a very ancient practice in England. It may be traced, it is fuppofed, as far back as the reign of Edward I. ; and it is certain, that in the year 1444, Cardinal Beaufort gave a ſum of money in loan to Henry VI. upon the ſecurity of the Cuſtoms of London and Southampton[18]. Various other inſtances of ſuch anticipations will occur in a ſubſequent chapter.

When any branch of the revenue is mortgaged, it may either continue under the management of public officers, as is the cafe in England, or it may be entruſted to the care of the creditor, as is the practice in France. The firſt is beſt adapted to a free ; the fecond, to a deſpotic government : but, under every government, it has been originally found neceſſary to farm the revenues, either to the creditors of the public, or to thoſe who make it their profeſſion. For, ſuch is the ingenuity of mankind, and ſuch their inclination to elude taxes, that they would never become productive, if intereſted perſons were not employed to difcover the means of counteracting the evaſion of them ; and the public may afterwards, through the medium of its own officers, reap the benefit of ſuch diſcoveries.

Another mode of borrowing money, is, by granting annuities for a certain fixed ſpace of time, at the end of which they are totally to ceafe. The experience of England tends to demonſtrate, that this is not an advantageous mode of procuring money : at leaſt the demand

Side notes:
3. By mortgaging the Public Domains.

4. By mortgaging Taxes.

5. By temporary Annuities.

[18] Noy's Rights of the Crown, p. 41.

of

of the creditor is proportionably higher for ſhort, or even long annuities, than when a perpetual annuity is granted ; and a nation which
adopts the funding ſyſtem, ought to conſider itſelf as a great and permanent corporation, and ought to adopt that plan, which, in the courſe
of many centuries, is the moſt likely to be of advantage to the community, without regarding immediate profit, or temporary conve-
niencies.

6. By Annu-
itieson Lives.
Annuities for lives is another mode that has been frequently practiſed, and by ſome is accounted the moſt advantageous. But it is
hardly poſſible for a nation, when it is in diſtreſs, by any means to
make a profitable bargain with a money-lender, particularly on the
principle of granting temporary annuities. Thus, when annuities for
lives are granted, the creditor takes care to pitch upon the perſons who
are the moſt likely to live long, and who conſequently will prove, for
the longeſt period, a burden upon the State. Nor have all the flattering hopes which Tontines hold forth to the avarice of mankind, been
able to procure money by life annuities, on advantageous terms to the
public.

7. By Con-
tingent An-
nuities.
When a State is in great neceſſity, it is eaſily induced to liſten to the
propoſals of any body of men, who offer to ſupply it with a conſiderable ſum, in conſideration of being inveſted with certain peculiar privileges, whilſt the money they advance remains unpaid. It was thus
that the Bank of England, the Eaſt-India Company, and other great
Corporations aroſe in this country. The grants of ſuch privileges
may ſometimes prove uſeful to the public, as well as profitable to thoſe
who engage in them. The two Companies above alluded to are un-
queſtionably of that deſcription. But the limits of that mode of borrowing money with advantage, are certainly confined ; for monopolies,
or peculiar privileges, cannot be carried to a great height, without injuring the commerce, and leſſening the induſtry of a country, and
conſequently diminiſhing the national capital, or fund of wealth.

8. By Per-
petual An-
nuities.
The laſt mode of borrowing money for national purpoſes, and the
climax of financial invention, is, when a nation grants certain annuities
to its creditors, *for ever*, ſubject to redemption at a certain price. This
is a modern invention, of which the ancients ſeem to have had no conception. It is, in fact, ſelling, for ever, a branch of the public re-

4   venue.

venue. It will appear in the farther progrefs of this Work, that by the ingenuity of the public creditors, this mode of raifing money has been rendered much more prejudicial, than otherwife it would be, from the practice of adding what may be called artificial, to the real capital. By this artful manœuvre, the nation cannot redeem fuch perpetual burdens, without paying fums confiderably greater than it ever received.

Such are the various modes of providing for the extraordinary ex- Conclufion. pences of a nation ; to which might be added, exchequer bills and debentures of every kind, the fale of offices, as thofe of judicature in France, and the alienation of the public domains fo univerfally practifed. On the whole, it is eafy to perceive, that every plan of raifing extraordinary fupplies, is attended with confiderable difficulties. Perhaps, in different periods of fociety, different plans ought to be adopted. At firft, wars are carried on in a defultory manner, and on a narrow fcale ; and a wife ftatefman will then endeavour to procure within the year, as great an addition to the ordinary income of the public, as the nation can be prevailed upon to pay. But in times like thefe, when hoftilities are extended over every quarter of the globe ; and when, from ten to fifteen millions of additional income are required, for military and naval operations, raifing the fupplies within the year, is a meafure, which, however defirable, can hardly be put in practice.

With regard to the beft mode of borrowing money, for the public fervice, it is propofed, to inveftigate that important queftion, in the following Chapter.

C H A P.

C H A P. II.

Of Public Debts in general.

THE moft fingular and important political feature of the prefent Æra, is undoubtedly the heavy load of public debts, with which almoft every nation in Europe is encumbered. It is therefore very natural to enquire, with fome degree of anxiety, into the circumftances that gave birth to their exiftence ; and into the advantages and difadvantages they have produced : a fubject on which many authors have written with great ability, but which ftill remains open to more ample difcuffion, and liable to much uncertainty and difpute.

I. Caufes of the Public Debts of Modern Europe.

It has already been remarked, that the ancient mode of providing for the expences of war, was that of collecting treafures in time of peace ; and many have accounted fuch a meafure highly politic. During tranquil periods, it is faid, that money is lefs neceffary for individuals, as well as for the public ; and if it were not thus locked up for national purpofes, it would probably be wafted in purchafing luxurious fuperfluities from other countries. When treafures thus collected, are iffued, they revive circulation ; and amidft all the calamities of war, give new vigour to a ftate ; and as the public is thereby enabled to give ready money for provifions, and other neceffary articles, it can always procure them upon eafy and moderate terms. But modern nations, it is faid, having no treafures collected, find themfelves reduced, at the very commencement of a war, to the neceffity of borrowing. The money they raife, when expended in diftant operations, inftead of being thrown into circulation, is actually taken out of it ; and at the fame inftant, that twelve millions are procured by the minifter, the manufacturer, and the hufbandman, are involved in the greateft mifery and diftrefs.

Such reafoning is plaufible, and it is certain, that if confiderable treafures were collected, they would, in a great meafure, prevent the neceffity of contracting debts, unlefs on very important emergencies.

It

It appears, however, from the preceding Chapter, that public hoards are necessarily productive of so many political evils, as greatly to outweigh any advantage that could possibly be derived from them.

But the heavy burdens with which the exifting powers of Europe are encumbered, are owing, not only to the want of public treasures, but also to the different manner of conducting hoftilities in ancient and modern times.

Formerly, one or other of the parties at war, boldly entered into the territories of his opponent; and marching directly to the capital, or to any spot where the enemy had affembled, the fate of a wealthy kingdom, or powerful republic, was often decided by a single engagement. But in modern times, the whole fury of the war is spent in befieging towns on the frontier, or in doubtful naval operations, or in the attack and defence of some remote colony, or diftant appendage ; the confequence of which is, that the war is protracted to a great length, and becomes progreffively more expenfive. Thus neither of the parties are able to procure any great fuperiority, or decided advantage ; and hoftilities are carried on, until the refources of one, or both of them, are exhaufted ; and it is found impoffible to raife money, either by augmenting the ordinary revenue, or by borrowing on the public faith.

In ancient times, wars were not only fhorter in their duration, but means were also taken, and principles were adopted, which rendered great pecuniary fupplies lefs neceffary than at prefent. Formerly, the whole was a fcene of plunder and devaftation. The perfons and the property of the enemy were at the entire difpofal of the conqueror; and the general eftimated the profits of the campaign, not only by the quantity of money, and other perfonal effects he had feized ; but alfo by the number of his prifoners, who were fold for flaves, and were accounted a very valuable commodity. The greater part of the plunder taken in the campaign, was accounted for to the public ; and many a Roman general, after defraying the charges of the war from the booty he had acquired, was alfo able to make confiderable additions to the public treafury, amidft the triumphal fhouts of his countrymen.

The arms now made ufe of, are alfo much more expenfive than thofe of antiquity. The fhield, the fpear, the lance, the javelin, and the
[C]   bow

bow and arrow of the ancients, cannot be compared, in regard to price, with the modern mufquet; particularly when the re-iterated expence of powder and ball is taken into confideration. And as to military engines, there can be no comparifon in point of coft, between a modern train of artillery, and a fet of battering-rams and catapultæ.

But the principal fource of national expences in thefe times, when compared to thofe of antiquity, arifes from naval charges. It is at fea, where all the modern nations have wafted their ftrength. It is on that element that thofe debts have in a great meafure been contracted, under the preffure of which they now groan. Had the rage of equipping numerous fleets, and building fhips of great magnitude and dimenfions, never exifted, hardly any ftate in Europe would have been at this time in debt. To that fatal ambition their prefent diftreffed and mortgaged fituation, ought chiefly to be attributed[1].

The nature of thefe national incumbrances, and the effects refulting from them, have given rife to political controverfies of the greateft public importance. By fome, the practice of borrowing money, to defray the extraordinary expences of a State, is extolled to the fkies, as equally neceffary and ufeful; whilft others confider it as big with every fatal and deftructive confequence. It is propofed to give a general view, of the various arguments which have been made ufe of, on both fides of the queftion.

II.   Advantages of the Funding Syftem.

Montefquieu, after ftating fome of the inconveniencies of public debts, fays, " I know of no advantages[2]." Such incumbrances, and the credit on which they are founded, are not perhaps fo beneficial, as fome authors have endeavoured to reprefent them; but this excellent Writer feems to have formed, on this occafion, by far too hafty a conclufion.

---

[1] It will appear in the farther progrefs of this Work, how confiderable a fhare of the revenue of England, has been expended on its navy.

[2] L'Efprit des Loix, l, xxii. c. 17.

It

It is hardly poffible for any perfon who attentively confiders the fubject, to deny the beneficial confequences refulting from public credit, in the profecution of a juft and neceffary war. The celebrated Bifhop of Cloyne well obferves, that credit is the principal advantage which England has over France, and indeed over all the other States of Europe; that it is a mine of gold to this country; and that any meafures taken to leffen it, ought to be dreaded [3]. In fact, the great fuccefs which has uniformly attended the arms of Great Britain, when its affairs have been wifely and prudently conducted, has been entirely owing to the eafe with which any fum, however great, could be procured for the public_fervice.

Indeed, when money can be raifed without difficulty, the greateft exertions may be made with the higheft probability of fuccefs. No attempt is rendered fruitlefs, from the inability of fending force fufficient to atchieve the enterprife. Pinto's obfervations upon this head are conclufive. " If a nation (he remarks) is able to raife only two thirds " of the money which any particular fervice demands, thofe two thirds " will probably be thrown away. If the Englifh, for inftance, had " fent a fleet and army, weaker by one third than it was, to conquer " the Havanna, the expedition would not only have mifcarried, and " the whole expence would have been loft, but that lofs would have " occafioned many others. Inftead of the treafure, and other advan- " tages produced by their fuccefs, every circumftance would have been " inverted [4]." By the magic of public credit, fleets are equipped, and armies are levied, with an expedition almoft incredible; and Pompey's boaft, that he could raife fo many legions by only ftamping with his foot, is completely verified [5].

It is even acknowledged by a refpectable Writer, who is no friend to the funding fyftem, that when money is borrowed to defray the expences of a war, the private revenue of individuals is neceffarily lefs burdened, than if the fupplies were raifed within the year; and confequently they are better enabled, at leaft whilft the war continues, to fave and accumulate fome part of their revenue into capital, and by their

---

[3] The Querift, N° 233, 234.
[4] Effay on Circulation and Credit, p. 41. The tranflation by Mr. Baggs is referred to on account of the valuable Notes which it contains.
[5] See Mortimer's Elements of Finance, p. 364, 365.

frugality

frugality and induftry, to repair the breaches which the wafte and ex-travagance of government may occafionally make in the general capital of the State[6].

But there are other advantages refulting from the funding fyftem, which it may be proper here to mention.

If fupplies were raifed within the year, and the expences of war were confiderable, every individual would be obliged, in confequence of the additional weight of his contributions, greatly to curtail his expences; and the employment of the poor, and the confumption of the rich, would be confiderably diminifhed. Whereas, when taxes are nearly equal, in times of peace and war (which can only be the cafe where the fyftem of funding is adopted), the value of every fpecies of pro-perty, the mafs of national induftry, and the circulation of national wealth, are maintained on as regular, fteady, and uniform a footing, as the uncertainty and inftability of human affairs will admit[7]. Indeed, before public credit is carried to too great a height, a war maintained by national loans and taxes, may be accounted even an advantage to the State. It is of fervice to the poor, becaufe the price of their labour increafes with the greater demand for labourers; it is of ufe to the rich, for the greater occafion there is for money, the greater is the profit of

---

[6] Smith's Wealth of Nations, vol. ii. p. 558. To illuftrate this point, let us fuppofe, that during a period of thirty years, we were to have twenty years of peace, and ten years of war; for the carrying on of which, ten millions of extraordinary fupplies muft annually be raifed. Is it moft for the public advantage, to levy the ten millions every year during the war, and pay nothing during peace; or to raife the money by loans, and pay an equal fhare of the expence in time of peace, as well as in time of war? If a common carrier has ten hundred weight to remove, is it not better for him, inftead of putting it at once upon his horfe's back, gradually to remove it? In the fame manner, when a State, for its fafety and protection, is obliged to make great exertions, and to load itfelf with heavy burdens, is it not preferable, by fpreading and extending the load, to render it as light as poffible? See Letter to a Member of the Houfe of Commons, p. 27.

[7] See Gale on Public Credit, part i. fect. 3. Nay, this intelligent Author contends, that borrowing money is not only the moft convenient method of raifing extraordinary fupplies, but is alfo productive of an actual faving to the State. But his arguments in fup-port of fuch a pofition are obfcure, and are not juftified by recent experience. Befides, he does not take into his confideration, the charges of management, nor the heavy expence of collecting the revenue neceffary to defray the intereft of a public debt, nor the com-mercial difadvantages with which taxes are accompanied; and particularly forgets, that duties on confumption, which muft at laft be reforted to, take confiderably more out of the pockets of the public, than comes into the exchequer.

thofe

thofe who have money to lay out: and foreign wars, though unavoidably attended with many private calamities; yet generally put an end to public difcord, and free the country of a number of turbulent and vicious characters, who are a peft to fociety[1].

Among the advantages of the funding fyftem, there is none which its friends have fo highly extolled, and its enemies have fo loudly reprobated, as its tendency to attract money from foreign countries, and the confequences with which that circumftance is attended. It may, perhaps, be of fervice to a ftate at war, to be able to draw fome refources from other nations; and the want of fuch aid (as Pinto obferves) might have checked and enfeebled all our military operations. Perhaps, alfo, the Bank of England, and the Eaft-India Company, the eftablifhment of which has added fo much to the wealth and commerce of this country, could not have been erected, or carried on with fuch effect, from the low ftate of the trade and refources of England at that time, if it had not been for the affiftance they originally received from foreigners: and perhaps, fo great is the amount of our public debts at prefent, that the quantity far exceeds our confumption or demand at home; and our funds could hardly be kept up at any tolerable price, without foreign purchafers[2]. At the fame time, whether foreign property in our funds, ought to be accounted of public detriment or advantage, is perhaps the moft difficult queftion of any connected with the funding fyftem.

I am apprifed of what a very intelligent author has faid, "That the "trading fubjects of this kingdom, from the Farmer to the Merchant, "make upon an average upwards of ten *per cent. per annum*, of the "money borrowed from foreigners, by our government, at little more than "four; and thence, that a profit arifes of nearly fix *per cent.* to enable "the people to bear the burden of an increafe of taxes, and to give "them a frefh contributive faculty of fubfcribing to new loans[10]." But it muft be acknowledged, that if the money borrowed is immediately wafted in foreign expeditions, and never comes into the circulation of

[1] Ramfay's Effay on the Conftitution of England, p. 70. Letter to a Member of the Houfe of Commons, p. 28.

[9] Effay on Credit, p. 9. alfo p. 35.

[10] Mortimer's Elements of Finances, p. 386. edit. 1772. See alfo Hope's Letters on Credit, p. 21. 30, 31.

I

the

2. Attracts money from abroad.

the country, the nation that borrows, pays intereſt to foreigners for a ſum of money, without reaping from it any ſolid advantage. The only benefit it can poſſibly produce is, that it renders it unneceſſary to raiſe the money at home, by which the commerce and circulation of the country would probably be injured ".

At the ſame time, it is proper to obſerve, that when foreigners are admitted into the public funds of a country, they become naturally intereſted in promoting its happineſs and proſperity. " Where their trea " ſure is, there will their hearts be alſo." And not only many wealthy individuals who are born in other countries, are gradually led to conſider the State in which their property is ſettled, as their home, and thence are induced to come and reſide in it ; but if any great revolution, or a long ſeries of deſtructive hoſtilities were to take place on the Continent (from which we might be happily exempted in conſequence of our inſular ſituation), the greater part of our foreign creditors might find it equally neceſſary and deſirable, to ſhelter themſelves in England from the ſtorm, and this country would receive a valuable addition to its population and wealth ".

3. Keeps money at home.

The public debts of a nation not only attract riches from abroad, with a ſpecies of magnetic influence, but they alſo retain money at home, which otherwiſe would be exported, and which, if ſent to other countries, might poſſibly be attended with pernicious conſequences to the State whoſe wealth was carried out of it. If France, for example, maintained its wars by borrowing money, and England raiſed all its ſupplies within the year, the neceſſary conſequence would be, that all the looſe and unemployed money of England, inſtead of remaining here, expoſed to the chance of being taken up by a government, who gave no intereſt in return for the uſe of it, would naturally be tranſmitted to France, where it could be placed out to advantage. It is well known, that the proſpect of high intereſt has tempted many unworthy Engliſhmen, to inveſt their property in the funds of that kingdom ; and we may judge from thence, what would be the caſe, if the funds of England were not in exiſtence. In every ſtate, however poor, laws are enacted to prevent the exportation of its ſpecie, and

---

" See Eſſay on Circulation, p. 35. Note.

" For many excellent obſervations on this part of the ſubject, ſee Sir James Stewart's Inquiry into the Principles of Political Oeconomy, vol. ii. p. 442, 443. 450, 451. 462, 463, 464.

the

the diminution of its circulating wealth. But the eſtabliſhment of public debts is the moſt likely means to hinder it. For none but profligate uſurers would think of ſending their property into another country, to ſupport the credit and conſequence of a foreign, and perhaps an inimical power, when it is poſſible to lay it out at home, with any tolerable advantage.

Public debts are particularly favourable to circulation. The taxes which they occaſion upon the property of the rich, and the encouragements which they hold forth to the avaricious, prevent the accumulation of private hoards, and bring the whole money, and perſonal property of a country, into the market. The beneficial conſequences reſulting from ſuch a circumſtance are well known. Unleſs the property of a nation circulates, it is of no real uſe to the community. Treaſures concealed and hoarded up, might as well ſtill remain in the bowels of the earth, for any benefit they yield to the public. *4. Brings money into circulation.*

We are told, that Eumenes king of Pergamus, one of the ableſt ſtateſmen of antiquity, finding that he had reaſon to diſtruſt ſome of his officers, borrowed money of them, with a view of inſuring their fidelity; as they might eaſily perceive, that they ſtood no chance of being repaid, if by their treachery his ruin was effected: and it is ſaid, that Biſhop Burnet, with ſimilar views, adviſed William III. to run the nation into debt, in order to ſecure the ſupport of the wealthieſt individuals in the kingdom". But it is probable, that the debts contracted at the Revolution, were more owing to the diſtreſſes of the times, and the difficulty of raiſing the neceſſary ſupplies within the year, without burdening the people, than to any political motives. When once debts, however, are incurred, it is evident that every individual creditor is led by his own intereſt to ſupport the government, on the proſperity and exiſtence of which the ſecurity of his property depends; and whoever conſiders for a moment, the many calamities with which revolutions are accompanied, will not probably regret, that an additional circumſtance ſhould take place, which contributes to confirm the ſtability, and to prolong the exiſtence of an eſtabliſhed government, whilſt it is conducted with ſufficient attention to the rights and happineſs of the people. *5. Attaches people to government.*

. '' Swift's Hiſtory of the Four laſt Years of the Reign of Queen Anne, edit. 1758. p. 158.

6. Encou-
rages com-
merce and
induftry.

The facility with which individuals, in a country where public debts exift, can lay out the property they have acquired by their labour or ingenuity, without the rifk of commercial bankruptcies, or the unavoidable expences and fmall profit which landed eftates yield, and without even abandoning their profeffions, is no fmall encouragement to induftry. To a certain extent therefore, fuch public fecurities are highly ufeful to a trading people[1]. It encourages a fet of men, defcribed by Hume, as half merchants, and half ftock-holders, who are able to carry on trade without great pecuniary advantages; becaufe commerce is not their principal or fole fupport, their property in the funds being a fure refource for themfelves and their families. " And " the fmall profit which fuch merchants require, when compared to " what otherwife would be neceffary, renders their commodities " cheaper, caufes a greater confumption, quickens the labour of the " common people, and helps to fpread arts and induftry throughout the " whole fociety[2]."

Nay, Pinto is fo enraptured with the funding fyftem as to contend, that every new loan, creates a new artificial capital, which did not before exift, which becomes permanent, fixed, and folid, and circulates with as much advantage to the public, as if fo much real additional treafure had enriched the kingdom[3]. And another author roundly afferts, that if our national incumbrances were paid off, we fhould be obliged to run ourfelves again, as faft as poffible, into debt; in order to recover our trade, our happinefs, and our profperity[4]. But fuch a whimfical mode of coining wealth, of amaffing treafure, or of infuring the profperity of a nation, no wife State will probably much depend on.

Such are the advantages which are commonly enumerated, as connected with the funding fyftem; and fo beneficial do they appear, that

[1] Blackftone's Commentaries, vol. i. p. 328.

[2] Hume's Effays, vol. i. p. 366, and 367. The whole paffage is admirable, and ought to be carefully examined.

[3] The national debt is as much a real poffeffion, as any property in filver or in gold. Its value is founded on the opinion of mankind, and on the difficulty of its acquifition, which alone make gold and filver of more eftimation than copper or tin. Hope's Letters on Credit. p. 19.

[4] Reflections on the National Debt, by J. Champion. See fuch ideas refuted, Smith's Wealth of Nations, p. 556.

one author, who has carefully inveſtigated the ſubjeċt, calls it a maſter-piece of human policy[17]; and another compares it to that ſpecies of inundation, which carries riches and fertility, as well as terror, along with it[18]. Let us next examine the arguments adduced by thoſe who conſider it in a very different point of view.

III. Diſadvantages of the Funding Syſtem.

It is difficult to arrange the numerous arguments, which, in various languages, and from authors almoſt innumerable, have at different times been thrown out, to prove the dangerous conſequences, and in-deed inevitable ruin, which neceſſarily attend public debts, when car-ried to any height. It is propoſed, however, to inveſtigate with as much brevity as poſſible, 1. The diſadvantages attending this mode of procuring money in caſes of emergency. 2. The pernicious conſe-quences reſulting from public debts, whilſt they remain unpaid : and 3. How far they have a deſtruċtive tendency to increaſe and accu-mulate.

The poſſeſſion of unbounded credit, like the accumulation of an immenſe treaſure, is too apt to make a nation inclined to engage in raſh and dangerous enterpriſes; and a State that can borrow fifty, or, if neceſſary, even a hundred millions, in the courſe of a war, thinks itſelf entitled to become an umpire among ſurrounding nations, and readily draws its ſword upon every trifling occaſion. Hence debts are often contraċted, not in ſupport of meaſures advantageous to the pub-lic, but in ridiculous quarrels, to gratify the humour of a headſtrong populace, or to carry on the viſionary projeċts, of the ſovereign, or his miniſters. " It is ſcarcely more imprudent (ſays Hume) to give a " prodigal ſon a credit in every banker's ſhop in London, than to em-" power a ſtateſman to draw bills in this manner upon poſterity[19]." Nay, this is a diſadvantage attending the funding ſyſtem, which its warmeſt advocate is under the neceſſity of acknowledging[20].

When a nation alſo borrows money, it is generally in a ſtate of diſ-treſs, and muſt ſubmit to any terms which the money-lender thinks

(margin note) 1. Diſad-vantages of public credit.

[17] Elements of Finance, p. 378.   [18] Eſſay on Public Credit, pref. p. 6.

[19] Eſſays, vol. i. p. 365.   See alſo Reynal, vol. iv. p. 453.

[20] Eſſay on Credit, p. 107, 108.

[D]   proper

proper to impofe. That unhappy fituation, the creditor uniformly takes advantage of, to make the public pay dear for the affiftance it receives.

" *Hinc ufura vorax, avidumque in tempore fænus,*
" *Hinc concuffa fides, & multis utile bellum*[22]..

Nay, if hoftilities are not carried on to maintain the effential interefts, or to preferve the very exiftence of a nation, it is no undefirable circumftance, that the public fhould feel the pecuniary calamities of war, fo as to render it defirous of peace, when reafonable terms can be obtained. When money however can eafily be procured, and the nation is only loaded with an annuity to pay the intereft of the debt that is incurred, war is a paftime to the people, which they are not defirous of giving up, whilft they are occafionally favoured with Extraordinary Gazettes, announcing the victories gained by their fleets and armies, and celebrating the valour of their troops, and the conduct of their commanders[23].

2. Pernicious confequences of public debts whilft they remain unpaid.

But if it were allowed that a nation, when it contracts public debts, may reap confiderable benefit by expending the money that it borrows, in well-judged and fuccefsful enterprifes ; yet it is evident that fuch incumbrances muft be attended with confiderable difadvantages, whilft they remain unpaid.

1. The income neceffary to pay the intereft of a public debt, is a heavy burden upon the wealth and induftry of a nation. The additional taxes, which it gives rife to, neceffarily occafion an increafe in the price of all the neceffaries of life, and renders it more difficult for the manufacturers of a mortgaged State, to carry on a fuccefsful competition with the fubjects of other powers, who may happen to be in a lefs embarraffed fituation ; and it is well known, that the ruin of the manufacturers of Holland, is univerfally attributed to the weight of taxes, which the public debt of that country has entailed upon it. Nay, what fome authors confider as the moft obnoxious of all the public evils, confequent to the funding fyftem, is, that the active and induftrious fubject fhould thus be loaded with heavy burdens, to maintain the ufelefs and indolent creditor in luxury and fplendor[24].

---

[22] Lucan.   [23] Wealth of Nations, vol. ii. p. 550, 551. 558, 559.

[24] L'Efprit des Loix, l. xxii. c. 17.   Blackft. Comm. vol. i. p. 329.   Hume's Effays, vol. i. p. 368.   Reynal, vol. iv. p. 454.

2. Public

2. Public debts have alfo a tendency to promote idlenefs and immorality among the people at large. The money neceffary to pay the intereft of fuch incumbrances cannot be raifed, unlefs the legiflature encourages, or at leaft winks at, immoderate expences in all the different ranks of the people. A large and voluptuous capital is therefore fuffered to encreafe, and meets with every poffible encouragement, notwithftanding its tendency to corrupt the manners, and to diminifh the numbers of the people. But every object of that nature, however important, muft be facrificed for the benefit of the revenue [23].

3. When a nation is encumbered with debts, a pernicious fpirit of gambling is introduced. Stock-jobbing, with all its train of dangerous confequences, neceffarily arifes: A monied intereft is erected, the fole employment of which, is that of drawing every poffible advantage, from the wants of individuals, or the neceffities of the public: felfifh and interefted principles fpread their deftructive influence far and wide: public fpirit either ceafes to exift, or becomes the object of ridicule [24].

Indeed, ftock-jobbing is faid to be a neceffary confequence of the funding fyftem, without which the public could not borrow fuch large fums of money, as may be neceffary for the enterprifes it has in view [25]; and unfortunately, to a certain extent, that circumftance muft be admitted. It is the hope of great advantage (and without gambling, much profit could not be acquired) which engages individuals to fubfcribe to new loans, and collects together the immenfe fums of money which are neceffary for that purpofe. The practice is at the fame time attended with fo much real injury to individuals, that no advantage can compenfate for the mifchiefs which it produces [26].

4. But a nation is not only heavily burdened, to defray the intereft of its debts, but is alfo obliged to maintain a number of officers to collect fuch branches of the revenue as are appropriated to that purpofe, and to defray the expences, with which the conducting or management

[23] Hume's Effays, vol. i. p. 367, 368, 369. Reynal, vol. iv. p. 454. L'Efprit des Loix, l. xxii. c. 17. Enquiry into the original of the Public Debt, p. 12.

[25] Original of Public Debt, p. 13. 14.

[27] Effay on Public Credit, p. 37, 38.

[28] See this fubject fully and ably difcuffed, in Mortimer's Elements of Finances, p. 374. 392.

of

of public funds is attended. And in a limited monarchy, like that of England, fuch a circumftance is peculiarly injurious ; for the creation of a number of places, and the entertaining a whole hoft of officers of the revenue, has a tendency to produce very important alterations in the nature of its government[19].

5. If public debts attract money from abroad, they are alfo attended with the pernicious confequence of rendering one State in a manner tributary to another. It is fuppofed that foreigners are at prefent pof-feffed of about a ninth part of the national debt of England, and con-fequently muft receive about a million a year from this country. If we were obliged (as one author very ingenioufly remarks) to pay a tri-bute of that amount to France, or to any other foreign State, every perfon would declare, that the nation muft infallibly be undone ; yet, the tribute paid to foreign creditors, is at prefent on a footing infinitely more pernicious[20] : for it is impoffible to get clear of it, unlefs by a public bankruptcy, or by paying above thirty years purchafe to the fo-reign annuitants ; a fum fully equal to the whole fpecie that circulates in the nation[21]. But the experience of England does not tend to juftify fuch political fpeculations ; and there is ftill fome reafon to hope, that permitting foreigners to acquire property in our funds, inftead of proving the means of tranfporting our people and our induftry to other climes, as Hume fo much apprehended[21], may be productive of very oppofite confequences, and may yet increafe the wealth and population of this country.

Laftly, When public debts are carried to a great height, they tend to weaken the nation by which they are incurred. Wars, though per-haps neceffary for the fafety of a State, muft be avoided ; for the re-fources by which they ought to be carried on, are already fpent. Among the other caufes therefore of national ruin, the practice of funding is

[19] Blackft. Comm. vol. i. p. 336. Elements of Finance, p. 373. 387, 388. Ori-ginal of the National Debt, p. 15.

[20] See Original of the Public Debt, p. 17. Blackft. Comm. vol. i. p. 329. L'Efprit des Loix, l. xxii. c. 17.

[21] Reynal (vol. iv. p. 452.) fays, that borrowing money from foreigners, is in fact, felling to them one or more of the provinces of the empire : and declares, that perhaps it would be a more rational practice to deliver up the foil, than to cultivate it folely for their ufe.

[21] Effays, vol. i. p. 369.

I   enumerated,

enumerated, as, fooner or later, the fource of weaknefs and defolation to every State where it has been adopted[11].

Every political fyftem may in two refpeéts be highly exceptionable. It may either be founded on improper principles in itfelf, or it may have a ftrong and natural tendency to be perverted. To the latter objection, it can hardly be denied, that public debts are particularly expofed. 3. Tendency to increafe and accumulate.

In faét, not an inftance can be produced from hiftory, of any nation having once begun to run itfelf into debt, that the burden was not perpetually increafing. No confiderable progrefs was ever made, excepting in France, under Sully's adminiftration, in diminifhing fuch incumbrances. The fame want of public zeal (which perhaps was the occafion of a national debt being originally contraéted) renders it popular to defer taking any manly and decifive meafures, for the liberation of the revenue. The parties principally interefted, become every day more callous and infenfible, to the dangers they are likely to encounter, or are ignorant how deeply they are concerned in preventing fuch delays. The creditor is in general fatisfied, with having his intereft punétually paid him; and at any rate is not entitled to demand the capital of his debt. The minifter, happy to be relieved from the moft obnoxious of all duties (that of adding to the burdens of the people in time of peace) employs his thoughts in concerting the means of preferving his own power, and of humbling his opponents, regardlefs of the immortal reputation he might acquire, by purfuing a different fyftem; whilft the public at large, loaded with accumulated burdens, hating the paft, and dreading the future; without zeal, and without fpirit, prone to floth, and incapable of exertion, fuffer matters to go on as they are, neither knowing what to hope, or what to fear.

Such are the principal objeétions which have been urged againft the funding fyftem; a general view of which, colleéted from the principal authors who have written upon the fubjeét, it was imagined, would not prove difagreeable to the reader. Many have been fo ftrongly impreffed with the folidity of thefe arguments, that a thoufand prophecies have been made, that our debts would prove the utter ruin of this country; Reflexion.

[11] Fergufon's Effay on Civil Society, p. 389. Smith's Wealth of Nations, vol. iii. p. 363, 364. Hume's Effays, vol. i. p. 369. 372. Blackft. Comm. vol. i. p. 329.

that

that a hundred millions was a greater burden than it could poffibly bear; and that the nation muft either deftroy its debts, or its debts would deftroy the nation. Notwithftanding all thefe gloomy predictions, it is evident, that the nation ftill remains in a flourifhing fituation; and confequently, that our national incumbrances are not quite fo deftructive as they have fometimes been reprefented. But the funding fyftem, on its prefent footing, is doubtlefs attended with many fatal confequences. It is a queftion therefore of confiderable importance, whether a plan of borrowing money *might not* be formed, liable to no material objection, productive of many public advantages, and capable of exalting a nation to the greateft degree of happinefs and profperity. With a few obfervations upon that fubject, it is propofed to conclude the prefent Chapter.

IV. Plan of eftablifhing the Funding Syftem on the moft beneficial Principles for a Nation.

When a nation refolves to defray its extraordinary expences by borrowing money, it ought to fet out upon certain fixed and unalterable principles, confirmed in the moft folemn manner by the whole legiflature, and from which it ought never to depart.

1. The firft principle that the public ought to eftablifh, is never to become bound to pay an *iota* more, than the fpecific principal fum which it originally borrowed. Adding an artificial to a real capital, or pledging the public to pay a hundred pounds, when perhaps only fixty were received, is the moft pernicious of all financial operations; and any minifter that propofed fuch a plan in Parliament, ought to be made liable to impeachment. It will probably be alledged, that it may be found impoffible to borrow money, without giving the creditor that ufurious advantage. That objection, however, ought not to be regarded. For when the money-lender knows, that every other plan is contrary to an eftablifhed law, which cannot fafely be infringed, his ideas will be regulated accordingly, and the difference will be made up by premiums, or, in the language of the Alley, by an additional *bonus* or *douceur*, on principles lefs pernicious to the public. Indeed, if money cannot be borrowed in fuch a manner, it is a fign, either that the minifter is defervedly

fervedly unpopular, or that the war is unneceffary, and confequently ought not to be perfevered in.

This rule, if invariably adhered to, will for ever prevent the accumulation of a great artificial capital, which terrifies the imaginations of mankind, depreffes the fpirit of the people, diminifhes their credit, and confequently impairs their ftrength.

2. It ought alfo to be an unalterable law of the land, that after the creditor has received the intereft originally agreed upon, for the fpace of five, or at the utmoft feven years, it fhall be in the power of the public to pay him off, if money can be borrowed for that purpofe at a lower intereft. This principle, if rigoroufly attended to, will gradually occafion, a great diminution, in the intereft of our debts. England, at this time, pays only three *per cent.* for money that was originally borrowed at eight; and where artificial capitals do not obftruct fuch a meafure, a nation can always borrow, in time of peace, at a cheaper rate, than in time of war, and thus the weight of its debts may be perpetually diminifhed[24].

3. A State determined to carry on its wars, by the funding fyftem, ought never to borrow money upon any other principle, than that of perpetual annuities. All long and fhort annuities, and annuities for lives, whether tontines or otherwife, ought to be avoided. They breed confufion in the public accounts; they occafion a great additional expence for management; and the money that is borrowed, is procured upon terms infinitely more difadvantageous to the public. Whether, in time of peace, fome money might not be raifed, in a favourable manner, upon life annuities, is queftionable; but, there can be no doubt that, in time of war, it is impoflible for the public to make any tolerable bargain with money-lenders, founded on any uncertain contingency.

[24] It is well known, that the intereft of money is perpetually decreafing, with the increafing wealth and commerce of a country, and of that circumftance the public is particularly able to avail itfelf: For when it regularly and punctually pays the intereft of its debts, it can always borrow in time of peace on better terms than private individuals, on account of the greater eafe and certainty with which the intereft of its annuities are received, particularly by thofe who refide in the capital.

It is alfo proper to remark, that diminifhing the intereft is not fufficient. It is alfo neceffary to leffen the capital, by feafonable and well-conducted operations.

Befides,

Befides, whatever may be faid in regard to calculations in the Alley, that an annuity for a hundred years, is equal to a perpetuity ; yet, as Dr. Smith well obferves, thofe who buy into the public ftocks, in order to make family fettlements, or to provide for remote futurity (and they are the principal buyers and holders of ftock), and corporations of every kind, are not fond of buying into a fund, the value of which is perpetually diminifhing. And though the intrinfic worth of an annuity for a long term of years, is nearly the fame with that of a perpetual annuity, yet it is not fo valuable in the market, is never fo much in requeft, and does not find the fame number of purchafers³⁵.

Indeed, if a nation is determined to perfevere in the funding fyftem, the wifeft and moft politic ftep it can poffibly take, is to adopt that mode of procuring money, which is the moft likely to be the cheapeft and moft advantageous in the courfe of ages. It may flatter itfelf, that when it borrows upon fhort or long annuities, it will reap confiderable advantages, when fuch annuities are extinguifhed. But it ought at the fame time to remember, that before the annuities can ceafe, more money, in all probability, muft be raifed ; and if the fame unprofitable fyftem is adhered to, the nation will always be borrowing money upon difadvantageous terms.

4. The eftablifhment of an unalienable finking fund, for the redemption of public debts, is another principle, which, in a State, where it is propofed to perfevere in the funding fyftem, cannot poffibly be difpenfed with ; and fuch a fund ought to arife, not from any little furplus of revenue, or the increafing produce of particular branches, but fhould be founded on fome great, folid, and productive tax, proportioned as much as poffible to the wealth of the nation, and the debts it has incurred. For that purpofe, no plan would be fo effectual, as a permanent regulation, by which every individual, having property in England, whether natives or foreigners, was under the neceffity of leaving to the public, at leaft *one half of his clear annual income* in this country, at the time of his death. No teftament ought to be valid, without fuch a bequeft ; and if any perfon died inteftate, a year's income fhould be exacted. A revenue of this kind, would always keep the debts of a nation within moderate bounds, and could hardly be evaded.

<hr>

³⁵ Wealth of Nations, vol. ii. p. 547.

5. The care of fuch an unalienable finking fund, fhould be entrufled to individuals peculiarly refponfible for its fuccefs. A fpecial commif-fion fhould be appointed for that purpofe alone. A different fet of in-dividuals fhould be pitched upon to pay off public debts, from thofe by whom they are contracted; and the progrefs made in difcharging the incumbrances of a nation, ought never to be fo involved with other operations of finance, as to become imperceptible to the eye of the public.

6. Every means fhould be adopted that might have a tendency to en-courage individuals, when they had no near relations, to leave their fortune and property to the public. The effects of fuch a meafure, particu-larly in wealthy and commercial nations, would be almoft incredible. But this is a fubject, which will afterwards require to be more fully invefti-gated. At prefent, it is fufficient to remark, that if fuch a fpirit had been encouraged, when our debts were originally contracted, and par-ticularly, if thofe fums had been left to the State, invariably appropri-ated, and accumulated at compound intereft, which were bequeathed to other public purpofes of lefs general utility, no inconfiderable fhare of our prefent immenfe incumbrances would have been long fince cancelled.

Laftly, peculiar checks, and additional fecurities ought to be con-trived, to prevent the wafte of the money that is borrowed[15]. It is the abufe of the funding fyftem; the fraudulent practices, and fhameful profufion of thofe who are entrufted with the guardianfhip of the public purfe, which occafion confufion and diftrefs in the finances of a country. Pinto afferts, that the Englifh might have done as much during all their wars, with one third lefs expence[17]. This is undoubt-edly exaggerated. But no one can poffibly deny, that if effectual fteps had been taken at the revolution, to check public frauds, and if the fame meafures had ever fince been perfevered in, a confiderable portion of our public debts would have been prevented.

---

[15] The beft check undoubtedly would be, to order fuch money to be paid to par-liamentary commiffioners, according to an ancient practice in this country. Such com-miffioners ought to have the whole charge of borrowing and expending the money. The confequences of trufting fuch powers to a minifter, muft ever be ruinous.

[17] Effay on Credit, p. 107.

[E]   Thefe

Conclufion.   Thefe are the principles on which public debts may, in general, be fafely contraſted, and which, if ſteadily adhered to, would always prevent the funding fyſtem from becoming burdenfome, or ruinous to a State. Nor ought the inveſtigation of fuch a fubjeſt to be accounted ufelefs to this country. For though our principal objeſt, at this time, ought to be, how to overcome the difficulties in which we are involved from paſt mifconduſt, yet an invariable plan of borrowing money for public fervices, in time to come, fhould be formed without delay ; and indeed our prefent incumbrances ought, if poſſible, to be reduced within the bounds of fuch permanent regulations, as the abilities of our ſtatef-men, and the wifdom of our legiſlature, may deem moſt conducive to the intereſt of the community.

C H A P. III.

Of the Public Debts of England, prior to the Revolution 1688.

THE public debts of a nation, when it is fubjeſt to a monarchical form of government, may be confidered in two different points of view : either as the perfonal debts of the fovereign, or as real incumbrances on the community.

A modern French author[1] (Monfieur Linguet) contends, that in an an abfolute government, like France, the reigning prince has only a temporary intereſt in the revenues of the State ; and confequently, that it would be not only a prudent and humane, but even a legal operation to annihilate the public debt at the commencement of every reign. But in England, where a limited monarchy exiſts, and where the money is borrowed by the reprefentatives of the people, he thinks that the whole kingdom ſtands pledged for the fecurity of the contraſt, and

---

[1] Linguet, Annal. politiq. du dix huitieme fiecle, tome i. p. 38.

that

that fuch a meafure would be a difgraceful and criminal bank-ruptcy.

It is impoffible to perceive, either the juftice of the diftinction ftated, or the benefit that would refult from it, to an abfolute government.

As to the juftice of the meafure that is propofed, it is evident that the money is borrowed in both cafes by the legal fovereign, and is fup-pofed to be expended for the public ufes of the State; and whether the fovereign that enters into fuch pecuniary engagements, is a def-potic monarch, or confifts of many individuals, does not feem to be material.

With regard to the advantage of fuch a diftinction, it would foon appear how unferviceable it muft prove. The credit of an abfolute mo-narch, who could only give fecurity to his creditors, during his own life, would be neceffarily unproductive and infignificant. Indeed fuch a principle would be equivalent to the eftablifhment of a perpetual inabi-lity of borrowing money, even in the moft preffing emergency, except on terms the moft ufurious and deftructive.

But the reader will be better enabled to form an opinion on this cu-rious fubject of political fpeculation, from examining the hiftory of our public debts prior to the Revolution, during which period they were only accounted the perfonal obligations of the fovereign, and weigh-ing the confequences they produced at that time, when put in compa-rifon with thofe perpetual national incumbrances which have fince taken place.

The unfortunate Henry III. is the firft monarch of England whofe debts are recorded in hiftory. In the fixteenth year of his reign, they had become fo great, that parliament was obliged to grant an aid to affift him in paying them off. His pecuniary diftreffes, however, were perpe-tually encreafing, in confequence of his folly and extravagance; and he in vain endeavoured to relieve them, by pawning the jewels of the crown, his robes of State, and other regal ornaments; nay, the fhrine of St. Edward, though at that time an object of particular veneration. Indeed, we are informed by Matthew Paris, that he owed fo much, to fo many different people, for the very neceffaries of life, that he durft hardly appear in public, for the clamours of his creditors. And other

Henry III. 1232.

[E] 2   hiftorians

hiftorians[2] reprefent him as publicly declaring, that fuch were his difficulties, that it was more charitable to give him money, than any beggar
at the door.

Edward I.   Henry died confiderably in debt; but his fon Edward I. was induced,
either from the generofity of his own difpofition, or from a fuperftitious
idea which prevailed at that time, that the foul of the deceafed remained
in purgatory until all his debts were paid, to make great exertions in
order to difcharge them[3]. And thofe incumbrances, which the many
wars he was engaged in, rendered it neceffary for him to incur[4], he was
always anxious to pay off, as fpeedily as his narrow revenue, and fmall
refources would permit.

Edward II.   It appears that Edward II. imitated his father's example, in refolving
to difcharge the debts of his predeceffor; for in the third year of his
reign, writs were iffued to the collectors of the cuftoms, requiring them
to pay certain vaft fums of money to his father's creditors, out of the
faid cuftoms, and 100,000l. befides, for the lofs and damage they had
fuftained, in confequence of the late and flow payment of the money
that was due to them[5].

Edward III.   The various military expeditions carried on by Edward III. neceffarily
involved him in the greateft difficulties. It is ftated in the very writ,
Anno 1340.   by which a parliament was fummoned in the fourteenth year of his
reign, that he had borrowed fo much money abroad upon his *perfonal
fecurity*, that if the fums for which he ftood engaged were not all paid,
he was obliged in his own proper perfon to return to Bruffels, and to
remain there, as a pledge to his creditors. Compulfive loans were not
unufual during his reign[6]; and pawning the royal jewels, nay the
crown of England itfelf, were meafures to which his neceffities compelled him.

Richard II.   Richard II. at firft endeavoured to eftablifh the credit of the crown,
by exerting himfelf to pay his grandfather's (Edward III.) debts, which

[2] See Stevens's Hiftory of Taxes, pref. p. 31. See alfo Parliamentary Hiftory, vol. i.
p. 27, 28. 44.
[3] In the words of the record, " ad exonerationem animæ Henrici regis, patris noftri."
[4] See Turner's cafe of the bankers and their creditors, p. 37.
[5] Cafe of the Bankers, p. 20.
[6] Parliament Hift. vol. i. p. 251.

were

were very confiderable. The commons had petitioned the crown for that purpofe, in the fourth year of his reign. They declared, that fuch a payment would be a ftrong encouragement to his Majefty's fub-jects, to lend him money on any great and unforefeen emergency. The anfwer from the throne was very gracious; the King declaring, that the requeft had been in a good meafure already fulfilled, and that the remainder fhould be done according to their petition[7].

It was in the reign of this monarch, that the firft attempt was made to raife money by the affiftance of Parliament. A plan had been form-ed of invading France with a formidable army; but fuch was the po-verty of the exchequer at that time, that it was found impracticable to attempt it, without borrowing money for that purpofe. The King therefore, had confulted with the principal merchants of London, and of other wealthy towns, about a loan. But fo many of them had fuftained fuch heavy loffes by former loans, that they refufed to lend any confiderable fum of money without the fecurity of Parliament. In order to procure the fanction of that affembly, a Parliament was Anno 1382. fummoned, and when the commons demanded what fum was neceffary to defray the charges of the intended expedition, they were anfwered *fixty thoufand pounds :* even that fmall fum could not be procured. The nobility pretended that they had no money; but they were willing to ferve the King perfonally in the war. The merchants on the other hand refufed to fupply the King's wants, unlefs they received the moft indifputable fecurity, and unlefs the nobility, clergy, and gentry would furnifh him with a confiderable fum without intereft. After an ineffectual attempt to raife the money, by granting foreign merchants the liberty of trafficking in England on eafy terms, the King was unwil-lingly compelled to give up the firft enterprife he had attempted, for the want of that inconfiderable fupply[8].

Among the articles for which Richard II. was depofed, his having Henry IV. extorted money under the pretence of borrowing, which was never repaid, is particularly infifted upon. It is no wonder therefore, that his fucceffor fhould be particularly anxious to avoid following his exam-

/

7 Rot. Parl. vol. iii. p. 96. Num. 45. Cafe of the bankers, p. 17.
8 Rot. Parl. vol. iii. p. 122, 123. Parl. Hift. vol. i. p. 394, 395.
9 Rot. Parl. vol. iii. p. 419.

ple

ple in that particular. Accordingly we find, that in the fixth year of his reign, when the commons prayed, that all tallies given by his Majefty for money lent to him by his fubjects, might be fatisfied, according to the true purport of the faid fecurities, notwithftanding any change made in the minifters of State, or officers of the exchequer, the King anfwered, that good payment fhall be forthwith made of the faid debts[10].

Henry V.

This gallant monarch did not purchafe his laurels in France, without oppreffing his people, and involving himfelf in the greateft pecuniary difficulties. In the fourth year of his fhort, but brilliant reign, his wants became particularly preffing; and a Parliament having been called for their relief, a fubfidy of two tenths and two fifteenths (about

Anno 1416. 60,000*l.*") was granted by the laity ; and two tenths from the clergy. But, as there was reafon to apprehend that the money would come in too flowly for the purpofes of the crown, it was propofed, that fuch as were willing to lend money to the King, fhould have letters patent to be paid out of the firft produce of the fubfidy that was granted ; and the Dukes of Clarence, Bedford, and Gloucefter pledged themfelves to fee this performed, in cafe the King fhould die before the fubfequent feaft of St. Martin's, in the year 1417. Notwithftanding this additional fecurity (which however was only contingent), the nation was either fo poor, or fo little accuftomed to propofals of that nature, that only half a tenth and fifteenth (about 14,500*l.*) could be raifed ; and the King was obliged to pawn the crown, and the royal jewels, to make up the deficiency". Another fubfidy, amounting to about 38,000*l.* was granted in the feventh year of his reign ; the produce of a part of which, the King found means to anticipate with fome difficulty". On the whole, it appears that Henry was not only ill-fupported by the grants of his Englifh fubjects, but alfo found the utmoft difficulty in borrowing money on the fecurity of the fubfidies which he received. Whereas, had the funding fyftem exifted in his reign, and could wealthy individuals have had full affurance that their money would be repaid, or an adequate intereft allowed for it, *even though the King fhould die* ; it is more than probable, that he would have completed the

---

[10] Cafe of the bankers, p. 17. Rot. Parl. 6 Henry IV. num. 53. vol. iii. p. 555.

[11] 60,000*l.* was about 116,000*l.* of our money.

[12] Rot. Parl. vol. iv. p. 95. Parl. Hift. vol. ii. p. 155.

[13] Rot. Parl. vol. iv. p. 117.

conqueft

conqueſt of France before he died. Whether that would have proved of advantage to this country, or otherwiſe, is a very different queſtion.

During the reign of this weak and unfortunate monarch, the debts of the crown were often brought under the conſideration of Parliament. Soon after his acceſſion, letters patent granted to the biſhop of Wincheſter, entitling him to receive twenty thouſand pounds, out of the firſt money ariſing from the cuſtoms, and other revenues of the crown, were confirmed by an act of the legiſlature; and the council were empowered by different votes of credit, paſſed at various times, to give ſecurity to the King's creditors, for ſums of money, which varied from 50,000 *l.* to 200,000 *l.* according to the amount of the ſubſidy that was granted[14]. But many of theſe ſecurities not being taken up, Henry's debts were perpetually accumulating; and they amounted at laſt to 372,000 *l.* ſuppoſed equal in value to 1,100,000 *l.* of our money[15]. The pecuniary difficulties in which this King was involved, joined to the ſhameful loſs of all the immenſe territories which had been acquired by his father on the Continent, were the great ſources of the revolution which afterwards took place in favour of the houſe of York.

We are told by lord Bacon, in his hiſtory of Henry VII. that he often borrowed money of his ſubjects, but punctually paid it back the very day it became due. It was a conſtant maxim with him, rather to borrow too ſoon, than pay too late. The ſums he had in loan, at leaſt in the beginning of his reign, were very inconſiderable. At firſt, he could only procure two thouſand pounds, and afterwards only four, from the city of London. But in order to keep up his credit, he was more anxious to repay ſuch inconſiderable debts, than the public is at preſent about diminiſhing the many millions which it owes[16].

In the preceding part of this work, ſome account was given of this monarch's compulſive loans, and other tyrannical exactions[17]; and of the acts that were paſſed, by which the debts he had incurred were diſcharged. The firſt ſtatute that was paſſed for that purpoſe, is not included in our printed acts of Parliament, but may be ſeen in Burnet's Hiſtory of the Reformation[18]. The grounds which are ſtated in the preamble to the bill, as the cauſes of its being enacted, are truly in-

Henry VI.

Anno 1425.

Henry VII.

Henry VIII.

[14] Parl. Hiſt. vol. ii. p. 195, 217. 222. 233. 241. 245. 249. 262.
[15] Ibid. p. 275, 276.
[16] Bacon's Hiſt. of Henry VII. Edit. 1676. p. 46.
[17] See part i. chap. 8.   [18] Vol. i. Append. No. 31.

famous.

famous. It is there declared, " That though divers of his fubjeds had
" lent his majefty great fums of money, *which had been all well em-*
" *ployed in the public fervice, and for the payment of which, the lenders*
" *had his fecurity ;*" yet, in confideration of the great things that the
King had done for the church and nation, which had involved him in
great expences, the Parliament offered him all the money he had thus received in loan ; difcharged him of the obligations he had come under ;
and of all fuits that might arife thereupon[19]. Another ad of a fimilar
nature was paffed, in the 35th year of his reign[20]. Fortunately the ftatute book cannot produce another example of fuch defpotic, arbitrary,
and difgraceful proceedings.

Edward VI.   During the reign of Edward VI. it became an ufual pradice to borrow money on the Continent; and it appears that he was indebted to
banks and to individuals abroad, in the fum of 132,372*l.* 10*s.* for which
he paid a heavy intereft of 14 *per cent.* His debts within the realm
amounted to 108,807*l.* 4*s.* 10*d.* the particulars of which were as
follows[21] :

						£.	s.	d.
To the houfehold	-	-	-	-	-	28,000	0	0
To the chambre	-	-	-	-	-	23,000	0	0
To the wardrobe	-	-	-	-	-	6075	18	0
To the ftable	-	-	-	-	-	1000	0	0
To th' Admiraltie	-	-	-	-	-	5000	0	0
To th' Ordinaunce	-	-	-	-	-	3134	7	10
To the Surveyer of the Works	-	-	-	3200	0	0
To *Calleys*	-	-	-	-	-	14000	0	0
To *Barwyck*	-	-	-	-	-	6000	0	0
To the Revels	-	-	-	-	-	1000	0	0
To *Silley* and *Alderney*	-	-	-	-	1000	0	0
To *Ireland*	-	-	-	-	-	13128	6	8
To *Winter*, for his Voyage to Ireland	-	-	471	4	6
To *Barthilmewe Campagni* (the King's Merchant)	4000	0	0
To *Portefmouth*, and the Ifle of *Wight*	-	1000	0	0
To the Men of Armes	-	-	-	-	800	0	0
To the Lieutenant of the Tower	-	-	997	7	10

£. 108,807   4   10

[19] Parl. Hift. vol. iii. p. 65.   [20] Cap. 12.
[21] Strype's Ecclef. Memorials, vol. ii. p. 312. Parl. Hift. vol. iii. p. 264.

The

The reader will naturally remark the ftriking difference between the fums then due on account of the Navy and the Ordnance, and the enormous outftanding or unfunded debts which now exift on thefe two departments.

Mary began her bloody reign, with an unufual act of grace to her fubjects. A fupply had been granted by Parliament to her brother Edward VI. for the purpofe of paying his debts. The money had not been raifed when fhe came to the throne; and by the advice of the artful Gardiner, fhe remitted the fubfidy, with a view of ingratiating herfelf with the people, and of rendering a Popifh Prince more acceptable to her Proteftant fubjects. But, fhort as her reign was, fhe was reduced to fuch pecuniary difficulties, as to be obliged to borrow fmall fums, even fo low as ten pounds, according to people's abilities. It is proper however to mention, that when fhe found it was unlikely that fhe could live long enough, to obtain any aid from Parliament to pay off the debts fhe had contracted, fhe made it one of her laft requefts to her fifter, to fee them fatisfied". *Mary.*

The conduct of Elizabeth, in regard to public debts, cannot be better defcribed, than in the words made ufe of by Sir Walter Mildmay, Chancellor of the Exchequer, on a motion for granting a fubfidy to that Princefs, in the Parliament held *anno* 1575. *Elizabeth.*

" Notwithftanding all thefe expences (alluding to the charges in
" Scotland, Ireland, and in other wars) her Majefty hath moft care-
" fully and providently delivered this kingdom from a great and
" weighty debt, wherewith it hath been long burthened; a debt be-
" gun four years, at leaft, before the death of Henry VIII. and not
" cleared until within thefe two years, and all that while running upon
" intereft : a courfe able to eat up not only private men, and their pa-
" trimonies, but alfo Princes and their eftates. But fuch hath been
" the care of this time, as her Majefty and the State is clearly freed
" from that eating corrofive ; the truth whereof may be teftified by
" the citizens of London, whofe bonds, under the common feal of the
" city, which have hanged fo many years to their great danger, and
" to the peril of their whole traffick, are now all difcharged, cancelled

" Parl. Hift. vol. iii. p. 288. 343. 357.

[F]   " and

" and delivered into the chamber of London, to their own hands. By
" means whereof, the realm is not only acquitted of this great burden,
" and the merchants free, but alfo her Majefty's credit thereby, both
" at home and abroad, greater than any other Prince for money, if fhe
" have need. And fo in reafon it ought to be, for that fhe hath kept
" promife to all men, wherein other Princes have often failed, to the
" hindrance of many[23]."

It is to be remarked, that Elizabeth, and indeed her fifter Mary,
were fometimes obliged, for the better fatisfaction of their creditors, to
mortgage their domains. Even with that additional fecurity, Mary could
not procure from the city of London, the fmall fum of 20,000*l.* under
12 *per cent.*[24].

James I.

James was hardly feated on the throne of England, before he found
himfelf involved in the greateft pecuniary difficulties, in confequence of
his own profufion, and the rapacity of his courtiers. It was ftated in
Parliament, that Elizabeth had died in debt, to the amount of 400,000*l.*
But it appears, that fhe left fubfidies due to her, amounting to 350,000*l.*
which her fucceffor actually received, and which confequently ought to
have been deducted[25]. A ftate of the King's debts, was reported to the
Houfe, 11th March, 1622 ; but the journals are fo defective, that it is impoffible now to difcover the particulars. During this Monarch's reign, it
fhould feem, that the fyftem of mortgaging grants, and anticipating
their produce, was perfectly well known. For in the Parliament held
anno 1624, the famous duke of Buckingham moved in the Houfe of
Lords, " That a meeting might be inftantly prayed with the Com-
" mons, to propofe to them, that certain monied men might be dealt
" with, to difburfe fuch a fum as was requifite for the prefent ufe ; the
" repayment of which to be fecured by parliament out of the fub-
" fidies intended in the grant, according to what has been heretofore
" done in the like cafes : concluding, that he doubted not, that fome
" would be found to difburfe the fame, upon that fecurity[26]."

Charles I.

The debts that were left by James I. upon his fucceffor, amounted
to about £360,000, without including arrears of penfions, and a confiderable fum due to the houfehold. So heavy a load, joined to the wars

[23] Parl. Hift. vol. iv. p. 211.   [24] Parl. Hift. vol. iii. p. 358.
[25] Parl. Hift. vol. v. p. 147. 219.   [26] Parl. Hift. vol. vi. p. 120.

which

which Charles attempted to carry on, involved him in the greateſt diſ-treſſes. Had this prince, however, followed the advice given to his father, a little before his death, by that excellent counſellor, the earl of Carliſle ; had he, at the commencement of his reign, caſt away but ſome crumbs of his crown, or beſtowed ſome grains of his prerogative on his people, they would probably have exerted themſelves to have rendered him happy and reſpectable[27]. But the haughty pretenſions of Elizabeth, which ſhe knew well how to maintain, when put into the hands of weaker and leſs able ſovereigns, could not eaſily be ſupported. This is a ſubject, however, which has been already ſtated at conſiderable length in the former part of this work.

From the commencement of the Civil War to the Reſtoration, no- Charles II.thing material occurs with regard to public debts. But, no ſooner was Charles II. ſeated upon the throne, than parliament was obliged to take into conſideration, the arrears due to the army and navy, which were very great: and the Commons ſeemed anxious not only to pay them off without delay, but alſo to prevent the dangerous conſequences that might enſue, from leaving even the remnant of a public debt in the kingdom. One member in particular declared, that the incumbrances of the nation would be found to reſemble that ſerpent in America, that could devour an ox at a meal, and then falling aſleep might eaſily be deſtroyed ; but unleſs his bones were broken to pieces, he grew again as big as before. In the ſame manner, the debts of the nation, though partially diminiſhed, would again increaſe, whilſt a veſtige of them remained : and he recommended to the Houſe, to pay off ſuch in-cumbrances, by one bold effort ; and not to imitate the fooliſh wo-man in the fable, who roaſted a hen with a faggot, ſtick by ſtick, un-til the faggot was all ſpent, and the hen ſtill continued as raw as ever. Much good ſenſe is couched under theſe odd alluſions[28].

But, however anxious the Commons were, *to break the bones of the ſerpent*, yet the ſyſtem of contracting temporary debts, by anticipating the produce of the grants of parliament, was frequently practiſed during

<hr/>

[27] For Lord Carliſle's excellent advice, ſee Parl. Hiſt. vol. v. p. 530.

[28] Parl. Hiſt. vol. xxiii. p. 11.

this monarch's reign, and met with every poffible countenance from the legiflature.

Indeed, fo far was a claufe of credit from being invented (as fome fuppofe to be the cafe) pofterior to the Revolution, that it was ufual, during the greater part of this Monarch's reign, to infert a claufe empowering the officers of the Exchequer to borrow money from all perfons, whether natives or foreigners, upon the fecurity of the fubfidy

Anno 1667. that was granted ; and a law was paffed, entitled, " An act for affign-" ing orders in the exchequer, without revocation"," which enabled the King to borrow money upon the credit *of any branch of the Revenue* ; becaufe in the words of the Statute, " it had been found by experience, " that the powers of affigning orders in the exchequer by former acts, " without revocation, had been of great ufe and advantage to the per-" fons concerned in them, and to the trade of the kingdom." Notwithftanding this act, an univerfal jealoufy prevailed, when the difgrace at Chatham took place, that fome ftop would be put to the payments at

18 June 1667. the exchequer. But the King iffued a proclamation, to diffipate all fuch apprehenfions; and not only declared, that no alteration or interruption fhould be made in regard to any fecurity already granted, but alfo pledged himfelf, that the fame refolution fhould be held firm and facred in all future affignments[20].

Here it is proper to give fome account of a tranfaction which contributed to the many heavy burdens under which we now groan, and which will for ever ftamp the character of Charles II. with the moft indelible infamy.

Shutting up the exchequer. The credit of the crown, in confequence of the acts of parliament, and the proclamation above-mentioned, was carried to a very confiderable height ; and the bankers, and other wealthy individuals, had made it a common practice to advance money to the exchequer, upon the fecurity of the fupplies voted by Parliament ; and they were gradually repaid, when the produce of the grants came into the treafury. The bankers, by this means, received from eight to ten *per cent.* for money, which their cuftomers had placed in their hands without intereft, or which they had borrowed at the legal rate of fix *per cent.* But an end

---

[20] 19 Car. II. cap. 3.

[21] See a copy of the declaration, Cafe of the bankers, p. 54.

was

was foon put to fuch vifionary profits: for on the 2d January, 1672, a proclamation was iffued, fufpending all payments upon affignations in the exchequer for the fpace of one year, a period which was afterwards prolonged, and never came to a conclufion. The confequences of fuch a meafure may eafily be conceived. Confufion overfpread the whole country. Many ftopped payment, or were ruined: diftruft every where prevailed; and a general ftagnation of commerce took place, by which the public was not only partially, but univerfally affected".

The fum of which the bankers and others were thus defrauded, amounted to 1,328,526 *l.*; and the King, by letters patent, charged his hereditary revenue with the intereft of that fum at fix *per cent.* amounting to 79,711 *l.* 11 *s.* 2 ¼*d. per annum*", which was punctually paid, until about a year before his death. The payment was then ftopped; and after vainly endeavouring to intereft the legiflature in their behalf, thefe unfortunate creditors were at laft obliged to maintain their rights before the courts of juftice". The fuit was protracted for about twelve years in the courts below, but judgment was obtained againft the crown, about the year 1697. The decifion, however, was fet afide by Lord Somers, then chancellor; though it is faid, that ten out of the twelve judges, whom he had called to his affiftance, were of a different opinion. The caufe was at laft carried by appeal to the Houfe of Lords, by whom the decree of the chancellor was reverfed; and the patentees would of courfe have received the annual intereft contained in the original letters patent, had not an act paffed *anno* 1699, by which, in lieu thereof, it was enacted, that after the 25th December 1705, the hereditary revenue of excife fhould ftand charged with the annual payment of three *per cent.* for the principal fum contained in the faid letters patent, fubject neverthelefs to be redeemed upon the payment of a moiety thereof, or 664,263 *l.*

The reader will naturally be anxious to know the amount of the lofs which the bankers fuftained in confequence of this tranfaction, and the

---

[31] Hume's Hift. vol. vii. p 4-6. Macpherfon's Hift. of Great Britain, vol. i. p. 451.

[32] Letter from a By-ftander, p. 88. See alfo Carte's full Anfwer to the By-ftander, p. 91. and 145. Alfo a Letter to the Rev. Mr. Thomas Carte, p. 81. and 98. And Carte's full Vindication, p. 104.

[33] Comm. Journ. vol. x. p. 224, 225.

effects of fuch proceedings upon the credit of the crown, and of the public.

The fum to which the bankers and their creditors were entitled, when the matter was thus fettled by the interpofition of the legiflature, was as follows [34]:

1. To the original fum ftopped in the exchequer, *anno* 1672, £.1,328,526
2. To 25 years intereft, at fix *per cent.* (about)   -   2,100,000

         Total, principal and intereft   -   £. 3,428,526

As by the act above-mentioned, their whole demand was reduced to the fum of 664,263 *l.* it is evident that the lofs they fuftained muft have been about 2,800,000 *l.*

With regard to the confequences of thefe tranfactions, we are told, that, notwithftanding fo violent a breach of the public faith, Charles was able, two years after he had fhut up the exchequer, to borrow money at eight *per cent.*[35] the fame rate of intereft which he had paid before that event; and Hume from thence takes an opportunity of remarking, " That public credit, inftead of being of fo delicate a na-" ture as we are apt to imagine, is in reality fo hardy and robuft, that " it is very difficult to deftroy it[36]." But the events at the time, were far from juftifying this pofition. In a tract written *anno* 1693 (attri-buted to the Marquis of Halifax), wherein, among other modes of raifing money, he takes into confideration, that of borrowing upon perpetual funds, it is obferved, " That the breach of the exchequer credit by " King Charles, will make men very fhy of parting with their money " upon new projects at a diftance" ;" and indeed, the great difficulty that was found in procuring money after the Revolution, and the high intereft that was paid for it, was in a great meafure owing to the fatal ftep taken *anno* 1672, which rendered men cautious in again con-fiding any confiderable fum to government, unlefs they were tempt-ed by exorbitant profit and ufurious advantages.

Amount of our public debt at the Revolution. It was the more neceffary to give an hiftorical account of this tranf-action, becaufe the above principal fum of 664,263 *l.* compofes a

---

[34] See a Modeft Vindication of the Memory of King Charles II. in relation to the flop at the exchequer.

[35] Danby's Memoirs, p. 65.   [36] Hume's Hift. vol. viii. p. 226.

[37] Somers's Collection of Tracts, vol. iv. p. 67.

part

part of the prefent national debt of this country, and indeed is the only portion of it that was contracted before the Revolution[37]. There was, it is true, a fmall fum (about 60,000*l.*) due to the fervants of Charles II. which was directed to be paid to them in three years, from the 24th of December, 1689[38]. But it was fuppofed, that little of it was paid, becaufe there was a provifo in the act, that no money fhould be given to any of that prince's fervants, who did not take an oath to the new government, before the 1ft of February, 1690; which, it is probable, many of them refufed or neglected to do[40]. There was alfo, on the 5th of November, 1688, an arrear of 300,000 *l.* due to the army, and about 280,000*l.* of the revenues of the crown had been anticipated. But the money that was found in the exchequer, and the fums which were in the hands of the different receivers and collectors of the revenue, fully compenfated thefe demands[41]. As to the intereft of the fum above ftated, it was originally at 6 *per cent.* and confequently amounted to 39,855*l.* 17*s.* 7*d. per annum;* but as the bankers debt was incorporated by 3 George I. cap. 7. into the general fund, at 5 *per cent.* and was afterwards fubfcribed, in confequence of 6 George I. cap. 4. into the South Sea ftock, which now bears only 3 *per cent.* intereft, 664,263 *l.* of principal, and 19,927*l.* 18*s.* 9¼*d.* of intereft, is the whole of our prefent debt, contracted prior to the Revolution.

Such are the moft material tranfactions which took place with regard to public debts, during the period of 450 years prior to the Revolution: from an attentive confideration of which, and of the circumftances ftated in the enfuing chapter, the reader will be enabled to determine, whether it is moft to be regretted, that the funding fyftem ever took place, or that it was not fooner adopted. Had it exifted at an earlier Æra, a fuccefsful conqueror, like Henry V. would never have been impeded in his progrefs, by the want of a few thoufand pounds, which feems to have been his unfortunate cafe. Whereas, on the other hand, had no money ever been borrowed, were we now free from the burden of thofe taxes, which have been impofed, to provide for the intereft of our prefent national incumbrances, the fituation of this country, at this time, would be truly happy and defirable.

Conclufion.

---

[37] Hiftory of the Public Revenue, by James Poftlethwayt, p. 107.
[38] 1 William and Mary, Seff. 1. cap. 28.
[40] Hiftory of our National Debts and Taxes, p. 6.   [41] Ibid. p. 7.

C H A P.   IV.

Of the Rife and Progrefs of our prefent National Debts.

THE three grand political objects that our ftatefmen feem to have had in view, from the Æra of the Revolution to the prefent time, were : Firft, to humble the power of France, which at that period threatened the reft of Europe with total fubjection : Secondly, to protect the Britifh Colonies in America, from the encroachments of that powerful monarchy : Thirdly, to preferve the allegiance, and maintain the connexions of thofe very colonies with their mother country, when, trufting to the promifes, and fupported by the arms of France, they lately declared themfelves independent States. The purfuit of thefe objects gradually brought on thofe heavy incumbrances, under which England now groans. Other caufes of lefs moment may indeed have occafionally contributed to increafe them : but upon the whole, it will hardly be denied, that our prefent national debts owe their origin, and the greater part of their amount, to the neceffity we have been under, either to oppofe the arms, or to guard againft the political intrigues of the houfe of Bourbon, for nearly a century paft.

The power that France had attained, and which rendered fuch exertions neceffary, is in a great meafure to be attributed to the wretched policy which has too often prevailed in the councils of this country. It began under the government of Cromwell, who, flattered by the artful Mazarine, and expecting to fecure acquifitions either on the Continent or in America, that would give luftre to his ufurped adminiftration, was induced to join his arms with France, againft the weakened and degenerate monarchy of Spain ; and by his additional weight, not only elevated the houfe of Bourbon on the ruins of that of Auftria, but alfo compelled the Spaniards to give their Infanta to Lewis XIV. an alliance which has fince been productive of many fatal confequences.

Unfortunately alfo, the reftoration of the royal family did not correct this miftake in politics. During their long refidence abroad, they had

2   imbibed

imbibed foreign manners and foreign principles, and felt little of the natural, and perhaps ufeful, prejudices of an Englifhman. Charles, diffatisfied with the neceffary reftraints of a limited government, which his own profufion and mifconduct alone could have rendered irkfome to him, inftead of endeavouring, with the affiftance of fome other States of Europe, to curb the power of Lewis, actually became his penfioner; and flattered himfelf with the hopes of being able, by that monarch's affiftance, to render himfelf defpotic. His parliament in vain recommended his entering into a war with France; and in vain was every motive held forth, that could have weight with an ambitious fovereign, panting for glory, or a virtuous prince, who wifhed to be accounted the real father of his people. Alive only to pleafure, infen- fible of the feelings of patriotifm, and callous to honourable fame, he fuffered an opportunity to efcape, which, had it been embraced, would have rendered all farther exertions, for reftraining the power of France, within reafonable bounds, unneceffary. Inftead of this, a peace was concluded at Nimeguen, not only highly favourable to that monarchy, but which alfo furnifhed it with an opportunity, of preparing for frefh wars, and new acquifitions[1].

When James II. fucceeded to the crown, fome expectations were at firft entertained of his acting a different part. He had more of the fpirit of an Englifh fovereign than his brother. His pride inclined him to afpire at being an independent monarch[2]; nor did he relifh the fuperiority which Lewis affected over the other powers of Europe. But unfortunately he was a bigotted Roman Catholic, and his fubjects had every reafon to apprehend that their Sovereign was refolved to deprive them of their civil and religious rights and privileges. The Dutch, and other nations in Europe, were at the fame time fenfible, that while James continued upon the throne of England, they could not depend

---

[1] It is certain (fays Hume) that this was the critical moment (May 1677) when the King might with eafe have preferved the balance of power in Europe, which it has fince coft this ifland a great expence of blood and treafure to reftore. Vol. viii. p. 31.

[2] Though he wifhed to be abfolute, yet he was defirous of acquiring unbounded autho- rity, without foreign affiftance. Macpherfon's Hiftory of Great Britain vol. i. p. 513. His ambaffadors told the States that he was too powerful a prince, to put himfelf under the protection of France, and that he had too much fpirit, as well as too high a birth, to be treated like the Cardinal of Furftenburg. Ibid. p. 511.

upon

upon his aid to preferve them from being fwallowed up by France ; and the confequence was, a general combination, both at home and abroad, to put an end to the reign of a prince, whofe conduct was fo likely to prove fatal to his own fubjects, and to Europe in general.

But this leads us to the acceffion of a monarch, who refcued this country from civil, religious, and political bondage ; under whofe government, however, our prefent financial burdens, at leaft to any great extent, had their commencement.

W I L L I A M   III.

Whoever confiders the fituation of England at the acceffion of William III. will eafily perceive that many circumftances, both foreign and domeftic, concurred to render the contraction of a public debt almoft unavoidable'; particularly as a war with France was neceffary to maintain a revolution, fo oppofite to the views, and fo contrary to the interefts of that powerful kingdom.

Caufes of our public debts at the Revolution.
The revenues of England at the time were evidently inadequate to the neceffities of the public in fo critical an emergency ; and yet they could not fafely be increafed. The Englifh were unaccuftomed to heavy taxes, and were not yet fenfible, that no nation ever enjoyed civil and religious liberty, without paying dearly for the bleffings it affords. Not many years before the Revolution, when the royal family was reftored, a vote of Parliament had paffed, declaring, that the permanent revenue of the crown ought to be made up 1,200,000 *l.* a year. But fo enormous did that fum appear, that the neceffary fteps were not taken for that purpofe, until fome time after. By different additions, however, the revenue had at laft been raifed to about two millions a year : but it was complained of as greater than the country could bear ; and the partizans of William, having unfortunately held forth the reduction of the revenue as a ftrong motive for a change in the government, it became neceffary, when the Revolution was accomplifhed, to gratify the people with the abolition of the productive duty of hearth-money, which happened to be particularly obnoxious.

The revenue at that period was not only fmall in itfelf, but alfo, in confequence of the calamities with which wars are always accompanied,

it

it was perpetually diminishing. Tunnage and poundage, which, during the reign of James, had produced 600,000 *l.* a year, fell, *anno* 1693, to 286,687 *l.* The other branches proportionably decreased, infomuch that the very fame taxes which before the Revolution had yielded 2,001,855 *l.* clear of all charges'; in the year 1693, had fallen to 1,104,115 *l.*; and in the year 1695, to 811,949 *l.*'; in which fums, however, no allowance is made for the abolition of hearth-money. Some additional cuftoms and excife had been added, but as they only amounted to 466,203 *l.* the whole revenue, *anno* 1693, did not exceed 1,570,318 *l.* It is eafy to perceive, how much fuch a circumftance muft have damped the fpirit of the people, diminifhed the vigour of their exertions, and increafed the burdens of the war.

The affairs of a nation can never be properly conducted, where a fpirit of felfifhnefs prevails; whether it arifes from attachment to the intereft of one man perfonally to himfelf, or to the intereft of what is called a party. In either cafe, the effects are much the fame, though the object may be more confined, or more extended. That fuch a fpirit prevailed in England, foon after William III.'s acceffion to the throne, can hardly be queftioned. The ufual confequences of a fac-tious difpofition quickly enfued. The intereft of the public was neg-lected; and nothing was thought of, that would not contribute to pro-mote the views of particular fets of men : nay, party was carried to fuch a height, that either one defcription of perfons, or another, were ever ready to rejoice when any event happened, tending to increafe the national diftreffes. Nor were the baneful effects of this fpirit con-fined to divided parliaments and fluctuating councils; they extended to our fleets and armies, and to the management of our revenue. " In " countries full of divifions (as Davenant well obferves), no man is " continued long enough in his employment, to gain experience in it. " He who begins to know a little, muft prefently make room for fome-

---

¹ Davenant's Works, vol. i. p. 233. But in this fum was included the duty of hearth-money, which yielded 245,000 l. *per annum*, and which was abolifhed before the year 1693. The decreafe in the revenue, however, was ftill very great, amounting, *anno* 1693, to 652,740 l. and *anno* 1695, to 944,906 l.

⁴ Ibid. vol. i. p. 20, 21. In Whitworth's edition, from fome miftake, hearth-money . is charged in the account 1693, though it had been previoufly abolifhed.

[G] 2   " body

" body more ufeful in other matters, or to gratify a fide; and hence
" the affairs of a prince will ever be difappointed, whilft the principal
" officers of the revenue, are frequently made a prey of, to each party,
" as they happen to be victorious'." This refpectable author, as a
proof of the juftice of this obfervation, mentions, that in confequence
of a fudden and improvident change in the commiffion of excife, the
revenue had fuffered, in that fingle branch, no lefs a decreafe than
256,000*l.* a year*.

In every factious country, public frauds will abound. Thofe who
get into power, are afraid that they fhall not long continue in the management of affairs, and therefore anxioufly embrace every opportunity of
enriching themfelves, at the expence of the public ; trufting either to
evade difcovery, or to efcape the punifhment they deferve, through
the ftrength and intereft of their party. The abufes and fraudulent
practices which took place in the various public offices, during the reign
of William, were very great. Some frauds were brought to light'; and
commiffioners of accounts were appointed, in hopes of difcovering other
public defaulters ; but with fuch little effect, that the commons came
to a refolution, *anno* 1701, " That it was notorious, that many millions
" of money had been given to his majefty, for the fervice of the pub-

---

⁵ Davenant's Works, vol. i. p. 180.   ⁶ Ibid. p. 184.

⁷ One fraud that was difcovered *anno* 1697, though clearly proved, and of an enormous nature, paffed unpunifhed. Exchequer bills, when firft iffued, were not entitled to
any intereft ; but when paid in, on account of any tax, they received upon the fecond
iffue (if indorfed by the proper officer), an intereft of 5 l. 12 s. *per annum.* This encouraged feveral of the officers of the excife and cuftoms to contrive together to get great
fums of money, by falfe indorfements, before fuch exchequer bills had been circulated.
Many officers had enriched themfelves by this fraud, and Duncombe, receiver general of
excife, had amaffed a fortune of 400,000 l. A bill paffed the Houfe of Commons, fining
this flagrant offender in about one half of that fum ; but it was rejected by the Lords,
in confequence of the exertions of a noble Duke, who was fufpected of having been
gained over by a golden facrifice. The other perfons guilty alfo efcaped. Life of Halli-
fax, p. 50.

It alfo appears, that many exchequer tallies were ftruck with intereft, for confiderable
fums of money, not only when there was no occafion to raife the money, but when part
of the produce of the tax, on which the tallies were ftruck, had come into the exchequer.
See an account of the proceedings of the Houfe of Peers, in regard to the public accounts,
printed *anno* 1702, p. 38.

" lic,

" lic, which remain yet unaccounted for[1]." And it is afferted, by an anonymous author, that, in the fpace of five years, the immenfe fum of 10,864,873*l.* 17*s.* 4*d.* had been actually mifapplied or embezzled[9]. Such abufes a foreign Prince was more likely to overlook, and would be lefs anxious to punifh, than a natural-born fovereign of the country.

There was alfo a want of public zeal and fpirit, not only among thofe who were in power, but even in the nation at large, which was attended with the moft unfortunate confequences. The landed intereft endeavoured to throw off the burden of the State from their own fhoulders; and procured an inftruction to the committee of fupply, that no money fhould be raifed upon land, without the fpecial leave of the houfe[10]. Even when a land-tax was eftablifhed at the rate of four fhillings in the pound, inftead of three, millions a year, which it ought to have produced, it only yielded two[11]; and every plan that was propofed in Parliament, for the general benefit, was rendered abortive. A bill had paffed the Houfe of Commons, for raifing a million upon the credit of the forfeited eftates in Ireland; but it was dropped in the Houfe of Lords; many of the leading members in that branch of the legiflature, trufting that they fhould procure thefe eftates for nothing, if they remained at the difpofal of the crown. The Commons alfo came to a vote, " That the falaries, fees, and perquifites of all " offices under the crown (leaving 500*l. per annum* to each refpective " officer), except the falaries of the judges, &c. and alfo all penfions " granted by the crown (with fome exceptions), fhould be applied to- " wards carrying on a vigorous war againft France." But fuch effectual meafures were taken, by thofe who would have fuffered by fuch a refolution, that a bill was not even fuffered to be brought in[12].

Jan. 19, 1692.

The fcarcity of fpecie, and the want of credit and circulation, which prevailed at that time, were circumftances which materially contributed to the pecuniary diftreffes of the nation, and to the decreafe of its revenues. The money that was recoined during the war (including

[1] Commons Journals.

[9] Letter to a new member of the Houfe of Commons, touching the embezzlements of the kingdom's treafure from the Revolution, p. 17. printed *anno* 1710.

[10] Hiftory of our National Debts, p. 14.   [11] Davenant, vol. i. p. 53.

[12] Hiftory of our National Debts, p. 20.

312,000*l.*

312,000l. worth of plate) amounted only to 8,136,000l." The whole
fpecie in the country, could not be eftimated at more than 16,000,000l.",
from five to fix millions of which were probably hoarded. Every fpecies
of credit was at the loweft ebb ; bank notes were at 20 *per cent.* and
tallies at 40, 50, nay 60 *per cent.* difcount". In fuch a fituation, with
only ten millions of circulating fpecie, and no fubftitute in its aid, how
was it poffible for this country to fpend five or fix millions *per annum*
in a foreign war, and to raife its fupplies within the year! Sir James
Stuart juftly remarks, that attempting, in thefe circumftances, to levy a
great revenue in England, was like putting a dumb man to the torture,
in order to extort a confeffion".

Whilft the public revenue was thus perpetually decreafing, the nation
was obliged to defray heavier charges than it ever had been accuftomed to before.

The expences of the Revolution itfelf were not inconfiderable. To
the Dutch alone were voted 600,000l. for the armament they had fitted
out, in order to bring about that event. The reduction of Ireland was
attended with great charges : nor were the partizans of the dethroned
Monarch driven from Scotland, without fome bloodfhed and expence.
The money that was thus required to place William upon the throne
of the three kingdoms, would have fully defrayed the charges of at leaft
one, if not of two campaigns. Had James II. therefore been a monarch who could have been trufted, and who would have cordially affifted in the accomplifhment of fo great a work, the balance of Europe
might have been reftored, without greater pecuniary exertions than
England could eafily have afforded : but our ftrength was unfortunately
at firft employed, rather in fettling our own government, than in humbling the power of France.

Another great and unforefeen expence to which the nation was put
at that time, was in order to remedy the diforder into which the coin
had fallen, and which was likely to be attended with the moft fatal

---

" Davenant, vol. i. p. 438.

¹⁴ Davenant, p. 441. fays, that the fpecie before the war amounted to about 18.500,000l.
but a good deal of it was exported in the courfe of the war. He alfo fays, that upwards
of 3,400,000l· of broad hammered money was hoarded in England, befides other kinds.
See p. 264. 439.

¹⁵ Life of Halifax, p. 36.   ¹⁶ Political Economy, vol. ii. p 365.

confe-

confequences to the commerce, induſtry, and revenue of the country. This great operation was obliged to be undertaken, in the midſt of an expenſive and dangerous war, and was fuccefsfully carried through by Montagu, then chancellor of the exchequer, afterwards created Lord Halifax ; but the diforder had proceeded to fuch a height, that the deficiency on the recoinage coſt the nation the enormous fum of 2,415,140 *l.* 16 *s.* 10 *d.*

Nor was reducing the power of France an eafy atchievement. Sir James Stuart is of opinion, that it was an enterprife far beyond the ſtrength of England to carry through at that time, though affifted by the great-eſt part of Europe [17]. That it was not beyond the power of England, appeared fufficiently evident during the reign of Queen Anne, though Spain, inſtead of being a friend, was under the dominion of the enemy. It muſt be acknowledged, however, that the enterprife, when it was under-taken by William, was attended with the greateſt difficulties. France was then at the very zenith of its power. Lewis had the good fortune to be furrounded with the ableſt generals and ſtatefmen of the age : his revenues were in good order, his troops were well paid, and his peo-ple were loyal and affectionate, confoling themſelves for their domeſtic miferies, by the greatnefs of their fovereign, and the glory he had attained [18]. A fingle power, poffeſſed of fuch refources, it is not a lit-tle difficult for any confederacy to fubdue.

But England was obliged to make greater exertions than otherwife would have been neceffary, in confequence of the languor and mifcon-duct of thofe States with whom fhe had confederated. The Dutch, on the whole, were not deficient ; but little affiftance was received from Spain, notwithſtanding the great riches that country was poffeſſed of ; and the Emperor, who was the perfon moſt intereſted in the war, was the leaſt ferviceable of the whole confederacy, and employed his arms, more in oppreffing his own fubjects in Hungary, than in maintaining the rights of his family, or defending the liberties of Europe [19].

Whoever confiders, therefore, the ſtate of our revenue, the magni-tude of our expences, and the various circumſtances, both foreign and

[17] Political Economy, vol. ii. p. 263.   [18] Davenant, vol. i. p. 8.
[19] Davenant, vol. i. p. 14.]

domeſtic, above enumerated, muſt clearly perceive, that contracting a
public debt, was a matter not of choice, but of neceſſity. Yet Bolingbroke, Swift, and after them other writers of the ſame party, have
contended that it was done with a view of ſecuring the additional
ſupport of wealthy individuals, to the government that was eſtabliſhed ¹⁰. Nay, we are told, that the ſupplies might have been raiſed
within the year, that a ſcheme to that effect was prepared and offered,
and that it was allowed to be practicable ; but that it was rejected, be-
cauſe the new government could not be ſo effectually ſecured, in any
other way, as by making the private fortunes of great numbers of people depend upon the preſervation of it. " Thus, (ſays Bolingbroke) the
" method of funding, and the trade of ſtock-jobbing began ; and great
" companies were created, the pretended ſervants, though in many reſpects
" the real maſters, of every adminiſtration." But a policy of that nature,
the conſequences of which it was impoſſible to foreſee, none but deſ-
perate miniſters would have attempted ; and when borrowing money
was firſt tried, it never was imagined that the war would have laſted ſo
long, or would have proved ſo expenſive.

Others have inſinuated, that the nation was involved in debts and
difficulties, in order that our trade might be loaded with heavy taxes,
and the Dutch the better enabled to rival us in commerce and manufactures ¹¹. But though the King was a Dutchman, and though his
principal friends and favourites were of that nation, yet he ſeems ever
to have maintained ſuch a degree of impartiality between the two countries, as to exempt him from ſuch ſuſpicions : and with regard to his
zeal for carrying on the war by land (which is commonly adduced in
proof of his predilection for Holland), that was evidently owing to his
greater attachment to military, than to naval operations.

Nay, ſome have ſuppoſed, that our glorious deliverer purpoſely ran
the nation into debt, not thinking it an evil, or, perhaps believing,
with ſome Dutch politicians, that it was for the intereſt of the public
to be incumbered : " and this might be true (ſays Swift) in a com-

---

¹ See Bolingbroke's Works, edit. 1773, vol iv. p 129. Swift's Hiſtory of the four
laſt years of the Queen, p. 159. Hiſtory of our National Debts, p 17.

· Hiſtory of our National Debts, p. 17. 27. 35, 36.

" monwealth,

" mon-wealth, fo crazily conftituted as Holland, where the governors
" cannot have too many pledges of their fubjects fidelity, and where a
" great majority muft inevitably be undone by any revolution, however
" brought about; but, to prefcribe the fame rules to a monarchy, whofe
" wealth arifeth from the rents and improvement of lands, as well as
" trade and manufactures, is the mark of a cramped and confined un-
" derftanding[12]." As William's underftanding was confeffedly intitled
to a different defcription, it is the lefs neceffary to trouble the reader
with any anfwer to fo groundlefs an allegation.

Let us next fee what were the modes of borrowing money adopted in
the reign of William III.

At firft, the practice, fo ufual in the time of Charles II. was adhered   Modes of
to, and the produce of the grants voted by parliament was anticipated,   borrowing.
without eftablifhing a fund, for the purpofe of paying a certain annual
intereft to the holders of the mortgage[13].

But refource was foon had to temporary annuities: for, *anno* 1692,   Temporary
an attempt was made to borrow a million upon annuities for 99 years,   annuities.
for which 10 *per cent.* was to be given, until the 24th of June 1700;
and 7 *per cent.* afterwards, with the benefit of furvivorfhip, for the lives
of the nominees of thofe who contributed[14]. So low, however, was the
credit of government at that time, that, even on thefe terms, only
881,493*l.* 12*s.* 2*d.* could be procured[15]. *Anno* 1693, a million was
raifed upon fhort annuities; and every fubfcriber received 14 *per cent.*
for fixteen years, with the additional benefits of a lottery[16]. So advantageous an offer, it is hardly neceffary to obferve, was eagerly grafp-
ed at.

Some money was alfo borrowed, during this reign, upon annuities for   Life annui-
lives; and 14 *per cent.* was granted for one life, 12 *per cent.* for two   ties.
lives, and 10 *per cent.* for three[17]. Such terms were to the higheft degree extravagant; particularly, as no attention was paid to difference of
ages. The original amount of thefe annuities, *anno* 1694, was about
22,800*l.*; and yet, in 1762 (fixty-eight years afterwards), they were

---

[12] Hift. of the four laft years of the Queen, p. 159.
[13] Hift. of our National Debts, p. 10.
[14] 4 Will. and Mary, cap. 3.   [15] See 4 and 5 Will. and Mary.
[16] 5 Will. and Mary, cap. 7.   [17] Hift. of our National Debts, p. 28.

reduced,

reduced, by deaths, no lower than 9,215 l.; and in 1782 only to 8,027 l. Dr. Price obferves, that borrowing at the rate of 12 *per cent.* for two lives, and 10 *per cent.* for three, is giving 10 *per cent.* for money in the one cafe, and 9 *per cent.* in the other [28].

Contingent annuities. In this reign, the Bank of England, and the Eaft India Company were eftablifhed: they paid to government the fum of 3,200,000 l., for which they received an intereft of 8 *per cent.*; and as the taxes impofed to defray that intereft, were to remain until the principal, and all the arrears of their refpective annuities, were difcharged, and confequently were unlimited in their duration, this naturally paved the way for thofe perpetual annuities which afterwards took place.

Perpetual annuities. The fuccefs with which the Bank of England was attended, had encouraged fome individuals to form the project of a *land bank*, with a view, not only of raifing a confiderable fum for the ufes of government, but alfo of lending money on landed fecurities at low intereft; a part of the fcheme being to give 500,000 l. on mortgage at 3 l. 10 s. *per cent.* to be paid quarterly, or 4 *per cent.* payable half yearly; but the project did not fucceed. The temptation, however, of mortgages at fo eafy a rate, induced the landed gentlemen to agree to the eftablifhment of perpetual taxes, to defray the intereft of the money intended to be raifed [29]. The ftatutes in the year 1695-6, furnifh the firft example in our hiftory of this climax of financial invention.

Lotteries. Lotteries began in this monarch's reign; and as all our evils were then attributed to Dutch counfels, the blame of Lotteries (thofe banes of induftry, frugality, and virtue, as they were called) was afcribed to an imitation of the example of Holland [30], and a wifh in the natives of that country, to ruin our morals, as well as cramp our trade.

Exchequer Bills. Exchequer bills furnifhed another mode of raifing money, firft adopted in the year 1697, which Montagu, when chancellor of the exchequer,

[28] Price, on Civil Liberty and the Debts of the Kingdom, edit. 1778, p. 134. Note 15. But it is faid that many of thefe annuities are wrongfully paid, owing to the frauds of the annuitants, and the careleffnefs of our public officers.

[29] 7 and 8 Will. III, cap. 31.   [30] Hift. of our National Debts, p. 27.

had

had the merit of inventing. Some fubftitute for money was particularly neceffary at that time, on account of its fcarcity during the recoinage. To render thefe bills more convenient, fome were iffued for only five, others at ten pounds"; a practice which, if now revived, might be attended with ufeful confequences.

It now only remains, to give an account of fome deftructive financial operations, adopted at this time.

It has already been obferved, that feveral life annuities were granted at 14 *per cent.* In order to raife a fmall additional fum upon the fame funds thus mortgaged, acts were paffed, by which thefe annuitants, or any other perfons for them, were offered a reverfionary intereft, after the failure of the lives, for ninety-fix years, from January 1695, on paying four and a half years purchafe (or 63*l.*), for every annuity of 14*l.*". Afterwards, *anno* 1698, four years purchafe (or 56*l.*), was only demanded for the converfion". The fame fyftem was afterwards adopted, in the reign of Queen Anne. Some of thefe long annuities were fortunately incorporated with the ftock of the South Sea Company; but fome ftill remain of thefe annuities to the amount of 131,203*l.* 7*s.* 8*d. per annum*, for which the fum of 1,836,275*l.* 17*s.* 10 ½*d.* had been originally contributed; and for the ufe of which, the public muft pay above thirteen millions before they are all extinct".

Rate of intereft.

The high rate of intereft at which money was borrowed during William's reign, in confequence of the fcarcity of fpecie, and the low ftate of public credit, was a fatal circumftance at the commencement of the funding fyftem in this country. At firft, attempts were made to raife money at only 6 *per cent.* intereft"; but it was found neceffary, the very fame feffion, to offer 7 *per cent.*": and, from the year 1690, during the remainder of the war, 8 *per cent.* was uniformly paid. *Anno* 1699, intereft was reduced fo low as 5 *per cent.* and continued at that rate until the value of money had again increafed, owing to a new war becoming inevitable.

" Life of Halifax, p. 43.   " 6 and 7 Will.III.cap. 5. 7 Will. III.cap. 2.
" 9 and 10 Will. III. cap. 24.   " Price on Civil Liberty, p. 134.
" 1 Will. and Mary, feff. i. cap. 3.   " Ibid. cap. 13.

[H] 2   Davenant

Davenant affirms, that the debt of the nation was fwelled more by high premiums than even by the exorbitant interest that was paid[17]; and that its credit was at fo low an ebb, that five millions, given by parliament, produced for the fervice of the war, and to the ufes of the public, but little more than two millions and a half[28]; and it is certain that the public paid dearly for eftablifhing its credit on fuch a footing, as to enable it to procure frefh loans. By an act paffed *anno* 1697, when tallies were at a very great difcount, a number of deficiencies, amounting to the fum of 5,160,459*l.* 14*s.* 9$\frac{1}{4}$*d.*, were accumulated into what was called the firft general fund or mortgage; and a variety of duties were confolidated together, in order to pay them off[29]. If this ftep had not been taken, public credit muft have been deftroyed; and yet, as tallies were at fo high a difcount, the meafure was attended with very great difadvantage. It is ftrongly afferted, that this evil was increafed by the arts of thofe who were in power; that it was a ufual practice to put off fettling a fund for any particular debt due by the public, until the fhares of thofe who were interefted as creditors, fold at a very great lofs. Thofe who were in the fecret then bought them up, and the deficiency was immediately fupplied[40]. If thofe fraudulent practices could have been prevented by raifing the fupplies within the year, it is furely much to be regretted, that fuch a plan was not carried through, notwithftanding the many difficulties attending fuch an attempt, and the various obftacles, which muft have been furmounted[41].

It

---

[27] Vol. i. p. 156.

[28] Vol. i. p. 264. But this feems to be contradicted in p. 284, where he fays, that four millions, within the year, would have gone as far as five millions upon diftant funds; more than one-fifth of what was granted upon credit, being confumed in difcount, high intereft, and exorbitant premiums.

[29] By 8 and 9 Will. III. cap. 20.

[40] Hift. of our National Debts, p. 35. Hift. of the four laft years of Queen Anne, p. 162.

[41] Davenant (vol. i. p. 157.) fays, that it would be greatly for the public benefit, by fevere penalties, to prohibit gratuities upon any loan, more than is allowed by parliament. Such a plan, he obferves, might bring difficulties at firft, but in the end would augment pub-

£   lic

It is not propofed to ftate minutely the loans of each year, or the money raifed by mortgaging each different branch of the revenue: fuch circumftances, not being interefting enough to thefe times, to render a particular difcuffion neceffary, it will be fufficient (it is hoped) to give a general view of the money borrowed, and repaid during this monarch's reign, and a ftate of the national debt at his deceafe. Thofe who wifh to obtain more minute and accurate information, may confult the ftatute book, or the authors who have profeffedly written on the fubject [42].

lic credit. Some regulation of that kind has become more neceffary than ever, in confequence of the great difcount upon our unfunded debts. The exorbitant profits attending the purchafing of which, are equally injurious to public and to private credit.

[42] See James Poftlethwayt's Hiftory of the Public Revenue, 1 vol. fol. printed *anno* 1759. Hiftory of our National Debts and Taxes, from the year 1688 to the year 1751, in four parts, the laft printed *anno* 1753; and Cunningham's Hiftory of Taxes, third edition, *anno* 1778.

ABSTRACT

ABSTRACT of the Money borrowed and repaid,
between the 5th November 1688, and Ladyday 1702.

	Borrowed upon various funds.	Produce of those funds.	Borrowed upon certain funds more than repaid.	Produce more than borrowed, but applied to other services.
From Nov. 5, 1688, to Mich'. 1691	£. 7,882,079	4,755,407	3,126,672	——
From Mich'. 1691, to ditto 1692	3,058,291	2,806,941	251,350	——
to ditto 1693	4,300,427	3,378,228	922,199	——
to ditto 1694	3,188,801	5,573,169	——	384,367
to ditto 1695	4,521,826	3,844,492	1,677,334	——
to ditto 1696	4,931,104	1,678,177	3,292,926	——
to ditto 1697	6,647,453	2,569,256	4,078,196	——
to ditto 1698	2,191,171	2,992,155	——	800,984
to ditto 1699	1,878,400	2,526,009	——	647,608
to ditto 1700	1,028,178	2,3121,10	——	1,192,952
to ditto 1701	2,064,937	2,250,506	——	185,569
From Mich'. 1701, to Ladyday 1702	1,408,128	1,538,548	——	130,420
Total borrowed	£. 44,100,795	34,034,518	13,348,677	3,341,900

From this account it might be inferred, that the funded debt of England, at the death of William III. did not much exceed ten millions;
but, unfortunately, when any fund produced more than was originally
impofed upon it, it was immediately re-mortgaged, or the income
arifing from it applied to the current fervices of the year.

It will next be proper to give a general view of the real ftate of our
national incumbrances, at this monarch's death.

CENERAL

GENERAL VIEW of the NATIONAL DEBT on 31st December, 1701.

I. PERPETUAL FUNDED DEBTS, for the Interest of which alone Provision was made.

	Principal.	Interest.
1. To the Bank of England, being their original stock, bearing an interest of 8 per cent.	£.1,200,000 0 0	96,000 0 0
2. To the East India Company, being their original stock of 8 per cent.	2,000,000 0 0	160,000 0 0
3. To the bankers debt, contracted in the time of Charles II.	664,263 0 0	39,855 15 7
	3,864,263 0 0	295,855 15 7

II. TEMPORARY ANNUITIES and DEBTS, which would have been extinguished by the Operation of the Funds on which they were placed.

	Principal.	Interest.
4. Annuities for 96 years, from 25th January, 1695	£.1,584,265 6 0	139,964 13 6
5. Ditto, for single lives, with survivorship	108,100 0 0	7,567 0 0
6. Ditto, for two and three lives	192,153 6 3	22,633 11 4
7. Short annuities for 16 years, from 29th Sept. 1694, consequently ending anno 1710	1,000,000 0 0	140,000 0 0
8. The first general fund or mortgage which it was purposed would be clear on 1st August 1706, producing above 800,000l. per annum	3,500,000 0 0	280,000 0 0
9. The second general fund, ending 1st August 1710	2,314,041 11 3	184,635 19 3¾
10. To sundry loans and deficiencies	1,162,486 18 8	78,321 14 7¼
	9,861,047 2 2	853,122 18 8¾

III. UNFUNDED DEBTS.

	Principal.	Interest.
11. The army and transport debts	1,123,258 7 9½	
12. The ordnance debt	94,985 0 2¼	
13. The navy debt	1,441,773 11 5¾	
14. Subsidies due to the elector of Hanover, and Duke of Zell	9,375 0 0	
Interest on the unfunded debt, at 6 per cent.	161,763 10 5	
	2,669,391 19 5	161,963 10 5

4) Total   £.16,394,702 1 7   1,310,942 4 8¼

4) Davenant (vol. i. p. 25.) supposes, that the national debt, anno 1698, amounted to about 17,552,000l. Postlethwayte, in his statement of the debt on 31st Dec. 1701, forgets the interest on the bankers debt, and calculates none on the unfunded incumbrances due at that time.

QUEEN ANNE.

The fituation of this country, at the acceffion of Queen Anne, even in the article of national incumbrances, was not greatly to be complained of. The perpetual debts which the public at that time owed, or thofe for which the intereft only was provided, amounted but to 3,864,263*l.* The temporary annuities, and other funded debts, whofe nominal capital was 9,861,047*l.* (with the exception of the Exchequer annuities), were likely foon to fall of themfelves, or to be extinguifhed by the produce of the funds appropriated for their redemption; and as for the unfunded debts (amounting to 2,669,392*l.*) they would probably foon have been paid off by œconomy and good management; and England might have feen itfelf again free from fuch difagreeable burdens, if another war with France had not unfortunately broken out, before fufficient time had elapfed to heal the wounds which former hoftilities had inflicted.

Caufes of the increafe of the public debts, during the reign of Queen Anne.

Two circumftances rendered fuch a war, if not neceffary, at leaft in a great meafure juftifiable.

By the treaty of Ryfwick, William III. was acknowledged king of England; and James's intereft having been abandoned by his ally, he had given up all hopes of being reftored to the throne, and had devoted his time to the ftricteft aufterities of religious enthufiafm. Whilft occupied in his ufual acts of devotion, he was fuddenly feized with a lethargy; and, after languifhing for fome days, expired on the 6th of September, 1701. Lewis was thrown off his guard by the fuddennefs of this event; and pity for a dethroned monarch, in fo diftreffed and miferable a fituation, led him to promife, that he fhould not only prove the protector of his family, but fhould alfo proclaim his fon the only legal fovereign of Great Britain and Ireland, after his deceafe [+]. This was an evident infraction of the treaty of Ryfwick. William therefore had recalled his ambaffador at the court of France, and was making every precaution to carry on a war, when his death prevented it. His fucceffor, however, upon her acceffion, was equally bound to

[+] Macpherfon's Hiftory of Great Britain, vol. ii. p. 214.

maintain

maintain her own title to the crown, by profecuting the fame meafures.

But this matter might eafily have been accommodated, and the
crown of England, to make ufe of the words contained in an Addrefs
from the Commons, " would have received reparation for the great
" indignity offered by the French king to his majefty and the nation,
" in owning and acknowledging the pretended Prince of Wales king
" of England, Scotland, and Ireland ","" without much bloodfhed or
expence, if it had not been thought neceffary, for the intereft of thefe
kingdoms, and the fecurity of Europe in general, to engage in a
war, in confequence of another event which took place about the fame
time.

When Lewis XIV. efpoufed the Infanta, he had renounced for himfelf and his pofterity, in the fulleft and ampleft manner, all right and
pretenfions of fucceeding to the throne of Spain ; and, after the peace
of Ryfwick, he had entered into different treaties of partition, by
which the Spanifh monarchy was to be fhared among the different
claimants, and had agreed to accept of certain territories belonging to
that crown, in lieu of all his rights. The king of Spain (Charles II.)
enraged at the propofed difmemberment, and refenting that foreign
powers fhould interfere in the domeftic concerns of his kingdom
during his own life, had nominated Philip duke of Anjou, fe-
cond fon of the dauphin of France, his heir; and when Charles died, 1 Nov. 1700.
Lewis without much hefitation abandoned the treaties of partition, and
accepted of a will, which put his grandfon in the peaceable poffeffion
of the whole dominions of Spain,. both in Europe and America.

Such an acceffion of power and ftrength to the Houfe of Bourbon,
and fo open an infraction of fuch folemn engagements, filled the
greater part of Europe either with indignation or difmay ; and an alliance was foon after formed, between the Emperor, Great Britain,
and Holland, the object of which was to fecure a barrier to the Dutch ;
to obtain fatisfaction to the Emperor for his pretenfions to the Spanifh
fucceffion ; and fufficient fecurity to Great Britain and Holland, for
their dominions, and for the commerce and navigation of their fub-

41 Comm. Journ. vol. xiii. p. 648. 3d Jan. 1701.

[I]   jects.

jects[46]. The treaty was concluded prior to William's deceafe; but his fucceffor perfevered in the plans he had entered into, as effential for the fafety and profperity of his kingdoms.

England, without doubt, was deeply interefted in the original objects of the grand alliance; and they might have been attained at a very early period of the war, before much blood or treafure was expended. But thefe objects were confidered as by far too narrow and confined, after the arms of the allies had triumphed, and the power of France was crufhed by the victories of Marlborough and of Eugene. Nothing then was heard of but the neceffity of dethroning Philip, who was at that time in full and quiet poffeffion of the whole Spanifh monarchy, and of fetting up his rival in his room[47]. A treaty for this purpofe was entered into with Portugal: a formidable army was fent to Spain, the operations of which were at firft fuccefsful; and addreffes came from both houfes of parliament, ftating, " that no peace could be fafe or honour- " able to her majefty or her allies, if Spain, and the Spanifh Weft " Indies, were fuffered to continue in the power of the houfe of Bour- " bon." But when the forces of the allies were defeated in Spain, and Charles, whom they had fet up, fucceeded to the Imperial crown upon his brother's death, fuch a plan became no longer advifable; particu- larly as feveral of the allies declared that they would never confent that the fame perfon fhould be king of Spain, and emperor of Germany.

The caufes which had formerly operated under the government of Wil- liam to fwell the public debts, contributed alfo, in the reign of Anne, to their increafe. The fame fraudulent practices prevailed at home; and a greater degree of lukewarmnefs to the caufe they were engaged in, and indeed neglect of the ftipulations they had entered into, took place amongft our allies on the Continent.

The profufe manner in which public money is wafted, when great fums are borrowed upon the national faith, is perhaps the moft unfor- tunate circumftance refulting from the funding fyftem. Ever fince the Revolution, it has in a greater or lefs degree prevailed. Some enquiry was made during this reign into thefe fraudulent practices. The Com-

Marginal notes:

16th May 1703.

An. 1711.

---

[46] See the fecond grand alliance, Collection of Treatifes, *anno* 1772, p. 42.
[47] Bolingbroke, vol. iv. p. 127.

mons thought it neceffary to expel one of their members ; refolutions were entered into, that might deter fuch practice for the future [48] ; and it was reprefented to her majefty, by the Commons, that there remained, at Chriftmas 1710, the fum of 35,302,107*l.* of public money unaccounted for. Though fuch charges were probably exaggerated, from the rage and malice of party, yet it cannot be doubted that there was too much truth in fome of their allegations.

We are told, that the earl of Rochefter, the queen's maternal uncle, had propofed in council, that England fhould only act as an auxiliary, and fhould leave the greater part of the burden upon the fhoulders of thofe who were moft interefted in its fuccefs [49]. But the intrigues and arts of the confederates, and the ambition of the duke of Marlborough, induced us to take, at firft, an active, and, afterwards, the principal part in carrying on the war : and whilft the Dutch were employing what forces they kept in pay, in fecuring a barrier for themfelves, and the emperor was endeavouring to conquer the Spanifh territories in Italy, the forces of England were fent to Flanders, to Germany, or to Spain, as fuited beft the views of the allies [50]. The Dutch alfo, no longer animated by their gallant Stadtholder, loft many opportunities, by their timidity, of bringing the war to a fuccefsful conclufion ; and threw away the favourable moment for making an advantageous peace, by indulging, in too great a degree, the natural infolence of conqueft [51].

---

[48] Hift. of our Nat. Debts, p. 129.   [49] Macpherfon's Hift. vol. ii. p. 234.

[50] We fo entirely neglected the advantages we might have reaped in America, that the French did us more mifchief in that part of the world than we did them. Hift. of our National Debts, part ii. p. 5.

[51] It is faid that the duke of Marlborough, after the victory at Ramilies, and the reduction of Oftend and Newport, had formed a plan, *anno* 1706, for paffing by Dunkirk, and for laying fiege to Calais (of which he expected to be mafter in a week's time), and then of marching coaftways by Dieppe and Rouen to Paris, in which attempt he might eafily have been fupported, and his army recruited from England. But the timidity of the Dutch (who were afraid that the French army, in the mean time, would have penetrated into the ircountry), prevented his attempting a plan, which would have brought the war to a fpeedy conclufion ; and as their infolence hindered the advantageous peace propofed by France at Gertruydenburg' from taking place, we had every reafon to complain of their conduct, both as to making peace, and carrying on the war.—See Hift. of our Nat. Debts, part ii. p. 67. 131.

They

They difplayed alfo too much of the fpirit of a mercantile people. They
wifhed to keep up their connexions with France, notwithftanding their
war with that country; and the commons were obliged to addrefs
the queen, that her majefty would *infift* with the States-general, that
the flop put to all correfpondence, trade and commerce with France or
Spain, fhould be continued. Addreffes alfo were fent to her majefty,
that the emperor fhould no longer opprefs his proteftant fubjects in
Hungary; and that the allies fhould be defired to furnifh their complete
quotas, both by fea and land, according to their refpective treaties [12].

Such are the caufes which are in general affigned for the increafe of
our public debts, during the reign of Anne. Let us next confider the
principles adopted by her minifters, in regard to borrowing money, and
the amount of the national debt at her death.

Mode of borrowing.   The old practice of raifing money, by anticipating the produce of
the taxes on land and malt, was perfevered in; and indeed has become
a permanent part in the fyftem of our finances.

Long annuities.   The deftructive mode of felling long annuities was alfo revived, and
only 210*l.* were demanded for an annuity of 14 *l. per annum*, for 99
years, being at the rate of fifteen years purchafe [13]. What renders
fuch a mode of borrowing money peculiarly difadvantageous to the
public, is, that fuch annuities are always irredeemable; nor can the
creditor be compelled to difpofe of them, but at his own price, however
able the nation may be to pay them off, or however anxious to get
free of fuch incumbrances.

Life annuities.   Annuities for lives were alfo granted during this reign. The terms
were more favourable to the public than formerly; one life felling at
nine years purchafe; two lives at eleven years, and three lives at twelve
years purchafe [14]: yet, on the whole, it furnifhes another example of the
impoffibility of making any advantageous bargain of that kind, particularly in time of war; and the difficulty attending the redemption of
fuch fecurities, with the confent of the creditor, renders them peculiarly
injurious.

[12] Comm. Journ. vol. xiv. p. 240.   Hift. of our Nat. Debts, part ii. p. 45. 59.
[13] 1 Anne, Seff. 2. cap. 3.   Hift. of our Nat. Debts, part ii. p. 38.
[14] Hift. of our Nat. Debts, p. 47.

During

During the greater part of the war, the fecurity granted to the cre- South Sea
ditor for the money that was borrowed, was continuing taxes which Company.
had been impofed in the reign of William, and borrowing upon funds
thus previoufly eftablifhed, and which otherwife would have expired.
The people were thus deceived into an opinion, that with hardly any
additional burden upon themfelves, they were holding the balance of
Europe, and acquiring immortal glory and reputation[55]. But this
procraftinating fyftem proved in the end fatal : a variety of unprovided
debts, tallies, and deficiencies came into the market[56]; were fold at
above 40 per cent. difcount, and had almoft ruined the credit of the
country, from the immenfity of the load. Thefe debts were at laft Anno 1710.
accumulated into one fund, and with the addition 500,000 l. raifed for the
current fervice of that year, amounted to 9,471,325 l. the intereft, of
which, at 6 per cent. came to 568,279 l. 10 s. per annum[57]. The proprietors of this ftock, having, in addition to that intereft a monopoly
granted to them of the trade propofed to be carried on in the South
Seas, thence obtained the name of the South Sea Company.

In this reign alfo, the Bank of England was permitted to increafe its Bank of
capital, and received a prolongation of its charter, in confideration of England.
400,000 l. which it advanced to government without intereft[58]. It ftipulated, however, for the repayment of the principal fum, though that
fum was properly a compenfation to the public for the privileges it had
beftowed. This, Dr. Price properly remarks, was a wanton and
unneceffary addition to the capital of our debt[59]. Nor was this all :
for the fame act contains the moft improvident bargain, on the part of
the public, and the moft ufurious one, on the part of the lender, that
can be produced in the hiftory of our revenue. The funds for difcharging the intereft of certain exchequer bills, which the Bank had
agreed to circulate, had been previoufly mortgaged for the fpace of four
or five years ; and inftead of impofing a new tax to defray the intereft
in the interim (left new burdens fhould irritate the people), it was
enacted, that both the intereft and the premium for circulating fuch

55 Swift's Hift. of the four laft years of the Queen, p. 164.   56 Ibid. p. 170.
57 9 Anne, cap. 21.   58 7 Anne, cap. 5.
59 Tracts on Civil Liberty, p. 125.

bills,

bills, fhould be paid *quarterly*, in frefh exchequer bills, until the fund was cleared[60]. When fuch meafures were countenanced by the legiflature, when compound intereft was thus paid quarterly, is it to be wondered at, that our public debts fhould have fo rapidly accumulated?

Eaſt India Company. Nor was the bargain made with the Eaft-India Company much more advantageous. They advanced, it is true, 1,200,000*l.* to the public, for which they were to receive no intereft[61]. But the nation became bound to repay the principal at the expiration of their charter; and thus, as Dr. Price well obferves, another unneceffary addition was made to the capital of its debt.

Perpetu 1 Annuities The nature of the funding fyftem began, during this reign, to be better underftood[62]. The advantages alfo of public credit, and the neceffity of giving undoubted fecurity to the creditor, were more generally acknowledged. *Perpetual annuities* became no longer an object of terror ; the new taxes impofed for the fecurity of the Bank, and the whole fund of the South-Sea Company being granted *for ever.* The public debts, however, either from the timidity of the minifters (who were afraid of irritating the people by frefh burdens, and confequently did not provide fufficient funds in proper time), or perhaps from the want of fpecie and refources in the country, fwelled to a height, which, in the apprehenfions of many, prognofticated a fpeedy bankruptcy, or national ruin.

Rate of Intereſt. At firft, money was borrowed, during this reign, at *5 per cent.* It afterwards rofe to 6, but, in fact, was much higher: for the South-Sea company received that intereft for tallies, which were incorporated into its ftock, at par, though they had fold in the market, a little time before, at 40 *per cent.* difcount.

Premiums. During the latter part of this reign money was principally borrowed by the mode of lotteries ; and confequently the profit of the fubfcribers greatly depended upon the fpirit of gambling at the time. In general, however, they were framed on very difadvantageous principles to the
Anno 1711. public ; and the laft, in particular, though it took place in the midft of

---

[60] Polit. Econ. vol. ii. p. 383. Hift. of our Nat. Debts, p. ii. p. 104.   [61] 6 Anne, cap. 17.
[62] Harley, afterwards created Lord Oxford, from two papers he wrote upon Loans and Public Credit, feems to have underftood the fubject. They may be feen in Somers's Collect. of Tracts, vol. ii.

the

the moſt profound tranquillity, has been often juſtly reprobated. For, of 1,876,400 l. raiſed at that time [63], only 1,400,000 l. was reſerved for the public ſervice; the remaining 476,000 l. being diſtributed among the proprietors of the fortunate tickets. This was a premium of about 34 per cent. upon the ſum actually received [64]. Such modes of raiſing money (as Hutchinſon well obſerves), though ruinous to the nation, was highly beneficial to private individuals, who, in a ſhort time, increaſed ſo much in wealth, as to out-top all the ancient gentry, and to vie with the firſt nobility in the kingdom [65].

Let us next ſee the amount of our national incumbrances at this Queen's death.

GENERAL VIEW of the NATIONAL DEBT, on 31ſt Dec. 1714.

1. PERPETUAL FUNDS.

	Principal.			Intereſt.		
1. To the capital of the Bank of England, at |6 per cent. — —	£ 1,600,000	0	0	96,000	2	0
2. To D', for cancelling exchequer bills at D'	1,775,027	17	10	106,512	13	5
3. To ſundry exchequer bills circulated by the bank . — —	4,676,812	10	0	335,557	8	5
Total to the bank	8,051,840	7	10	538,070	1	10
4. To the Eaſt India Company at 5 per cent.	3,200,000	0	0	160,000	0	0
5. To the South Sea Company at 6 per cent.	9,177,967	15	4	550,678	1	3
6. To the bankers debt, contracted in the reign of Charles II. —	664,263	0	0	39,855	15	7
	£ 21,094,071	3	2	1,288,603	18	8

2. TEMPORARY ANNUITIES.

7. By various lottery funds, granted for thirty-two years — —	13,223,910	0	0	990,249	12	0
8. By various other temporary annuities	12,793,132	13	4	871,134	12	10
	£ 47,111,113	16	6	3,149,988	3	6

3. UNFUNDED DEBTS.

9. To the navy and victualling debt, with intereſt at 4 per cent.	795,901	19	8	31,836	1	7
10 To army debentures by 3 Geo. I. cap. 7. charged upon the general fund	1,604,572	15	2	64,182	18	2
11. To the army debt, including the ſums paid off by grants, anno 1714 and 1715	550,000	0	0	22,000	0	0
12. Deficiencies on the old funds, made good by parliament, after the Queen's death	2,083,775	0	0	83,351	0	0
	£ 52,145,363	11	4			
13. Suppoſed addition to the capital upon converting the temporary into redeemable annuities —	2,000,000	0	0			
	£ 54,145,363	11	4	3,351,358	3	3

[63] By 12 Anne, ſeſſ. 2. cap. 9. [64] Hiſt. of our National Debts, part iii. p. 161. [65] Treatiſes of the National Debt, p. 61.

This

This is as accurate a ſtatement, as it is now poſſible to furniſh, of our public debts at the acceſſion of the preſent royal family. It is extracted from various accounts, drawn up by different authors, who do not entirely agree with each other as to the amount of the debt[66]; a circumſtance, however, the leſs material, as minuteneſs of accuracy, in ſuch remote tranſactions, is hardly to be expected, and is far from being eſſential. In regard to the value and real burden of theſe national incumbrances, Hutchinſon ſuppoſes, that the funded debts alone, in April 1717, at the market price of the day, were worth 50,106,611 *l*. But the total of the national debt, funded and unfunded, in December 1717, he calculates at 54,026,865 *l*.[67] : and indeed, 54,145,363 *l*. of principal, bearing an intereſt of about 3,351,358 *l*. ſeems to have been pretty nearly the ſtate of our debts at the death of Queen Anne : conſequently they received, during her reign, an addition of about 37,750,661 *l*. 8 *s*.[68]

In all the computations drawn up of the value of the national debt, at that time, there is no circumſtance with which the reader will be more ſtruck, than with the addition which is always made to the capital,

[66] See the account of the public debts at the exchequer, March 14, 1716, Commons Journals, vol. xviii. p. 498. From the death of the queen till that period, there was little difference in the amount, excepting, that by 1 George I. cap. 21. 822,032 *l*. 4 *s*. 8 *d*. was added to the ſtock of the South Sea Company, which made it up complete ten millions ; and byt he ſame act, in conjunction with cap. 19. of the ſame ſeſſion, 1,079,000 *l*. was added to the redeemable annuities, bearing an intereſt of 5 *per cent*.

Poſtlethwayt's Hiſtory of the Public Revenue, p. 106. The hiſtory of our National Debts, Part iv. p. 15. The collection of treatiſes, relative to National Debts, by Archibald Hutchinſon, Eſq; p. 8. ; and the abſtract of our public funds, by Mr. Aſgill, printed *anno* 1715, may alſo be conſulted.

[67] See Treatiſes on the National Debt, p. 12. He afterwards adds 8,582,500 *l*. to the above ſum, on account of the increaſed value of the temporary annuities. Poſtlethwayt, in his Hiſtory of the Public Revenue, p. 152, computes the national debt, on the 25th December 1716, at 54,542,545 *l*. 11 *s*. 1 *d*. conſequently, about 54,000,000 *l*. ſeems to be the general idea entertained of the amount of the debt at that time.

[68] Poſtlethwayt, in his Hiſtory of our Revenue, computes the difference in regard to the amount of our debts, between the 31ſt December 1701, and 31ſt December 1712, at only 35,488,293 *l*. 7 *s*. See p. 107. But it appears from p. 152, that there was a difference between the 31ſt December 1712, and 25th December 1716, of 2,670,231 *l*. 1 *s*. the greater part of which falls to be added

upon

upon the fuppofition that the temporary annuities were to be bought up. Though many of them commenced in the reign of William, and, confequently, from fifteen to twenty years had elapfed fince they were originally granted; yet it was computed, that it would require 4,415,189 *l.* 2 *s.* 1 *d.*, more than the nation had originally received, to re-purchafe them at the prices for which they fold in December 1717 [19]: and fuch of thefe temporary annuities as were fubfcribed into the South Sea Stock, in confequence of two acts of parliament, paffed *anno* 1719, and 1720 [19], coft the nation an additional capital of 3,034,769 *l.* 11 *s.* 11 *d.* though 1,836,275 *l.* 17 *s.* 10 *d.* of Long Annuities, befides fome life annuities, were not included. The holders of fuch of thefe annuities as were granted *anno* 1694, Hutchinfon calculates, were not only repaid both their principal and intereft at 6 *per cent.* in December 1717, but alfo had received about 30 *per cent.* more than they had originally paid [71]. The lofs which the public has fuftained by thefe annuities, fince the period above-mentioned, it is impoffible to think of with any degree of patience.

GEORGE I.

Whoever contemplates the hiftory of this country under the government of thofe princes who were attached to Roman Catholic principles, or connected with the court of France; the various grievances which the people at home had fo much reafon to complain of, and the difgraces which the nation had fuffered abroad, will not hefitate to acknowledge, that the acceffion of the Houfe of Hanover to the throne, was the moft fortunate event that could poffibly have happened to Great Britain at that time; and nothing was wanting to have crowned our happinefs as a nation, but fuch an attention in the fervants of the crown to the public credit and finances of the country, as might have laid the foundation of our being once more free from a confiderable fhare of thofe burdens to which we were then fubjected. But fuch were the timidity, the carelefs-

---

[69] See Hutchinfon's Treatifes, p. 59.

[70] See 5 George I. cap. 19. and 6 George I. cap. 4.; and Poftlethwayt's Hift. p. 104. 106.   [71] Treatifes of the National Debts, p. 60.

nefs,

nefs, or the mifconduct of thofe who were in power, that, though the
reign of George I. was, on the whole, a period of tranquillity, little
difturbed by foreign wars, and thofe not of a very expenfive nature, yet
fo favourable an opportunity was fuffered to efcape; and though the intereft of our debts, in confequence of the decreafe in the value of money, and of the bargain with the South Sea Company, was confiderably
diminifhed, yet the capital unfortunately underwent no material reduction.

It is propofed briefly to explain, from what caufes this circumftance
proceeded.

At the clofe of the reign of Queen Anne, the people of this country were divided into two great parties, one of whom was defirous of
reftoring the Houfe of Stuart, the other, of maintaining the rights of
the proteftant fucceffion. When George I., therefore, came to the
throne, he was naturally led to truft the entire management of public affairs in the hands of thofe who had profeffed themfelves his
friends, and indeed had perfevered in their attachment to his intereft,
even when fuch principles were not the immediate road to preferment.
It is to be regretted that fuch a monopoly of power was judged neceffary: for fuch a fyftem promoted difaffection, and encouraged violence
and party rage in thofe who confidered themfelves as profcribed..
Whereas, had William's example been followed, and had an adminiftration been compofed out of both parties, it is probable that no man
would have attempted to have difturbed the eftablifhed government
of his country[71].

But fuch meafures, though warmly recommended to his majefty at
his acceffion to the throne, were confidered to be either dangerous or
impracticable; and a formidable party, finding themfelves thus totally
excluded from all hopes of authority and power, joined the warm partizans of the exiled family, and raifed an infurrection, which, though foon
quelled, involved the nation in confiderable expences; injured the credit of the government, and juftified their delaying to take the methods
that were neceffary for the re-eftablifhment of our finances. The
delay might alfo arife in part from an abfurd notion propagated
during this reign, that the reduction of the national debt might prove
prejudicial to the family upon the throne, by diminifhing the number

---

[71] Hift. of our Nat. Debts, part iii. p. 2.

of thofe who were attached to it from interefted motives, and whofe fortune would be materially injured, fhould any revolution take place ".

It was carefully propagated by the partizans of a particular party, about the middle of the reign of George II., that, fince the acceffion of the prefent royal family, the interefts of Great Britain had been conftantly facrificed to that of the electorate, and that this country had been ever fince fteered by the rudder of Hanover ". It is certain, that our connexions with that country neceffarily involved us, more than otherwife would have been neceffary, in the affairs of the continent: and the firft of the Brunfwick family that fat upon the Englifh throne, having acquired the poffeffion of the dutchies of Bremen and Verden, and being anxious to fecure an acquifition of fuch great importance to his hereditary dominions, we were thence led into a war with Sweden, to which Bremen and Verden properly belonged; but all pretenfions to which fhe was compelled to renounce, in confequence of our exertions ". Nor was this all; for as thefe dutchies compofed a part of the German empire, it was neceffary to procure the inveftiture of them; and this brought on a train of negociations with the emperor, and with other powers, which, whilft they did no credit to the abilities of our ftatefmen, proved highly prejudicial to our finances ": for having guarantied, by the quadruple alliance, the territories of the emperor in the Italy, we were thereby involved in a war with Spain, begun in July 1718, which, after having been fignalized by a victory obtained on the coaft of Sicily over the Spanifh fleet, was terminated by a treaty of peace, figned June 13, 1721.

But the principal caufe of our public debts remaining undiminifhed during this period, undoubtedly was—mifmanagement in our domeftic

---

⁷³ See Treatifes on the Nat. Debt, p. 117. Hutchinfon juftly ridicules the idea, that a load of fifty millions of debt upon the nation was a fecurity to the proteftant fucceffion.

⁷⁴ See Faction Detected by the evidence of Facts, 2d edition, p. 121. fuppofed to be written by the famous Pulteney, Earl of Bath.

⁷⁵ See the Treaty of Peace, dated Nov. 20, 1719. Collection of Treaties, vol. i. p. 345.

⁷⁶ Bolingbroke, vol. iv. p. 132. and Faction Detected, p. 26. in which it is remarked, that, anno 1731, in confequence of thefe negociations, we employed a fquadron of Britifh men of war to efcort fome Spanifh troops into Italy, at the expence of 200,000 l.

[K] 2   affairs.

affairs. Little care was taken to raife fuch a revenue as the nation could afford; and what was raifed, was expended in a greater peace eftablifhment than Britain had ever been accuftomed to fupport. Our unneceffary expences, during this monarch's reign, are calculated to have amounted to 13,730,000 l.[17]; a fum which, had it been properly applied to the redemption of the debt, would not only have diminifhed the principal to that amount, but would alfo have enabled us to have reduced the intereft of the remainder, and would have raifed a finking fund, capable of producing the greateft effects, in alleviating our burdens.

It is not propofed to give any account at prefent of the financial operations, during this reign, as they more properly belong to the enfuing chapter, where it is intended to explain the different meafures taken, for reducing either the capital, or the intereft of our debt. We fhall, therefore, give, without farther preliminary obfervations, a general view of the national incumbrances at this monarch's death..

GENERAL VIEW of the NATIONAL DEBT, on Dec. 31, 1727..

1. PERPETUAL FUNDS.

	Principal.	Intereft.
1. To the capital of the Bank of England, at 6 per cent. — —	£ 1,600,000 0 0	96,000 0 0;
2. To ditto, for cancelling Exchequer bills, reduced at Midfum. 1727, to 4 per cent.	1,775,027 17 10½	71,001 2 3½
3. For cancelling Exchequer bills, reduced at Midfum. 1727, to 4 per cent. —	2,000,000 0 0	80,000 0 0.
4. Purchafed from the South Sea Company, reduced to 4 per cent. at Midfum. 1727	4,000,000 0 0	160,000 0 0.
Total to the Bank	£ 9,375,027 17 10½	407,001 2 3½
5. To the Eaft India Company —	3,200,000 0 0.	160,000 0 0.
6. To the South Sea Company ——	33,802,203 5 6½	1,352,088 2 7½
	£46,377,231 3 5	1,919,089 4 10½

2. TEMPORARY ANNUITIES.

7. To various long, fhort, and life annuities	2,433,942 4 4½	182,932 14 11
8. To various Exchequer bills, &c. charged on different furplufes —	1,543,780 15 4	46,038 6 4½.
	£50,354,954 3 1½	2,148,060 6 1½

3. UNFUNDED DEBT.

9. To fundry Navy and Victualling bills, at 4 per cent. — —	1,737,281 2 3½	69,491 4 10½
	£52,092,235 5 4½	2,217,551 11 0

[17] Hift. of our Nat. Debts, part iv. p. 14.

Thus

Thus it appears, that the capital of the national debt in the year 1714, and in the year 1727, were nearly the fame; particularly if no addition is made to the principal, in the former period, on the fuppofition, that the temporary annuities ought to be valued at the price they would fetch in the market, and not at the fum that was originally paid". The reader, at the fame time, will perceive how much the two periods differ in regard to the interest. In the reign of Queen Anne, the fame capital of about fifty-two millions, was paid annually the fum of 3,351,358l., which, at the death of George I., was reduced to 2,217,551l. The difference amounting to 1,133,807l. is a full proof of the flourishing credit which this country enjoyed, and of what might have been done at that time for retrieving our finances, by an able, decided, and public-fpirited minifter.

GEORGE II.

The reign of George II. may be divided into four periods. The firft, from his acceffion to the beginning of the Spanifh war, *anno* 1739; the fecond, terminates at the peace of Aix la Chapelle, *anno* 1748; the third, with the breaking out of the French war, *anno* 1755; and the laft may be extended to the treaty of Paris, *anno* 1762. As it was during this reign that our debts began to put on the formidable appearance they now wear, it is the more neceffary to trace their progrefs in each of thefe periods.

If any one æra, fince the revolution, were to be pointed out in which our minifters were peculiarly culpable for neglecting to take folid and fubftantial meafures to reftore good order in our finances, it muft be that of the commencement of this monarch's reign. The nation was then acknowledged, on all hands, to be in the moft profperous and flourishing condition: its glory and reputation were at the highest pitch, and it never was better able to vindicate the honour of the crown, and to de-

The firft period.

" Poftlethwayt, in his Hiftory of the Revenue, p. 122, fuppofes, that about 2,670,231l. 1s. of principal was paid off on the 25th of March 1728. But he includes, in the National Debt, at the death of Queen Anne, the additional value of the temporary annuities.

fend its juft privileges and poffeffions[7]; and yet little advantage was reaped from fo fplendid a fituation. The minifter at the time, (Sir Robert Walpole,) though fupported by the whole influence of the crown, and by a formidable party in parliament, did not enjoy the general confidence of the people; and inftead of adding to the public revenue, and diminifhing the national incumbrances, he preferved his tottering authority, by reducing the land tax to one fhilling in the pound, in order to ingratiate himfelf with the landed intereft, and by alienating the produce of the finking fund, from thofe purpofes to which it had been originally deftined, and applying it to the current fervices of the year. There is alfo too much reafon to believe, that thofe refources which ought to have been employed in difcharging the public incumbrances, were fhamefully wafted in purchafing the votes of the venal, and in hiring mercenary writers, to defend the caufe of the minifter, and to rail againft his opponents[8]. · The confequence was, that, during a period of profound peace, and which lafted for the fpace of twelve years, the reduction in the capital of our debt was very inconfiderable, in comparifon of what it ought to have been, confidering the many advantages which we enjoyed.

But, as the national debt, *anno* 1739, was lower than it has been at any time fince the death of Queen Anne, it may not be improper to ftate the particulars of which it confifted.

---

[7] Thefe are expreffions contained in one of this monarch's firft fpeeches from the throne, July 17, 1727. Comm. Journ. vol. xxi. p. 14.

[8] From 1707, to 1717, the money paid for fecret fervices, amounted only to 337,960*l.* 4*s.* 3½*d.* But, from 1731, to 1741, being another period of ten years, no lefs a fum than 1,453,400*l.* 6*s.* was iffued for the fame purpofes. See Commons Journals, vol. xxiv. p. 295.

GENERAL

GENERAL VIEW of the NATIONAL DEBT on December 31, 1739.

I. PERPETUAL FUNDS.

	Principal.	Intereſt.
1. To the capital of the Bank of England, at 6 per cent. — —	£. 1,600,000 0 0	96,000 0 0
2. For cancelling Exchequer bills, at 4 per cent. —	500,000 0 0	20,000 0 0
3. Purchaſed of the South Sea Company, at 4 per cent. — —	4,000,000 0 0	160,000 0 0
4. Annuities at 4 per cent. from Midſummer 1728 — —	1,750,000 0 0	70,000 0 0
5. Annuities at 4 per cent. from ditto 1729	1,250,000 0 0	50,000 0 0
Total to the Bank	£. 9,100,000 0 0	396,000 0 0
6. To the Eaſt India Company, at 4 per cent.	3,200,000 0 0	128,000 0 0
7. To the South Sea Company, at ditto	27,302,203 5 6½	1,092,088 2 7¼
	£. 39,602,203 5 6½	1,616,088 2 7½
8. To various long and ſhort annuities, Exchequer bills, &c. —	6,527,735 2 4	314,949 19 8
9. The Navy and Victualling debt, at 4 per cent. — —	824,684 15 6	32,987 7 9½
Total	£. 46,954,623 3 4½	1,964,025 10 1½

	Principal.	Intereſt.
Debt on Dec. 31, 1727	£. 52,092,235 5 4½	2,217,551 11 0½
Ditto on Dec. 31, 1739	46,954,623 3 4½	1,964,025 10 1½
Difference	£. 5,137,612 2 0	253,526 0 10½

If, inſtead of this inconſiderable reduction, the miniſter had proceeded to the great work of diminiſhing the debt with firmneſs and vigour, and, indeed, had he not alienated the ſinking fund, and defeated Sir John Barnard's plan, for reducing the intereſt of the greater part of the redeemable annuities, from 4 to 3 per cent. (which might have been carried into effect anno 1737, as well as anno 1749) our finances would have been put in ſuch a ſtate, that no power in Europe would have ventured to incur our reſentment; and we might have avoided a war, equally unneceſſary and inglorious, which added above thirty millions to our national incumbrances.

An idea had become not a little prevalent, in foreign countries, The ſecond during the latter part of Sir Robert Walpole's adminiſtration, that this period. country, notwithſtanding all its power and riches, might be inſulted with

impunity;

impunity; becaufe the minifter knew well that a war muft prove fatal to his authority. The court of Spain embraced fo favourable an opportunity of difplaying that antipathy to Great Britain which it had long entertained, and the fources of which it is neceffary briefly to explain.

By an exprefs article in the fecond grand alliance, concluded *anno* 1701, it had been ftipulated, that Great Britain and Holland fhould retain whatever cities and territories belonging to the Spanifh dominions in the Indies fhould be conquered by their arms". But, though fuch an opportunity of making valuable acquifitions to the crown of England, had never before, or, indeed, fince exifted, yet our exertions were almoft entirely dedicated to European conquefts; and, inftead of Hifpaniola and Cuba (poffeffions almoft invaluable to a commercial nation), Gibraltar and Minorca were thofe about which we were occupied; and, as it was eafily perceived that no plan of a treaty would fucceed, unlefs this country was gratified with fome important acquifitions, the King of Spain was thence compelled, by certain articles in the treaty of Utrecht, to furrender Gibraltar and Minorca, in full right and property, to the crown of Great Britain.

It is probable, however, from the conclufion of the article by which Gibraltar was ceded (in which it is declared, that if ever the property of that fortrefs was to be alienated, the preference fhall be given to the crown of Spain), that there was fome fecret underftanding between the parties at the time, with refpect either to an exchange or a fale; and Philip King of Spain, in confequence of fome fuch agreement, was perpetually importuning the Britifh minifters, that Gibraltar might be reftored. Nay, on the 1ft of June 1721, George I. wrote a letter to that monarch, in which it is faid, " I do no longer balance to affure your " majefty of my readinefs to fatisfy you with regard to your demand, " touching the *reftitution* of Gibraltar; promifing you to make ufe of " the firft favourable opportunity to regulate this article with the confent " of my parliament"."

" See Art. 6.

   See the original letter in French, and a tranflation of it, Comm. Journ. vol. xxi. p. 285.

Gibraltar,

Gibraltar, however, was a poffeffion too dear to the Englifh nation to be eafily relinquifhed; and fuch advantage would have been taken of their attachment to it by thofe who were in oppofition to government at the time, that no fteps could be fafely purfued for a reftitution of that fortrefs. This naturally excited chagrin and refentment in the court of Madrid, which were perpetually breaking out when any favourable opportunity occurred of infulting us with impunity.

But the war more immediately arofe from the treatment which our fhips and mariners, and thofe of our colonies in particular, received on the American feas. The Spaniards, anxious to monopolize the whole trade of their colonies in America, treated, in the harfheft and moft cruel manner, fuch Britifh veffels as ventured near their fettlements, whether for the purpofes of commerce, or when driven by neceffity. Thefe circumftances at laft attracted the attention both of the crown and of parliament; and the examination of an old failor at the bar of the houfe of commons, who was maimed by the cruelty of the Spaniards, roufed the indignation of that affembly, and filled the whole nation with a fpirit of refentment; in confequence of which, war was declared againft Spain on the 19th of October 1739.

An event foon afterwards took place, which involved all Europe in confufion.

On the 9th of October 1740, Charles VI. Emperor of Germany (the laft prince of the houfe of Auftria), expired at Vienna. Little doubt was at firft entertained that his eldeft daughter (Maria Therefa, married to the grand Duke of Tufcany) would enjoy an undifturbed fucceffion. But, though the principal powers of Europe had guaranteed her rights, difputes arofe with regard to the poffeffion of the greater part of her father's dominions; and the Elector of Bavaria was fet up by France as a competitor for the imperial crown. In this extremity, her whole dependence refted on the fupport of Great Britain; by whofe affiftance fhe at laft triumphantly furmounted all her difficulties. But to eftablifh that princefs, and to preferve the prefent imperial family, in oppofition to the intrigues and the armaments of France, was attended with charges, the burden of which this country feels at this hour.

[L]   Great

Great Britain has, in general, enjoyed this advantage, that the wars in which fhe has been engaged have not been carried on within the boundaries of the ifland. In the year 1745, however, we felt all the horrors of inteftine war, in confequence of a bold and defperate attempt to raife a new rebellion in favour of the exiled family. The warlike fpirit for which the northern parts of Scotland have been fo long diftinguifhed, inftead of being employed to maintain the rights and to extend the fame and glory of the Britifh empire, had been fuffered to ruft in floth, and to brood over its caufes of difcontent. A brave and hardy race, thus neglected by their legal fovereign, confidered themfelves as a profcribed and devoted people; and, preferving their old attachments, flew to arms with alacrity and zeal, to fupport the only caufe for which they were fuffered to bleed; flattering themfelves with the vain expectation of being able, by their valour, to replace the houfe of Stuart upon the throne. The infurrection, though at firft fuccefsful, was at once quelled by the decifive victory at Culloden. Befides the great expences which this rebellion occafioned, and the injury which it did to the national credit, it was attended with another unfortunate circumftance. The troops employed for that purpofe being drawn from the armies of the allies on the continent, this circumftance weakened our forces there to fuch a degree, as to difable us from reaping thofe advantages which otherwife we had every reafon to expect.

This war with Spain and France, which had lafted nine years, was at laft terminated by the treaty of Aix la Chapelle; and it is now propofed to give fome account of the principles upon which money was borrowed to defray the extraordinary expences it occafioned, and alfo a general view of the amount of our public debt, when the war was brought to a conclufion.

Mode of borrowing.

It was during this period that a practice which began in the reign of Queen Anne, of adding an artificial to the real capital, was firft carried to any great height. The funds were now confidered as a permanent fpecies of property, which it was fuppofed the nation could never totally redeem; and it was, therefore, thought better to difpofe of a certain quantity of a 3 or 4 *per cent.* ftock; and thus to make a bargain at one determinate intereft, than to eftablifh new funds at different rates, in

proportion

proportion to the fluctuation of the value of money, which during a long war, was perpetually increasing [81]. The plan was at firſt leſs pernicious than it has ſince proved. The price of ſtocks, during this whole period, did not greatly differ from the capital. Indeed, until the rebellion of 1745, the 3 *per cents.* had never been below 89. But the ſame practice has ſince been purſued, when theſe funds ſold at little above one half of their nominal value; and the State has acknowledged itſelf indebted in a hundred pounds, when, perhaps, it only received ſixty. The ignorant might be thus deceived into an opinion, that we were borrowing at a lower intereſt than in fact was the caſe. We have dearly paid, however, for this imaginary advantage, by a great and ſolid addition to our national incumbrances. How much of our preſent debts ought to be attributed to this deſtructive mode of raiſing money, will be the ſubject of future enquiry.

It was alſo uſual, at this time, when money was borrowed, to give *Premiums.* douceurs to the creditor in the ſhape of lottery tickets, or of life annuities; a mode adopted, not only with a view of concealing from the people the real burdens of the war, but alſo of enabling the moneylender to make the greater profit of his bargain with the public, by furniſhing him with every ſpecies of ſecurity, and putting it in his power to pleaſe the palate of every different purchaſer.

It has been an unfortunate circumſtance for this country, that we have *Eaſt India* hardly ever concluded a bargain with any of thoſe great companies *Company.* which were originally inſtituted with a view to facilitate the reduction of our debts, but at a time when the public was involved in difficulties, and conſequently neceſſitated to accept of any terms they thought proper to propoſe. Thus, in order to procure a million from the Eaſt India Company, the excluſive charter which it had obtained, was continued from 1766 to 1780; and conſequently prolonged for fourteen years, twenty-three years before the former term of the monopoly was to have ceaſed. For this million, they were to receive an intereſt of 3 *per cent.*; and, as 3 *per cents.* were then at 97, the whole value they gave for this grant did not exceed 30,000*l.* [84]. The company, it is

---

[81] Polit. Econ. vol. ii. p. 393.   [84] Ibid. p. 392.

[L] 2   believed,

believed, would have paid in a million, and would have readily accepted of 750,000*l.* of capital, bearing what was then the usual interest of 4 *per cent.* But those who managed these contracts for the public (as Dr. Price well observes) did not attend to the absurdity and extravagance of loading posterity with a debt for money paid to enjoy the exclusive possession of certain valuable privileges, and of thus *borrowing*, in the very act of *selling*, a very important monopoly[13].

During this period, also, the charter of the Bank was prolonged, until the 1st of August 1764, in consideration of which, they lent to government, *anno* 1742, the sum of 1,600,000*l.* without interest; the greater part of which would have been paid for the prolongation of its exclusive charter, had the former interest of 6 *per cent.* on their original stock been continued. Thus another wanton and unnecessary addition was made to the capital of our debts[14].

Let us next see the amount of our national debt, when the war was brought to a conclusion.

---

[13] Tracts on Civil Liberty, p. 132.   [14] Ibid. p. 125.

GENERAL

GENERAL VIEW of the NATIONAL DEBT, on 31st Dec. 1748.

1. FUNDED DEBTS.

	Principal.			Interest.		
1. The capital of the Bank of England, at 3 *per cent.* — —	£ 3,200,000	0	0	96,000	0	0
2. For cancelling Exchequer bills, at 4 *per cent.*	500,000	0	0	20,000	0	0
3. Purchased of the South Sea Company, at ditto — — —	4,000,000	0	0	160,000	0	0
4. Annuities at 4 *per cent.* from Midsum. 1728	1,750,000	0	0	70,000	0	0
5. Annuities at ditto, from ditto 1729 —	1,250,000	0	0	50,000	0	0
6. For cancelling and circulating exchequer bills — — —	1,486,400	0	0	54,450	0	0
	£ 12,186,400	0	0	450,450	0	0
7. To the East India Company, for its stock and annuities — —	4,200,000	0	0	158,000	0	0
8. To the South Sea Company, at 4 *per cent.*	27,302,203	5	6½	1,092,088	2	7¼
9. To various long and short annuities, payable at the exchequer —	2,042,723	6	1½	218,117	11	8
10. To various redeemable annuities, at different rates of interest —	3,079,071	5	1¼	104,561	7	9
11. To various Bank annuities, at different interests — —	22,530,000	0	0	829,200	0	0
	£ 71,340,397	16	9¼	2,852,417	2	0¼

2. UNFUNDED DEBTS.

12. To navy, victualling, transport, and ordnance debts, at 3 *per cent.* —	5,748,264	17	5¼	172,447	18	11
13. Debts and deficiencies provided for posterior, to Dec. 31, 1748, at 3 *per cent.*	1,204,650	7	8¼	36,139	10	2½
	£ 78,293,313	1	10¾	3,061,004	11	1¾

	Principal.			Interest.		
Debt on Dec. 31, 1739	£ 46,954,623	3	4	1,964,025	10	1¼
Ditto on Dec. 31, 1748	78,293,313	1	10¾	3,061,004	11	1¾
Increase	£ 31,338,689	18	6¾	1,096,979	1	0½

Thus it appears, that the war occasioned an addition of 31,338,689*l.* 18*s.* 6¾*d.* to the principal; and of 1,096,979*l.* 1*s.* 0½*d.* to the interest of our debts; to which are to be added the money taken from the sinking fund, and the additional taxes which were imposed, in order to carry on a war, which, after all, was productive of not one solid advantage, and was concluded by a peace, in every respect inglorious.

From

Thirdperiod.   From the treaty of Aix la Chapelle, we enjoyed the bleſſings of peace for about ſeven years; a period diſtinguiſhed by the boldeſt and moſt uſeful operation of finance recorded in the hiſtory of this country: for, by the judicious meaſures taken by that able and patriotic miniſter, Mr. Pelham, who at that time had the management of our revenue, aided by the counſels of that excellent citizen, Sir John Barnard, no leſs a ſum than 57,703,475 l. 6 s. 4¼ d. was gradually reduced from an intereſt of 4 to 3 per cent. This is a ſubject, however, which more properly belongs to the enſuing chapter. At preſent, it is only neceſſary to remark, that our debt, anno 1755, amounted to 74,571,841 l. 0 s. 2¼ d., bearing an intereſt of 2,416,717 l. 0 s. 4¼ d. Conſequently, 3,721,472 l. 1 s. 8¼ d. of principal, was paid off, in addition to the great reduction of intereſt that took place at this time.

Fourth period.   The Britiſh colonies in North America, after long ſtruggling with various difficulties, ariſing from the nature of the climate, the ruggedneſs of the ſoil, and the barbarity of their Indian neighbours, began about this time, in conſequence of their own exertions, and aided by the ſupport and encouragement which they received from the mother country, to enjoy a conſiderable degree of happineſs and proſperity; and when nothing ſeemed likely to have diſturbed the tranquillity of England for many years, ſhe was alarmed with intelligence, that theſe colonies, which ſhe had reared at ſuch an expence, and protected at ſuch heavy charges, were in a ſtate of the utmoſt danger and diſtreſs, the French having, by their intrigues, united the various tribes of Indians againſt them; and having conſtructed forts, ſurrounding the frontiers of all the ſettlements, ſome of them within 225 miles of Philadelphia". Theſe circumſtances were firſt publickly taken notice of in his majeſty's ſpeech from the throne, on the 13th of November 1755; and the Commons, in their addreſs, thanked the Crown, " for having, at the ha-" zard of all events, taken meaſures for the defence of the Britiſh do-" minions in America, not only encroached upon, but openly attacked " by the French, in a time of full peace, and farther threatened and en-" dangered by a large embarkation of troops from Europe." And they alſo declared, " that they would vigorouſly and chearfully ſupport " his majeſty, in his reſiſting ſuch unjuſtifiable encroachments"."

17 Mort. Hiſt. of England, vol. iii. p. 512.
18 Comm. Journ. vol. xxvii. p. 301.

Attempts

Attempts have recently been made to afcribe the origin of this war to other motives, in order to palliate the ingratitude of the new American States. Pofterity will be able to judge with more impartiality than we can at prefent, how far their reafonings are well founded, but it will be difficult for it to be convinced, that the war did not arife from a paffion-ate defire on the part of the Englifh nation, to defend thofe whom they confidered as their brethren, and who would either have been de-ftroyed by the tomahawks of the Indians, or driven into the fea by the French, had it not been for our affiftance. A war thus fpringing up, foon fpread its deftructive influence far and wide; and occafioned an expence to this country, much greater than it ever had before incurred; the fatal confequences of which were greatly encreafed from the perni-cious manner in which our debts were contracted.

The enormous charges with which this war was attended, put go- Mode of vernment fo much in the power of the money lenders, that the moft ^{borrowing} difadvantageous terms were agreed to, without hefitation. The firft million that was borrowed, was obtained at an intereft of only 3 *per cent.*; and as every addition to that intereft, or augmentation of capi-tal, for which no value was received, is to be accounted an additional premium or douceur, the lofs which the public fuftained in this man-ner will appear almoft incredible.

GENERAL VIEW of the PREMIUMS upon the NEW LOANS,. in the courfe of the War, begun *anno* 1755.

	£		
1. On the loan 1756, an additional intereft of 1-half *per cent.*	90,000	0	0
2. Ditto 1757, being a life annuity of 1 *per cent.*[8] —	472,500	0	0
3. Ditto 1758, an additional intereft of 1-half *per cent.* for 24 years	495,000	0	0
4. Ditto 1759, 990,000*l.* of capital, bearing an intereft of 3 *per cent.*			
which, in 9 years only, amounted to — —	1,257,300	0	0
5. Ditto 1760, by various douceurs — — —	1,852,800	0	0
6. Ditto 1761, by ditto — — —	4,296,375	0	0
7. Ditto 1762, by ditto — — —	5,820,000	0	0
[9]	£ 14,283,975	0	0

[8] Sir James Stuart remarks (Polit. Econ. vol. i. p. 397), that Mr. Grenville has calculated thefe life annuities at too low a rate.

[9] See the Prefent State of the Nation, fuppofed to be written by the Right Honourable George Grenville, 3d edition, p. 11.

It

It is evident that fome part of this fum cannot juftly be placed to the account of thofe minifters by whom the money was borrowed; becaufe the value of money neceffarily increafes with the demand for it in a time of war. But if loans had been made at a high intereft, and with a low capital, the public would have been, perhaps, *twelve millions and a half* lefs incumbered than it was; and, at the fame time, the annual charges in no refpect greater[91]; and fome part of the debt might eafily have been redeemed by parliament at the return of peace, or borrowed upon lower intereft.

Let us next fee the amount of our debts, funded and unfunded, at the conclufion of the peace, *anno* 1762.

GENERAL VIEW of the NATIONAL DEBT, at the conclufion of the War, begun *anno* 1755, and ending *anno* 1762.

	Principal.	Interest.
1. To the national funded debt, on the 5th of January 1755 (See Commons Journals, vol. xxvii. p. 167), with the intereft payable thereon, fince the reduction, *anno* 1755 and 1757 — — — —	£73,289,673	2,378,252
2. To the Navy debt, Jan. 17, 1755 (ditto p. 108), at 3 *per cent.*	1,282,167	38,465
	£74,571,840	2,416,717

	Principal.	Interest.
3. To the debt funded during the war, including the value of the long annuities, granted *anno* 1761 and 1762 —	£58,129,375	2,036,300
4. To unprovided debts, funded prior to 1764 —	6,983,553	279,342
5. Unfunded debt, remaining *anno* 1763, deducting the navy debt of 1755 — —	6,998,076	108,462
	72,111,004	2,424,104
[92] £	146,682,844	4,840,821

[91] Tracts on Civil Liberty, p. 108.

[92] Mr. Grenville, in his State of the Nation (p. 28), fuppofes, that the debt, funded and unfunded, at the conclufion of the peace of Paris, amounted to 148,377,618 *l.*, bearing an intereft of 4,993,144*l. per annum.* But the above is the fum at which it is ftated by the learned Dr. Price, who has more recently examined the fubject (See the Account of the Progrefs of the National Debt, Tracts on Civil Liberty, p. 147). The difference feems to have arifen from the former including the deficiencies of grants and funds *anno* 1763 and 1764, and the whole of the extraordinaries of the army, which the latter does not take into its computations.

Thus

. Thus, for the fake of protecting from the power of France thofe very colonies who have lately thought proper to throw themfelves into the arms of that country, we were led into a train of meafures which al-inoft doubled the incumbrances of the nation, and required an addition of above two millions and a half to pay merely the annual intereft of the debt incurred; and when a peace was concluded, and Guardeloupe and Canada came to be put in competition (however preferable the former in every commercial view), the interefts of Great Britain were not fuffered for a moment to ftand in competition with providing for their fecurity. Thefe are circumftances which, it is to be hoped, in their cooler moments, when they are fatiated with the imaginary blef-fings of independence, and of the friendfhip of their new allies, they will recollect, with the natural fenfations of generous minds awakened from prejudice and paffion, and alive to the genuine dictates of gratitude and of honour.

G E O R G E   III.

At the conclufion of the war, in 1762, the fituation of this country was, to all appearance, fplendid and flourifhing. It was incumbered, it is true, with a heavy debt, but in no degree beyond what it could bear; and we might have enjoyed as high a pitch of profperity and happinefs as any nation could have defired, if a fatal fpirit of anarchy and of inteftine difcord, if a luft of power among the great, and an impatience of fubordination among the people, had not arifen, which, after raging for fome time at home, at laft broke out, with redoubled violence, in our American colonies, and produced a conteft equally pernicious to both countries. Even before the difpute with America had broke out into hoftilities, our diffentions had been attended with the moft deftructive confequences to the nation. They occafioned, in the management of our affairs, an inattention to every thing but parliamentary influence, a prodigality in our public expenditure, and a fyftem of adopting tem-porary expedients, inftead of purfuing fome great, uniform, and deci-five line of conduct. The fame unhappy divifions made us neglect to cultivate the friendfhip, or to conciliate the affections of thofe powers with whom we were naturally connected: whilft, on the other hand, we feemed afraid to offend our enemies, unmindful of that found politi-

[M]   cal

cal maxim, " when difcord rages at home, to give it an opportunity of " fpending its violence againſt other ſtates." Indeed, if the rupture with Spain, for the poſſeſſion of Falkland iſlands, had not been unfortunately prevented, thoſe reſources which Great Britain and her colonies waſted in deſtroying each other, might have been employed in curbing the power, and in conquering the territories of their mutual enemies. It will appear alſo, from the following ſtate of the national debt at Midſummer 1775, that the continuance of peace was not attended with thoſe great effects, in reducing our incumbrances, which might have been expected.

GENERAL VIEW of the NATIONAL DEBT at Midſummer 1775.

I. PERPETUAL FUNDS.

	Principal.	Intereſt.
1. To the capital due to the Bank of England —	£ 11,686,800	350,604
2. To the Eaſt India Company — —	4,200,000	126,000
3. To the South Sea Company — —	25,984,674	779,541
	£ 41,871,474	1,256,145
4. Perpetual Bank annuities, at 4 per cent. which in January 1781 fell to 3 per cent. —	18,986,300	759,452
5. Ditto, at 3 and a half per cent. which fell to 3 per cent. anno 1782 — — —	4,500,000	157,500
6. The 3 per cent. conſolidated annuities —	38,251,696	1,147,551
7. The 3 per cent. reduced annuities —	18,353,774	550,613
8. The 3 per cents 1726 — —	1,000,000	30,000
	£ 122,963,244	3,901,261

2. TEMPORARY ANNUITIES.

9. Bank long annuities, for 99 years, from 1761 —	6,702,750	248,250
10. Exchequer long annuities — —	1,836,276	131,203
11. Various life annuities — — —	840,781	88,107
	£ 132,343,051	4,368,821

3. UNFUNDED DEBT.

12. Exchequer bills, 1,250,000l., Navy debt, 1,850,000l., Civil Liſt debt, 500,000l., the intereſt only 2 per cent.	3,600,000	72,000
Total Debt at Midſummer 1775 £ 135,943,051		4,440,821

	Principal.	Intereſt.
Debt, anno 1762	£ 146,682,844	4,840,821
Ditto, anno 1775	135,943,051	4,440,821
52 Diminiſhed, during the Peace	£ 10,739,793	400,000

91 Tracts on Civil Liberty, p. 119. Of this boaſted diminution, one half did not ariſe from the ſurplus of the revenue.

2   Thus

Thus it appears, that little more than ten millions of our debt were paid off during the peace: a fmall fum, compared to what might have been difcharged with eafe, had the refources of this country been fully exerted; and, indeed, if only one half of thofe taxes to which the nation has lately been made fubject, had been impofed *anno* 1763, when tranquillity was fully reftored, our finances would have been brought into fuch order, before the year 1775, that no ftate in Europe, nor any colonial confederacy in America, would have ventured to have incurred our refentment. But a nation that will not look its dangers and its burdens in the face, and purfue great and decifive meafures for its liberation, when in its power, muft ever expect to feel the bitter confequences of indolence and timidity.

The fources of the war with our colonies, and the events with which it has been accompanied, are circumftances too recent, and too well known, to require being enumerated in this work; and as neither the relation, nor the perufal of them, can furnifh any friend to the happinefs and profperity of this country with any pleafing fenfations, it is therefore hoped, that the following ftatement of the debt which we have incurred, in confequence of our late hoftilities, will be deemed fufficient.

GENERAL.

GENERAL VIEW of the DEBT incurred to defray the Expences of the American War.

Year	Stock price	Money received	Annual interest	Nature of the Stock	Additional Capital	Premium per 100l.
1776	£ 2,150,000	£ 2,000,000	£ 64,500	3 per cents	£ 150,000	10 sh. short annuities.
1777	5,000,000	5,000,000	225,000	4 per cents	—	2¼ per cent. for 30 years.
1778	6,000,000	6,000,000	330,000	3 per cents	—	3¼ for 29 years, or for life.
1779	7,000,000	7,000,000	472,500	3 per cents	—	1l. 16s. 3d. for 80 years.
1780	12,000,000	12,000,000	697,500	4 per cents	—	
1781	21,000,000	12,000,000	660,000	18,000,000 3 per cents 3,000,000 4 per cents }	9,000,000	17s. 6d. for 78 years.
1782	20,250,000	13,500,000	793,125	13,500,000 3 per cents 6,750,000 4 per cents }	6,750,000	13s. 4d. for 77 years.
1783	15,000,000	12,000,000	560,000	12,000,000 3 per cents 3,000,000 4 per cents }	3,000,000	5s. 6d. for 75¼ years.
1784	9,000,000	6,000,000	316,500	6,000,000 3 per cents 3,000,000 4 per cents }	3,000,000	
	£97,400,000	£75,500,000	£4,119,125		£21,900,000	
Navy bills funded, anno 1784, at 5 per cent. 127l. 10s. 6d. in stock per 100l.	6,879,341	6,449,383	343,967	5 per cents	429,958	
Unfunded debt, now remaining; (deducting the unfunded debt anno 1775), at 4 per cent. suppofed.	6,000,000	6,000,000	240,000	—	—	
Debt contracted during the war	£110,279,341	87,949,383	4,703,092		22,329,958	

Debt, anno 1775   £ 135,943,051   4,440,821
Ditto, incurred during the laſt war   110,479,341   4,703,092

Total of the preſent national debt   £ 246,222,392   9,143,913

* It is hoped that the unfunded debt (deducting 3,600,000l. due at the commencement of the war) will not be quite ſo conſiderable. But in ſuch calculations, it is better to be a million over than under.

Such is the *nominal* amount of the exifting incumbrances of the nation, the real nature and burden of which will be the fubject of future difcuffion. At prefent, it is only propofed to give a fhort view of the progrefs of the public debts from their commencement to the prefent time.

	Principal.	Interest.
National debt at the revolution — —	£ 664,263	39,855
Increafe during the reign of King William —	15,730,439	1,271,087
Debt at the acceffion of Queen Anne — —	16,394,702	1,310,942
Increafe during the reign of Queen Anne —	37,750,661	2,040,416
Debt at the acceffion of George I. — —	54,145,363	3,351,358
Decreafe during the reign of George I. —	2,053,128	1,133,807
Debt at the acceffion of George II. — —	52,092,235	2,217,551
Decreafe during the peace — —	5,137,612	253,526
Debt at the commencement of the Spanifh war 1739 —	46,954,623	1,964,025
Increafe during the war — — —	31,338,689	1,096,979
Debt at the end of the Spanifh war 1748 —	78,293,312	3,061,004
Decreafe during the peace — — —	3,721,472	664,287
Debt at the commencement of the war 1755 —	74,571,840	2,396,717
Increafe during the war — — —	72,111,004	2,444,104
Debt at the conclufion of the peace 1762 —	146,682,844	4,840,821
Decreafe during the peace — —	10,739,793	400,000
Debt at the commencement of the American war —	135,943,051	4,440,821
Increafe during the war — — —	110,279,341	4,703,092
Amount of our prefent national debt — —	£ 246,222,392	9,143,913

One circumftance alone furnifhed the author with any confolation whatfoever during the whole courfe of this painful inveftigation, which has arifen from the wealth and refources of this country having been found infinitely fuperior to the expectations even of the moft fanguine. There is hardly a period, fince the revolution, in which as great apprehenfions were not entertained of the ftability of the funds, and as loud complaints made of the intolerable weight of taxes, as at the prefent hour: and

and if the public are but convinced that our incumbrances, however
enormous, are not beyond the ability of the country either to bear or to
redeem, and at the fame time that the burden has grown to fuch a height
that palliatives can be no longer effectual, but that great and fubstantial
meafures muft be taken for their redemption without delay, it is apprehended there will be little difficulty in carrying fuch plans into effect as
will foon render Great Britain as happy, flourifhing, and powerful, as
ever; and Europe (in the words of Raynal) will yet be able to fhow
the world one nation, of whom fhe has reafon to be proud.

C H A P. V.

*Of the Steps hitherto taken to diminifh the Capital, and to
reduce the Intereft of the National Debt, with fome
account of the different Plans fuggefted for that purpofe.*

ANY perfon, unacquainted with the hiftory of England, who was
told that, in lefs than a century, it had involved itfelf in a debt of
upwards of 240,000,000*l.* would naturally enquire whether any fteps
had ever been taken to prevent fo immenfe an accumulation. He
would be apt to afk—Were there no generous patriots to warn the nation of its danger? Were there no minifters who had either wifdom to
apply a remedy, or magnanimity to check this cancerous humour[1], before it grew to fuch a height; or were the people fo felfifh and interefted,
that they would not bear the fmalleft additional burden for the fake of
their pofterity?

To fatisfy the curiofity of thofe who may be defirous of knowing
what meafures were purfued for difcharging the capital, or reducing the
intereft of our national incumbrances, is the object of the prefent
chapter.

[1] Bolingbroke, vol. iv. p. 130.

From

From the preceding part of this work, it appears that, during the King Wil-
reign of William, our perpetual funded incumbrances did not amount liam.
to four millions; and as the remaining burdens of the country at that
time, either confifted of long annuities (which would be annihilated in
the courfe of time), or of loans upon funds which yielded fo great a
furplus, after defraying their refpective interefts, that they were likely
foon to be paid off, it was the lefs neceffary to form any plan for a more
fpeedy redemption: the only reduction, therefore, that took place during the whole period, was that of annihilating, by act of parliament, one
half of the capital and annual intereft of the bankers debt, which
Charles II. had left behind him.

The great addition to our national incumbrances, which took Queen Anne.
place in the reign of Queen Anne, not a little alarmed the public.
Propofals were made for raifing between two and three millions *per
annum*, to be applied as a finking fund to pay them off[a]: and one
member in the houfe of commons (Archibald Hutchefon) thought it
incumbent on him to point out the deftructive confequences of our
public debts, and to fuggeft the means that might be taken for their redemption. But the attention of minifters was taken up with matters
which they confidered to be of much greater importance; namely, in
political intrigues for preferving their own power, and fecuring a fucceffor to the crown, on the enjoyment of whofe confidence they might
fully depend; confequently no fteps were taken for that purpofe.

Soon after the acceffion of the prefent royal family, Mr. Hutchefon George I.
prefented to George I. his famous plan for the payment of the public
debts, which, as it is drawn up with great concifenefs, and with much
ability, is well entitled to infertion in a hiftory of our finances.

A Propofal for the Payment of the Public Debts.

1. That the fums feverally affeffed on the lands of Great Britain for
the land-tax of the year 1713, be made payable as a rent charge in fee

---

[a] See Propofals for a very eafy Tax, to raife between two and three millions *per annum*,
to begin to pay the Public Debts; by Ephraim Parker. London, printed *anno* 1713. It
was by a tax upon the linen, woollen, and filk manufactures.

for

for ever, out of the faid feveral refpective lands, redeemable, notwithftanding, at any time, by the proprietors paying twenty-two years purchafe for the fame.

2. That the faid rents, or the money raifed by redemption or affignments of the fame, be applied towards the difcharge of the public
debts.

3. That one-tenth part of all annuities for life, or other eftate; and
all other rents iffuing out of the aforefaid lands, and of all fums of
money fecured by mortgage, and of all other debts which affect lands,
be entirely remitted to their refpective proprietors.

4. That the proprietors of fuch lands be empowered, notwithftanding any difability by fettlements, to fell fo much of the faid lands as
fhall be fufficient to redeem the aforefaid refpective rent charges.

5. That one-tenth part of all the debts fecured by the public funds,
be remitted.

6. That one-tenth part of all the other nett perfonal eftate of all the
inhabitants of Great Britain, exclufive of the aforefaid debts which affect lands and public funds, be applied to the payment of the public
debts.

7. That two fhillings in the pound be made payable yearly out of
the falaries and perquifites of all offices and places which are now in
being, or fhall at any time hereafter be created, and to remain during
the continuance of fuch offices and places refpectively.

8. That the legal intereft be reduced to 4 *per cent. per annum.*

9. That, for the effectual fecuring of the payment of fuch public
debts, for which there either is at prefent no provifion, or the provifion
made by parliament appears to be deficient, that all funds granted for
any term of years be made perpetual, until the principal and intereft of
all the faid public debts be fully paid off; and that the intereft of fuch
public debts as at prefent have defective or no fecurities, be paid out of
the yearly produce of the faid funds, and that the remainder only of
fuch produce, over and above the intereft of the faid public debts, be
applied towards the finking of the principal money.

10. That provifion may be made by an excife on apparel, or fome
other excife, fufficient to produce one million *per annum,* in lieu of the
land-tax, to continue till all the public debts are difcharged'.

³ Hutchefon's Collection of Treatifes, p. 27.

It

It is unneceſſary to trouble the reader with any obſervations upon ſo excellent a propoſal, the propriety of which muſt ſtrike every perſon who is in the leaſt acquainted with the ſubject. It contains a ſyſtem alſo, which, with little alteration, might be accommodated to theſe times. Notwithſtanding the immenſity of the preſent load, were it thus transferred from the public to the ſeveral individuals in their juſt proportions, the burden would be little felt, in compariſon of what it is; and, in the ſpace of a few years, the whole would be totally extinguiſhed. It propoſes, it is true, an attempt of a bold and daring nature; but if it came recommended by a popular miniſter, or a reſpectable committee of the houſe of commons, it might yet meet with a favourable reception from the public. It is a matter alſo that may be diſcuſſed with the utmoſt propriety, not only by thoſe who are in power, and thoſe who are in parliament, but by the public in general: for there is not a ſingle individual in the country, whatever his ſtation may be, who is not materially affected by the debts with which the nation is loaded, and whoſe comfort and happineſs will not, in future, depend upon the ſteps that muſt ſoon be taken in regard to theſe incumbrances.

Nor was Hutcheſon the only perſon, during this reign, who ſuggeſted the neceſſity of adopting effectual meaſures for diminiſhing the national debts.

In the year 1715, Mr. Aſgill publiſhed his plan, for the more ſpeedy redemption of all the perpetual funds, excepting the original ſtock of the Bank of England*. His idea was, that two millions ſhould be raiſed in ſpecie, and depoſited in a bank, to ſupport the circulation of twenty millions of Exchequer bills, bearing an intereſt of 3 per cent., with which all the redeemable debts were to be paid off. As an annual intereſt, amounting to 1,182,454l. 10s. 5d. was then paid for theſe redeemable debts, and as the intereſt of the two millions to be borrowed, at 6 per cent., and of twenty millions of Exchequer bills, at 3 per cent., amounted only to 720,000l. it is evident that the public would thus have acquired a ſinking fund of 462,454l. 10s. 5d. It is ſaid, that the Bank, notwithſtanding the variety of difficulties it had to ſtruggle with in the infancy of public credit, and of paper currency,

Mr. Aſgill's plan.

* Abſtract of the public funds, printed for J. Roberts. An. 1715.

[N]   and

and the fituation of public affairs at the time, was able to fupport a circulation of 1,200,000*l.*, by means of 300,000*l.*, which it had called in from the proprietors. Mr. Afgill therefore computed, that two millions would be fufficient to maintain the credit of twenty millions of Exchequer bills. The plan was undoubtedly too extenfive; perhaps were it tried on a more limited fcale, it might be attended with fuccefs.

Stephen Barbier's propofal.　　When paper circulation was firft fet on foot, it was viewed with great jealoufy and apprehenfion: but when the minds of men had become more reconciled to it, and the beneficial confequences attending it were more clearly perceived, the world rapidly run into a very oppofite extreme, and it began to be imagined, that the greateft operations might be effected by means of this new power[5]. Impreffed with thefe ideas, Stephen Barbier prefented his expedient to pay the public debts to George I. on the 6th of May 1719.

The object of this propofal was to convert forty millions of the national debt into notes, bearing 1 *per cent.* lefs intereft than the original fund, which was thus to be converted: the converfion was only to take place at the requeft of the creditor, who might thus, at any time, obtain both his principal and intereft. Thefe notes were to be current in all pecuniary tranfactions, and were to be paid in fpecie in fix months after they were prefented for payment. Every perfon muft perceive, that the only poffible advantage which this plan afforded, was that of reducing the intereft of the funds 1 *per cent.* when the creditor chofe to convert his ftock into notes, which would not probably be done to any great extent; and yet the author flattered himfelf, that he had pointed out treafures more valuable than the mines of Peru, and fuggefted the means of rendering this country, by a fingle ftroke of finance, the moft powerful in the univerfe[6].

[5] A very ingenious propofal, founded on thefe ideas, entitled, " A method that will enable the government to pay off that part of the public debt which is redeemable by " parliament," was privately printed in April 1715, and diftributed among the minifters and members of parliament. By this plan, twenty-one millions was to be paid in feventeen years, by bills of credit, without intereft.

[6] See an expedient to pay the public debts, by Stephen Barbier, gentleman, printed *anno* 1719. As George I. was not very converfant in the Englifh language, it was printed both in French and Englifh.

Having

Having thus feen the various plans that were propofed, let us next confider what meafures were really adopted.

The firft ftep that was taken for relieving the nation undoubtedly was, that important regulation, by which legal intereft was reduced from 6 to 5 *per cent.* On the 18th of June 1714, a member of the Houfe, whofe name is not known, had propofed to reduce the intereft of the public funds; but it was dropped, no perfon having feconded the motion. On the contrary, Mr. Hutchefon, and other members, were ordered to prepare and bring in a bill for reducing the rate of intereft, without prejudice to parliamentary fecuritics[7]. We are much in the dark, as to the grounds on which it proceeded. It appears, however, that fo large a fum as 20,000 *l.* had been lent at only 4 *per cent.* on private fecurity[8]; and confequently, there could hardly be any well founded objection on the part of the monied intereft, to the law being enacted.

(margin: The rate of legal intereft on private fecurities lowered.)

The reduction of the intereft of the public debts, though not the avowed, yet was the neceffary confequence of the legal rate on private fecurities being thus diminifhed. Government began immediately to borrow money upon lower terms. Of this, a fingular inftance occurs *anno* 1715. By an act that paffed that year, 54,600 *l. per annum*, was fet apart, as the intereft that muft be provided for in confequence of a loan of 910,000 *l.* propofed to be raifed at that time. But as it was afterwards found, that money could be procured at 5 *per cent.*; another act was paffed that very feffion, by which the annuity was reduced to 45,500 *l. per annum*[9]. When new loans were thus raifed at 5 *per cent.* no good reafon could be affigned why the old debts, redeemable by parliament, fhould remain at fix.

(margin: Reduction of the intereft of the public debts.)

The merit of eftablifhing a Sinking Fund in this country has, in general, been afcribed to Sir Robert Walpole, but erroneoufly; for other funds of the fame nature had previoufly exifted, and in particular, the furplus of the aggregate fund had been dedicated to purpofes exactly fimilar[10]. But he, as chancellor of the exchequer, had the charge of the firft important operation of that nature, and undoubtedly, managed it with

(margin: Origin of the Sinking Fund.)

[7] Comm. Journ. vol. xvii. p. 689.
[8] See Chandler's debates of the Commons, vol. vi. p. 131.
[9] 1 Geo. I. feff. 2. cap. 19.   [10] Ibid. cap. 12.

[N] *   great

great dexterity and judgment. For he not only prevailed upon the Bank, and the South Sea Company, to make a confiderable reduction in the intereft they received from the public, but alfo voluntarily to offer 5,500,000 l. to government, if it fhould be neceffary, to be applied for paying off the redeemable debts of fuch creditors as were unwilling to accept of 5 per cent. for their principal ". Such an advance however was not neceffary; and the advantage which the public received from this reduction, will appear from the following ftatement :

STATE of the REDUCTION of the INTEREST on the PUBLIC FUNDS, *Anno* 1716.

	Principal.	Interest.	Reduced.
1. To exchequer bills cancelled by the Bank, *anno* 1710.	£ 1,775,027 7 10½	106,501 14 5	88,751 7 10½
2. To fundry other exchequer bills due to the Bank, being originally at the rate of 7l. 4s. ¼d. interest	4,561,025 0 0	328,561 15 6	215,779 13 5
3. To the South Sea capital	10,000,000 0 0	600,000 0 0	500,000 0 0
4. To other redeemable debts, reduced to 5 from 6 per cent. ¹²	£ 9,392,311 4 2½	563,538 13 5½	469,615 11 2½
	£ 25,728,364 2 1	1,598,602 3 4½	1,274,146 12 6
		£ 1,274,146 12 6	
Total annual furplus		£ 324,455 10 10½	

Claufe appropriating the furplufes of the funds.

A confiderable furplus being thus procured, the next queftion was, how it fhould be difpofed of? The Commons, on the 23d March 1716, had refolved ¹³, that all favings that fhould arife from the reduction of the intereft, fhould be applied towards difcharging and diminifhing the

" A reduction of intereft was, at that time, not unpopular even among the creditors; at leaft, it is faid, that old Bateman (a great ftockholder) told Lord Stanhope, that he was glad the refolutions had been taken; becaufe, though his intereft was diminifhed, he fhould think his principal more fecure than ever. Bolingbroke's Works, vol. iv. p. 150.

¹² There was afterwards added to this fum 140,844 l. 6 s. 5¼ d. of intereft, converted into capital. See Poftlethwayt, p. 252.   ¹³ Comm. Journ. vol. xviii. p. 513.

national

national debt. But on the 10th of April, Sir Robert Walpole refigned his fituation in the treafury ; and as the plan of one minifter is feldom relifhed by another, this important regulation was actually left out of the bill that was brought in. The omiffion, however, was fupplied, by an inftruction to the committee, by which they were directed to provide, that the furplufes of the feveral funds fhould be ftrictly appropriated to the difcharge of the national debts[14]; and the act itfelf, contained the following memorable claufe[15]: "And be it further enacted, that all the " monies to arife, from time to time, as well of the excefs, or furplus " of an act made this feffion, for redeeming the funds of the Bank of " England, and of the excefs, or furplus, by virtue of one other act, . " made likewife this feffion, for redeeming the funds of the South Sea " Company, as alfo of the excefs or furplus of the duties and revenues " by this act appropriated as aforefaid, and the overplus monies of the " faid general yearly fund by this act eftablifhed, fhall be appropriated " to the difcharging the principal and intereft of fuch national debts as " were incurred before the 25th of December 1716, and are declared " to be national debts, and are provided for by parliament, in fuch " manner as fhall be directed by any future act, or acts of parliament, " to be difcharged therewith, or out of the fame, *and to or for none* " *other ufe, intent, or purpofe whatfoever.*"

Thefe furplufes have ever fince been known under the name of *The Sinking Fund*; and if, in addition to them, new taxes to the amount of half a million *per annum* had been impofed at the fame time, and if the whole had been invariably appropriated to the purpofes above mentioned, the progrefs that would have been made in difcharging our public incumbrances would have been rapid indeed.

The debts of the nation, at the acceffion of the prefent royal family, confifted either of *redeemable* annuities, which could at any time be paid off by parliament, whenever money could be procured for that purpofe, or of certain annuities for life, or for terms of years, which might be called *irredeemable*, as they could not be difcharged without the confent of the proprietors. It has been already feen, that the former had undergone a very confiderable reduction in point of annual intereft ; and it was always in the power of the public, to take advantage of its increaf-

Origin of the South Sea fcheme.

[14] Comm. Journ. vol. xviii. p. 611.   [15] 3 Geo. I. cap. 7.

ing

ing wealth and credit, to reduce them ftill lower. But the irredeemable debts were a burden, which it was difficult to form any plan effectually to remove.

The South Sea Company was, at that time, by far the greateft public creditor ; and it had procured an act *anno* 1717, by which the proprietors of certain fhort annuities (amounting to 134,998 *l.* 12 *s.*) who had yet to run above twenty-three years of their term, from Chriftmas 1718, were permitted to fubfcribe the refidue of the term, at the rate of eleven and one-half years purchafe into the South Sea ftock, and were to receive 5 *per cent.* for the principal [16]. In confequence of this circumftance, and of an additional advance of about 544,142*l.* 0*s.* 10½*d.* the capital of the South Sea Company, was increafed to 11,746,844*l.* 8*s.* 10½*d.*

The fuccefs with which this operation was attended, induced the company, about the middle of November 1719, to prefent to Earl Stanhope, then firft Lord of the Treafury, a fcheme " for advancing the " public credit, and for a certain reduction of the intereft of the whole " debt of the nation to 4 *per cent. per annum*, at the end of feven years, " from Midfummer 1720 ; alfo, for rendering it practicable to alter, " change, or even fink the moft burdenfome funds; and to reduce the " feveral branches of the cuftoms and excife, into one entire duty." The plan underwent confiderable alterations, in confequence of the obfervations made by that noble lord, and Mr. Aiflabie, then chancellor of the exchequer ; and it was particularly infifted upon, that the company fhould advance to the public no lefs a fum than 3,500,000*l.* for the liberty of enlarging their ftock, in the manner that had been propofed. This propofal was unfortunately acceded to. I fay unfortunately ; for the higher the public raifed its demands, the lefs profpect there was of the plan proving fuccefsful.

When the South Sea fcheme, thus altered, was prefented to parliament, the national debt ftood nearly as follows :

[16] 5 Geo. I. cap. 17.

1. Due

1. Due to the Bank, being their original fund — -	£ 1,600,000
2. Redeemable annuities due ditto — —	3,775,000
	5,375,000
3. Eaſt India Company's capital — — —	3,200,000
	8,575,000
4. The South Sea capital - — —	11,746,844
	20,321,844
5. To all the other public debts and annuities propoſed to be taken in by the South Sea Company, and computed at -	30,981,712
	51,303,556
6. To be paid by the South Sea Company, for reducing the national debt	3,500,000
	£ 47,803,556

In addition to this reduction of the principal, the plan, in proceſs
of time, would have produced a ſinking fund, which, when added to
the former ſurpluſes, would have been productive of the greateſt advantages to the public.

STATE of the ANNUAL SAVINGS.

1. By converting the long annuities into redeemable ſtock -	£ 133,541
2. The intereſt of the £ 3,500,000 advanced by the South Sea Company at 5 per cent. - - - -	175,000
	£ 308,541
3 To the reduction of intereſt from 5 to 4 per cent. upon the Company's original capital, and the redeemable annuities, to be incorporated in their ſtock, which reduction was to take place at Midſummer 1727	235,426
Total annual ſaving	543,967
4. The Sinking Fund, then produced per annum - -	636,000
Total Sinking Fund	£ 1,179,967

Thus, anno 1727, a ſinking fund of near 1,200,000 l. was provided, by which the whole debt of the nation would have been ſoon
extinguiſhed, had it been invariably appropriated.

It is neceſſary to attend to a very important diſtinction between the
South Sea plan, as it was originally formed, and as it was afterwards
perverted. The original plan was, merely to induce the irredeemable
creditors

Perverſion of
the South Sea
ſcheme.

creditors to part with their annuities, confifting of 667,705 *l.* 8 *s.* 1 *d.*
per annum, in long annuities, which did not terminate till the year 1708,
and of 121,000 *l.* 8 *s.* in fhort annuities; the value of both of which
was perpetually rifing, and proportionably increafed, as the intereft on
the other funds was reduced. No effectual meafures could be taken
for leffening the public debts, whilft thefe annuities remained irredeemable. It was an object, therefore, of the utmoft confequence to
the public. But unfortunately, other advantages were expected, which,
it was imagined, a competition between the Bank and the South Sea
Company, would not a little promote.

It is faid, that, at firft, the Bank difcouraged all ideas of that nature.
But afterwards being chagrined, that an upftart company fhould thus
propofe a plan fo likely to prove beneficial, they were induced to give
in propofals, by which they offered no lefs a fum than 5,500,000 *l.* for
the fame privilege which the South Sea Company were to have acquired;
and it was reprefented on their behalf, that if any advantage was to be
obtained by a bargain with the public, confidering the many great and
eminent fervices which their corporation had done to government, in
the moft difficult times, they flattered themfelves that they ought to be
preferred. The South Sea Company were fo much irritated by this oppofition, that at a general court, they inftructed their directors, not to
lofe the fcheme *coft what it would;* and accordingly, they offered propofals, fecuring a profit of 4,667,000 *l.* to the public; and by which,
if all the irredeemable annuities were fubfcribed, the enormous fum of
7,567,500 *l.* would be gained ". Terms fo advantageous were immediately accepted of; and a bill was accordingly brought in, which, after
fome oppofition, at laft received the full fanction of the legiflature ".
But the competition between the two companies, and the great offers
which they had refpectively propofed, made the public imagine, that
there muft be fomething more profitable in the fcheme than was at firft
fuppofed, or could be fathomed by thofe who were not in the fecret;
and hence, " The imaginations of mankind became eafily heated, and
" their paffions fo animated with ideas of *inconceivable advantages,* that

---

[1] See the propofal, Comm. Journ. vol. xix. p. 246. The propofals given in by the
Bank, may be feen in the Hiftorical Regifter for the year 1720, p. 31 and 38.

[15] 6 Geo. I. cap. 4.

" they

" they threw away all reafon, and gave themfelves up wholly to
" humour "."

The profits of the South-Sea Company, were to arife, 1. From the
intereft they were to receive from the Public on their capital, which
was to continue at 5 *per cent.* for feven years: 2. From the advantages
of their trade to the South-Sea : 3. From a monopoly of the trade
to Africa, and the property of Nova Scotia, and of that part of the
ifland of St. Kitt's which had belonged to the French. But in the
fervour of their competition with the Bank, they had been prevailed
upon to give up thefe latter advantages for the prefent, trufting to the
promife of the minifter, that they fhould afterwards be procured. And
fuch was the dilemma to which the company was reduced from thefe
circumftances, that nothing but taking advantage of the blindnefs and
infatuation of the people, and of that phrenzy of avaricious enterprife
in pecuniary fpeculations, which prevailed at that time, could give
them any profpect of fulfilling their engagements with the public. Accordingly, a variety of infamous artifices were put in practice, to enhance the value of their ftock ; imaginary advantages were held forth ;
a thoufand groundlefs reports were circulated with regard to acquifitions
in the South-Seas, &c. &c. and dividends were voted, which the directors very well knew could never be paid, and for which there was
no folid foundation.

The fteps that were taken for the relief of thofe individuals who
fuffered by thefe tranfactions, and for the punifhment of the directors,
and their affociates in guilt, is not within the object of this work to'
relate. It is proper, however, to ftate the advantages which the nation
reaped. At firft, an act was paffed, by which (in full for the claims
which the public had upon the company) two millions of its capital
were funk. Thefe two millions, however, were afterwards revived,
together with the annuity attending the fame*. But the public, in the
firft place, received this advantage, that 535,362 *l.* 15 *s.* 7¼ *d.* of long
annuities, and 97,335 *l.* 5 *s.* of fhort annuities, were converted into
redeemable ftock (which at this time bears but 3 *per cent.* intereft;) and
by the bargain with the company, their capital was reduced, at Mid-

¹' See a true ftate of the South-Sea fcheme in folio, p. 30.

²' 6 Geo. I. cap. 6.

[O]   fummer

fummer 1727, from 5 to 4 *per cent.* by which the following profit was gained :

State of the Annual Profit gained by the Public, in confequence of its bargain with the South-Sea Company.

1. By One *per cent.* on 13,061,878 *l.* of South-Sea capital, reduced by the bargain at Midfummer 1727, from 5 to 4 *per cent.*	£ 130,618 15 7
2. By one *per cent.* on the South-Sea annuity, the principal being 16,901,241 *l.* 17 *s.* — — —	169,012 8 4
3. By one *per cent.* on 4,000,000 *l.* purchafed of the South-Sea Company by the Bank of England — — —	40,000 0 0
Total	£ 339,631 3 11

This annual faving, calculated at 25 years purchafe, yielded a profit to the public of 8,490,780 *l.* : a fmall fum, compared to the advantages of which this meafure might have been produ&tive, but much greater than what is generally fuppofed [21].

Progrefs of the finking fund during this reign. The great obje&t which minifters feem to have had in view, fince the commencement of our public debts, was not to difcharge the principal, but to diminifh the intereft, fo as to render their adminiftration as little burdenfome to the people, and confequently, as popular as poffible. Notwithftanding principles of a nature fo very unfavourable, to the exiftence of a finking fund ; yet during the whole reign of George I. it was invariably appropriated to the purpofes for which it had been formed ; and, rather than encroach upon it, money was borrowed upon new taxes, when the fupplies in general might have been raifed, by dedicating the furpluffes of the old taxes to the current fervices of the year [22]. Little progrefs, however, was made in difcharging the public debts ; for at the fame inftant that old incumbrances were thus paid off, new debts were contra&ted. The finking fund alfo, until the five *per cents.* were reduced to four, in the year 1727, hardly amounted to 600,000 *l. per annum* ; and in the infancy of fuch a fund, its operations are

[21] Advantages which have accrued to the public, by the execution of the South-Sea fcheme, printed *anno* 1726, p. 8. It may be faid, that by 11 Geo. I. cap. 9. 3,775,027 *l.* 17 *s.* 10 *d.* was reduced at the fame time to 4 *per cent.* But that was probably owing to the example given by the South-Sea Company of fuch a redu&tion.

[22] Price's Appeal on the National Debt, edit. 1762. p. 29. note B.

very

very limited and confined. It appears, however, from a vote of the Houfe of Commons, on the 12th of March 1727, that from Chriftmas 1716 to Lady-day 1728, there was, or would be, iffued, for diminifh-ing the national debts, no lefs a fum than 6,648,762 l. 5 s. 1 d. ²³

About the latter end of the former reign, it was a queftion which George II. became not a little controverted, whether the public creditors had a right to infift, that the finking fund fhould be folely applied to dif-charge the principal of their debts. On the one hand, it has been pofitively afferted, that no condition of that nature was either ex-preffed or underftood, in all the conferences that were held between the minifter and the public creditors, when that fund was originally efta-blifhed ²⁴. On the other, nothing can be ftronger in fupport of fuch a claim, than the words of the act of parliament, particularly when joined to the fpeeches from the throne, and the addreffes of both houfes of parliament ²⁵. It is well known alfo, that in the year 1726, a very able and intelligent member, connected with the minifter at the time, publifhed an elaborate performance, to prove the utility of fuch a fund, and to refute all apprehenfions in regard to its being perverted ²⁶. The fact feems to have been, that at firft it was fuppofed equally for the ad-vantage of the creditor and the public, that it fhould be thus invariably applied. But when it was no longer infifted upon by the creditor, and when the competition came to be, not who fhould be *firft*, but who fhould be *laft* paid, it was eafy to forefee, that the finking fund would foon be alienated, unlefs protected from the rapacity of minifters, by much ftricter regulations than had as yet been enacted.

²³ Comm. Journ. vol. xxi. p. 81.

²⁴ Confiderations concerning the Public Funds, &c. 2d edit. printed anno 1735, p. 13. Nor is it fo much as hinted at in the propofals given in by the Bank, or South-Sea Company. Hift. Regift. an. 1717. p. 208.

²⁵ See the extracts of the fpeeches and addreffes, in Price's Appeal, p. 26. Note A.

²⁶ Effay on the Public Debts of the Kingdom; fuppofed to be wrtten by Sir Na-thaniel Gould, 2d edit. printed anno 1726, reprinted for B. White, Fleet-ftreet, anno 1782. This tract was twice anfwered, firft by a pamphlet intitled, Remarks on the Effay, &c. Printed by A. Moore, anno 1727; and fecondly, by Mr. Pulteney's well-known State of the National Debt, printed for R. Franklin, in the fame year. Sir Nathaniel fupported his former opinions in a paper, intitled, A Defence of the Effay, &c. Printed for J. Peele, anno 1727.

[O] 2 The

Perverfion of the finking fund.

The firſt encroachment may be traced to the year 1728-9[27]. It was ne-ceſſary to raiſe 1,250,000 *l.* for the current ſervice of the year ; and the miniſters boaſted, that ſuch was the flouriſhing condition of the finking fund, that it was very well able to pay the intereſt of that ſum, and that there was no occaſion to impoſe any new taxes upon the people. In vain did a member of the houſe move, that the ſupplies ſhould be raiſed, without creating a new debt upon any exiſting fund[28]. The motion paſſed in the negative without a diviſion, and is ſtigmatiſed as having been made, merely with a view of diſtreſſing government. So little was the public at large ſuppoſed to be intereſted in this important tranſaction.

The ſecond encroachment took place *anno* 1730-1[29], when certain duties impoſed in the reign of king William, for paying the intereſt due to the Eaſt-India comfany (which became no longer neceſſary for that purpoſe, in conſequence of their intereſt being reduced), was made uſe of as a fund for raiſing 1,200,000*l.* inſtead of being thrown into the finking fund, as it ought properly to have been ; but the final perverſion of this fund took place, *anno* 1732-3. The land-tax in the former year, had been reduced to one ſhilling in the pound ; and the miniſter (Sir Robert Walpole) had by this means rendered himſelf ſo popular with the landed intereſt, that he was determined to perſevere in the ſame unfortunate ſyſtem of ſecuring his own power at the expence of the revenue. Accordingly he moved, that the land-tax ſhould be continued at one ſhilling in the pound, and that 500,000*l.* ſhould be taken out of the finking fund, and applied to the current ſervices of the year[30].

It is to the credit of parliament, that the meaſure propoſed met with a violent oppoſition in both houſes : but it is unneceſſary to enter into the particulars of debates, which every perſon may eaſily obtain, and

---

[27] By 2 Geo. II. cap. 3. Mr. Pulteney ſays, that the firſt encroachment made upon this fund, was by an increaſe of the civil liſt ; and the ſecond, by taking off the ſalt duty. See Chandler's Debates, vol. vii. p. 228.   But theſe were rather circuitous than direct encroachments.   [28] Comm. Journ. vol. xxi. p. 206.

[29] 4 Geo. II. cap. 9.   [30] Comm. Journ. vol. xxii. p. 16.

perufe ". The parliament, however (as Dr. Price obferves), not accuftomed to refufe the minifter any thing, agreed to the propofal;
" and thus expired, after an exiftence of about eleven years, the finking
" fund, that facred bleffing—once the nation's only hope—prematurely
" and cruelly deftroyed by its own parent. Could it have efcaped the
" hands of violence, it would have made us the envy and the terror of
" the world, by leaving us at this time, not only tax-free, but in pof-
" feffion of a treafure, greater perhaps than ever was enjoyed by any
" kingdom ²²." This learned and refpectable author, has perhaps
carried his enthufiafm too far, with regard to the advantages refulting
from an invariable appropriation of this fund; but he fpeaks with that
honeft warmth which every real patriot feels, in a matter fo interefting
to the public.

It is unneceffary to enquire very minutely into the application of the
finking fund, after it was thus fatally perverted; for though it has been
occafionally applied for difcharging fome part of our incumbrances, yet it
has been much oftener expended in the current fervices of the year, and confequently has not been productive of any material advantage; on the contrary, has loaded the public with a heavy burden, to encourage the profufion of minifters, and to difcourage, fo far as a weight of taxes is able
to do it, the general induftry of the people.

Sir Robert Walpole was not only the perfon by whofe means the
finking fund was perverted, but he alfo exerted his abilities and influence in parliament, to prevent the reduction of a confiderable part
of the public debt from 4 to 3 *per cent.* which might have been eafily
effected in the year 1737. The 3 *per cents.* at that time, bore a premium at the market; confequently there could have been no difficulty
in procuring money at that rate, to pay off fuch of the creditors as were
unwilling to agree to the reduction. But the meafure being fuggefted
by that inflexible patriot Sir John Barnard, who was generally in oppofition to the minifter, the whole power of government was exerted to
deprive him of the juft applaufe he would have acquired by bringing
fuch a meafure to bear. The motions, however, which were made,
" that all the public funds, redeemable by law, carrying intereft at

*Rejection of
the plan for
reducing the
intereft of the
public funds,
An. 1737.*

²¹ See Hiftorical Regifter, p. 218. Comm. Debates, publifhed by Chandler, vol. vii.
p. 285; and Lords Debates, publifhed by ditto, p. 489.
²² Appeal on the National Debt, p. 38.

" four,

" four, fhould, with the confent of the proprietors, be reduced to three
" *per cent.*," and, " that his majefty fhould be enabled to borrow any fum
" of money that might be neceffary for redeeming the debts of thofe
" who refufed to confent to the reduction," were voted, after fome oppofition. But the bill that was brought, in in confequence of thefe refolutions, was not even fent to a committee ". It is aftonifhing what
abfurd arguments were made ufe of to prevent this propofal paffing into
a law. It was urged, that fuch a reduction, inftead of tending to increafe our trade, and to improve the landed property of the nation,
would probably contribute to the ruin of both. The pitiable cafe of
widows and orphans, whofe income would be thus diminifhed, was
loudly deplored ; and in particular, it was afferted, that it would prove
deftructive and ruinous to the capital, in whofe neighbourhood the
greater part of the ftockholders and annuitants could no longer afford
to live, but would be obliged to retire to remote and cheap diftricts in
the country. It was alfo contended, that the fcheme was impracticable,
though a fimilar one had been carried into effect, *anno* 1716, and
was again put in practice under Mr. Pelham's adminiftration. It is
difficult to eftimate the lofs which the public fuftained in confequence
of this propofal having been rejected. The capital of the South Sea
company at Chriftmas 1738, when the reduction would have taken
place, amounted to 27,300,000 *l.* one *per cent.* on which was 273,000 *l.*
per annum. It continued at four *per cent.* till December 1750, and at
three one-half *per cent.* until December 1757. The difference of intereft which the public paid in the interval, amounted to four millions
and a half ; and when it is confidered, that the other four *per cents.*
might alfo have been reduced about the fame time, we may in fome
degree calculate what the minifter facrificed from a fpirit of oppofition.

Reduction of
intereft,
An. 1749.

But the fame meafure, which, when it was propofed by a private individual, was accounted vifionary and impracticable, was no fooner put
into the hands of a minifter, than it inftantly became the beft and

---

¹³ Comm. Journ. vol. xxii. p. 834. The divifion was 222 in favour of the firft
motion, and 157 againft it. But the fecond divifion was very oppofite to the firft ; 249
being againft the bill, and 134 only for it. This proves how efficacioufly the minifter had
made ufe of his influence to overturn the plan. Ditto, p. 368.

wifeft

wifeft plan that could be devifed; and was actually carried into execution, though in the courfe of the Spanifh war, which began *anno* 1739, an addition of above thirty millions had been made to the national debt. The hiftory of this important financial operation it is proper briefly to explain.

In the feffion of parliament, which began in November 1748, Mr. Pelham, as chancellor of the exchequer, publicly intimated his intention of embracing the firft favourable opportunity that fhould offer, to reduce the intereft then payable on the greateft part of the national debt; and as fuch a meafure was afterwards recommended to the confideration of parliament, in a fpeech from the throne on the 16th November 1749, thofe who were interefted in the public funds, had due notice of the intentions of the miniftry. Every ftockholder was put on the fame level; confequently no unfair advantage could be well taken of any individual.

The four *per cent.* annuities, at that time, were as follows:

1. Due to the Bank of England — —	— £ 8,486,800	0 0
2. Due to the South-Sea Company — —	— 27,302,203	5 6
3 Due to the Eaft-India Company — —	— 3,200,000	0 0
4. Annuities transferrable at the Bank of England	— 18,402,472	0 10
5. Annuities on the plate act, tranferrable at the Exchequer	312,000	0 0
	£ 57,703,175	6 4½

The firft refolution of the houfe of commons, in regard to this reduction, paffed on the 29th of November 1749. The purport of it was, that fuch public creditors as received an intereft of 4 *per cent.* upon their capital, redeemable by parliament, who would fignify, on or before the 28th of February 1749-50, their acceptance of 3 *per cent.* intereft from December 1757, fhould have their debts made irredeemable until that period, and fhould receive in the interval, 4 *per cent.* till December 1750, and three one-half *per cent.* from that time until the whole reduction took place. It met with no oppofition; and the commiffioners and officers of the Treafury, and Sir John Barnard the original propofer, were ordered to bring in the bill.

Every perfon muft perceive, that to difcharge fo immenfe a capital at once, was totally impracticable. Yet fuch was the influx of money into

into this country, and the high credit which it then enjoyed, that new loans could have been obtained at 3 *per cent.* to pay off fome part of the creditors; and as money would naturally grow cheaper, and more plentiful every year, during the continuance of peace, larger fums might have been borrowed at the fame rate every fucceeding year, and the reduction to 3 *per cent.* would probably have taken place fooner than it actually did. The 3 *per cent.* annuities then fold at 101; and as fuch 4 *per cent.* creditors as were paid off (if they replaced their money in the funds), could not receive even 3 *per cent.* for their money, the offer was evidently in their favour. But an idea being prevalent, at the time, that the peace would be of fhort continuance, and a variety of objections having been made on the part of the creditors, fome propofing one plan, and others recommending another totally different, the fcheme was likely to have failed, very few of the ftockholders having fignified their approbation of the terms propofed, when the period approached.

It was at this crifis (6th February 17$\frac{4.9}{5.6}$), that Sir John Barnard, wrote his famous " Confiderations on the Propofal for reducing the " Intereft of the National Debt "[34], in which, he proved fo clearly, the general utility of the meafure, and the advantages which it would yield to the fubfcribers themfelves, that, before the 28th of February, about forty millions were fubfcribed.

Little difficulty would have been found to procure money for paying off, in the fpace of a few years, thofe annuities which remained un-fubfcribed. It was therefore refolved, to punifh fuch as fhowed a dif-pofition, by their tardy acceptance, to defeat fo beneficial a propofal to themfelves and the public. Accordingly, a bill was brought in, by which the fecond fubfcribers were reduced from 3$\frac{1}{4}$ to 3 *per cent.* at December 1755; two years fooner than thofe proprietors who had fig-nified their affent to the original propofal. Above eight millions, ex-

---

[34] Printed by J. Ofborn, *anno* 1750. In this tract, the diftinction between a public and private creditor, is taken notice of. " The latter (he fays) has a right to demand " his money when he wants it, which the creditor of the public cannot do." P. 7. He was alfo the author of another excellent tract, publifhed on the fame fubject, *anno* 1737, entitled, " Reafons for the more fpeedy leffening the National Debt, and taking " off the moft burthenfome of the Taxes."

clufive of the India and South Sea ftock ", were fubfcribed on thefe reduced terms; and the remainder, amounting to three millions and a half, was paid off by new loans at 3 *per cent.*, and by the produce of the finking fund, " Thus (fays an intelligent writer), thefe acts were " paffed, which received their currency from the fair character, both " for knowledge and integrity, of that diftinguifhed patriot Sir John " Barnard, whofe concurrence with the miniftry, procured fuch a quick " paffage through the Houfe to the laws themfelves, and whofe judg- " ment, in matters of that nature, has for many years had fuch weight " with the public, that the fuccefs of the meafure much depended upon " his affiftance²⁶."

The nature of this great operation, will appear in one view from the following ftate:

	1. *Subfcription.*	2. *Subfcription and pofterior acts.*	*Unfubfcribed.*
1. Bank ftock	£ 8,486,800 0 0	— — —	— — —
2. Eaft India ftock	— — —	3,200,000 0 0	— — —
3. South Sea ftock	— — —	3,662,784 8 6½	— — —
4. South Sea annuities	15,335,740 5 0	6,026,785 0 5	2,276,893 11 7
5. Bank annuities	14,857,455 18 4	2,714,117 18 0	830,898 4 6
6. Annuities on the plate act -	126,500 0 0	3,250 0 0	182,250 0 0
Firft fubfcription	£ 38,806,496 3 4	15,606,937 6 11½	3,290,041 16 1
Second ditto	15,606,937 6 11½		
	£ 54,413,433 10 3½		
Unfubfcribed	3,290,041 16 1		
	£ 57,703,475 6 4½		

As this was the laft important reduction that took place, it may not be improper to give a general view of the three great operations of that nature, with fome obfervations upon the queftion, how far fuch meafures ought to be adopted.

²⁵ The South Sea Company, however received (in confequence of 24 Geo. II. cap. 11.) intereft upon their capital of 3,663,784 *l.* 8 *s.* 6½ *d.* at the rate of 4 *per cent.* until the 25th December 1757.

²⁶ See a difpaffionate remonftrance on the nature and tendency of the laws now in force, for the reduction of intereft. Printed *anno* 1751, p. 11 and 16.

GENERAL

GENERAL VIEW of the Principal Reductions which have taken place in the Interest of the Public Funds.

1. REDUCTION.

To the reduced interest of various funds, from 6 to 5 *per cent.* *anno* 1717   -   -   -   -   £ 324,455 10 10½

2. REDUCTION.

1. To the reduction, by the bargain with the South Sea Company, from 5 to 4 *per cent.* commencing Midsummer 1727   -   -   -   -   339,631 3 10

2. To the reduction on part of the debt due to the Bank at ditto, in consequence of a separate agreement, exclusive of the four millions purchased from the South Sea Company   37,750 5 6½

3. REDUCTION.

1. To various annuities, reduced from 4 to 3 *per cent.* at different periods, from Dec. 1750 to ditto 1757, including only the annuities subscribed, or afterwards admitted   544,134 6 8½

2. To 2,100,000 *l*, borrowed at 3 *per cent.* to pay certain unsubscribed 4 *per cent.* South Sea annuities   21,000 0 0

                                 £ 1,266,971 6 11½

For the propriety of such reductions, Sir John Barnard has ably contended; nor is it possible to state the arguments in their behalf in a clearer light.

" When the nation (says he) is under a necessity of raising money, " more than can be supplied by taxes paid within the year, they mort- " gage some particular taxes for payment of the interest of a sum of " money borrowed; and they are obliged to give such interest and pre- " miums, as will induce people to lend their money, let the terms be " never so extravagant; and if the public was always to continue to pay " the highest interest exacted at the times of lending the money, the " nation must become overloaded with debts. But care is taken to make " it a condition, and a stipulation, in the very act which borrows the " money, that the parliament shall be at liberty to redeem the annuity " attending the debt, by payment of the principal money, in such " manner as the act provides. And the parliament is not tied down " to redeem the annuity by the produce of the fund only. If that was

                                                 " the

" the cafe, almoft all the debts contracted, would be for ever irredeem-
" able.· But the parliament may raife money by what means they can,
" and apply it to the difcharge of the capital; and whenever money
" can be borrowed, cheaper than the intereft paid by the public, it is
" incumbent on the parliament (with great deference be it fpoken), and
" what the nation have a right to expect from them, to make ufe of the
" opportunity, in order to give the people in general all the cafe in their
" power".."

Notwithftanding fuch convincing arguments, and the important circumftance in favour of reductions, that the public, by adopting fuch
meafures, is above 1,200,000 l. a year lefs loaded than it would otherwife be, yet a modern author, whofe opinions are defervedly refpected,
afferts, " that the nation is likely to fuffer by them, much more than it
" has gained;" and, indeed, is for making all future loans irreducible ".

I am ready to confefs, that fuch reductions, joined to the inattention
of our financial minifters, to every thing but providing for the prefent
moment, regardlefs of the burdens of pofterity, have been the means of
accumulating an artificial capital to a confiderable amount ; but, furely
that circumftance, however unfortunate, is amply compenfated, by an
addition of 1,200,000l. *per annum*, to our unencumbered revenue.

" The favings produced by fuch reductions (we are told by the fame
" author) being expended on current fervices, tempt to extravagance ;
" give a fallacious appearance of opulence, and by making our debts
" fit lighter, render us lefs anxious about redeeming them, and lefs
" apprehenfive of danger from their increafe ."." All this may be very
true, yet ftill the gain of 1,200,000 l. *per annum*, counterbalances thefe
evils. · If it tempts to extravagance, it alfo furnifhes the means of wafte,
without additional burdens upon the people ; if it makes our debts fit
lighter, it prevents the induftry of the people from being overloaded
with taxes, and enables them the better to increafe the wealth and

³⁸ Confiderations, &c. p. 3.

³⁹ See Dr. Price's Tracts on Civil Liberty, p. 201 and 203. The firft reduction anns
1717, the Doctor thinks, was neceffary in order to begin a finking fund. The others,
he totally difapproves.

⁴⁰ Ibid. p. 202. Alfo the conclufion of Sir Nathaniel Gould's Effay on the Public
Debts of this Kingdom.

capital of the country ; and with regard to the appearance of fallacious
opulence, which it is faid to afford, nothing but *real opulence* could
furnifh a nation with the ability of reducing the interest of its incumbrances; nor are there any means by which its debts could be more
fpeedily difcharged, than by taking advantage of any favourable opportunity that may occur of diminifhing the interest, and applying the
favings, thus obtained, to the payment of the capital.

The pofition above mentioned, feems to have been founded upon a
principle contained in the learned author's treatife on reverfionary
payments; in which it is faid, " That it is of lefs importance what
" interest a nation is obliged to give for money ; for the higher the
" interest, the fooner will a finking fund, properly applied, pay off the
" principal ".'' This idea has been already fully confidered, and in my
apprehenfion, folidly anfwered by two writers who have animadverted
upon it. They have urged, that there are certain bounds to the
refources of all ftates, beyond which they cannot go without ruin. That
if a nation owes a hundred and forty millions, and its refources can only
furnifh fix millions towards paying the interest, and difcharging the principal, if the rate of interest was 6 *per cent.*, it muft become immediately
bankrupt. Whereas, if by any means the interest came to be reduced
from 6 to 3 *per cent.*, it could not only difcharge the interest, but could
alfo, annually, diminifh the capital. Hence, it appears, that a nation
may be fo circumftanced, that the reduction of interest may be of fuch
importance, that its very exiftence may depend upon it ".

There is one circumftance, however, that cannot well be difputed ;
namely, that too little attention has been paid to the reduction of the
capital. In the whole hiftory of our finance, there is not a fingle attempt of that nature to be met with, except the compulfatory diminution of the bankers debt in the reign of King William ; and that went
both to the principal and interest. It is to that fpecies of reduction,
therefore, to which our views muft now be extended, as the beft means

---

⁴¹ Obfervations on Reverfionary Payments, edit. 1ᵗ83, vol. i. p. 187. In the firft
edition of that work, *anno* 1771, inftead of *lefs*, the Doctor had ftated, that it was of *little*
importance ; and in the firft edition of the Appeal on the Subject of the National Debt,
the interest paid upon loans, is reprefented to be a matter of little or *no* confequence.

⁴² Remarks on Dr. Price's Obfervations on Reverfionary Payments, *&c.* printed for
J. Lowndes, *anno* 1782, p. 23. and Remarks on his Appeal, p. 37.

of putting our revenue in good order, and of retrieving that credit, which is fo likely to be overwhelmed by artificial, as well as real burdens.

When the reduction was propofed *anno* 1749, there were two important queftions which were the fubject of much difcuffion. 1. Whether the faving fhould be unalienably applied to the difcharge of the capital? Or, 2. Whether taxes to that amount fhould be taken off?

We find, in the tract attributed to Sir John Barnard, that many of the creditors were willing to fubfcribe, provided the intereft thus reduced, was tied down to the payment of the principal, and could not *by any means* be diverted from it; and that excellent citizen himfelf, declares, that the beft ufe to be made of the finking fund, is to tie down abfolutely a good part of it to the payment of the debts[43]. But he is at the fame time of opinion, that this is not the *only* good ufe which may be made of it; nay, he goes fo far as to affert, " that to whatever ufe " the finking fund may be applied, the nation muft be benefited. That " when part of it is appropriated to the current fervice of the year, it " prevents fo much being raifed by new taxes; and that it is beft to be " in poffeffion of the intended favings, before the ufes be determined."

Unfortunately, however, when once the favings were fecured, no fteps were taken to tie down the inviolable appropriation of fo confiderable a furplus, for the extinction of our incumbrances.

Nor did another plan, agitated at that time, meet with a better fate.

It was urged, with confiderable ftrength of argument, that by fuch a reduction, the income of the creditor was curtailed; and yet his expences continued the fame; whereas, if the taxes, which enhance the price of every commodity were taken off, the lofs which the native refident creditor fuftained, would be greatly diminifhed, and the nation in general would be relieved from many of thofe burdenfome duties which check its induftry and commerce, and by which, more than double the fum that is paid to the exchequer, is extracted from the pockets of the people[44].

Every friend to the intereft of this country will regret, that one or other of thefe meafures was not adopted. If an unalienable finking

---

[43] Confiderations, &c. p. 28.
[44] See a difpaffionate Remonftrance on the Nature and Tendency of the Laws now in force, for the Reduction of Intereft, p. 23.

fund

fund had been eftablifhed, it would have been fully afcertained before
this time, how far fuch a plan is entitled to all the praifes which have
been lavifhed on it; or if taxes to the amount of above half a million
had been taken off, the effeds of diminifhing the burdens of the people,
would not have been at this hour problematical. Every difficulty with
regard to the proper application, or the entire abolition of a finking
fund, would have been removed; and the fteps now to be purfued,
would have refted, not on arguments (which are too often fallacious),
but on experience, which cannot err.

It would be improper to conclude this fubjed, without taking notice
of a very important circumftance; namely, that the plan propofed in
1749, for reducing the intereft of the funds, was as loudly exclaimed
againft, as being contrary to the faith of parliament, and likely to
deftroy the whole credit of the nation, as any meafure could well be.
When the ftockholders were affembled to take it into their confideration, it was generally reprobated. The Bank refufed its confent; the
Eaft India Company were greatly diffatisfied *; and from the account already given, it appears, how many other difficulties it had to ftruggle
with. By this example, our minifters fhould be encouraged, not to be
alarmed by groundlefs clamour, nor terrified from carrying ufeful meafures into effed, from ideal apprehenfions, that public credit is of fo
tender and delicate a nature, that it cannot bear the flighteft touch, or
minuteft alteration. If that had been the cafe, our credit could never
have furvived the operation we have been confidering.

Mr. Hooke's
plan.
An. 1750. There is nothing farther, of any great importance, conneded with
the prefent fubjed, during the reign of George II., which deferves to
be particularly taken notice of; except Mr. Hooke's admirable Effay
on the National Capital, and the plan that he propofed for difcharging
the national debt.

The debt, which then amounted to nearly eighty millions, this ingenious author calculated was not a twelfth part of the national capital, nor
the annual intereft of it at 4 *per cent.*, a thirtieth part of the national
income. To pay off, therefore, fo flight an incumbrance, when com-

---

*· Difpaffionate Remonftrance, p. 29. Annotations on Sir John Barnard's Trad,
p. 1. 16, &c.

3   pared

pared to the national capital,·he contended was of lefs confequence to the community than was generally imagined; and the debt, he afferted, might be increafed to double the fum without any real danger of a national bankruptcy⁴⁶. But, as others might be of a different opinion, he added a plan well entitled to the moft mature confideration.

" Let the *eighty* millions debt be divided into *eighty* equal parts of a
" million each, to be paid off feverally, by an equal number of fepa-
" rate and independent claffes of fubfcribers, whofe refpective confti-
" tuents fhall, in confideration of fuch fubfcriptions, be jointly and fe-
" verally interefted in an equivalent annuity, to be granted to each clafs,
" for the term aforefaid, with benefit of furvivorfhip.

" Let it be enacted, then, that the intereft of *one* million, at
" *three one-half per cent.*, be converted into a capital annuity of *thirty-*
" *five thoufand* pounds, and granted, for *ninety-nine* years abfolute, to
" any body or clafs of fubfcribers, who, in confideration thereof, will
" advance the fum of *one* million towards difcharging fo much of the
" national debt.

" That the *one* million, fo to be fubfcribed, be divided into *four thou-*
" *fand* parts or fhares of *two hundred and fifty* pounds, and the capital
" annuity of *thirty-five thoufand* pounds, into *four thoufand* leffer an-
" nuities of *eight* pounds *fifteen* fhillings each, anfwerable to the faid
" number of fhares, and vefted in the individuals of each clafs, in
" proportion to the number of fhares fubfcribed by them feverally and
" refpectively.

" That every perfon fubfcribing *two hundred and fifty* pounds, or
" one fhare, be entitled to one of the faid leffer annuities during the life
" of any perfon he fhall nominate, fubject to the limitation in the faid
" grant, and fo in proportion to any greater number of fhares, pro-
" vided always, that the number of his nominees be ever equal to the
" number of his fhares.

" That, in confideration of his finking the principal money, every
" fubfcriber be further entitled to fuch annual augmentation of his an-

---

⁴⁶ See an Effay on the National Debt and National Capital, by Andrew Hooke, Efq. Printed for W. Owen, *anno* 1750. p. 44.

" nuity,

" nuity, or annuities, as fhall, from time to time, accrue by cafualties of
" mortality among the nominees of fuch clafs; fo that, before the ex-
" piration of the original term, the whole capital annuity of *thirty-five*
" *thoufand* pounds may veft in fuch fubfcriber or fubfcribers, or his or
" their reprefentative, as the cafe fhall happen, whofe nominee, or no-
" minees, fhall be the laft furvivor, or furvivors, of the faid clafs.

" That the government creditors have the preference to all other fub-
" fcribers, for fo much principal money as fhall, at the time of fuch
" fubfcription, be actually and *bona fide* due to them from the crown;
" and that, notwithftanding the claffes, as fuch, are, by this plan, to
" be independent of each other, yet, that individuals may become fub-
" fcribers in as many claffes as they pleafe, and their nominees in one
" clafs be nominees in every other clafs, as they fhall think fit. And
" laftly,

" That the government, on payment of the capital annuities of
" *thirty-five thoufand* pounds to the feveral claffes, be abfolutely dif-
" charged from all future claims of individuals, touching their refpec-
" tive fhares, proportions, and interefts, therein; and that all matters
" relating thereto be tranfacted among themfelves, and determined by a
" court of directors, to be elected and appointed in fuch manner as
" fhall be thought fit, who, by law, fhall be fully authorized and em-
" powered to make the refpective dividends, and, from time to time,
" adjuft all claims thereto; fubject, neverthelefs, to an appeal to the
" Lords of the Treafury, who, in a *fummary way*, fhall finally hear
" and determine the fame ".".

It is in general to be remarked, on every plan that has been propofed
for paying off the whole of the national debt, with the voluntary confent of the creditors, that no one fcheme will fuit the ideas of every individual of which that numerous body is compofed. Each different
fpecies of ftock has its refpective friends and favourers. Some prefer
perpetual, others temporary annuities. One fet of men look no farther
than themfelves; whilft another is anxious to fecure fplendor and opulence to their pofterity. And in regard to Mr. Hooke's fcheme, as no
inconfiderable part of our public funds belongs to corporations, to whom

---

[47] Effay, p. 46.

an annuity of 99 years would in no refpect be eligible, it is probable, that nothing but compulfion would induce them to agree to fuch a propofal.

But though it is liable to thefe objections, when carried to an extreme, yet, on a more limited fcale, and with fuch alterations as would be fuitable to the prefent ftate of our funds, the plan might be tried with perfect fafety to the public. Though borrowing money on temporary annuities is wretched policy in time of war, when the ftate is in the power of the money-lender; yet, in a time of peace, *the lender is the fervant of the borrower*, and better terms may be procured. And if there were a fet of men fpecially appointed for the fole purpofe of difcharging the incumbrances with which the nation is loaded, great advantage might be reaped, by embracing favourable opportunities of altering the nature and form of our fecurities, in the manner the moft advantageous to the public, and the beft calculated to gratify the views and wifhes of individuals.

At the conclufion of the war, which ended *anno* 1762, the unfunded debt amounted to about fixteen millions. Until that unfhapen mafs was brought into fome form, no effectual fteps could be taken for diminifhing our incumbrances. But when that object was accomplifhed, no good reafon can be affigned, why fome effectual fyftem was not purfued for bringing our finances into good order. A more favourable opportunity never exifted. At firft, indeed, our funds (for reafons which are ftated by an excellent political author[47]) did not rife in the fame proportion that they did after the peace of Aix la Chapelle: but wealth abounded in the country; the value of the ftocks was increafing every day; and mortgages were obtained, for immenfe fums, on private fecurity, at 3 and a half *per cent.* Thefe profperous times, however, were fuffered to pafs away unheeded, amidft the fquabbles of party.

During the late peace, 10,739,793*l.* of debts, funded and unfunded, were paid off[48]. But that reduction did not take place from favings out of the ordinary revenues of the ftate: for it is calculated,

George III.

Debt paid off.

[47] Polit. Econ. vol. ii. p. 399.
[48] Dr. Price's Tracts on Civil Liberty, p. 177.

by a moſt reſpectable author, that above five millions of that ſmall diminution aroſe from extraneous articles, ſuch as the balances in the
hands of different public accountants; the produce of the French
prizes; compoſitions for French priſoners; the ſum paid by the Bank
for the renewal of its charter; and two millions received from the Eaſt
India Company, in lieu of the claim which the public had to the terri-
torial acquiſitions, &c. &c.[50]. We were beginning, however, to ſurmount
our financial difficulties, when the late unfortunate war again threw us
into a gulph of miſery and oppreſſion, from which it will be difficult to emerge, unleſs every individual in the great veſſel of the ſtate
lends his moſt ardent and zealous aſſiſtance.

It is propoſed to conclude the preſent chapter with a general view of
the *funded* debts that have been paid off ſince a ſinking fund was eſtabliſhed, and with a few obſervations on the neceſſity of making ſome alteration in that branch of our finances.

State of the Funded Debt paid off ſince the firſt eſtabliſhment of a Sinking Fund[51].

Year.				
1723	-	-	-	£ 1,204,786 3 $4\frac{1}{4}$
1724	-	-	-	333,447 18 4
1727	-	-	-	650,453 2 $8\frac{1}{4}$
1728	-	-	-	1,000,000 0 0
1729	-	-	-	1,275,027 17 $10\frac{1}{4}$
1730	-	-	-	1,000,000 0 0
1731	-	-	-	1,000,419 16 4
1732	-	-	-	1,000,000 0 0
1733	-	-	-	913,115 15 $3\frac{1}{4}$
1734	-	-	-	86,884 4 $8\frac{1}{4}$
				£ 8,464,134 18 $7\frac{1}{4}$

[50] Wealth of Nations, vol. ii. p. 555.
[51] Prior to the year 1723, the finking fund was applied to cancelling exchequer bills,
and other unfunded debts.

1736

Year.				Brought over	£ 8,464,134	18	7¼
1736	-	-	-		1,000,000	0	0
1737	-	-	-		1,000,000	0	0
1738	-	-	-		1,000,000	0	0
1751	-	-	-		368,771	2	4
1752	-	-	-		821,270	13	9
1765	-	-	-		870,888	5	5¼
1766	-	-	-		870,888	5	5¼
1767	-	-	-		2,616,776	10	11
1768	-	-	-		1,750,000	0	0
1769	-	-	-		875,000	0	0
1770	-	-	-		1,500,000	0	0
1772	-	-	-		1,500,000	0	0
1774	-	-	-		1,000,000	0	0
1775	-	-	-		1,000,000	0	0

$$^{33}£\ 24,637,729 \quad 16 \quad 6¼$$

It is unneceffary to trouble the reader with an account of the *un-funded* debts which have been difcharged, and the manner in which the finking fund has in general been expended, as that fubject alone would require a volume to elucidate, and may be feen in another work dedicated to that fpecial purpofe[33]. We fhall now, therefore, proceed to confider that important and interefting queftion—What is the beft mode of applying the furplus revenue of a ftate?

There are two methods which a nation might purfue, and by adopt- Two modes ing either of which, the funding fyftem might be carried on without of employing much inconvenience to the public. The firft is, employing the furplus revenue. of its revenues in promoting fuch meafures as may augment its wealth,

*

52 The fums put down in the years 1751 and 1752, were to difcharge exchequer bills iffued to pay off certain annuities unfubfcribed, when the reduction of intereft took place, *anno* 1749.

53 Sir Charles Whitworth's Annual Abftract of the Sinking Fund, to the 10th of October 1763; printed *anno* 1764. This, and other ufeful compilations, publifhed by the fame author, ought to be continued at the public expence.

[Q] 2   population,

population, induftry, and commerce: the fecond, employing the fame .
furplus in a perpetual diminution of its public incumbrances. By the
firft, public debts are rendered lighter and more fupportable; by the fecond, their accumulation is prevented.

1 Firft mode.
Encouraging
private accu-
mulation.

Whoever confiders the financial hiftory of this country, muft be
aftonifhed at the immenfe refources it has poffeffed, and the great
wealth which has been amaffed in it, by the induftry of its inhabitants.
It is, therefore, a curious fubject of political fpeculation, whether the
furplus of its revenue, inftead of being employed in diminifhing its
debts, would not have been better expended in the encouragement of
induftry; in promoting the cultivation of the foil, and in extending
commerce and navigation: if, for example, twenty-four millions,
which have been applied to difcharge our public debts, had been dedicated to fuch beneficial public purpofes, whether the nation would not
have been, at the prefent moment, in a richer and more flourifhing
fituation?

The mercantile fyftem, as it has been called, has received fuch a blow
from the writings of a refpectable modern author[54], that it is with
confiderable diffidence we venture to fuggeft the poffibility of its being
extended to advantage. But the happieft theory, fupported by the
moft plaufible arguments, may be invalidated by a fingle fact. Notwithftanding every objection which has been urged againft this fyftem,
" though its mean and malignant expedients have diminifhed, inftead
" of increafing, the whole quantity of manufacturing induftry main-
" tained in Great Britain; though it difcourages the improvement of
" land, and hurts the intereft of every order in the ftate, to promote
" the little intereft of one little order of men; nay, though it is un-
" favourable to the revenue of the fovereign[55];" yet, with all thefe
difadvantages, the country has flourifhed under it. Its riches have
multiplied without bounds; its revenue, in lefs than a century, has
increafed about twelve millions *per annum*; nor has any one attempted
to affign any other reafon for all this profperity, but the commercial
encouragements which have been enacted by the legiflature, and the at-

54 Wealth of Nations, by Dr. Adam Smith, vol. ii.
55 Ibid. vol. ii. edit. 1. p. 217, 218, 219, and 497.

tention:

tention which has been fhewn to promote the induftry and exertions of the people.

Among the regulations of the mercantile fyftem, none feems to have been more unjuftly reprobated, than the meafures it has propofed of employing fome part of the furplus of the revenue in promoting induftry where induftry is unknown, in bounties upon the exportation of our commodities, or in the encouragement of ufeful undertakings, which, without fome public affiftance, could not be attempted.

The northern parts of Scotland are furrounded by an ocean, in which the moft valuable fifheries might be carried on with profit. But the inhabitants of thofe diftricts, ignorant of the bleffings of induftry, unacquainted with the means of conducting commercial undertakings fuccefsfully, and without capital to enable them to begin, have long enjoyed this natural advantage, without reaping from it any real benefit. How foon might the fcene be altered, were proper encouragement given to their exertions! Nor would the general wealth of the country alone be augmented. The addition that might be made to the maritime ftrength of the kingdom, by adopting fuch a meafure, would be ineftimable[16].

England has been under the neceffity of impofing upon itfelf fuch a heavy load of taxes, that neither the products of its land, nor all the manufactures of its people, can ftand a competition with thofe of other powers in foreign markets. The exportation therefore of grain, and of fome other articles, has met with encouragement from the legiflature; and bounties have been given, " which have operated, like the warmth " which, in a human body, one member communicates to another, when " it ftands in need of it [17]." Were thefe bounties to be increafed from the furplus of the national revenue, how much might not agriculture be extended; to what a height might not our commerce be raifed; and how foon might not Great Britain become the emporium of Europe!

---

[16] Some bounties have been given to buffes and on herrings exported, but the expence has been great without any real benefit. The high price of falt, proper for the purpofe of curing, and the difficulty of obtaining cafks in a diftant and indigent country, are the principal obftacles to the fuccefs of the fifhery, and to remove which the legiflature ought to be the more attentive, as it may be done at little expence.

[17] Poftlethwayte's True Syftem, vol. ii. p. 380.

But

But the queftion to which the reader's attention is more particularly called at prefent, is, if the fum that has been taken from the finking fund, and applied to the difcharge of our funded incumbrances, had been expended folely in making Great Britain one populous and cultivated field or garden; whether the nation could not have borne the whole debt with lefs difficulty than it now can fupport the debt as it has been reduced? Twenty-four millions laid out in promoting the improvement and cultivation of the foil, would have rendered every acre in the kingdom productive of fome valuable article. The whole country would have exhibited one uninterrupted fcene of labour and fertility. No more well-founded complaints would be heard, that the number of the people had decreafed, that the poor wanted encouragement to induftry, or the means of employment.

But laying afide the farther difcuffion of a fubject which it is probable the conduct of a neighbouring kingdom will foon clear up by the fureft of all tefts, that of experience[18]; let us next fee by what arguments another mode of applying the furplus revenue has been fupported.

2. Mode. Public accumulations.

There is no axiom in Euclid more felf-evident than this, that if the debts of a nation are never diminifhed, and if no fteps are taken to promote the increafe of its wealth, it muft foon be involved in the greateft mifery and diftrefs. If the furplus of its revenue therefore cannot fafely be expended in the encouragement of its agriculture, its induftry, and its commerce; " if the fovereign, in attempting to perform fuch a " duty, is expofed to innumerable delufions; and if directing the induftry " of the people towards employments the moft fuitable to the general " interefts of fociety, is a tafk for which no human wifdom or know- " ledge could ever be fufficient," nothing then remains, but to ftrain every nerve to leffen the public debts by the annual application of a fum, not like the prefent finking fund, fometimes to one purpofe, and fometimes to another, but *invariably* to the difcharge of our incumbrances.

To prove how efficacious fuch a fund would be, let it only be confidered, that if a million were inviolably appropriated, it would difcharge

18 In Ireland the furplus of the revenue is in general applied to fuch public purpofes, and the effects of fuch a fyftem in that country, will eftablifh it in Great Britain fome years hence; if the example of France does not render the eftablifhment of an unalienable finking fund abfolutely neceffary.

in

in the fhort fpace of fixty years, a capital of nearly three hnndred and feventeen millions of 3 per cents., at the price of feventy-five per cent. " : confequently, if we were engaged in wars equally expenfive with thofe which have taken place for fixty years back, namely, fince the year 1723, which is hardly to be conceived ; and if thofe wars were to coft the nation two hundred millions for extraordinary expences, yet, at the end of that period, we fhould be *one hundred and feventeen millions lefs in debt*, than we are at prefent; and at the end of an hundred and twenty years, if the fame plan were perfevered in, the whole of the prefent national debt would be paid off, together with another additional two hundred millions, which it might be neceffary to borrow, in the fecond period of fixty years, for the public defence.

The firft objection to an unalienable finking fund, is, that it would be abfurd to employ money in the paying off old debts, if a nation is at the fame time under the neceffity of contracting new incumbrances. This argument is too plaufible not to carry with it fome weight. But the plan may be formed fo as to remove this obftacle, without deftroy-ing the certain advantages of an unalienable finking fund. Let the public, in times of emergency, borrow from that fund what money it can fpare, *but let it at the fame time provide a fund for defraying the in-tereft of the money that it borrows*, giving the finking fund a propor-tionable fhare of the new loan. If that rule is obferved, the public will not be deprived of fo important a refource, whilft the certain effects of an unalienable finking fund will not be diminifhed. In the fpace of fixty years, it will be poffeffed of a capital of three hundred and feven-teen millions of 3 per cents., and it muft be indifferent to the public, whether that capital confifts of old debts, or of more recent burdens.

By fuch a plan alfo, a very plaufible objection is removed, that it would be impoffible to protect fuch a fund from the rapacious vio-lence of minifters. For, let it be made ufe of when the public fervice requires it ; but at the fame time, let not its beneficial effects be put an end to, by annihilating the fum that is taken from it. Render that fum productive ; let it enjoy a certain annual intereft, and the procefs cannot be defeated.

<hr/>

59 Maferes on Life Annuities, vol. i. p. 294.

The

The fecond objection refts upon the many evils with which a load of taxes is accompanied; and which an unalienable finking fund has in fome degree a tendency to accumulate. It has been urged, " that " taxes are taken, not out of a *dead, barren, unproductive* fund, but out " of the moft *prolific* of all funds; out of the national flock of induftry, " and taxable capacity. They are a part of that flock, which, if " left in the hands of the individual, would, at the end of the year, " have produced him an *intereft*, which intereft would have again " become the parent of *another intereft*, and would have accumulated juft " as much fafter in his hands, than in the hands of the public, as the " rate of intereft which he may make in his private affairs, is fuperior " to that in the public funds. Adding at the fame time to his fide of " the account, the expences of collection and management on the part " of government:" and we are told, " that the people lofe *compound* " *intereft* of every fhilling which they fend into the exchequer; and " that too at a much higher rate of intereft in general, than can poffibly " be made of it after it has got hither ⁹⁹."

So plaufible an objection, nothing but experience could refute. But it is now indifputably afcertained, that this country was poffeffed of refources which rendered all apprehenfions of that nature ideal. Who can now doubt, that an additional fum fufficient to have extinguifhed the whole of our prefent debt might have been annually raifed in former times without oppreffing the people? It would have required, it is true, more popular or abler minifters. They muft have facrificed, perhaps, fome fhare of their own emoluments, to have rouzed a proper fpirit in the nation; and the public muft have been convinced, that the management of their affairs was in the hands of men who had nothing but their intereft at heart, and who had devoted their time and labours for the benefit and falvation of their country. In fuch a cafe, it will be hardly difputed, that no backwardnefs would have been found in the Britifh nation in fubmitting to any tax that would have been neceffary for that purpofe.

Befides, taxes do not alone affect the induftrious part of the community. When wifely impofed, they in general fall upon the idle confumer, who feldom thinks of making *compound intereft* of the money he might fave, if no fuch tax exifted. I fay *might fave :* for if the tax did

⁹⁹. Remarks on Dr. Price's Appeal to the People, printed anno 1772, p. 8, and 10.

2   not

not exift, the money, inftead of being faved, would probably be wafted in the purchafe of luxurious foreign fuperfluities. A fmall additional duty upon porter, an additional land-tax of only fix-pence in the pound, or (according to Dr. Price), a tax upon celibacy, impofed at the acceffion of the prefent Royal Family, would, before this time, have extinguifhed a confiderable portion of our debts. What poffible evil could have arifen from any of thefe taxes? Would lefs porter have been confumed; fewer of our fields been cultivated; or would the population of the country have been decreafed? Every one muft anfwer thefe queftions in the negative.

The only remaining objections to an unalienable finking fund, are the power which it is fuppofed it would put into the hands of the minifter; the encouragement that it would afford to ftock-jobbing; and the fluctuations which it would occafion in the price of the funds, according as fmall or great fums were fent into the market.

But thefe objections are eafily removed. For in the firft place, fuch a fund ought to be confided to the care of commiffioners appointed for that fpecial purpofe, and not entrufted to any of thofe fluctuating boards which at prefent exift. Such commiffioners ought to confift partly of certain great officers of State, who fhould be entitled, *ex officio*, to a feat at the new board (to act occafionally as a check upon the efficient commiffioners), and partly of refpectable individuals, to whom the real management of the bufinefs fhould be committed. To give the latter every chance for permanency, the number fhould be fo few, that their removal could be no object to a party in oppofition, fhould it chance to prove victorious. The money to be applied for purchafing ftock, or difcharging any particular branch of the funds, fhould be laid out monthly, and not brought at once into the market; and before any ftock was purchafed, public intimation of it fhould be iffued: every ftockholder fhould be invited to give in his propofals for the ftock he held; and the commiffioners fhould be tied down, under the ftricteft penalties, to accept of the loweft offer, or to divide the fum to be laid out proportionably among thofe whofe terms were equal.

Under thefe regulations, unalienable finking funds may be fafely and ufefully eftablifhed.

[R] Whoever

Whoever has attentively confidered the fubject treated of in this and the preceding Chapter, will probably be of opinion, that our prefent diftreffes are in a great meafure owing to our want of experience in regard to the funding fyftem. Neither our minifters nor the public, had the example of any ftate, in ancient or in modern times, to guide them through fo intricate a labyrinth. The object, therefore, they kept in view, was merely to relieve the preffure of the prefent moment, trufting that pofterity would find out what remedy fhould be applied, to prevent a ruinous accumulation of the burden. But had we now the fame courfe to run, our ftatefmen, inftructed by paft events, would find little difficulty in conducting the greateft and moft complicated operations of finance; nor would the public at large be at a lofs to know, what meafures were neceffary to be taken, for the general intereft of the community.

※.

END OF PART II.